In 1866, the mighty Austrian Empire was attacked by the armies of Prussia and Italy. In a lightning campaign, the Prussians overran Austria's German allies – Hanover, Hessia, Bavaria, and Saxony – and then thrust into the Habsburg province of Bohemia. In a sequence of well-executed flanking attacks, the Prussians drove the Austrians from good defensive positions at Trautenau, Vysokov, Skalice, Münchengrätz, and Jicin, and forced them back to the Elbe River fortress at Königgrätz. While the Prussians encircled Austria's North Army, the Italians attempted the same maneuver against Austria's South Army in Venetia, but – in a humiliating, disastrous battle – were routed at Custoza. The Austro-Prussian War culminated at Königgrätz on July 3, 1866. There the Prussians hit the Austrians in front and flank and nearly annihilated them, driving North Army and its hapless commandant – General Ludwig Benedek, a pre-war celebrity accounted the best general in Europe – back to Vienna in a shattered, demoralized state. While the Austrians girded for a last stand on the Danube, the Italians thrust again into Venetia and drove past Venice to the Isonzo in July. Caught between two pincers, the Austrians capitulated, ceding control of the German Confederation to Prussia and all of Venetia to Italy. The war of 1866 thus fledged two new Great Powers – Prussia-Germany and Italy – and forever consigned its victim – Habsburg Austria – to the fringes of European power.

In a style at once riveting and scholarly, Geoffrey Wawro recounts the story of this crucial European war, from its diplomatic origins to its pivotal battles. This is the first history of the Austro-Prussian War in more than thirty years, and the first ever to be based upon extensive research in the political and military archives of Austria, France, Germany, Italy and England. Wawro has reconstructed the Austrian campaign, blow-by-blow, hour-by-hour. He divulges the secrets of Prussian military success, as well as the dismal, sometimes lurid reasons for Austria's military collapse and Italy's near collapse. The book is most notable for the light it sheds on the Habsburg war effort. Wawro reveals how Benedek and his deputies fumbled away key strategic advantages and ultimately lost a war – vital to the fortunes of the Habsburg Monarchy – that most European pundits had predicted they would win.

The Austro-Prussian War

Austrian Infantry, 1866. Lithograph by Rudolf von Ottenfeld, 1895. Courtesy of Oster-
reichisches Kriegsarchiv.

The Austro-Prussian War

Austria's War with Prussia and Italy in 1866

GEOFFREY WAWRO

Oakland University

CAMBRIDGE
UNIVERSITY PRESS

Published by the Press Syndicate of the University of Cambridge
The Pitt Building, Trumpington Street, Cambridge CB2 1RP
40 West 20th Street, New York, NY 10011-4211, USA
10 Stamford Road, Oakleigh, Melbourne 3166, Australia

First published 1996
Reprinted 1997
First paperback edition 1997

Printed in the United States of America

Photographs courtesy of Österreichische National-Bibliothek-Bildarchiv

Library of Congress Cataloging-in-Publication Data

Wawro, Geoffrey.
The Austro-Prussian War : Austria's war with Prussia and Italy in
1866 / Geoffrey Wawro.
p.   cm.
Includes bibliographical references and index.
ISBN 0-521-56059-4
1. Austro-Prussian War, 1866.   2. Germany – Politics and
government – 1858–1870.   3. Austria – Politics and
government – 1848–1870.   4. Italy – Politics and
government – 1849–1870.   5. Custoza, Battle of, 1866.
6. Königgratz, Battle of, 1866.   I. Title.
DD438.W39   1996
943'.076 – dc20   95-50529
CIP

A catalog record for this book is available from the British Library

ISBN   0-521-56059-4 Hardback
ISBN   0-521-62951-9 Paperback

To my mother and father

Contents

List of illustrations   *page* ix
Acknowledgments   xi
List of abbreviations   xiii

Introduction   1
1. Strategy and tactics in 1866   6
2. Origins of the Austro-Prussian War   36
3. War plans and mobilization   50
4. Italy declares war   82
5. Custoza   100
6. Podol, Vysokov, and Trautenau   124
7. Münchengrätz, Burkersdorf, and Skalice   156
8. Jicin and Benedek's flight to Königgrätz   181
9. Königgrätz: Benedek's stand in the "Bystrice pocket"   208
10. Königgrätz: Moltke's envelopment   238
11. Aftermath: The peace and Europe, 1866–1914   274

Bibliography   297
Index   309

Illustrations

FIGURES

Austrian Infantry, 1866, by Rudolf von Ottenfeld   *frontispiece*
1. General Helmuth von Moltke (1800–91), Prussian General Staff
   chief in 1866   14
2. General Ludwig Benedek (1804–81), commander of the Austrian
   North Army in 1866   26
3. General Alfred Henikstein (1810–82), Austrian General Staff chief
   in 1866   28
4. Habsburg Emperor Franz Joseph (1830–1916) in 1866   33
5. General Gideon Krismanic (1817–76), "operations chief" of the
   Austrian North Army in 1866   58
6. Field Marshal-Archduke Albrecht Habsburg (1817–95), commander
   of the Austrian South Army in 1866   66
7. General Franz John (1815–76), staff chief of Austria's South Army
   in 1866   68
8. General Alfonso La Marmora (1804–78), commander of the Italian
   Mincio Army in 1866   85
9. General Enrico Cialdini (1811–84), commander of the Italian Po
   Army in 1866   91
10. Custoza and the Belvedere   101
11. General Eduard Clam-Gallas (1805–91), commandant of the
    Austrian I Corps until Königgrätz   132
12. The Austrian attack on Vysokov, June 27, 1866   141
13. The final Austrian assault at Trautenau, June 27, 1866   149
14. The Austrians storm the railway embankment at Skalice, June 28,
    1866   172
15. General Leopold Edelsheim (1826–93) and the staff of Austria's 1st
    Light Cavalry Division in 1866   206

16. General Wilhelm Ramming (1815–76), commandant of the
Austrian VI Corps and Benedek's principal rival   239
17. The rout of the Austrians at Königgrätz, July 3, 1866   264

MAPS

Austria, Prussia, and the German States, 1815–66   37
Austria, Piedmont, and the Italian States, 1815–59   46
The Prussian mobilization, June 1866   54
The mobilization of Austria's North Army, June 1866   60
The Italian front, June 1866   69
West Army's push to Langensalza, June 1866   76
Custoza: La Marmora and Albrecht deploy, June 23, 1866   97
Custoza: La Marmora's passage of the Mincio, June 24, 1866   103
Custoza: The struggle for the Mincio Heights   113
The Battle of Vysokov, June 27, 1866   140
The Battle of Trautenau, June 27, 1866   146
The strategic situation on June 27, 1866   152
The Battle of Münchengrätz, June 28, 1866   157
The Battles of Burkersdorf and Rudersdorf, June 28, 1866   161
The Battle of Skalice, June 28, 1866   168
The strategic situation on June 28, 1866   177
The Battle of Jicin, June 29, 1866   185
The strategic situation on June 29, 1866   192
Benedek's Dubenec position on June 30, 1866   194
Benedek's flight to Königgrätz on July 1, 1866   198
Königgrätz: Benedek's position on the Bystrice, July 2, 1866   209
Königgrätz: Attack of the Prussian Elbe and First Armies, July 3, 1866   217
Königgrätz: Mollinary's bid to envelop the Prussian First Army, July 3,
1866   223
Königgrätz: Moltke envelops Benedek, July 3, 1866   244
Königgrätz: North Army's collapse, July 3, 1866   256
Benedek's retreat to Olmütz and Moltke's drive on Vienna, July 1866   275

Acknowledgments

I was able to undertake most of the archival research for this book thanks to a two-year research fellowship from the Austro-American Fulbright Commission in Vienna. I am also indebted to the MacArthur and Mellon Foundations and to the Yale Council on West European Studies for their generous summer research grants, which permitted me to use archives in London, Paris, Munich, Rome, Milan, and Budapest. After my stint in Vienna, I was fortunate to receive an Andrew W. Mellon Doctoral Fellowship, which provided me with the time and funds to convert several duffel bags full of notes into this book.

My advisor and mentor at Yale University, Professor Paul Kennedy, was a careful reader, a helpful critic and a powerful teacher. He brought order and clarity to my first drafts and showed me the way whenever I became lost in thickets of detail. I must also thank Professor Michael Howard for reading the manuscript and giving me much useful advice along the way. What I know today about the Habsburg Monarchy is in many ways owed to Professor Ivo Banac, who broadened my horizons and proved a wise teacher and a good friend during my years at Yale. My attempts to make sense of Italian life and politics have been eased by the insights of Professor Brian Sullivan, who has been a most sympathetic friend and confidant for the past ten years.

Throughout my two years in Austria, I benefited from the kind attentions of Dr. Johann Christoph Allmayer-Beck, who received me several times in his apartment on the *Parkring* to review my research over glasses of old sack. Other Austrian academics, Dr. Manfried Rauchensteiner and Dr. Lothar Höbelt in particular, were very good to me, as were the employees of the *Kriegsarchiv* and the *Haus-Hof-und Staatsarchiv*. The wheels of my research would have turned very slowly indeed had it not been for the assistance of Drs. Rainer Egger and Peter Broucek, who produced an unending stream of documents for me in the Kriegsarchiv. In the Staatsarchiv, Dr. Horst Brettner-Messler explained the inexplicable – the Habsburg police bureaucracy – and guided me through its various indexes. Research in other countries would have been difficult without the unstinting hospitality of a number of good friends: Jun Hiraga and David Noble in London, Isabelle Lecasble and the Bataillon family in Paris, Leni von Rospatt in Munich, and, back in Vienna (Perchtoldsdorf, actually), all the Bergmanns.

Here in Michigan, I am grateful for the various kinds of support Oakland University has lent me during the actual writing of this book. Thanks are also due the Austrian Cultural Institute in New York, which recently dignified my Yale dissertation – the backbone of the book – with its 1994 Prize for Best Dissertation in Austrian Studies. I have been aided in the conversion of that sprawling dissertation into this cogent book by three erudite readers, Professors Holger Herwig, Williamson Murray and Dennis Showalter, and by the assistance of a superb editor at Cambridge University Press, Dr. Frank Smith. Beyond the archives, universities, and institutes, *un gran abrazo* for my wife, Cecilia Schilling, who renounced a dulcet life in Argentina to join me in Vienna and Detroit and has never failed to relieve the tedium of research and writing.

Much of my enthusiasm for this work came from visits to the battlefields in Venetia and Bohemia, places that have hardly changed since 1866. In Italy, I was foolish enough to set out from Villafranca on foot for Custoza under a midday sun well supplied with bread, salami, and cheese, but without a drop of water. By the time I reached Custoza – tormented the whole way by gurgling brooks turned green by fertilizers – I was done in and restored thanks to the Adami and Brentegani families, who threw open their doors on a Sunday, filled me with mineral water and peach pie, and then conducted me down to the village church, where the priest – Giancarlo Piatelli – no less stunned than his neighbors by the apparition of an American historian in Custoza, presented me with an album of photos and lithographs depicting Italy and its army in 1866. On the northern front – in Bohemia and Moravia – I was able to visit all of the camps and battlefields, from Jicin and Königgrätz east to Skalice and Olmütz, thanks to a tireless chauffeur with the patience of Job: my mother. I dedicate this book to her, along with my dear, departed father, who was himself a great adventurer and a potent source of inspiration. On the road in Bohemia, my mother endured frequent changes of route and mood, and forbore to answer when, at one point, under a driving rain, on a bad road in the Iser river valley, I turned to her and screamed: "You mean *you* don't know the way to Münchengrätz?"

Rochester Hills, Michigan
April 1995

Abbreviations

AAT   Archive de l'Armée de Terre, Vincennes.
AFA   Alte-Feldakten (KA), Vienna.
AdHP   Actes de Haute Police (HHSA), Vienna.
BKA   Bayerisches Kriegsarchiv, Munich.
CK   Centralkanzlei (KM), Vienna.
CP   Correspondance Politique (Quai d'Orsay), Paris.
FO   Foreign Office (PRO), London.
HHSA   Haus-Hof-und Staatsarchiv, Vienna.
IB   Informationsbüro, Vienna.
KA   Kriegsarchiv, Vienna.
KM   Kriegsministerium, Vienna.
MKSM   Militärkanzlei Seiner Majestät (KA), Vienna.
MR   Mémoirs-Reconnaissances (AAT), Vincennes.
ÖMZ   Österreichische Militärische Zeitschrift.
PA   Politisches Archiv (HHSA), Vienna.
PÖM   Protokolle des österreichischen Ministerrates.
PRO   Public Record Office, London.

Introduction

The Austro-Prussian War of 1866 would more accurately be called the Austro-Prussian-*Italian* War, for Italy – determined to have the Habsburg provinces of Venetia and South Tyrol – seized the opportunity presented by Austria's war with Prussia in Bohemia and the German states to invade Austria from the south. Though this history shuns the longer title, it covers both fronts of the war of 1866 by focusing on the central power in the conflict, the Austrian Empire, which fought for its survival as a dynastic, historical collection of nations in the face of armed attacks by the budding nation states of Prussia-Germany and Piedmont-Italy.

Physically, Austria was well situated to repel these attacks. The monarchy was shielded in the south by Europe's most redoubtable fortress group – the Quadrilateral forts on the Po and Mincio rivers – and by the high Alps. In the north, Austria was protected from Prussian invasion by its imposing *"Reichs-Barrière,"* the line of the Carpathian, Tatra, and Sudeten mountains extending from Ukraine west to Bavaria. Behind these formidable mountain ranges, the Austrian emperors of the eighteenth century had built their so-called northern Quadrilateral, the Elbe fortresses in northeastern Bohemia at Theresienstadt, Königgrätz, and Josephstadt. A good Austrian general would have made the most of this promising position in 1866: a central deployment, internal lines, an intact railroad net, and the ability to divide one's forces to north or south as the need arose and rush to the threatened point along the shortest possible line. Yet somehow, despite these advantages and the unforeseen bonus of French and Russian neutrality, Austria managed to lose the war of 1866 and, in the process, its stature as a Great Power. All for the want of a good general? Perhaps. This is the story of Austria's military collapse in 1866, and of the rise of Prussia-Germany and national Italy.

It is the first history of the war to appear since the 1960s and the first ever to undertake extensive archival research in Austria, Germany, and Italy. Explaining the triumph of Prussian arms has been relatively easy, not least because the best archival materials in Berlin were destroyed by an American air attack in 1945. When the smoke cleared, little was left besides the already published papers of Moltke and Bismarck and the official Prussian history of the war – *Der Feldzug von*

1

1866 in Deutschland — that had been distilled in 1867 from the very General Staff records that were subsequently destroyed. Yet with or without the old Prussian *Heeresarchiv*, the scarcely alterable fact remains that General Helmuth von Moltke — Prussia's General Staff chief in 1866 — devised a controversial but effective operations plan, which his generals in the field ultimately implemented to good effect.[1] What new research there has been on Prussia's victory in 1866 has tended to take Moltke's military genius for granted, and to seek for continuities in Prusso-German nineteenth- and twentieth-century strategy, "Moltke to Schlieffen" and, in some cases, on to Guderian.[2]

Italy's records of the war are more difficult to fathom because of the fathomless bureaucracy that guards them. This historian, armed with an invitation from the Italian General Staff and letters of accreditation from Yale University and the American government, was turned away from the Italian army archive in Rome for want of a supplementary authorization from the Italian *foreign* minister. Despite this vexing interference, I was able to glean valuable information with far less trouble at Rome's central state archive, and at provincial archives in Milan, Venice, and Naples. Italy's printed literature on the war proved another good source, for the army's embarrassing defeat at Custoza in 1866 prised off its hard shell of decorum, loosing a storm of "insider" revelations.[3] Italian army reformers did not hesitate to reap this whirlwind, using Custoza as a prime example of everything that was wrong with the unprofessional, nepotistic army of King Vittorio Emanuele II.[4] Writing in this charged enviroment, the authors of the Italian General Staff history — *La Campagna del 1866 in Italia*, belatedly published in 1875 — had little choice but to explain frankly just how it was that the Italian army managed to "liberate" Habsburg Venetia in 1866 despite having lost its only major battle with the Austrians.

Austria's reaction to the events of 1866 was less forthright. For three years the Habsburg General Staff pondered the war, then released its five volume official history — *Österreichs Kämpfe im Jahre 1866* — in 1869. The Austrian staff history was most remarkable for its many evasions. Rather than place blame for Austria's defeat where it belonged — in the Habsburg army itself, which fought the war

1 Gordon A. Craig, *The Battle of Königgrätz* (Philadelphia: Lippincott, 1964). Martin Van Creveld, *Command in War* (Cambridge, Mass.: Harvard University Press, 1985).

2 Gunther E. Rothenberg, "Moltke, Schlieffen and the Doctrine of Strategic Envelopment," in Peter Paret, ed., *Makers of Modern Strategy* (1943; Princeton: Princeton University Press, 1986). Arden Bucholz, *Moltke, Schlieffen and Prussian War Planning* (New York: Berg, 1991). Larry H. Addington, *The Blitzkrieg Era and the German General Staff, 1865–1941* (New Brunswick: Rutgers University Press, 1971). Martin Kitchen, *A Military History of Germany* (Bloomington: Indiana University Press, 1975).

3 Alfonso La Marmora, *Un po più di luce sugli eventi politici e militari dell'anno 1866* (Florence: Barbèra, 1873). Luigi Chiara, *Ancora un po più di luce sugli eventi politici e militari dell'anno 1866* (Florence: Barbèra, 1902). Pio Calza, *Nuova luce sugli eventi militari del 1866* (Bologna: Zanichelli, 1924).

4 Alberto Pollio, *Custoza 1866* (Città di Castello: Unione Arte Graphiche, 1914).

with brutish tactics and directed it with amazing laxity – the authors, all imperial officers, sought instead for scapegoats. In their biased view, the Habsburg army was beaten in 1866 less by its own flawed organization and leadership than by sheer numbers of Prussian and Italian troops, by Prussia's superior rifle, by faithless allies, and by a stingy parliament.

Although Austria's official historians did find fault with General Ludwig Benedek – commander of the Austrian North Army – they did not explain how it was that Austria's emperor could have sanctioned the rise of such a mediocre strategist to the supreme command of his army. Though the Austrian staff historians attributed Prussia's victory to the superior war plans of General Moltke, they never explained how it was that Moltke's vital post came to be filled in Austria by a frivolous, inexperienced banker's son – General Alfred Henikstein – who, predictably, made a hash of Austrian war planning in 1866 and had to be recalled from the field army in the midst of the campaign for incompetence. Finally, though Austria's official historians cited the Habsburg army's failure in 1866 to adopt a breech-loading rifle and Prussian-style fire tactics as factors in its defeat, they did not explain just how the Austrians could have ignored Prussia's fearsome display of fire tactics in the Danish War of 1864, then gone to war with Prussia in 1866 armed with muzzle-loading rifles and formed in deep, easily targeted shock columns. All in all, *Österreichs Kämpfe* was so vague or misleading on the vital questions of Austrian command, strategy, and tactics that Lieutenant-Colonel Eduard Bartels – a dissident Habsburg staff officer – likened the book to the military disaster that had broken the Austrian Empire in 1866. He pronounced it a "historiographical Sadova, contrived in the poisonous atmosphere of the [Habsburg] war ministry."[5]

Although there have been newer attempts to describe and interpret the Austro-Prussian War, they have all relied upon the nineteenth-century staff histories for their military details and have consequently broken little or no new ground. Heinrich Friedjung's two-volume *Struggle for Supremacy in Germany, 1859–66* – revised several times in the years between 1897 and 1912 – was far more a Liberal critique of Franz Josephan Austria than a serious study of Austria's war effort.[6] Friedjung, an outspoken Liberal in the Austrian parliament at the *fin-de-siècle*, saved his best barbs for the "feudals," the "Jesuits," the "Slavs," and the "émigrés" he held responsible for Austria's collapse in 1866 and propagated the myth that General Benedek – a Germanized and therefore good Hungarian in Friedjung's rather bigoted view – had been the victim not of his own monumental vanity and incompetence but of "court creatures" and machinations.[7] Friedjung never enjoyed free access to the

---

5 Eduard Bartels, *Der Krieg im Jahre 1866* (Leipzig: Otto Wigand, 1867), p. 11.
6 Heinrich Friedjung, *The Struggle for Supremacy in Germany, 1859–66*, trans. A. J. P. Taylor (1897; London: Macmillan, 1935). Original, unabridged German editions: *Der Kampf um die Voherrschaft in Deutschland*, 2 vols. (Stuttgart, Berlin: Cotta, 1897–1912).
7 The popularity of Friedjung's sociopolitical explanation for Austria's defeat in 1866 prompted Karl Krauss, the great Viennese wit, to quip: *"Ohne Friedjung kein 1866; ohne 1866 kein Friedjung. In vielen Kreisen wird das Dasein Friedjungs als hinreichende Entscheidung für Königgrätz aufgefasst."* Die

free access to the Habsburg *Kriegsarchiv* and thus relied on what uncontroversial documents were shown him by his chaperone, General Friedrich Fischer, the very man who had written *Österreichs Kämpfe* thirty years earlier.[8]

Since the fall of the Habsburg Monarchy and the opening of its archives to all, few historians have undertaken new archival research on the Austro-Prussian War to extend Friedjung's narrow foundation. In 1960, Oskar Regele, an officer in Austria's Federal Army, published a book called *Feldzeugmeister Benedek und der Weg nach Königgrätz*, which made the unlikely argument that "Austria's diplomats and politicians were far more culpable [for the defeat in 1866] than their mere agent, General Benedek."[9] This unoriginal thesis – it had been, after all, the Habsburg army's own rationalization for its defeat at the hands of Prussia and Italy – was altogether unsatisfactory. It took no account of the Austrian army's own considerable political influence under Franz Joseph, nor of its hugely wasteful bureaucracy. Principally concerned as it was to absolve General Benedek and the army of blame for the disaster, Regele's book did not begin to explain just how Benedek and his handpicked staff *chef*, General Henikstein, could have squandered so many excellent chances in 1866.

The centennial of the Austro-Prussian War saw new books but little new research on the war beyond a fine essay by Johann Christoph Allmayer-Beck based on research in the archive of Emperor Franz Joseph's military cabinet.[10] Emil Franzel's two-volume *1866 Il Mondo Casca* was derived from published material as was Gordon Craig's *Battle of Königgrätz* and Adam Wandruszka's *Schicksalsjahr 1866*.[11] None of these historians questioned the official version of Austria's crushing defeat. None of them peered *inside* the Austrian army to determine just why and how it broke under pressure. This book aims to do just that. It is the first unofficial history of the war to base itself on documentary evidence, and it usefully blends a social-historical perspective with a more conventionally military one. Using private, newly discovered diaries and the Austrian army's own detailed field correspondence – plans drafted at the army and corps levels and battle reports submitted by brigades, regiments, and battalions – I have been able to reconstruct the "everyday life" of the Austrian army in 1866. At the army's

Fackel, 6, February 5, 1913, pp. 4–5. Michael Derndarsky, "Das Klischée von 'Ces Messieurs de Vienne,'" *Historische Zeitschrift* 235 (1982), pp. 288–90. Toilow [F. Karl Folliot-Crenneville], *Die österreichische Nordarmee und ihr Führer im Jahre 1866* (Vienna and Leipzig: Wm. Braumüller, 1906), pp. 150–3. Sigismund Schlichting, *Moltke und Benedek* (Berlin: Mittler, 1900), p. iii.

8 Alfred Krauss, *Moltke, Benedek und Napoleon* (Vienna: Seidel, 1901), pp. 2–5. Oskar Regele, *Feldzeugmeister Benedek und der Weg nach Königgrätz* (Vienna, Munich: Verlag Herold, 1960), pp. 10–11.

9 Oskar Regele, *Feldzeugmeister Benedek*. Oskar Regele, "Staatspolitische Geschichtsschreibung: Erläutert an Königgrätz 1866," *Mitteilungen des österreichischen Staatsarchivs (MÖSA)* 3 (1950), p. 305.

10 J. C. Allmayer-Beck, "Der Feldzug der österreichischen Nordarmee nach Königgrätz," in Wolfgang Groote and Ursula Gersdorff, eds., *Entscheidung 1866* (Stuttgart: Deutsche Verlags Anstalt, 1966).

11 Craig, *The Battle of Königgrätz*. Adam Wandruzka, *Schicksalsjahr 1866* (Vienna: Verlag Styria, 1966). Emil Franzel, *1866 Il Mondo Casca*, 2 vols. (Vienna: Verlag Herold, 1968).

highest and lowest levels, I have been able to chart its downfall in precise, sometimes lurid detail.

This book, based as it is on firsthand, candid testimony, exposes for the first time the awful ineptitude of General Benedek's command, and the various ways in which Benedek transmitted his ineptitude to Austria's regiments, strategically, tactically, and psychologically. The book thus offers fresh, intimate insights into a war that, until now, has only been studied from a polite, unknowing distance, and only in its strategic and operational aspects. Austria did lose in 1866 for many reasons, but chiefly because, in the clinch, its largely Slavic and Hungarian regiments fought badly – through no fault of their own – and because Ludwig Benedek, Austria's supreme commander on the Prussian front, revealed himself to be a supremely incompetent general.

1

~~~~~~

Strategy and tactics in 1866:
The state of the art

Until 1866, the whole history of modern warfare had been one of ever increasing troop numbers and ever more sophisticated fortress and weapons systems. The average army fielded in the wars of the seventeenth century had numbered just 20,000 men. To shield and supply these small arrays of well-trained mercenaries, military engineers like France's Vauban built constellations of star-shaped fortresses along the frontiers and at the crossroads of their kingdoms. Warfare developed precise rules as small, professional armies let loose in vast countries with few supplies unfailingly marched to the enemy and attempted either to engage him or force him back on his forts, where a siege would ensue until the mounting cost in lives, money, and material persuaded one party or the other to cede a province, a daughter, or a sum of bullion.

During the eighteenth-century wars of Louis XIV and Frederick the Great, armies – manned and funded by wealthier, more populous states – grew to an average strength of 60,000 men. They were, however, rarely able to commit more than half that number to the field because of the need to "mask" or keep under observation all the Vauban-style forts that had sprouted along their routes of march. Set-piece battles and sieges remained the norm because it took pharaonic labors just to deploy a thirty-pound howitzer, let alone move it, and because the flintlock musket, introduced in the eighteenth century, though faster-firing than the arquebus it replaced, was still hopelessly inaccurate at ranges beyond 100 meters.[1] Thus, line regiments had to be marched to within a stone's throw of each other at which point they would raise their muskets and fire volleys at terrifyingly short range. Here the advantage went to the line that fired last, for, after absorbing the enemy's volley, it could shuffle forward, shortening the range still more and, with the proverbial "whites of the enemy's eyes" in sight, deliver a devastating salvo of .70 caliber balls. Crude tactical considerations like this one accounted for a notorious incident at Fontenoy in 1743, when French and English officers

---

1 Martin Van Creveld, *Technology and War* (New York: Free Press, 1989), pp. 87–95, 113.

closed up their opposing lines and then, with exaggerated politeness, each invited the other to fire first.[2]

War changed dramatically in the nineteenth century, when Napoleon Bonaparte introduced "batteries" of lightweight, eight- and twelve-pound cannon, which fired light projectiles and could be limbered up and moved quickly by horse teams. The new French "battery system," which concentrated the fire of eight guns on a single target, wrought havoc everywhere it struck and accounted for the rapid adoption of this system by all armies. In the French Revolutionary and Napoleonic Wars, the ratio of field guns to infantry increased on all sides, making war a much more dangerous business. By 1815, with his regiments thinned by twenty years of war, Napoleon increasingly used massed batteries of artillery to compensate for his shrinking numbers of men.[3] Carl von Clausewitz's *On War*, published in 1832, contained the classic synopsis of Napoleonic combat, describing the descent of a man from the rear echelons of a battle to its front line. At each interval – corps, division, and brigade – he remarked upon the mounting ferocity of artillery fire, as cannon balls plowed the ground, shells hurled their lethal splinters, and "grape shot" rattled off buildings and screamed overhead.[4]

Troop numbers also increased in the course of the French Revolutionary and Napoleonic Wars. Assailed by a coalition of Great Powers in 1793, the French Jacobins had decreed universal conscription as a last resort to raise sufficient men to fend off the combined armies of Austria, Prussia, England, Holland, Spain, and Piedmont.[5] Napoleon took this ready-built system and used it to man and replenish his own "Grand Army" from 1804 until his downfall in 1815.[6] Initially reluctant to adopt the French system, which entailed arming large numbers of untrained, politically unreliable men, rival armies were forced by attrition to embrace all or parts of it. Thus, in 1814 the Prussians introduced universal conscription and the Austrians created a *Landwehr* or reserve army of national guards.[7]

Bigger armies needed new tactics, for the old ones had been devised for small, professional armies, which had devoted years to the perfection of complex linear formations. Confronted with droves of green recruits and advancing enemies on every frontier, the generals of the French Revolution – Napoleon included – had hit upon an ingenious solution: columnar tactics. Whenever an enemy regiment

2 Hew Strachan, *European Armies and the Conduct of War* (London: Allen and Unwin, 1983), pp. 8–22, 32–3, 55, 111.

3 Van Creveld, *Technology*, pp. 94–6. Strachan, *European Armies*, pp. 51–2.

4 Carl von Clausewitz, *On War*, trans. J. J. Graham, ed. Anatol Rapaport (1832; New York: Penguin, 1985), 1/iv, "Of Danger in War," pp. 158–60.

5 Strachan, *European Armies*, pp. 39–40.

6 Larry H. Addington, *The Patterns of War since the Eighteenth Century* (Bloomington: Indiana University Press, 1984), pp. 21–7.

7 Hajo Holborn, "The Prusso-German School: Moltke and the Rise of the General Staff," in Peter Paret, ed., *Makers of Modern Strategy* (1943; Princeton: Princeton University Press, 1986), p. 282. Strachan, *European Armies*, pp. 56–8.

deployed in line and prepared to fire, a French attack column would sprint at it with the bayonet. The astonished line infantry, armed with muzzle-loading muskets, would be lucky to get off one or two volleys before the "shock columns" of howling French peasants and *sans-culottes* burst through their midst, wrecking their formation and trampling the old regime musketeers underfoot.[8]

The first triumph of these new French "shock tactics" was Valmy in 1792, when a rapidly assembled army of French conscripts advancing behind a heavy cannonade put an army of Prussian professionals to rout. Rough and dirty though the French tactics were, the Prussians, Austrians, and Russians could not afford to ignore them. Indeed, only British infantry proved bold and skillful enough to "hold the line" against French columnar assaults. After Valmy, all other powers gradually adopted shock tactics, which would remain the standard Continental tactic until 1866.

Backed by his mass armies, which initially made up with zeal what they lacked in experience, Napoleon committed ever larger forces to battle. After 1800, Bonaparte regularly campaigned with 100,000 men or more and tended to ignore enemy fortresses that appeared on his flanks. Thrusting impatiently past these eighteenth-century relics, he dared their small garrisons to sally against his big armies. This emphasis on mass, speed, and mobility was yet another of Napoleon's innovations. If an unsubdued fortress blocked a march route or interrupted French lines of supply, Napoleon rarely wasted time besieging the obstacle, but improvised instead, lurching round the fort and making up any deficit in supplies by requisitioning at the expense of local populations.

Swollen with fresh-faced drafts and fed by an eighteenth-century agricultural revolution that introduced the potato and more bountiful crop yields, armies grew and grew in the early 1800s, becoming so large that, in 1805, Napoleon was compelled finally to slice them into manageable, self-sufficient pieces the size of seventeenth-century armies. These were the first army "corps." They were, in turn, subdivided into two or three all-arms "divisions," each comprising twelve infantry battalions, five cavalry squadrons, and thirty-two guns.[9] This decentralization of command and logistics permitted Bonaparte to build even *bigger* armies. In 1812, he marched to Moscow with 600,000 men. One year later, he engaged 300,000 Allied troops with 130,000 of his own at Leipzig. This so-called battle of the nations would stand as the biggest battle of all time until 1866, when 450,000 Austrians and Prussians bestrode the field at Königgrätz.[10]

The growth of armies and the attendant devolution of command from army to corps to division to brigade accentuated as never before the function of the

---

8 Gunther E. Rothenberg, *The Art of Warfare in the Age of Napoleon* (Bloomington: Indiana University Press, 1978), pp. 98–102, 114–18.

9 Strachan, *European Armies*, pp. 40–4. Cyril Falls, *The Art of War* (London: Oxford University Press, 1961), pp. 30–4.

10 Vincennes, Archive de l'Armée de Terre (AAT), 7N848, Gaston Bodart, "Die Stärkeverhältnisse in den bedeutesten Schlachten." Craig, *The Battle of Königgrätz*, p. x.

professional general staff. Once despised by their regimental colleagues as mere mappers and theorists, staff officers of the Napoleonic era, like Bonaparte's Berthier and Schwarzenberg's Radetzky, became the very glue of modern armies. By plotting lines of operation and supply they contributed decisively to a campaign's outcome by moving troops efficiently to a theater of war.[11] If line troops arrived on their battlefield fit and well fed after a sequence of reasonable, well-supplied marches, then it was fair to say that the general staff had taken the first, essential step to victory and conferred an inestimable advantage on its field commanders.

In terms of actual fighting, general staffs were no less important, for troop movements became more complex as crowds of unruly infantrymen, cavalry mounts, field guns, and ammunition wagons were crammed into growing armies, extending the frontage of the average European corps in the first decade of the nineteenth century from 1.2 to 2.5 kilometers. As a result of this more than two-fold growth, the *time* needed for a Napoleonic corps to deploy for battle also more than doubled, from two to five hours, as frantic staff officers toiled to separate an army's guns and reloads from its infantry, cavalry, and food stocks and to make contact with neighboring units. It was a difficult task, usually completed under fire amid confusion, and it required cool heads and rigorous organization from the initial mobilization until the decisive battle.[12]

These major organizational changes carried strategic ones in their train. By 1815, with new, better-managed regiments advancing along the hundreds of new roads that had been laid down as a part of Europe's modernization under Napoleon, it was fair to say that the old eighteenth-century practice of fighting from fortress to fortress for control of the intervening turnpikes and waterways was obsolete. Troops parked inside the old forts were easily contained by enemy "observation corps" and kept from joining decisive battles beyond their walls. Generals who hewed too closely to eighteenth-century rules of war in the nineteenth century found themselves outnumbered and vulnerable in the field.[13] Thus Clausewitz's *On War* recommended a strategy of "unbridled violence" for the new century.[14] Clausewitz was for restless offensives aimed not at an enemy's forts or capital but at his *army*, which, once destroyed, would compel the surrender of the enemy state.[15] *On War*, which, significantly, was a Prussian production, discarded all the old truths of the eighteenth century – especially the belief in the efficacy of defensive fortifications and limited war aims – and presaged a new era of war on a

11 Strachan, *European Armies*, p. 53.

12 Wolfgang von Groote, "Moltkes Planungen für den Feldzug in Böhmen und ihre Grundlagen," in Wolfgang von Groote and Ursula von Gersdorff, eds., *Entscheidung 1866* (Stuttgart: Deutsche Verlags-Anstalt, 1966), p. 90.

13 Helmuth von Moltke, *Moltke on the Art of War*, ed. Daniel J. Hughes (Novato: Presidio, 1993), pp. 22–35. Strachan, *European Armies*, pp. 34–5.

14 Strachan, *European Armies*, pp. 92–6.

15 Clausewitz, *On War*, 4/v, "The Significance of Combat," pp. 316–18.

grand scale, where whole populations would be mobilized and politics and war would mingle with dangerous implications for Europe's ancient dynasties.[16]

In 1848, a revolution toppled the throne of France and nearly overthrew the monarchs of Austria and Prussia. Even the most reactionary European generals and statesmen, some of whom had taken Clausewitz for a rabble-rouser bent on arming the masses, awoke to the fact that armies like politicians had to move with the times.[17] Symbolic of this realization was the fact that France's new Republican government had crushed a Socialist insurrection in Paris in June 1848 not with local garrison troops − many of whom had fraternized with insurgent workers − but with French national guards trucked in from the provinces in record time on steam trains.[18] Just as road-building and improved crop yields had aided the first Napoleon in his campaigns at the turn of the century, a new Napoleon at mid-century would be able to exploit the military potential of two new innovations: the railway, which permitted rapid movement, and the electric telegraph, which, for the first time, permitted instant communication across vast spaces.

Shunted by railroads and coordinated by telegraphs, Europe's armies resumed their growth after 1848, this time aided by deadly new developments in weapons technology. In the 1840s and 1850s, most European armies discarded their smoothbore muskets and rearmed with rifled ones, which extended the range of an infantryman from 120 to 1,200 meters. The French and the British, followed by the Austrians, Prussians, Italians, and Americans, applied rifle technology to their artillery, which pushed maximum gun ranges out from 1,000 meters in 1848 to 7,000 in 1859, raining chaos and death far behind enemy lines.[19] Asked by his company captain at Shiloh in 1862 why he did not make for the safety of the rear, a wounded Union soldier pointed to shells screaming overhead and replied: "Because, cap'n, this battle ain't got no *rear.*"

In the Crimean War, fought from 1854−6, 600,000 French, British, Turkish, and Piedmontese troops were mobilized to fight 600,000 Russians. The British were armed for the first time with rifles, with which they inflicted horrible casualties on the Russians. Although contemporaries ridiculed the Russians for their inability to drive the Allies off their remote Black Sea beachheads, they were in no doubt as to the reason why. The Russians were still armed with a musket, still formed in Napoleonic shock columns, and still marching on foot. Tsar Nicholas I had never built a railway to connect his depots in Moscow and St. Petersburg with his Crimean ports, which meant that Russian reinforcements and

---

16 Michael Howard, *War in European History* (Oxford: Oxford University Press, 1976), pp. 94−7.
17 Strachan, *European Armies*, pp. 69−70.
18 And in Baden in 1849, a Prussian counterrevolutionary army had been unable to come to grips with a Badenese revolutionary one, which had skipped backward out of reach on the railway each time the Prussians attempted to engage. Dennis E. Showalter, *Railroads and Rifles* (Hamden: Archon, 1975), pp. 36−7.
19 Vincennes, AAT, MR 845, Paris, January 1862, Maj. Auguste Châtelain, "Etudes historiques et militaires sur la guerre d'Italie en 1859."

supplies never arrived in sufficient quantity to defeat the French and British, who ended up winning the Crimean War almost by default in 1856.[20]

In 1859, the world witnessed its first great railroad mobilization, as French Emperor Napoleon III, a nephew of the great Napoleon, transported 130,000 troops – half his total strength – to Italy by rail. In June, 300,000 French, Piedmontese, and Austrians clashed at Solferino in Lombardy, a battle that exhibited all the problems modern European armies were experiencing as they struggled to adopt new arms, tactics, and organizational methods. The French army of 270,000 gained the Po basin only after what one commentator called a "Xerxes march" to Milan, a straggling caravan of mixed-up arms and supplies that was able to form for battle only because of the no less sluggish approach of Austria's five corps, one of which proved so muddled that it was able to cover no more than three miles a day in the critical weeks before Solferino.[21]

Three inconclusive battles were fought before Solferino – at Montebello, Palestro, and Magenta – and the Austrians fumbled away good chances in all three. This was due in large part to the ineptitude of Austria's infantry, which had only just rearmed with a rifle and had no idea how to use it to good effect. Thus, though armed with older rifles technically inferior to Austria's new ones, the French were able to rout the Austrians employing the shock tactics of the last century. Some Austrian battalions literally dissolved before French bayonet charges, as panic-stricken Habsburg troops tried to load, aim, and fire rifles that, in many instances, were still slick with factory grease.[22] At Palestro, where French and Austrian troops battled for control of the Sesia river bridges, foreign observers marveled that many units actually fought with their bare hands, as columns of French infantry crashed into lines of bewildered Austrian riflemen, who solved the technical problem posed by their relatively sophisticated rifles by casting them away and fighting with their fists.[23]

In 1859, Austrian tactics – revised by Field Marshal Joseph Radetzky in 1849 to take full advantage of the monarchy's new "precision rifle" – had proven too complicated for Austria's largely Slavic, uneducated peasant conscripts. Although there were nine different "languages of instruction" for peace-

20 Strachan, *European Armies*, pp. 72–3.
21 Vincennes, AAT, MR 845, Anon., "Précis historique de la campagne d'Italie en 1859." Wolf Schneider von Arno, "Der österreichisch-ungarische Generalstab," (Kriegsarchiv Manuscript), vol. 7, pp. 18, 54–5. Michael Howard, *The Franco-Prussian War* (1961; London: Granada, 1979), p. 23.
22 Helmuth von Moltke, "Der italienische Feldzug des Jahres 1859," *Moltkes kriegsgeschichtlichen Arbeiten*, ed. grosser Generalstab, 3 vols. (Berlin: Mittler, 1904), vol. 3/2, pp. 114-15. Eduard Bartels, *Der Krieg im Jahre 1859* (Bamberg: Buchner Verlag, 1894), pp. 6–8. k.k. Generalstab, *Der Krieg in Italien 1859*, 3 vols. (Vienna: Druckerei des Generalstabs, 1872), vol. 1, pp. 411 and 438.
23 Vincennes, AAT, MR 845, Paris, January 1862, Maj. Auguste Châtelain, "Etudes historiques et militaires sur la guerre d'Italie en 1859." Col. Charles Ardant du Picq, *Battle Studies*, trans. J. Greely (1880; New York: Macmillan, 1921), pp. 268-70.

time use in the polyglot Austrian army – languages like Czech, Serbo-Croatian, Hungarian, Rumanian, and Italian – in battle the army employed just one: German. Conceive, then, the terror that engulfed Austria's non-German troops of the line as French storm columns converged on them while their German-speaking officers bellowed orders in what was, for most, an unfamiliar tongue. One Austrian officer later noted that at Solferino his company of Slavs had been unable to comprehend even the command "*Halt.*"[24] Thus France and Piedmont triumphed in 1859, due in large measure to Austrian fumbling with a new rifle, new tactics, and horribly mismanaged lines of supply. So wretched had been the Austrian war effort that, after Solferino, Emperor Franz Joseph, who served for the first and last time in his long reign as commander in the field, took the unusual step of suing for an immediate peace rather than retiring over the Mincio river to continue the war from Austria's formidable Quadrilateral fortress group in Venetia.

Franz Joseph capitulated in July 1859 and agreed to cede the rich Habsburg province of Lombardy to Piedmont, a French client and a budding Great Power. In his Laxenburg Manifesto – drafted to explain the Austrian fiasco to a disbelieving public – Franz Joseph blasted Austria's principal ally in the German Confederation, Prussia, for failing to aid Austria in the conflict. Yet the sad fact was that the Prussians had *tried* to help but, like the Austrians, had been derailed by logistics, which had slowed Prussia's mobilization on the Rhine to a crawl and convinced the Prussian regent, Crown Prince Wilhelm, of the need to entrust reforms of Prussia's army to its two most most able administrators, Generals Helmuth von Moltke and Albrecht von Roon.[25]

The French, although victorious, suffered horribly in the campaign. With just one ambulance per regiment of 3,000 men, most French wounded were abandoned to the heat and vultures. Food was always in short supply; most French troops subsisted on coffee and cold gobs of *vercelli*, starvation rations that produced a debilitating flow of men to the army's sick bays. France's shock tactics, though acclaimed for their audacity, were often nothing more than a desperate tactical correction to the army's strategic floundering. At Magenta, for example, French troop commanders stormed ahead all along the line because Napoleon III had issued conflicting orders – one set made his left the "turning wing" the other, the right. The predictable result was a deadlock, as French attack columns battered for hours against Austria's *front* and broke through only at the cost of heavy, avoidable casualties.[26] In sum, on all sides, the Italian War of 1859 furnished further proof of the need for modern armies to streamline their organizations, accelerate their deployments, and improve the tactical performance of their

24 D. N., "Über die Truppensprachen unserer Armee," *Österreichische Militärische Zeitschrift (ÖMZ)* 2 (1862), pp. 365–7.
25 Showalter, *Railroads and Rifles*, pp. 44–8.
26 Vincennes, AAT, MR 845, Paris, January 1862, Maj. Châtelain, "Bataille de Magenta."

troops.[27] Victory in the next war would almost certainly go to the army that grasped the lessons of this one.

Prussia's regent, Crown Prince Wilhelm, ascended to the throne in 1861 upon the death of his elder brother. The new king, Wilhelm I, though not noted for his sagacity, had the good sense to employ brilliant advisors, foremost among them Count Otto von Bismarck at the foreign ministry, Moltke at the General Staff, and Roon at the ministry of war. In just seven years, Moltke and Roon would not only grasp but *institutionalize* the lessons of 1859, a task they completed in time for the war of 1866, which would pit a thoroughly professional Prussian army against a scarcely reformed Austrian version of the force that had fallen to the French at Solferino.

Born in Mecklenburg in 1800 and educated at Berlin's *Kriegsakademie*, Moltke took Clausewitz's offensive precepts and, in the decade between his promotion to Prussian staff chief in 1858 and Prussia's war with Austria in 1866, worked them into hard-hitting war plans, which he successfully communicated to most of the Prussian officer corps.[28] Convinced of the urgent need to reform Prussia's military establishment after the technical and military embarrassments of the 1830s, 1840s, and 1850s, when the Prussian army had stumbled through its deployments and snared itself in its own limited operations against a Polish insurrection and minor revolutions in Baden and Hessia, Moltke first expanded the Prussian regular army, then revolutionized its strategic, operational, and tactical doctrines in the years between 1862 and 1866.

Throughout his long career, Moltke was driven by the fear, shared by Bismarck, that Prussia could all too easily be overrun by any of its larger neighbors. In the reign of Frederick the Great (1740–86), Voltaire had dismissed Prussia as a mere "kingdom of border strips," for its eastern heartland – Brandenburg and Prussia – was riven from its western enclaves in Westphalia and the Rhineland by the north German free cities and the princely states of Saxony, Hanover, and Hessia. In the south, Prussian Silesia and Lusatia, prized for their textile mills and coal mines, overlapped the Austrian Empire and its Saxon ally. In the east, Prussia was flanked by the Russian Empire's Baltic and Polish provinces. In the west, it was bounded by France. In short, of all the European Great Powers, Prussia was the most vulnerable to invasion, and the expansion of railroads and telegraphs in the 1840s only accentuated this vulnerability. In 1859, Berlin's efforts to win a reprieve for its Austrian ally in Lombardy by threatening Napoleon III with a Rhine mobilization had been met with the cool French assurance

27 Howard, *Franco-Prussian War*, pp. 17–18.
28 Strachan, *European Armies*, pp. 98–9.

1.   General Helmuth von Moltke (1800–91), Prussian General Staff chief in 1866

that since France's railways could muster 200,000 men to the Rhine in a matter of *days*, the Prussians, who would require weeks, ought perhaps to desist with their threats, which they had.[29]

Such embarrassments had been the stuff of Prussian army life in the 1850s, a decade that had begun for Berlin with what Bismarck called the "humiliation of

29 Showalter, *Railroads and Rifles*, p. 48.

Olmütz," a crushing diplomatic setback occasioned by the army's failure to deploy in time to defend Prussia against a threatened Austrian invasion from Bohemia in November 1850. With an Austrian army on their frontiers, Prussian negotiators at the Austrian town of Olmütz had been forced to drop Hohenzollern plans to dissolve the Habsburg-run German Confederation of 1815 and reorganize north Germany under Prussian hegemony. Ridiculed for the climb-down, Prussia's generals protested that they had no choice, for Prussia's march routes, telegraph roads, and railways were everywhere interrupted and flanked by Austria and its German Confederate allies.

This precarious strategic situation accounted for Prussia's timid approach to international affairs in the first half of the nineteenth century. Rather than challenge Austria's control of the thirty-nine state German Confederation, a privilege that had been granted Austria by all the European Great Powers at the Congress of Vienna in 1815, the Prussians had loyally maintained the treaties of 1815 and generally collaborated with the Austrians to uphold a European "balance of power" that was premised upon Habsburg supremacy in Germany and Italy. Thus, Austro-Prussian cooperation was taken for granted in the Polish crisis of 1831, in the revolutions of 1848, throughout the Crimean War, and even as late as the Franco-Austrian War of 1859, when the Prussian king had refused Bismarck's suggestion that he take advantage of Austria's defeat at Solferino to dissolve the German Confederation, link up the scattered provinces of Prussia, and push the Protestant kingdom's frontiers deep into Germany's Catholic south.[30]

Prussian military doctrine had long mirrored this political conservatism, which explained the army's capitulation to Austrian threats in 1850 as well as King Wilhelm's decision to replace Prussia's unimaginative old guard with daring new reformers in the late 1850s.[31] Upon assuming the post of Prussian General Staff chief in 1858, General Moltke immediately remarked that whereas a vast Continental power like Russia or Austria could absorb a whole series of defeats while retiring on its interior, Prussia, that "kingdom of border strips," would not be so fortunate. Its flat, sandy plains offered few obstacles to an invader, and Berlin, with its carefully husbanded treasury, its vital rail terminals, and its efficient ministries, had no natural features to defend it against a determined enemy, who, like Napoleon in 1806, would be able to dash across the entire kingdom in a matter of days.[32]

Moltke understood that the only way for Prussia to break from its dependency on Austria and its subordination to England, France, and Russia, was to make Prussia what it had briefly been under Frederick the Great: the premier military

---

30 Otto Pflanze, *Bismarck and the Development of Germany*, 3 vols. (1963; Princeton: Princeton University Press, 1990), vol. 1, p. 136. Lothar Gall, *Bismarck*, trans. J. A. Underwood, 2 vols. (Frankfurt 1980; London: Allen and Unwin, 1986), vol. 1, pp. 98–9.

31 Gall, *Bismarck*, vol. 1, pp. 73–7. Showalter, *Railroads and Rifles*, pp. 37–8.

32 *Moltke on the Art of War*, ed. Daniel J. Hughes, pp. 102–7.

state of Europe. To do this, Moltke hurried to implement strategic and tactical changes that rival powers were only slowly adopting. It was the English historian A. J. P. Taylor who described the rise of barren Prussia as "a triumph of man over nature," and this was no less true of Moltke's strategic conceptions after 1857.[33] Like Frederick the Great, Moltke sought to overcome Prussia's geographical weakness by mobilizing more quickly than his enemies, then launching his army into enemy territory to deflect and destroy hostile forces aimed at Berlin.[34]

This, again, was pure Clausewitz, but it was accomplished thanks to momentous reforms conceived and enacted by Moltke and Roon. In the years between 1859 and 1866, these two men staked their careers in a bitter fight with Prussia's Liberal-controlled parliament waged to bring the Prussian regular army up to the strength of its Austrian rival and to subject Prussia's notoriously easygoing *Landwehr*, the kingdom's middle-class national guard, to strict royal supervision. With the help of Bismarck, a domineering *Junker* whom the Prussian king appointed minister-president in 1862 to ram these controversial army reforms through parliament, Moltke and Roon were able to add fifty regiments to Prussia's army and triple its effective wartime strength, from 100,000 bayonets in 1859 to 300,000 in 1866. They also succeeded in developing for Prussia the most efficient, rapidly deployable army of any European power. Whereas the French, Austrians, and Russians still practiced "extraterritoriality," posting regiments not in their home districts but far away in order to make the army a "school of the nation," Moltke and Roon devised a territorial system of army corps that could be increased to war strength locally, then mobilized and deployed in a fraction of the time required by Prussia's rivals.[35] This enlarged, uniquely efficient army would enable Prussia, which disposed just half the population of the Austrian Empire in 1866, to risk war with its much more populous neighbor.

To ensure the professionalism of their enlarged army, Moltke and Roon sheared the army's *Landwehr* battalions away from its regular regiments and assigned them easy tasks like fortress duty and the defense of depots and supply lines. Although this raised another storm of protest from Prussia's Liberals, who wanted *Landwehr* units mixed with regular ones in order to dilute the *Junker* aristocracy's control of the royal army, Roon, Moltke, and Bismarck simply ignored parliament's annual vetoes of army bills and *forced* their changes through in time for 1866, giving Prussia the steep increase in troop numbers it would need to beat Austria and its principal German federal allies: Bavaria, Württemberg, Saxony, and Hanover.

33 A. J. P. Taylor, *The Course of German History* (New York: Capricorn, 1946), pp. 27–30.
34 Groote, "Moltkes Planungen," in *Entscheidung 1866*, pp. 78–81.
35 Hajo Holborn, "The Prusso-German School," in *Makers of Modern Strategy*, pp. 286–7. William Carr, *The Origins of the Wars of German Unification* (London: Longman, 1991), pp. 49–53. Gerhard Ritter, *The Sword and the Scepter*, trans. Heinz Norden, 4 vols. (Munich 1954–68), vol. 1, *The Prussian Tradition, 1740–1890*, pp. 121f.

While Bismarck battled Prussia's parliament on the *Landwehr* question, Moltke and Roon quietly brought Prussia's railways and telegraphs under state control and adapted them for military use. Railroad wagons were equipped with detachable benches so that seats could be removed and soldiers crammed inside in the event of mobilization, and freight cars were fitted with rings and breakaway partitions to accomodate cavalry horses and gun carriages. Lines were expanded and, in some cases, double-tracked to permit movement in two directions along the same railway. Lines that bypassed fortresses or regimental depots were equipped with extra sidings and prepared for military use, and telegraph cables were strung over the rails to ensure that army orders arrived in time to meet speeding trains.[36]

In 1864, Austria, Prussia, and the German states declared war on Denmark in order to free the provinces of Schleswig and Holstein from Danish rule and incorporate them into the German Confederation. This Danish War, which lasted a year, convinced Moltke of the need to hurry the integration of railroads into Prussian military planning. The Austro-Prussian force sent to Denmark to liberate Schleswig-Holstein traveled by rail, which spared the men much fatigue and landed them in the theater of operations in time for a spring 1864 offensive.[37]

Once mobilized and deployed in Denmark, Moltke came to appreciate the combat function of railroads no less than their logistical one. Instead of maneuvering, the Danes had fought the war with Austria and Prussia from a series of trench works, first from the Dannevirke in Schleswig, then from the royal forts at Fredericia and Dybbøl. In these places the Danes had concentrated and entrenched their guns and rifles, inflicting heavy casualties on Austrian and Prussian attackers. Witnessing first hand the range and destructiveness of rifled weapons, Moltke resolved in future to maneuver around fortifications, using railroads to move and concentrate his armies quickly. Railroads were essential to such operations because the range and accuracy of rifled guns and the continued growth of modern armies tended to make flank attacks and envelopments *strategic* rather than purely operational or tactical tasks. Now that a cannon could hurl a shell seven kilometers and an infantry rifle could bring a man down at 1,000 paces, it would be difficult to redirect a regiment from an enemy's center to his flank in the heat of battle. In the 1860s, such a classically Napoleonic maneuver would have resulted in prohibitive casualties.[38]

Moltke also recognized that since the Prussian army of the 1860s was three times larger than the Prussian army of the 1850s – 300,000 versus 100,000 men – it would be impossible to move it efficiently if it were deployed *en masse*.

36 Showalter, *Railroads and Rifles*, pp. 38–46. *Moltke on the Art of War*, ed. Daniel J. Hughes, pp. 107–21. Van Creveld, *Technology*, pp. 153–9.
37 Vincennes, AAT, MR 60/1470, Copenhagen, May 7, 1864, Lt-Col. Février to Marshal Randon. Bucholz, *Moltke, Schlieffen*, pp. 43–4.
38 Rothenberg, "Moltke, Schlieffen, and the Doctrine of Strategic Envelopment," pp. 299–300.

That had been just one of the many lessons taught by Solferino in 1859, when the Austrians had tried and failed to deploy more than a fraction of their densely packed army of 150,000 in the Mincio hills.[39] Armies of 100,000 or more had posed logistical problems even for Bonaparte, for a single corps of 30,000 men required fifty kilometers of open road to accomodate its march columns and trains. If infantry corps, cavalry divisions, artillery regiments, and supply wagons were simply stacked up one behind the other, most of the army would never see battle. Recognizing all this, Moltke resolved to use the mobility and speed afforded by Germany's excellent road, rail, and telegraph nets to move his armies separately to their jumping-off stations, where they would then hasten along uncluttered march routes to the point of attack, joining themselves wing-to-wing *in battle*, when a decisive result was in sight.[40]

For most of the world's military establishment, this Moltkean doctrine seemed heretical, for in the 1860s old soldiers still hewed to the precepts of Antoine Henri Jomini. Jomini, who had campaigned with Napoleon and then summarized his experiences in *Précis de l'art de la guerre* published in 1838, insisted that the secret of Bonaparte's success had been his "strategy of the central position," his tendency to mass troops on the "internal lines" *between* converging enemy armies to beat them separately. With the Napoleonic examples of Lodi, Marengo, and Austerlitz in mind, Jomini postulated that "simple and interior lines enable a general to bring into action . . . upon the important point a stronger force than the enemy." He cautioned nineteenth-century generals against repeating the errors of Napoleon's adversaries, who, too often, had failed to *concentrate* their coalition armies and thereby allowed themselves to be isolated and overwhelmed, one after the other, by Napoleon's massed columns.[41]

What Moltke perceived, however, was that the nineteenth century's ever growing numbers, weight and bulk of soldiers, guns, and material tended to clog Napoleon's "internal lines" and make rapid movement along them impossible. Indeed, Moltke, who insisted that "the *normal* state of an army is its separation into corps," took as his inspiration Bonaparte's famous victory at Ulm in 1805. There the French emperor – his army spread across a front of 200 kilometers – had converged quickly upon a slow-moving Austrian army massed on the Danube and had strangled it.[42] The example of Ulm must have symbolized for Moltke the many contradictions contained in Jomini's *Précis*. Had not Napoleon created the marshalate and the corps system to facilitate the *dispersal* of armies, which would permit them to march more quickly? And did not the examples of Ulm and Jena

39 Edward Bruce Hamley, *The Operations of War* (Edinburgh and London: Wm. Blackwood, 1866), pp. 364, 395.
40 Hajo Holborn, "The Prusso-German School," in *Makers of Modern Strategy*, p. 287.
41 "An undue number of lines divides the forces, and permits fractions to be overwhelmed by the enemy." Strachan, *European Armies*, pp. 44–6, 60–4. Howard, *War in European History*, p. 83.
42 Hajo Holborn, "The Prusso-German School," in *Makers of Modern Strategy*, p. 287. Strachan, *European Armies*, pp. 43–4, 64, 99.

suggest that armies massed in concentrated positions could easily be enveloped by dispersed, well-coordinated flanking armies?[43]

Moltke – like his American contemporary, Ulysses S. Grant, who never read Jomini and scorned "fixed laws of war" – appreciated that the intangible elements of surprise and flexibility had been far more vital to Napoleon's success than Jominian principles.[44] Moltke would make these elements instrumental in his own success by harnessing the railroad and the electric telegraph to make the rapid, *prolonged* movement and concentration of dispersed units possible. This distinguished Moltke from Napoleon, who, occupied as he usually was shuttling between two enemy armies, rarely found the resources to pursue and *destroy* either of them. In the post-Napoleonic period, Moltke felt certain that he could use the railway and the telegraph to mount unprecedentedly *wide* envelopments that would sweep the entire enemy front line and reserve into their jaws.[45]

Moltke also predicted the disappearance of charismatic captains like Bonaparte. The growth of armies, Moltke discovered, necessitated a devolution of command from headquarters to officers at the front. Headquarters, Moltke believed, had no business other than to deploy a field army wisely and direct it to its strategic objectives, where field commanders would plan and fight its battles to their conclusion. Later this Moltkean concept would be enshrined as *"Auftragstaktik,"* the Prusso-German practice, born in 1866, of limiting instructions to subordinates to a description of an army's ultimate objectives, leaving junior officers considerable tactical freedom for their attainment.[46] Though Moltke's prescriptions made perfect sense, they seemed to be the very antithesis of Napoleonic practice, which had landed sledgehammer blows with massed armies under the watchful eyes of the emperor himself.

Though Moltke's views were controversial, Prussia's King Wilhelm I believed in his staff chief and helped clear away obstacles to change put up by Prussia's high-ranking veterans of the wars with Napoleon. These influential "old sweats," officers like Field Marshal Friedrich von Wrangel and General Eduard Vogel von Falckenstein, submitted reluctantly to Moltke's reforms, and only just in time for a conflict with Austria that arose from the question of how to divide and administer the duchies of Schleswig and Holstein, which Prussia and Austria had jointly detached from the Kingdom of Denmark in 1864.[47] In 1865, Moltke and Roon began planning in earnest for a war with the Austrian Empire for control of the two disputed "Elbe Duchies." In the pending conflict, Austria would enjoy several advantages. The Habsburg province of Bohemia formed a salient that thrust northward into Prussia's hostile neighbor Saxony, which, assuming an

43 John Shy, "Jomini," in *Makers of Modern Strategy*, pp. 174–6.
44 Strachan, *European Armies*, pp. 73, 99.
45 Strachan, *European Armies*, pp. 46, 99.
46 *Moltke on the Art of War*, ed. Daniel J. Hughes, pp. 156–7. Strachan, *European Armies*, pp. 98–9.
47 Wilhelm Ritter von Gründorf von Zebegény, *Mémoiren eines österreichischen Generalstäblers, 1832–66*, 2 vols. (Stuttgart: Verlag Robert Lutz, 1913), vol. 2, p. 198.

Austro-Saxon alliance, would permit the Austrians to deploy just three days' march from Berlin. Any Prussian attempt to flank such an Austrian deployment from Upper Silesia would have been hindered by the physical barrier formed by Bohemia's Giant Mountains. Prussian march columns small enough to pass through the half dozen passes connecting Prussia and Austria could have been easily overpowered by the concentrated Austrian army in Bohemia.[48]

Despite these formidable obstacles to a Prussian invasion of Austria, Moltke decided in 1866 to risk one anyway. Over the opposition of Prussia's eldest generals – and old Jomini himself, who, from his study in Paris, recommended a defensive Prussian concentration in Silesia – Moltke opted for an offensive.[49] Prussia's last great expansionist, Frederick the Great, had never failed to beat the notoriously slow-moving Austrians through the mountains, and Moltke reasoned that Prussia's six railroads to the Austrian frontier would give him as a much as a six weeks' head start against the Austrians, who would have to rely on foot marches and a single railway – the *Nordbahn* – to convey troops and war material from Vienna to the Prussian border. Moltke understood that so long as he were left with the strategic initiative in the war, with full powers to initiate mobilization and thus beat Austria "to the draw," he would have ample time to overrun Saxony, seize its vital north-south railways, and pass through the Giant Mountains and into Bohemia, the granary and industrial core of the Austrian Empire.

To implement this daring plan, Moltke would have to move swiftly, to prevent the Austrians from completing their own mobilization and deployment, and to block cooperation between the Austrian army and its German federal allies – Bavaria, Württemberg, Baden, Saxony, Hanover, and Hessia – who, collectively, could furnish the Austrians with an additional 150,000 bayonets.[50] In a memorandum prepared in the winter of 1865–6, Moltke insisted that in any war with Austria and its German cohorts, Prussia's "first day of mobilization must coincide with the declaration of war . . . and as soon as one of our neighbors begins to arm, we must declare war and announce mobilization simultaneously, for in no case can we permit ourselves to lose the initiative."[51] Moltke, in short, pinned his hopes on a *Blitzkrieg*, a lightning strike into Austria and the German states by fast-moving Prussian columns that would seize the Habsburg army and the federal contingents in the midst of their deployments, swarm round their flanks, and crush them. Moltke later called this process of strategic envelopment, begun weeks before a battle by mobilization on an extended front, the "*Kesselschlacht*" or

48 Groote, "Moltkes Planungen," in *Entscheidung 1866*, pp. 78–83. Showalter, *Railroads and Rifles*, pp. 52–6.
49 Strachan, *European Armies*, p. 99.
50 Vienna, Kriegsarchiv (KA), Militärkanzlei Seiner Majestät (MKSM) 1866, Karton 342, 69–8, Vienna, May 1866, k.k. Generalstab, "Kriegsstärke des VII. und VIII. Bundes-Armee Korps und des sächsischen Contingents."
51 Craig, *Königgrätz*, pp. 27–9.

"pocket battle." Enemy forces would be driven into a narrow "pocket" by the broadcast wings of the Prussian army and annihilated.

Tactics would be instrumental in the execution of a Prussian *Kesselschlacht*. To engulf a nineteenth-century army of 300,000, Moltke would have to approach it on a precariously broad front, with his own *corps d'armée* stretched thin. In the days before the intended pocket battle, while the Prussian center attempted to pin the enemy army in a pocket, where the wings could settle around it and sever its lines of retreat, those central Prussian units would be exposed to potentially devastating counterattacks by the entire enemy force. With their wings splayed, the Prussians would be unable to reinforce their weakened center in depth.

This danger of an enemy breakthrough accounted for the preference most nineteenth-century commanders had for Jominian strategy. Safety, it seemed, was to be had in troop numbers and mass, in closed order and prepared positions. Moltke, however, saw a way around this dilemma. By exploiting modern fire-power and improving the tactical performance of the Prussian soldier, he would enable the Prussian infantryman to cut his way *tactically* through even the most unfavorable *strategic* obstacles to reach Moltke's ultimate goal: the narrow *Kessel* or pocket, where overwhelming Prussian numbers could be wrapped around the densely arrayed enemy army to destroy it with their fire.[52] In the Prussian General Staff's history of the Austro-Prussian War published in 1867, Moltke would summarize his views on the matter: "An army hit in front and flank finds that its strategic advantage of internal lines has been beaten *tactically*."[53]

Moltke's resolve to make the Prussian infantryman the best and most resourceful in Europe was aided by the coincidence that, in 1866, Prussia was the only European Great Power armed with a breech-loading rifle, the Dreyse *Zündnadelgewehr*, or needle rifle, so-called because of its needle-shaped firing pin. Although the bolt-action needle rifle could be loaded and fired four times more quickly than the muzzle-loading rifles used by other European armies, none of Prussia's rivals adopted the Dreyse rifle after it was introduced in 1849. This curious fact was attributable to flaws in the Prussian rifle that made it suspect in the eyes of foreign powers. It was crudely constructed, with a fragile firing pin, a stiff bolt action that had sometimes to be hammered open with a rock, and a leaky breech that blasted sparks into the faces of its own handlers. This defective gas seal, which was the basic defect of all early breech-loaders, also dissipated much of the rifle's blast and velocity, making long-range Prussian fire, in the no doubt exaggerated judgement of an Austrian medical expert, "scarcely more hazardous than a handful of pebbles."[54] As for the rifle's rapid rate of fire, this too was perceived by most European officers to be a flaw, not a strength, for in

52 London, Public Record Office (PRO), Foreign Office (FO) 120/907, Vienna, December 8, 1913, Maj. Cuninghame to Bunsen.
53 Grosser Generalstab, *Der Feldzug von 1866 in Deutschland* (Berlin: Ernst Mittler, 1867), p. 99.
54 "Über die Misserfolge bei der österreichischen Nordarmee," *ÖMZ* 2 (1866), pp. 353–4. Craig, *Königgrätz*, pp. 20–1.

all but the coolest hands, such a rifle would be fired *too* quickly, exhausting ammunition stocks with skirmishing, before a battle was fully joined.[55]

Rifle cartridges of the 1860s were heavy, large-caliber tubes the size of a man's finger, and line infantry in the field, laden with all sorts of kit, could carry no more than sixty of them. For muzzle-loading infantry, sixty rounds amounted to an hour's fire, for it took a minute to stand a percussion rifle on its end and load it with a ramrod. However, for a breech-loading Prussian rifleman, who could load his rifle in *any* posture – standing, kneeling, or lying prone – and still get off four or five aimed shots in a minute, sixty rounds would last no more than fifteen minutes, not enough time for a platoon to skirmish, let alone battle the enemy's main force.

In view of this disturbing fact, all armies save Prussia's rejected the early breech-loaders. Since reloads had to be conveyed in ammunition wagons that, in battle, unfailingly ended up at the wrong end of an army's baggage train, commanders thought it wiser to forgo the possible advantages of rapid fire for the certainty of fire *control*: the methodical delivery of salvos aimed by a company's NCOs – who strode down a line of riflemen calling out ranges – and triggered on the command of an officer. Volley fire was always more accurate than individual fire because it was supervised, and its *moral* effect often proved decisive. Whereas individual fire merely pecked at enemy formations, salvo fire scythed them to the ground in an instant. Met with a volley, whole files would collapse amid spurting blood and shattered limbs, the cries of the wounded inducing reserve companies to retire rather than press an attack.[56]

"Fire as little as possible with the infantry, and then charge with the bayonet," Frederick the Great had counseled a century earlier, and this remained the view of most European generals in the 1860s. Had not all European armies taken on sufficient "light infantry" to do the work of "skirmishing" in the course of the Frederician and Napoleonic Wars?[57] By the 1860s, France had added sixty-three battalions of *chasseurs*, Prussia fifty battalions of fusiliers, Italy forty battalions of *bersaglieri*, and Austria forty battalions of *Jäger*, which, like "*chasseur*," meant "hunter," and perfectly described the function of light infantry: to stalk an enemy's skirmishers, drive them off, and provide covering fire for the advance of the line infantry, who would otherwise, given their dense formations, be easy marks for enemy sharpshooters.[58]

In the years before 1866, which would mark a watershed in infantry tactics, most generals believed that skirmishers, advancing in a protective screen before their comrades of the line, knew all that an army needed to know about range-taking and musketry. Loading and firing their stubby carbines at twice the speed

55 Strachan, *European Armies*, p. 112.
56 Jay Luvaas, *The Military Legacy of the Civil War* (Chicago: University of Chicago Press, 1959), pp. 42, 173.
57 Strachan, *European Armies*, pp. 27–32.
58 Vincennes, AAT, MR 47/1634, Strasbourg, November 30, 1855.

of line infantry, actually *using* their backsights, and ducking in and out of cover, light infantry battalions would be able to rock an enemy force back on its heels, throw off its aim, and permit their own massed line regiments to come up and put the enemy to rout with the bayonet.

Such was the tactical orthodoxy in 1866, which Moltke would shortly transform as radically as he was transforming strategy. In all of their mobilizations, wars, and maneuvers between 1848 and 1864, the Prussians had wavered uncertainly between the "shock tactics" they and other European armies had employed in the Napoleonic Wars and the revolutionary new "fire tactics" that their needle rifle, with its high rate of fire, made possible. This vacillation accounted for the scorn a French officer heaped upon the Prussian army after observing its maneuvers in 1861: "Prussia," he sneered, "is compromising the military profession."[59] The low opinion France and the other European powers had of Prussia began to change three years later, when Prussian rifles shredded the Danish army in a series of bloody clashes and staff chief Moltke decided to abandon shock tactics altogether and trust instead in fire.

Moltke's tactical innovation, which split the massed Prussian battalion column into more nimble rifle companies and platoons that could be deployed in skirmish lines to bring every quick-firing rifle to bear, was at first ridiculed by contemporaries. Prussia's first soldier in the 1860s, eighty-year-old Field Marshal Friedrich von Wrangel, who briefly commanded the Prussian contingent in Denmark in 1864, considered Moltke's fire tactics "uncontrollable" and "dishonorable," for they dispersed troops in ragged lines and dealt deadly blows not face-to-face but from concealment and at a distance.[60] Much more serious than Wrangel's cavils was an objection raised in early 1866 by General Adolf Schönfeld, the Austrian staff officer who had been attached to Prussian headquarters in Denmark. Schönfeld considered Moltke's tactical reforms reckless: "In Denmark," he wrote, "I repeatedly overheard Prussian officers worrying about the inability of their men to conserve ammunition for the *second, decisive* phase of a battle."[61]

Here was much cause for anxiousness. In 1864, in their first experience of combat, many Prussians had, in fact, done just what all unseasoned infantry were prone to do: wasted their precious rounds in skirmishing, where only light infantry, who took more target practice than line infantry in peacetime, could be confident of scoring a hit. In Denmark, the Prussians had been able to replace units that had emptied their cartridge pouches with fresh reserves. Against a Great Power like Austria, however, the Prussians would not enjoy this luxury. Most of their reserves would have to be committed to battle at the outset, and units that expended their ammunition prematurely would be overrun and bayoneted by Austrian "storm columns."

59 Howard, *Franco-Prussian War*, p. 18.
60 Gründorf, vol. 2, p. 198.
61 KA, Nachlässe, B/572:1 (Nosinic), Vienna, March 1866, GM Schönfeld, "Charakteristik preussischer Armee."

In short, the arguments against fire tactics were compelling. Was it not safer and more sensible to develop battles in the traditional style? "Traditional" in the 1860s meant beginning with a cannonade, throwing out skirmishers and dragoons to harass the enemy and pinpoint his positions, battering through weak spots with massed columns of line infantry, then pursuing with the entire cavalry and gun reserve once the line regiments had breached or flanked the enemy's formation. In the pivotal 1860s, only Moltke had the courage to defy this model by recasting Prussian infantry tactics.

Whereas the Austrians ruled out fire tactics from the start, believing it all but impossible to teach uneducated peasant recruits to measure ranges and aim fire at moving targets, Moltke believed that, given sufficient training, all Prussian recruits, not just the fusiliers, could learn to use their rifles to deadly effect at short, medium, and even long range.[62] Thus between 1862 and 1864, while the Austrians actually reduced their annual expenditure on target practice and began to rely upon cheap, easily managed shock tactics instead, the Prussian army went on a shooting spree. At a time when Austrian recruits were allotted just twenty practice rounds per year, Prussian recruits fired 100. And while Austrian recruits fired their twenty rounds at fixed targets over fore- and backsights aligned by vigilant NCOs, Prussian recruits were made to rove back and forth and side to side on the rifle range, learning to use their own sights to compensate for the arc of a bullet and recording the success or failure of each practice shot in a "shooting log."[63]

Moltke's intensive shooting practice was accompanied by an emphasis on small-unit tactics. Whereas the Austrians, Russians, French, and Italians rarely exercised line infantry in formations smaller than the half-battalion, Moltke realized that such massed formations would only squander the needle rifle's unique advantage, its rapid rate of fire. If Prussian infantrymen were crammed together like Russians or Austrians in narrow, deep shock columns, the majority of them would never be able to use their rifles for fear of shooting their comrades in the back. Thus, over opposition from conservatives like Wrangel, who thought shock columns an essential element in any order-of-battle, Moltke decentralized the Prussian regiment, encouraging its battalions to subdivide as circumstances required into half battalions, companies, platoons, and sections. Thus divided, even small Prussian units would be able to outflank massed enemy formations and destroy them with cross fire.[64]

Moltke's emphasis on fire and the small unit was, in sum, a smaller, *tactical* version of his larger, *strategic* doctrine of envelopment. Exploiting the flexibility and firepower of the Prussian battalion, he would aim to make every brush with

---

62 Geoffrey Wawro, "An 'Army of Pigs': The Technical, Social, and Political Bases of Austrian Shock Tactics, 1859–66," *The Journal of Military History* 59 (July 1995), pp. 407–34.

63 "Die Schiessübungen der k. preussischen Infanterie," *ÖMZ* 3 (1865), p. 20.

64 Vincennes, AAT, MR 3/1537, Paris, June 1866, Capt. de Mille, "Notice sur l'Armée Prussienne."

the enemy a *Kesselschlacht*, regardless of the numerical odds arrayed against him. Firing four rounds in the time it took the enemy to fire one, Prussian infantrymen would, in theory, be able to shoot their way through four times their strength in order to keep their rendezvous with Moltke's rolling envelopment of an enemy army.[65] Most considered Moltke's theory preposterous, but it would prove itself in 1866 and become the tactical basis of Prusso-German strategy thereafter.

AUSTRIAN STRATEGIC AND OPERATIONAL DOCTRINE, FROM ARCHDUKE KARL TO BENEDEK

Austria in the 1860s had no Moltke. This was not for lack of native talent, but was rather a consequence of the peculiar culture of Habsburg Vienna. Though well-meaning, Emperor Franz Joseph I was in 1866 what he would remain until his death in 1916, an ineffectual trimmer. He dreaded conflict and, after an early and unsuccessful experiment with authoritarian rule in the 1850s, tended to preempt every possible source of discord with a compromise. As the emperor's politics went, so went his military affairs. In 1860, under pressure from public opinion to atone for the monarchy's humiliating defeat in Italy, the emperor rudely jettisoned his General Staff chief of ten years, seventy-two-year-old Field Marshal Heinrich Hess, and replaced him with a younger, more *popular*, but much less qualified man.

The general Franz Joseph selected to replace Hess was fifty-seven-year-old Ludwig Benedek, the only Austrian hero to have emerged from the Habsburg defeat at Solferino, where Benedek's corps had bravely covered the Austrian army's retreat over the Mincio river bridges to safety. Prodded by imperial propagandists, who made the most of this single bright spot in an otherwise dreary campaign, the Vienna press dubbed Benedek Austria's "second Radetzky," and the emperor responded by rather too hastily making Benedek a *Feldzeugmeister*, a lieutenant-general, promoting him over a half dozen more capable officers and putting him simultaneously in charge of Austria's largest standing army – the Army of Italy in Verona – as well as the imperial General Staff in Vienna.[66]

Benedek's meteoric rise was fraught with danger, for the Feldzeugmeister was a notoriously incompetent strategist. His promotion had been a political ploy by Emperor Franz Joseph to win popularity among Austria's newly enfranchised middle class, who revered Benedek for his colorful personality and common origins and tended to overlook the Feldzeugmeister's obvious shortcomings as a staff officer. Benedek, the son of a provincial doctor, loudly disdained military

---

65 Royal instructions for Prussian maneuvers in 1863 conjectured that "with the needle rifle, 300 men armed with the needle rifle are equal to 900 men with muzzle-loaders." Moltke, "De l'influence des armes perfectionées sur le combat," *Militär-Wochenblatt*, July 8, 1865. "Die Waffenwirkung in der preussischen Gefechten im Feldzuge 1864," *ÖMZ* (1865), pp. 126–7.

66 Eduard Heller, "Benedek und Benedek-Legenden," *Militärwissenschaftliches Mitteilungen* (Vienna, 1937), pp. 2–3.

2.   General Ludwig Benedek (1804–81), commander of the Austrian North Army in 1866

science and often joked that he had not read a book since leaving Vienna's war college decades earlier. Among his aphorisms on war was the observation that "the only talents required in a staff chief are a strong stomach and a good digestion."[67]

67 Hans Delbrück and Emil Daniels, *Geschichte der Kriegskunst im Rahmen der politischen Geschichte*, 7 vols. (Berlin: Georg Stilke, 1907–36), vol. 5, p. 421. Klaus Koch, *Franz Graf Crenneville* (Vienna: Österreichischer Bundesverlag, 1984), p. 182. Wolf Schneider von Arno, "Der österreichischer-ungarische Generalstab." Vienna Kriegsarchiv Manuscript, n.d., vol. 7, p. 12.

Though well liked by his enlisted men, who relished the occasional taunts Benedek directed at the "blue-blooded baboons" and "bookworms" on his staff, the Feldzeugmeister cut a different figure among his officer colleagues, many of whom despised and feared Benedek for his vulgarity and the powerful hold he exercised upon the romantic young emperor's imagination.[68] This influence peaked in the early 1860s, when Franz Joseph first made Benedek imperial staff chief and then, at the Feldzeugmeister's request, relieved him of the post in 1864 and gave it to Benedek's best friend and adjutant, General Alfred Henikstein – the rather dissolute, fifty-four-year-old scion of a Jewish banking house – who very reluctantly made the move from Verona to Vienna to take charge of Austrian strategic planning as Austria's war with Denmark wound down.

The weakness of character that would mark Emperor Franz Joseph's entire reign was never more apparent than in this fateful decision to ratify Benedek's careless choice of Henikstein. Henikstein's army career had been undistinguished, and he had nothing to recommend him for his new responsibilities save his friendship with the Feldzeugmeister. Bewildered Austrian officers, who sought a new course after the débâcle of 1859, rightly saw in this bizarre appointment the triumph of court politics over efficiency. Benedek, it was whispered, felt isolated in Verona and wanted someone from his personal circle installed at Vienna to deflect challenges to his power within the Habsburg army.[69] What *other* explanation could there have been for the appointment of a man as hapless as Henikstein to such a crucial post?

In the years between his appointment in 1864 and the war of 1866, Henikstein did little to improve Austrian preparedness for the two-front war with Prussia and Italy that looked increasingly likely after Italy began demanding Habsburg Venetia in 1861, and after Prussia began pressuring Austria to sell or cede it Vienna's half share in Schleswig-Holstein, which the two German powers had wrested from Denmark in 1864. Despite the clear and present danger of these explosive German and Italian questions, Benedek did nothing to correct Henikstein's drift. On the contrary, in 1865 he wrote Henikstein that he was using his influence in Vienna to have his friend assigned an industrious *sous-chef*, who would see to Austrian strategic planning so that Henikstein, whom Benedek valued above all for his qualities as "paterfamilias, gigolo, gourmand, gambler and stag hunter," could devote his time to more important pursuits.[70]

Ludwig Ritter von Benedek, *Benedeks nachgelassene Papiere*, ed. Heinrich Friedjung (Leipzig: Grübel und Sommerlatte, 1901), pp. 373–4.

68 Antonio Schmidt-Brentano, *Die Armee in Österreich* (Boppard: Harald Boldt, 1975), pp. 318–19, 382. Koch, *Crenneville*, p. 163. Eduard Bartels, *Kritische Beiträge zur Geschichte des Krieges im Jahre 1866* (Zurich: Caspar Schmidt, 1901), p. 247. Antoine Mollinary, *Quarante-six ans dans l'armée austro-hongroise, 1833–1879*, 2 vols. (Paris: Fournier, 1913), vol. 1, pp. 96–7. Alfred von Schlieffen, "Benedeks Armee-Führung nach den neuesten Forschungen," *Vierteljahrshefte für Truppenführung und Heereskunde* 8 (1911), p. 180.

69 Bartels, *Kritische Beiträge*, p. 24. Arno, vol. 7, pp. 81–5.

70 Delbrück, vol. 5, p. 241.

3.   General Alfred Henikstein (1810–82), Austrian General Staff chief in 1866

Although an Austrian war minister of Prussian General Albrecht von Roon's caliber might have offset the staff chief's weaknesses, Franz Joseph entrusted his war ministry to an even weaker vessel than Henikstein: fifty-eight-year-old General Karl Franck, a tractable bureaucrat whom the emperor selected in 1864 precisely for his tractability in order to quash Prussian-style army reforms attempted by the emperor's outgoing minister of war, General August Degenfeld.[71] The emperor rejected Count Degenfeld's reform proposals, which ranged from a promotion exam for officers to the creation of twenty new infantry regiments, on the dubious grounds that such innovations violated army "tradition." A promotion exam, Franz Joseph protested, would have interfered with his "imperial prerogative" to appoint courtiers to key military posts. New regiments, he objected, would have been like "bastards," hastily formed rucks of men without the stirring example of a centuries-long regimental history. Bucking the trend of the nineteenth century, which was toward smaller, more flexible, and fire-intensive units, the emperor and his powerful young adjutant general, forty-five-year-old Count Franz Folliot-Crenneville, ultimately agreed to create just half the number of new regiments recommended by Degenfeld and, for the rest, insisted that new recruits simply be layered over old ones in the existing, increasingly unmanageable battalions of Austria's "ancient regiments."[72]

With a leading mind like Franz Joseph's tracing the outlines of Austrian strategy and army organization, Benedek, Henikstein, and Franck can hardly be assigned the entire blame for Austria's military stagnation in the 1860s. Nevertheless, their own papers confirm that none of them was nearly as prolific or energetic as Moltke or Roon. Indeed, by 1865, the usually jovial Henikstein, who sometimes had to escort the sickly Franck to ministerial councils in order to speak for him, seemed himself demoralized by the Austrian high command's slack performance. Early that year he actually recommended that the vital post of General Staff chief be folded up and merged in the Habsburg war ministry's "operative department," which was managed by one of Franck's sixteen deputies.[73] Needless to say, less redoubtable contrasts to Moltke and Roon could scarcely be imagined.

Austria, in short, failed to fashion effective responses to Moltke's new strategic and tactical concepts. For want of anything better, Austrian strategists of the 1860s fell back upon the Restoration prescriptions of Jomini and Archduke Karl Habsburg. Karl, who had defeated Napoleon in battle at Aspern in 1809, had written prolifically on war until his death in 1847. The archduke's strategic *pensées*, though set down in the 1830s and 1840s, were not actually published in Austria until 1862, when, rather unwisely, they were seized upon by Austrian staff officers as a home-grown basis for Austrian strategy.

The Austrian and Prussian strategic schools could not have been more different. Whereas Clausewitz had gone so far as to commend war as an "extension of policy," Karl rejected war as a grand strategic option under all but the most

71 Koch, *Crenneville*, p. 188. Bernhard Ritter von Meyer, *Erlebnisse*, 2 vols. (Vienna: Carl Satori, 1875), vol. 2, pp. 63–5, 95.

72 Koch, *Crenneville*, pp. 161–4, 178–80. Mollinary, vol. 1, p. 104.

73 Eugen Frauenholz, "FML Alfred Freiherr von Henikstein im Jahre 1866," *Münchener Historische Abhandlungen* 2/3 (1933), pp. 34–5.

desperate circumstances. "War," Archduke Karl judged, "is the greatest evil a state can experience."[74] Noting that Napoleon had overextended himself in the course of his wars, Archduke Karl posited a more cautious, *defensive* alternative to Napoleonic-Clausewitzian theory. Clausewitz's insistence that the goal of all armies ought to be the destruction of the enemy's armed force derived from Napoleon's maxim that the task of an army was no more complicated than "to march, fight, and camp." The French emperor had often ignored lines of supply and retreat in order to land annihilating blows. By regularly flouting the "rules of war," Napoleon had consistently achieved the element of surprise and won major victories over more numerous enemies.[75]

Nevertheless, Austria's Archduke Karl considered that Napoleon's constant improvisations had ultimately undone him. Restless offensives had wasted the energies of France and opened it to invasion in 1814. For Austria, Karl sought a more sustainable system of defense and found it in the seventeenth-century proposition that "the occupation of strategic points is the decisive factor in war."[76] To block the punches of a future Napoleon, Archduke Karl conceived a defensive strategy based upon improved fortresses, fixed lines of communication, and the assumption that Austria and Europe contained a finite number of "keypoints," the control of which would ensure victory regardless of enemy maneuvers. "Every state," Karl opined in 1840, "contains strategic points that determine its fate. These points are the keys of the land."[77]

A more complete rejection of Napoleonic, Clausewitzian, and *Moltkean* doctrine could scarcely be imagined. The archduke called for Austria's transformation into "a defensive system" girded by fortresses, "which would protect the whole by protecting the parts," a recommendation that was implemented at tremendous expense by the Habsburg army in the decades after Waterloo.[78] Menaced by the Russians in the east, the Italians in the south, the French in the west, and the Prussians in the north, the Austrians spent a billion florins (c. $13.5 billion in 1995 dollars) to construct new fortresses and renovate old ones in the years between 1815 and 1866. Between 1833 and 1849, the Austrian army spent 100 million florins ($1.35 billion) just to construct the four Quadrilateral forts in Venetia, which sealed Austria's Italian flank with polygonal works at Mantua, Peschiera, and Legnago, and an entrenched camp at Verona.[79] In the German Confederation, Austria contributed 60 million florins ($810 million) to the con-

74 Strachan, *European Armies*, pp. 66, 93–4.
75 Delbrück, vol. 4, pp. 488–93, 504. Hamley, p. 56.
76 Erzherzog Karl, "Verteidigungssystem des Kriegsschauplatzes," *Militärische Werke*, 3 vols. (Vienna: k.k. Hof-und-Staatsdruckerei, 1862), vol. 1, p. 89. Günter Brüning, "Militär-Strategie Österreichs in der Zeit Kaiser Franz II. (I.)," (phil. Diss. Münster, 1982), pp. 60–2, 267–72.
77 Cited in Joszef Zachar, "Die Frage des Verteidigungs-Krieges im Gebirgsland," in *Clausewitz, Jomini, Erzherzog Carl*, ed. Manfried Rauchensteiner (Vienna: Österreichischer Bundesverlag, 1988), p. 131.
78 Erzherzog Karl, "Verteidigungssystem," *Militärische Werke*, vol. 1, p. 9 ("ein Defensionssystem").
79 Aresin, *Das Festungsviereck von Oberitalien* (Vienna: k.k. Hof-und Staatsdruckerei, 1860), pp. 7–8.

struction of modern forts at Mainz, Luxemburg, Ulm, Rastatt, and Landau to deter a French (or Prussian) grab at the left bank of the Rhine and a descent on the Danube by either foe.[80] Along Austria's border with Prussia, the Habsburg war ministry elected not to subsidize the construction of better roads or railways to speed foot regiments to threatened points in the Prussian style but, instead, to maintain Empress Maria Theresa's "northern Quadrilateral," the antiquated Elbe forts at Theresienstadt, Königgrätz, and Josephstadt, which, in Frederick's day, had blocked Prussia's march routes to Vienna.

The maintenance of so many facilities that had long since been circumvented by new roads and railways highlighted the essential difference between Austrian and Prussian war planning in the 1860s. The Prussians had begun decommissioning their old forts as early as the 1840s and had transferred some of the savings to their strategic railways. In 1861, Moltke argued for an acceleration of this process, reiterating words he had first set down in 1843: "Every new development in railways is a military advantage; and for the national defense, a few million on the completion of our railways is far more profitably employed than on our fortresses."[81] The Austrians took the opposite course, doggedly plowing military appropriations into fixed fortifications rather than railroads.[82] In 1861, Franz Joseph plucked Field Marshal Hess from retirement and entrusted him with the job of pushing a *new* cycle of fortress construction through parliament, a 140 million florin ($1.89 billion) project that, the emperor argued, would "close the gaps" once and for all in Austria's straggling frontiers.[83] And in 1865, when called upon to pass judgement upon Moltke's cut-and-thrust methods in the Danish War, Colonel Ferenc Vlasits, who had planned Austria's invasion of Denmark, condemned Prussian operations as "too turbulent. . . . Although Prussian strategists appreciate the value of initiative, the rash deed and an exploited victory," Vlasits scolded, "they do not understand the critical, nay, *decisive* importance of lines of communication. They are incorrigible optimists, and have failed to organize life-sustaining arteries to the rear in the course of their tumultous, forward operations."[84]

In tactics, Franz Joseph and the Austrian high command proved no less retrograde. They had been too easily impressed by the winning example of French shock tactics in 1859, when Austria's unskilled line regiments had been routed by

---

80 Hans Kramer, *Österreich und das Risorgimento* (Vienna: Bergland Verlag, 1963), p. 54. Heinrich Benedikt, *Kaiseradler über dem Appenin* (Vienna: Verlag Herold, 1964), p. 128.

81 Howard, *Franco-Prussian War*, pp. 2–3.

82 *Stenographische Protokolle über die Verhandlungen des Abgeordnetenhauses (SPA)* (Vienna: k.k. Haus-Hof-und Staatsdruckerei, 1865), 3. Session, 54. Sitzung, p. 1460.

83 KA, Nachlässe, B/2:127 (Beck), "Antrag im Herrenhause des FM Frhr. von Hess über die höchsten und wichtigsten militärischen Interessen der Monarchie, 1863." SPA, 3. Session, 192. Sitzung, November 26, 1862, p. 4767. Edmund von Glaise-Horstenau, *Franz Josephs Weggefährte* (Zurich and Vienna: Amalthea, 1930), p. 80.

84 KA, Nachlässe, B/572 :1 (Nosinic), Vienna, March 26, 1866, Col. Vlasits, "Über die preussische Armee." Vlasits concluded his summary of Moltkean strategy thus: "Although the Prussian *Operationskrieg* has a hearty appetite, once it plucks the fruit, it does not know how to bear it safely home."

columns of hard-charging French infantry. After Solferino, Franz Joseph had vowed never again to trust in fire, irrationally insisting that "only *motion* will bring victory."[85] What the Austrian emperor failed to appreciate was that the Italian War of 1859 told far less about tactics than it did about the ineptitude of the Austrian army. Though flush with cash in the 1850s, when the Habsburg military had joined with the emperor's civil bureaucracy to rule Austria "neo-absolutistically," the army had squandered most of that wealth on luxuries, forts, and superfluous offices. Precious little money had trickled down to the line troops, most of whom had not even been instructed in the use of their new Lorenz rifles when war broke out in 1859. Thus, though armed with the best rifle in Europe and deployed in small battalion "divisions" of 300 men, which, in theory, were able to maneuver in groups of three to enfilade France's massed battalions of 600, the Austrians had actually shot badly in 1859 and, exhibiting a stolid disregard for their own tactical manual, had refused to maneuver jointly, permitting the French battalions to infiltrate between the Austrian "divisions" to rout them one after the other.[86]

To what was this bungling attributable? Friend and foe alike ascribed the poor performance of the Austrian regiment in battle to two things: the profligacy of the Habsburg high command, which spent lavishly on bureaucracy and sparingly on troop exercises, and the benightment of the average Austrian foot soldier, who grew up in poor, rural areas without even a primary education and could thus not be expected to grasp the science of musketry or even the Habsburg army's German "language of command."[87] In the years between 1859 and 1866, the Habsburg war ministry budgeted far more for bureaucracy and office buildings than it did for fighting men, weapons, and training.[88] Under the indulgent gaze of Franz Joseph, who viewed the imperial army as a political strut in his ceaseless struggle with antidynastic parties, the Habsburg army became a flabby, over-officered, over-administered jobs bank. Each year, more money was appropriated for "provincial commands," "supernumerary officers," and pensions than was taken for Austria's eighty infantry regiments of the line, which never learned to shoot, use cover, or fight in small units – the three things that Moltke was emphasizing in Prussian infantry training after 1859.[89]

Rather than spend at the Prussian rate for tactical exercises, Franz Joseph opted

---

85 Delbrück, vol. 5, p. 404.

86 KA, AFA 1866, Karton 2275, 13–165, 1936, "Vor 70 Jahren: Waffe, Taktik und Strategie."

87 Geoffrey Wawro, "An 'Army of Pigs': The Technical, Social, and Political Bases of Austrian Shock Tactics, 1859–66," *The Journal of Military History* 59 (July 1995):407–34. István Deák, *Beyond Nationalism* (New York: Oxford University Press, 1990), pp. 98–100. D. N., "Über die Truppensprachen unserer Armee," *ÖMZ* 2 (1862), pp. 365–7. V. R. Streffleur, "Österreich am Schlusse des Jahres 1866," *ÖMZ* 1 (1867), pp. 2–7.

88 *SPA* (1865), pp. 1442–3, 1469–81. *Stenographische Protokolle über die Verhandlungen des Herrenhauses* (Vienna: k.k. Haus-Hof-und Staatsdruckerei, 1862), p. 911.

89 Geoffrey Wawro, "Inside the Whale: The Tangled Finances of the Austrian Army, 1848–1866," *War in History* 3 (February 1996):42–65.

4. Habsburg Emperor Franz Joseph (1830–1916) in 1866

for shock instead. It was a cheap, simple substitute for Prussia's fire tactics. Shock spared the emperor the considerable cost of rifle training and gave him the means to preempt language and morale problems by literally herding his ethnically mixed regiments together like cattle.[90] After 1861, only Austria's light infantry

90 "Vorschläge zur taktischen Vervollkommung der Infanterie," *ÖMZ* 1 (1860), pp. 31–2. KA, Nachlässe, B/214:2 (Krismanic), 494, Verona, February 6, 1860, FML Degengeld, "Truppen-Instruktion Nr. 5." Walter Wagner, *Von Austerlitz bis Königgrätz* (Osnäbruck: Biblio Verlag, 1978), pp. 148f.

(*Jäger*) would use their rifles. The line infantry — with the intervals between their columns reduced from fifty-four paces in 1859 to just twelve in 1866 — would function as steamrollers.[91] Although Austrian tacticians allowed that "battalion masses" would suffer heavy casualties in their front files if deployed against quick-firing Prussian rifles, they reasoned that the *bulk* of each shock column would survive to trample dispersed enemy rifle companies as cruelly as the French had trampled Austria's scattered "battalion divisions" in 1859.

The results of the Austro-Prussian invasion of Denmark in 1864 ought to have given Austrian tacticians pause, for Denmark's army resembled Austria's in many ways and was easily beaten by the Prussians. The Danish army of 1864 embodied a high percentage of German officers and NCOs — career soldiers from the German Confederation — yet most of its line infantry were untrained Danish peasants. Like the Austrians, the Danes viewed shock as the easiest, most economical way to organize big drafts of green conscripts.[92] However, each time Danish "storm columns" charged Prussian firing lines, they were driven off with heart-rending losses. In early 1864, a small action at a place called Lundby in Jutland furnished a textbook example of the futility of shock against well-handled rifles. At Lundby, 180 Danes encountered 124 Prussians on an open moor, formed in two company columns, fixed bayonets, and charged the Prussians, who deployed in line, waited till the Danes had closed to within 250 meters' range, then fired a salvo. The Danes, weary from their long run, staggered, but came on. The Prussians fired a second salvo at 200 meters, a third at 150 meters. The Danes halted, fired a ragged volley, and retired in confusion. In a minute's time, they had lost three officers and eighty-five men, half their effectives. To press their attack, the Danes would have had to cross the final 150 meters into three or four more Prussian salvos and a final burst of individual fire; it was impossible. Even the Austrian war ministry, a dévoté of shock, had to applaud "the awesome result of the Prussian rifle at Lundby, achieved by the methodical, quick delivery of aimed salvos . . . against two Danish companies in closed order."[93] Colonel Ferenc Vlasits, staff chief of the Austrian expedition to Denmark, recalled a similiar episode elsewhere in Jutland. "I saw one Prussian company hold off two Danish companies with rapid fire. The Danes could not even *launch* a storm attack."[94]

Immediately after the Danish War, the Austrian war ministry evaluated Prussia's needle rifle afresh, but concluded that the "purely theoretical claim" of the superiority of Prussian fire tactics had "not been tested in the Danish War." Why? Because the Danish War offered "no great pitched battles involving large numbers

91 Vincennes, AAT, MR 54–55/1634, 1869, "Composition des armées permanentes en Prusse, Autriche, etc."
92 Vincennes, AAT, MR 53/1478, Augustenborg, April 13, 1864, Lt-Col. Février to Marshal Randon.
93 "Die Schiessübungen der k. preussischen Infanterie," *ÖMZ* 3 (1865), pp. 19–20.
94 KA, Nachlässe, B/572 :1 (Nosinic), Vienna, March 26, 1866, Col. Vlasits, "Über die preussische Armee."

of troops in the open field. . . . It was largely a war of *tirailleur* skirmishes."
When the Danes were not potting from behind trees and stone walls, they were
entrenched or holed up in fortresses.[95] These cavils were partly justified. Moltke
himself allowed that "in the Danish War . . . our rifle never proved itself in a *real*
battle."[96] Nevertheless, how could the Austrian war ministry overlook the import
of its own observations at Lundby and other combats like it; namely, that against
densely packed, large troop masses traversing open fields without adequate skirmishers, the Prussian needle rifle would be optimally effective?

Overall, Austria's response to the Danish War was profoundly superstitious.
Noting that Austrian shock tactics had garnered no fewer victories than Prussia's
fire tactics in Denmark, though at a much higher cost in casualties, the Austrian
General Staff concluded that the *moral* advantage of shock far outweighed the risk
of casualties. When the emperor asked General Adolf Schönfeld – a Hofburg
adjutant and staff officer who had campaigned with the Prussians in 1864 – to
juxtapose Austrian and Prussian battle tactics, Schönfeld submitted a revealing
memorandum. "Prussian troops," he wrote, "are just *too* intelligent, *too* methodical. They lack the Austrian's *moral* factors: peace of mind, *sang-froid*, stamina and
the resolve to give and take hard blows without regard for the price." Schönfeld
had come to this conclusion at Prussia's siege of Dybbøl in 1864, where he
contrasted the "caution, methodicism and pedantry" of the Prussian with the
"fresh, happy soldier's courage" of the Austrian. Prussians, Schönfeld concluded,
lacked *"élan,"* Austria's motive force.[97]

While the Austrian General Staff completed its analysis of the Danish War and
Prussian fire tactics, Feldzeugmeister Benedek, who would shortly be given
command of the Austrian army, persisted in viewing massed frontal attacks as the
best way to proceed against Prussian infantry. Storm attacks would succeed, he
rather stupidly insisted, "because given the excellent Prussian rifle, the Prussians
will never *expect* us to attack their front." Ignoring the well-publicized example of
Lundby, Benedek instructed his corps generals to proceed against Prussian units
thus: "Close resolutely to within 300 paces and then sprint at the enemy and
overthrow him."[98] France's army attaché in Vienna was understandably skeptical:
"High military men here assert that Austria will fall on the Prussians with the
bayonet. To me, it seems more a question of whether or not the Austrians will
ever actually *reach* the Prussians."[99]

95 "Die Waffenwirkung in der preussischen Gefechten im Feldzuge 1864," *ÖMZ* (1865), pp. 126–7.
96 Vincennes, AAT, MR 61/1536, Moltke, "De l'Influence des armes perfectionées sur le combat,"
    Militär Wochenblatt, July 8, 1865.
97 KA, Nachlässe, B/572: 1 (Nosinic), Vienna, March 1866, GM Schönfeld, "Charakteristik
    preussischer Armee."
98 KA, MKSM-SR 1866, 24/5, Vienna, May 19, 1866, FZM Benedek, Corps-Befehl Nr. 8,
    "Gefechtsweise der Preussen und Normen für das eigene Verhalten." Toilow, *Die österreichische
    Nordarmee*, p. 28.
99 Vincennes, AAT, MR 68/1606, Vienna, April 25, 1866, Col. Merlin to Marshal Randon.

2

Origins of the Austro-Prussian War

The Austro-Prussian War was a quick and violent solution to the German and Italian questions, two European disputes that had been simmering since the French Revolutionary Wars. Of the two, the German question was the more pressing, for a united Germany had the potential to become the richest, most industrialized state on the European continent. The German question therefore weighed most heavily on the delicate European balance of power struck at the Congress of Vienna in 1815.

In 1866, "Germany" referred to a loose federation of thirty-nine states collectively called the German *Bund* or Confederation. The *Bund* had been founded by the five European Great Powers – England, France, Russia, Austria, and Prussia – in 1815 upon the ruins of the old Holy Roman Empire, which had been abolished and dismantled by French Emperor Napoleon I in 1806. Although the German Confederation joined the ethnically German provinces of Austria and Prussia to the small German states, its mission was essentially negative, not to unite Germany, but to deny its immense wealth to a single Great Power by dissipating Germany's human and material resources among thirty-five princely states and four free cities. Although votes in the German federal diet at Frankfurt were weighted in favor of Austria and Prussia, the two German powers agreed on little after 1848, and thus spent most of their energy at Frankfurt cultivating antagonistic, mutually destructive coalitions of petty and "middle states," small and medium-sized principalities like Mecklenburg, Bavaria, Saxony, Hessia, and Baden.[1]

The Confederation frustrated progressive Germans, for it wasted the energies of the country in costly, overlapping bureaucracies and interminable debates at the federal diet on the most trivial matters. And yet the *Bund* of 1815 was an indispensable pillar of the European balance of power, for its legal existence placed much of Germany "off limits" to Europe's four Continental powers, and

---

1 James J. Sheehan, *German History, 1770–1866* (Oxford: Clarendon, 1989). Thomas Nipperdey, *Deutsche Geschichte 1800–1866* (Munich: C. H. Beck, 1983).

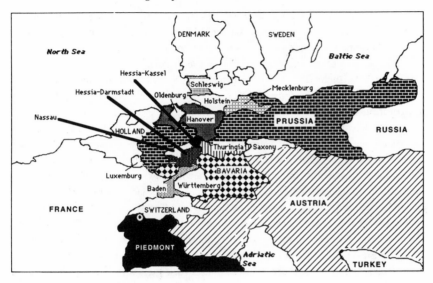

Austria, Prussia, and the German States, 1815–66

thus prevented them from increasing their economic and military might at the expense of the others.[2]

Such at least was the theory behind the German Confederation conceived in 1815 by Austria's foreign minister, Prince Klemens Metternich, who had doggedly resisted Prussian attempts to annex all of north Germany in the aftermath of the first Allied capture of Paris in 1814. Aware that Prussia was a likely nucleus for German unification, Metternich proposed the Confederation as a safe repository for the lands of Germany. The other powers, far more concerned at the time with the possibility of French, not Prussian, encroachments in Germany, consented to this Austrian arrangement. As a final touch, Lord Castlereagh, Britain's foreign minister, who wished to strengthen Austria as a bulwark against France and Russia, saw to it that the Austrian emperor, who for 400 years had worn the crown of the Holy Roman Empire, was made honorary president of the new Confederation, with the hereditary right to preside over the federal diet in Frankfurt.

The Prussians cooperated in this Austrian-run *Bund* until 1848, when Metternich's "Confederation of princes" was briefly dissolved by popular revolt in the course of Europe's year of revolution. While German Liberals tried in vain to found a German nation state, imitating similiar efforts in Italy, Hungary, and Poland, Prussia seized upon the brief dissolution of the federal diet in 1848–9 as an opportunity to take control of Germany while Austria was distracted by armed revolts in its Czech, Hungarian, and Italian crownlands. In April 1849, the

2 W. E. Mosse, *The European Powers and the German Question, 1848–71* (Cambridge University Press, 1958), pp. 4–6.

Prussian King, Friedrich Wilhelm IV, offered to replace the Confederation of 1815 with a more authoritarian version that would exclude Austria – disparaged by most German Liberals as a largely Slavic "mongrel state" – center itself on Berlin, and give broad executive powers to the Prussian king.[3]

Friedrich Wilhelm IV's so-called Erfurt Union amounted to a naked grab for power by Prussia. Thus, once he had crushed his own national revolts, Austrian Emperor Franz Joseph hastily marched an army to the Prussian frontier in November 1850. With an Austro-Prussian war in sight, Friedrich Wilhelm IV thought better of his plans to unify Germany and rather meekly agreed to scuttle the Erfurt Union and restore Metternich's Confederation of 1815. Flushed with victory, the Austrian government, led by a newly crowned emperor and an able minister of state, Prince Felix Schwarzenberg, proposed to bury the Prussian threat once and for all and at the same time satisfy German desires for more unity and more power by reorganizing Germany along *Austrian* lines. Thus, in the 1850s, Franz Joseph's minister of trade, Baron Ludwig Bruck, proposed a vast "Middle European" trading bloc administered from Vienna. It would be nothing less than a "Reich of seventy millions," in Bruck's grandiloquent phrase, that would extend "from Antwerp to the Adriatic," uniting the economies of all thirty-nine German states.

Although Bruck's *"Mitteleuropa"* plan excited interest in parts of Germany, it was no more acceptable to the other European Great Powers than had been Prussia's short-lived Erfurt Union. Hence, it too came to nothing, first undercut by Austria's rivals, then shattered by Austria's military collapse in the Franco-Austrian War. In 1859, Austria had launched an army into Piedmont to stop Turin's support for Italian nationalists in the Habsburg provinces of Lombardy and Venetia, which Austria had inherited at the Congress of Vienna in 1815. France had joined the conflict to defend "brave little Piedmont," and the rather surprising result was a humiliating series of defeats for an Austrian army that had just emerged from a decade of unprecedentedly heavy military spending. Forced to cede Lombardy to the Piedmontese after a brief, dispiriting campaign, Austria lost considerable ground in Germany, where the monarchy was, not without reason, viewed as a decadent power hopelessly undermined by its dozen, fractious non-German nationalities. When Austrian Emperor Franz Joseph summoned a "Congress of Princes" to Frankfurt in 1863 to consider *new* Austrian reform proposals for the Confederation of 1815, Prussia's decision to abstain from the proposed congress was enough to ensure its failure.

While Austria's stock declined in Germany, Prussia's quickly recovered from the diplomatic humiliation of 1850. Whereas Austria emerged from the Italian War of 1859 buried in debt and verging on bankruptcy, Prussia entered the 1860s an economic juggernaut, propelled by the *Zollverein* or Prussian Customs Union, which had been founded in Berlin in 1834. Though Metternich had always

3 Sheehan, *German History, 1770–1866*, p. 866.

opposed the Zollverein on the grounds that it could be nothing other than a stalking horse for the gradual Prussian conquest of Germany, it grew in the 1840s to embrace most of the German states, with the deliberate exception of Austria. Prussia's economy thus became an iron link joining Germany's Protestant north and Catholic south. By sheer coincidence, Germany's deepest, richest seams of coal and iron – the stuff of industrialization – were lodged beneath *Prussian* soil, in the Ruhr, the Saar, Lusatia, and Upper Silesia. Thus by 1860, Prussia had become the motor of the German economy, producing no less than 80 percent of the Confederation's coal and iron, and quite strong enough to wrestle all the German states – save Austria – into a low tariff Anglo-French-Prussian trading zone in 1862. In this way, Rudolf Delbrück, Prussia's answer to Ludwig Bruck, succeeded in isolating the economically inefficient, highly protected Austrian Empire from the rest of Germany and Europe.[4]

Prussia's attempt to sunder Austria economically from Germany was accompanied by a no less aggressive political program. In 1862, Count Otto von Bismarck became prime minister of Prussia and, in a speech to the Prussian parliament, announced his intention to reorganize and consolidate the German Confederation by "blood and iron" if need be.[5] Bismarck was by no means a conventional nationalist. He accompanied his notorious "blood and iron" speech with a reminder that his goal was not to unify the German nation but to "liberate Prussia from the web of [German] federal treaties" spun round it by Metternich in 1815 and thereby to "exert the full force of Prussia's weight in Germany."[6] What distinguished Bismarck from his no less ambitious predecessors was his pragmatic willingness to make selective use of the language and slogans of liberal German nationalism to get what he and Prussia's King Wilhelm I wanted: an enlarged Prussia that would grow to hegemonic proportions by abolishing the Austrian-led Confederation of 1815 and annexing all of the German states.[7]

Like Frederick the Great, Prussia's last great expansionist, Bismarck believed that the "first duty of Prussia was to expand" in order to overleap the indefensible natural frontiers of the Brandenburg march and plant new ones on the best mountain barriers and river lines of Central Europe. But whereas "Old Fritz" had been content to consolidate and buttress Prussia's eastern space at the expense of Poland, Austria, and Saxony, Bismarck looked west. In 1865, he resolved to annex the duchies of Schleswig and Holstein at the mouth of the Elbe and to unite Prussia's western and eastern halves by conquering the intervening princely states and free cities – Hanover, Hessia-Kassel, Hamburg, and their neighbors – which interrupted Berlin's communications with the Prussian Rhineland around Bonn, Düsseldorf, and the Ruhr.

---

4 Carr, *Origins*, pp. 104–10. Helmut Böhme, *Deutschlands Weg zur Grossmacht* (Cologne: Kiepenheuer and Witsch, 1966).
5 Pflanze, *Bismarck*, vol. 1, pp. 183–4.
6 Gall, *Bismarck*, vol. 1, p. 217.
7 Gall, *Bismarck*, vol. 1, pp. 98–9.

Bismarck's strategic aim to forge a contiguous north German state and dominate the Baltic Sea brought Prussia into renewed conflict with Austria, legal guardian of the German Confederation. In the 1860s, the Austrians feared Bismarck like none of his Prussian predecessors. He was monstrous: a big, powerful man with quick wits, a biting tongue, and a dangerous fascination with Frederick the Great, Prussia's eighteenth-century *conquistador*. Bismarck had served as Prussia's delegate to the Frankfurt diet from 1851 to 1859 and there had impressed his colleagues with nothing so much as his hatred for Austria, which he characterized, in one of his more charitable moments, as a weary "old fox," who clung to ancient privileges by craft and guile, not power. Prussia, Bismarck warned in 1856, would not "forever play Leporello to Austria's Don Juan," a reference to Prussia's official subordination to Austria in the German Confederation.[8] Although this tiered arrangement had been justified in 1815, when Prussia, which had fared badly in the Napoleonic Wars, was a second-tier power, it no longer squared with economic, military, or political reality in the 1860s. Hence, when Bismarck faced his first crisis with Austria in 1864, he did not shy from it. "Great crises," he liked to say, alluding to the way modern Prussia was hemmed in by the borders of 1815, were "the weather most conducive to Prussia's growth."[9]

THE SCHLESWIG-HOLSTEIN QUESTION, 1848–66

The Austro-Prussian crisis of 1864 arose from the disputed status of Germany's northernmost territories, the "Elbe Duchies" of Schleswig and Holstein. Although the two duchies had been a part of the Kingdom of Denmark since 1460, their legal ties to the Danish crown differed. Holstein, ethnically German and an ancient duchy of the Holy Roman Empire, was only nominally controlled by the Danes. Indeed in 1815 Holstein, though a province of Denmark, was admitted to the German Confederation, where its German population was represented by a delegate appointed by the Danish king. Schleswig, in contrast, was 50 percent Danish and had never been a member of the Holy Roman Empire. Although the Danish government in Copenhagen was willing to consider independence for German Holstein, it clung stubbornly to Schleswig, which it considered an integral part of the Danish kingdom and a strategic necessity, for Schleswig's Schlei river estuary closed the entrance to Denmark from Germany to a narrow, defensible gap.[10]

A Danish-German War therefore threatened in 1848 when the intermittently oppressed Germans of Schleswig and Holstein formed themselves in a "Schleswig-Holstein party," which insisted upon Danish observances of a fifteenth-century law that held Schleswig and Holstein to be indivisible units. Although the ancient Danish law had been intended to prevent the feudal partition of the

---

8 Gall, *Bismarck*, vol. 1, pp. 98–9, 129.
9 Carr, *Origins*, p. 70.
10 Site of the Dannevirke fortifications. Carr, *Origins*, p. 83.

duchies into myriad, ungovernable fiefs and thus preserve them as manageable provinces of the Danish kingdom, the modern *"Schleswig-Holsteiner"* aimed to unite the duchies in order to *detach* them from Denmark and join them instead to the German Confederation as its fortieth state.

In 1847, King Christian VIII of Denmark died without a male heir, offering German nationalists in the two duchies the opportunity first to unite, then to secede altogether from the Danish kingdom amid the chaos of Copenhagen's succession crisis. In 1848, the Danish government, despairing of a compromise that would induce the Germans of Holstein to remain in the *Helstat* – the unitary Danish state – offered independence to Holstein but vowed not only to retain Schleswig but to eliminate its home rule and linguistic privileges and bind it tightly to the Kingdom of Denmark. When the Danish army, trailed by a regiment of Danish-speaking bureaucrats, entered Schleswig to enforce this centralization, the German federal diet at Frankfurt voted to authorize north Germany's "gendarme," the Prussian army, to invade Denmark and defend the autonomy and language rights of Schleswig's Germans. After a successful campaign, the Prussians dictated the Malmø Armistice to the Danes in 1850, which restored the pre-war *status quo*. Schleswig, Holstein, and the latter's southern outcropping, Lauenburg, would remain provinces of the Danish crown, but would each enjoy local autonomy administered by popularly elected assemblies.[11]

However, this partial solution to the Schleswig-Holstein question proved no solution at all. Agitation for a German nation state was on the rise in every land of the German Confederation in the 1850s and 1860s, and Denmark, itself no stranger to aggressive nationalism, had its own version of "Pan-Germanism," called "Eiderdanism," which sought to push the frontiers of the centralized *Helstat* to the Eider river separating Schleswig and Holstein. These conflicting nationalisms provoked a second Danish War in 1863, when King Frederick VII of Denmark, prodded by "Eiderdanes" in Copenhagen, rather rashly promulgated a new constitution that, for the first time, attached Schleswig to the unitary *Helstat*. Every German government was affronted by this clear Danish violation of the treaties that had ended the last Danish War in 1850.[12]

At Frankfurt, the German diet appealed again to Austria and Prussia for military support against the Danes, who, though by no measure a Great Power, still mustered an army of 50,000 bayonets. To appease mounting German nationalist sentiment in the Confederation and put paid to the continual crises on Prussia's northern border, 60,000 Austrian and Prussian troops invaded Schleswig in February 1864 and, in four months' fighting, cleared the Danes out of the Elbe Duchies. Although Austria and Prussia had embarked on the war with the limited aim of forcing Denmark to restore home rule to Schleswig, Bismarck, Prussia's prime minister resolved early on to exploit the crisis to Berlin's advantage.

11 Carr, *Origins*, pp. 39–42.
12 Carr, *Origins*, pp. 40–1.

Whereas the Austrians hoped, after a victorious campaign, to unite Schleswig and Holstein under an Austrophile German prince – Duke Friedrich von Augustenburg – Bismarck plotted throughout the war to annex the two duchies to Prussia, for they would round out Prussia's northern frontier and give it control of the Baltic Sea. These contrary Austrian and Prussian plans for the future of Schleswig-Holstein became a bone of contention in October 1864, when Denmark admitted defeat in the Danish War and ceded Schleswig, Holstein and Lauenburg jointly to the Emperor of Austria and the King of Prussia. [13] Although joint Austro-Prussian rule of the duchies was regarded in Vienna and Berlin as a mere provisional arrangement, neither power would agree to cede or sell the other its half share in the formerly Danish provinces. After a year-long diplomatic struggle, during which Franz Joseph replaced his Prussophile foreign minister with a Prussophobe, General Alexander Mensdorff, Austria and Prussia agreed finally to split the two duchies in the Gastein Convention of August 1865. [14] Prussia would take Schleswig and Austria Holstein, but Bismarck wrung so many concessions from the Austrians that the deal was far less balanced than it seemed. Austria agreed in future to treat the question of the duchies as an exclusively Austro-Prussian affair, which ruled out an appeal on Augustenburg's behalf to the German middle states, and then closed the deal by selling the Prussians Lauenburg. [15] These two decisions served only to alienate potential Austrian allies in the German Confederation, who might otherwise have been expected to join Austria in a preventive war against Prussian expansion. Austria also conceded Prussia the right to dig a canal through Holstein to link Prussia's Baltic ports with the North Sea and gave Berlin use of Holstein's principal roads and telegraph facilities. [16]

BISMARCK'S DIPLOMACY ON THE EVE OF WAR

Given the massive Prussian investment that would inevitably flow from this solid foothold in the duchies, it had now become exceedingly difficult for Austria to dislodge Prussia from Schleswig-Holstein. By ignoring the wishes of the German middle states and all but inviting Bismarck into the northern duchies, General Mensdorff had painted himself into a corner. In October 1865, his room for maneuver narrowed still further, when Bismarck held secret talks with French Emperor Napoleon III at Biarritz. Having already neutralized Russia for the event of an Austro-Prussian War by helping Tsar Alexander II suppress a Polish revolt in 1861, Bismarck neutralized France in 1865 by *seeming* to promise Louis-Napoleon Belgium and Luxemburg in return for a free Prussian hand in a future

---

13 Carr, *Origins*, pp. 82–3. J. C. Clardy, "Austrian Foreign Policy during the Schleswig-Holstein Crisis of 1864," *Diplomacy and Statecraft* 2 (July 1991).

14 Lawrence Steefel, *The Schleswig-Holstein Question* (Cambridge, Mass.: Harvard University Press, 1932). Pflanze, *Bismarck*, vol. 1, pp. 253–8.

15 Fritz Stern, *Gold and Iron* (1977; New York: Vintage, 1979), pp. 65–9.

16 Carr, *Origins*, pp. 124–6.

German war.[17] By the dawn of 1866, Mensdorff and the Austrians were diplomatically isolated, virtually friendless in Europe. Their plight took a drastic turn for the worse in April 1866, when Bismarck concluded a military alliance with Italy. Prussia had only to declare war upon Austria within ninety days and Italy – which coveted Austria's Italian provinces – would be obliged to open a second front in Habsburg Venetia and Tyrol.[18]

To apply still more pressure to the Austrians, and to force the German federal princes to submit to Prussia's will, Bismarck took another radical step in April 1866. He proposed to abolish the German Confederation's governing "diet of princes" and replace it with a popularly elected German parliament. According to Bismarck, this would have been the first, consensual step in the creation of a united, democratic Germany. Though a patently cynical ploy in view of Prussia's own voting law, which reserved the vote for holders of wealth and property, Bismarck's proposal did arouse popular enthusiasm in the German states. It thus raised the stakes still higher in Bismarck's struggle with the reactionary Habsburg Monarchy – which dreaded manhood suffrage – as well as with the German princes themselves, the kings of middle states like Hanover and Bavaria, who feared for their survival in a more democratic Germany unified and centralized by Prussia.[19]

Pushed to the wall by Bismarck's bold maneuvering, Mensdorff made two desperate decisions in the spring of 1866. In a bid to recapture the waning friendship of the German states and drive Prussia out of Schleswig-Holstein, the Austrian foreign minister unilaterally ditched the bilateral Gastein Convention on June 1, 1866. Although he was clearly violating his agreement with Bismarck to treat the Elbe Duchies as an exclusively Austro-Prussian affair, Mensdorff turned the question of Schleswig-Holstein over to the German federal diet at Frankfurt in the hope that the grateful middle states would show their appreciation by putting their armies at Austria's disposal in the looming Austro-Prussian War. This done, Mensdorff advised Prince Richard Metternich, his ambassador in Paris, that Austria was prepared to *purchase* French neutrality in an Austro-Prussian conflict by ceding France the Austrian province of Venetia. Although this secret Austrian cession – pledged by Vienna on June 9 and delivered on July 5 – did not render the coming Austro-Italian War pointless – the Italians desired Habsburg South Tyrol in addition to Venetia, and the Austrians aimed to smash Italian unity once

17 Dietrich Beyrau, "Russische Interessenzone und europäisches Gleichgewicht, 1860–70." Wilfried Radewahn, "Europäische Fragen und Konfliktzonen im Kalkül der französischen Aussenpolitik vor dem Krieg von 1870," both in, Kolb, ed., *Europa vor dem Krieg von 1870*, pp. 33–9, 72–5. Mosse, *European Powers*, pp. 110–23. Carr, *Origins*, pp. 125–6. Robert van Roosbroeck, "Die politisch-diplomatische Vorgeschichte," in Groote, Gersdorff, eds. *Entscheidung 1866*, pp. 31–4.

18 Alfonso La Marmora, *Un po più di luce sugli eventi politici e militari dell'anno 1866*, pp. 1–5. The "secret" alliance was signed in Berlin and Florence on April 8, 1866, but was immediately detected by the Austrians. Vienna, Haus-Hof-und Staatsarchiv (HHSA), IB, Karton 364, BM 1866, 35, Berlin, April–May 1866, Agenten-Rapports. Gall, *Bismarck*, vol. 1, pp. 283–4.

19 Stern, *Gold and Iron*, pp. 24, 75. Gall, *Bismarck*, vol. 1, p. 278.

and for all – it did indicate a lack of brilliance in Austrian diplomacy.[20] All Mensdorff received in return for Venetia was Napoleon III's "benevolence" and the vague, ultimately empty assurance that France would do what it could to uncouple Italy from its military pact with Prussia.[21]

Mensdorff's consignment of the Schleswig-Holstein question to the German diet on June 1 violated the Gastein Convention of August 1865 and was the excuse Bismarck needed to declare war on Austria and drive it out of Holstein and the German Confederation. The Prussian king, however, was less bellicose than Bismarck. Awed by Austria's army and ancient traditions, Wilhelm I at first refused to give his sanction to what he rather romantically called a *"Bruderkrieg,"* a "war of Germanic brothers." Hence, a nerve-wracking week passed, while Bismarck and General Moltke pleaded with their royal master to take full advantage of Prussia's faster mobilization by declaring war promptly. Finally, on June 8, while Austria's extraterritorial regiments dribbled into Moravia, Bohemia and Venetia from their faraway garrisons in Galicia, Hungary, and Croatia, Bismarck and Moltke overcame King Wilhelm's fears and launched Prussian troops into Holstein to shut the local assembly and provoke a battle with the Austrian brigade garrisoned at Kiel. Heavily outnumbered, Austria's Holstein garrison refused the challenge and withdrew by rail to Bohemia, where, as in 1850, an Austrian army had begun to mass for a punitive strike at Berlin.

At Frankfurt, on June 14, Austria asked the German states to mobilize and deploy their armies to punish the Prussian invasion of Holstein. When Bavaria, Württemberg, Saxony, Hanover, and Hessia-Darmstadt voted the Austrian proposal, Bismarck replied by dissolving the German Confederation, a purely symbolic gesture that Austria and its German federal allies chose to ignore. With the bulk of the German *Bund* thus ranged against him, Bismarck's deputy in Frankfurt stormed out of the federal diet on June 14, vowing to humble the Habsburg Monarchy, smash the Confederation, and reorganize Germany under Prussian control.[22]

THE ITALIAN QUESTION IN 1866

Although the German question was the European dispute that *ought* to have preoccupied Austrian strategists in the 1860s, many, Feldzeugmeister Benedek included, preferred to puzzle over its Italian variant instead, for Venetia, Austria's last Italian outpost in the 1860s, was a magical place. "Only in Italy," General Karl Moering confided to his diary in July 1866, "was the Austrian soldier truly

20 Geoffrey Wawro, "Austria versus the Risorgimento: A New Look at Austria's Italian Strategy in the 1860s," *European History Quarterly* 26 (January 1996):7–29.
21 Frank J. Coppa, *The Origins of the Wars of Italian Independence* (London and New York: Longman, 1992), pp. 124–6.
22 Carr, *Origins*, pp. 132–3.

happy."[23] "At last, back in Italy," another officer breathed in 1866, taking in the splendid food and climate, the Palladian billets, the rich *Virginia* cigars rolled in Venice, and the pretty women.[24] "O Italy, you made bad things good/ There we cracked open the nut of southern pleasure," went a popular army ditty.[25] It was no coincidence that senior Habsburg archdukes in the Austrian army stationed themselves in Italy in the 1860s: Ernst and Heinrich at Vicenza, Joseph at Rovigo, and Albrecht at Padua.[26] Benedek, who, in April 1866, attempted to refuse the command of Austria's North Army on the grounds that he knew "every tree from Verona to Milan" but nothing of Germany, literally relished his Venetian command. The result was what one of Franz Joseph's adjutants called the typical "Radetzkyan staff officer," Austrian officers who, for atmospheric reasons, "ignored Germany and Russia to focus on Italy."[27] Indeed, the best, the most senior, and the most celebrated Austrian generals had themselves posted to Italy in the early 1860s : Archduke Albrecht, Ludwig Benedek, Alfred Henikstein, Ludwig Gablenz, Wilhelm Ramming, Anton Mollinary, Gideon Krismanic, and Franz John. They were there to defend Venetia against the Italian invasion Vienna believed inevitable after the loss of Lombardy in 1859, but also to cultivate useful contacts and play army politics. As Adjutant General Franz Crenneville's nephew recalled: "After 1850, all talented [Austrian] officers strove for a post in Italy, where they stood the best chance of finding war and promotion. The result? Attention was lavished on the periphery and the center was neglected. With the best men in Italy, mediocrities ruled at Vienna and the army had no clearly defined goals."[28]

This Habsburg focus on Italy had deep historical roots. Most of Italy had belonged to the Habsburg-run Holy Roman Empire in the Middle Ages and early modern period, and the Austrian army had intervened in Italy throughout the eighteenth century to check the spread of French influence on the peninsula. At the Congress of Vienna in 1815, Austria received Lombardy, Venetia, and Dalmatia, which "rounded off" Austria's southern border and gave it control of the rich

23 Cited in Emil Franzel, vol. 2, p. 415: "In Italien allein war das österreichischen Soldaten-Geist noch frei."

24 Eduard von Kählig, *Vor und nach Custozza: Alte Tagebücher aus dem Feldzüge 1866* (Graz: Verlag Leykam, 1892), pp. 6–10.

25 "O Walschland, du hast uns/Wol gmacht viel Verdruss/Do hama aufknakt/Du wellische Nuss." Alexander Baumann, *Ehrenbuschn für d'österreicher Armee in Italien* (1853; Dortmund: Harenberg, 1980), p. 87.

26 Vienna, KA, Nachlässe, B/1003: 1 (Hirsch), pp. 34f.

27 Heinrich Srbik, "Erinnerungen des Generals Freiherrn von John, 1866 und 1870," *Aus Österreichs Vergangenheit* (Salzburg: Otto Müller Verlag, 1949), p. 45. When Franz Joseph ordered Marshal Joseph Radetzky, Benedek's mentor, to organize the Austrian mobilization against Prussia in November 1850, the old field marshal wrote his mistress: "*Mein fatales Schicksal ist, nach Böhmen zu gehen und das dumme Kommando der grossen Armee zu übernehmen, oder nach Italien zurückzukehren – ich wünsche von Herzen und von der Seele das letztere.*" Schmidt-Brentano, p. 178.

28 Toilow, *Die österreichische Nordarmee*, p. 33.

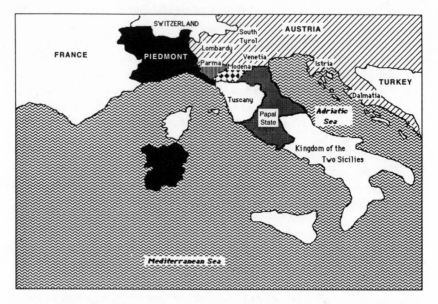

Austria, Piedmont, and the Italian States, 1815–59

Po basin, the Adriatic, and the western Balkans. Napoleon Bonaparte's "Kingdom of Italy," which had included Lombardy, the northern Italian duchies, and much papal territory, was dismantled, and Habsburg archdukes were installed in Tuscany, Modena, and Parma. To buttress this reactionary, Austrian-run league of Italian states, Metternich extorted a French indemnity to build the Quadrilateral forts – strategic bridgeheads sited along the intersecting arms of the Po, Adige and Mincio rivers – which secured Venetia for the Austrians and put the entire Italian peninsula under Habsburg control.[29]

The Pope, restored in 1815 to Rome, Lazio, the Marches, and Romagna, gave Austria the right to push over the Po at any time to occupy his restive cities of Ferrara and Ancona. The Austrians were also invited to intervene at will in the Habsburg duchies of Tuscany, Modena, and Parma. King Ferdinando Bourbon, returned by the Great Powers to his twin capitals of Palermo and Naples in the oddly named "Kingdom of the Two Sicilies," gravitated naturally into the conservative Austrian orbit.[30] King Carlo Felice of Savoy, restored by the Great Powers to Piedmont after 1815, declared, in the spirit of most restoration princes, that

29 Hans Kramer, *Österreich und das Risorgimento* (Vienna: Bergland Verlag, 1963), pp. 9, 140–3. Benedikt, *Kaiseradler*, p. 111. Oskar Regele, *Feldmarschall Radetzky* (Vienna, Munich: Verlag Herold, 1957), pp. 320–2.

30 Lucy Riall, *The Italian Risorgimento* (London and New York: Routledge, 1994) pp. 11–28. Kramer, pp. 14–17, 56.

"educated people are evil; only the ignorant are good."[31] It all added up to a suffocating tyranny best described by Stendhal, the French consul in papal Civitavecchia in the 1830s, who himself had been expelled from Italy by the Austrian police in 1821. In the *Charterhouse of Parma*, Stendhal's Fabrizio crept from Milan to Naples and back again, yet never managed to elude Baron Binder, chief of the Austrian police at Milan. Fabrizio ended in a dark Habsburg cell, and Stendhal rued the fact that Italian life was nowhere more scrupulously detailed than in the "fat, green, leather-bound registers of the Austrian police . . . stained with wine and ink and black with finger-marks."[32]

For a time, Italy was good business for the Austrians. In the 1840s, the Habsburg state pushed ahead an industrial revolution in Lombardy and Venetia in textiles, silk, glass, and tobacco. Jobs were created in the public sector to drain marshes and build bridges, roads, railways, schools, and facilities to shelter and employ the expanded bureaucracy and Army of Italy. Big new taxes were levied to pay for administration and troops. Although the taxes and bureaucracy gradually choked off economic growth and contributed to an upsurge in tax evasion and brigandage, they actually increased Austria's stake in north Italy as Field Marshal Joseph Radetzky's police, functionaries, and troops spilled over the Alps in growing numbers to man a reaction that only intensified in the face of civil disobedience and economic depression.[33] In 1855, Lombardy and Venetia alone furnished 25 percent of Austrian tax revenues, and all arms of the Habsburg bureaucracy fattened themselves on the bounty. The Patriarchate of Venice and the Archbishopric of Milan expanded to become two of Austria's richest dioceses, and the Habsburg Army of Italy quartered 70,000 non-Italian troops in the plain around Verona.[34]

In the years between 1815 and 1859, the Habsburg Monarchy served as the "gendarme of Italy." Austria sent troops over the Po in 1815, 1821, 1830, and 1831 to crush opposition to the restored regimes in Piedmont, Rome, Naples, and the Italian duchies.[35] In 1847, the Austrians put an end to Pope Pius IX's brief flirtation with liberal nationalism by dispatching an Austrian corps to disarm

---

31 Luigi Barzini, "Italy and Its Aristocracy," *Memoirs of Mistresses* (New York: Macmillan/Collier, 1986), p. 16.

32 Stendhal, *The Charterhouse of Parma*, trans. M. R. B. Shaw (1839; London: Penguin, 1983), pp. 195, 197.

33 Alvise Zorzi, *Venezia Austriaca, 1798–1866* (Rome, Bari: Laterza, 1985), pp. 66–73, 106–113.

34 Friedrich Engel-Janosi, "Der Monarch und seine Ratgeber," *Probleme der franzisko-josephinische Zeit, 1848–1916,* eds. Friedrich Engel-Janosi and Helmut Rumpler, 2 vols. (Vienna: Verlag für Geschichte und Politik 1967), vol. 1, p. 10. Zorzi, pp. 44–5. Kramer, pp. 102, 123. Benedikt, *Kaiseradler,* pp. 122, 140. Regele, *Radetzky,* p. 245.

35 William A. Jenks, *Francis Joseph and the Italians, 1849–1859* (Charlottesville: University Press of Virginia, 1978), pp. 3–4. Kramer, pp. 19, 24–5, 128, 150–1. Benedikt, *Kaiseradler,* pp. 114–117, 125, 443, 447. Regele, *Radetzky,* p. 261. Policing the Papal State alone cost the Austrians 30,000 florins (cir. $405,000 in 1996 dollars) a month in the 1850s. Schmidt-Brentano, p. 208.

upstart papal brigades at Vicenza and Ferrara.[36] In 1848, the Habsburg army put down Italian nationalist revolts in Lombardy, Venetia, Tuscany, Parma, and Modena, prompting France's minister at Parma to remark that "the sovereigns of Italy have been, and still are, the prefects and proconsuls of the Austrian government."[37]

France's decision to side with Piedmont against Austria in 1859 effectively ended Austria's control of Italian affairs, for the Habsburg defeat at Solferino in 1859 shortened the monarchy's reach. Just how much was revealed in 1860, when General Giuseppe Garibaldi and his little army of Italian nationalists invaded Bourbon Sicily. The Austrians, still prostrate in the wake of their war with France and Piedmont, could do nothing more than demand that the *other* Great Powers resist Garibaldi's "illegal revisions" of the borders of 1815. However, Austria's fellow powers not only refused to aid the Habsburgs, they went so far as to recognize the "Kingdom of Italy," which was founded by a vastly expanded Piedmont in 1861 in barefaced contravention of the Vienna treaties of 1815.[38] Though only Spain and the Pope sided with Austria in its struggle against Italian nationalism after 1861, Emperor Franz Joseph grimly persisted in his determination to revive Austria as the "gendarme of Italy" and dismantle the newly joined Kingdom of Italy, which exerted constant pressure on Austria's Italian-speaking crownlands.[39] In the years after 1859, Franz Joseph increased his Army of Italy in Venetia to a permanent strength of 100,000 bayonets. By 1866, his generals in Verona fairly yearned for an Austro-Italian War, for, as Austria's Roman ambassador explained in April 1866, "a victorious campaign for Austria would give the *coup de grâce* to this phantasmal Kingdom of Italy and prepare the peninsula for the prompt, complete restoration of the old régime."[40]

This arrant Austrian conservatism combined with the young Kingdom of Italy's concomitant resolve to drive the Austrians over the Alps forever made the Italian question as explosive as the German one in the 1860s. In 1859, King Vittorio Emanuele II of Piedmont and his brilliant prime minister, Count Camillo Cavour, had allied with France to seize Lombardy, one of Austria's richest provinces. After taking Lombardy, Cavour had, in league with General Garibaldi's volunteers, annexed Tuscany, Parma, Modena, most of the Papal State, Naples, and Sicily and, in 1861, renamed Piedmont the "Kingdom of Italy."[41] In

---

36 Kramer, p. 130. Regele, *Radetzky*, pp. 234, 303.

37 Michael McDonald, "Napoleon III and His Ideas of Italian Confederation, 1856–60" (Ph.D. diss., University of Pennsylvania, 1968), p. 30.

38 Richard Blake Elrod, "The Venetian Question in Austrian Foreign Relations, 1860–66" (Ph.D. diss., University of Illinois, 1967), pp. 17–38.

39 HHSA, PA XI, Karton 207, Vienna, October 25, 1865, Mensdorff to Hübner, "Instructions." PRO, FO 45/85, no. 41, Florence, February 10, 1866, Elliot to Clarendon.

40 HHSA, PA XI, Karton 208, Rome, April 3, 1866, Hübner to Mensdorff. Geoffrey Wawro, "Austria versus the Risorgimento: A New Look at Austria's Italian Strategy in the 1860s," *European History Quarterly* 26 (January 1996):7–29.

41 Denis Mack Smith, *Vittorio Emanuele, Cavour and the Risorgimento* (London: Oxford University Press, 1971), pp. 92-189.

1864, King Vittorio Emanuele moved the Italian government from Turin to Florence and announced his intention to acquire the last foreign-controlled enclaves in Italy: Austrian Venetia and Papal Rome. This was "irredentism," the Piedmontese determination to "redeem" the entire Italian peninsula from foreign domination, but it could be accomplished only after a war with the Austrian Empire. Thus five successive Italian governments in the years between Cavour's death in 1861 and the war of 1866 vowed as a matter of principle to wrest Venetia from Austria *at any price*. They backed this pledge with a vast military build-up, increasing the Italian army from 50,000 to 200,000 bayonets and constructing Europe's third largest ironclad fleet from scratch in the first five years of national unification.[42]

In April 1866, Italy and Prussia signed a military alliance that direly threatened the "Metternich system" of 1815. Metternich's order had been based upon Habsburg bluff, occasional applications of force in Italy, and the active sympathy of Austria's fellow Great Powers. By 1866, the Prussians and Italians saw clearly that Austria was isolated. Distracted by domestic and colonial concerns, none of the other Great Powers shared Austria's conviction that German and Italian disunity were absolutely essential to the balance of power in Europe. Though the other powers would later repent of their short-sightedness in this regard, in the spring of 1866 they left Austria alone against the combined armies of Prussia and Italy. Thus threatened in north and south, Emperor Franz Joseph summoned his most famous general, Feldzeugmeister Ludwig Benedek, and ordered him to prepare for a two-front war in which the very survival of the Austrian Empire, assailed by a half million enemy troops, would be at stake.

42 John Gooch, *Army, State and Society in Italy, 1870-1915* (London: Macmillan, 1989), pp. 13–14. HHSA, IB, Karton 364, BM 1866, 33, Vienna, April 24, 1866, Belcredi to Mensdorff, Franck. KA, MKSM 1866, Karton 338, 33–1/8, no. 5, Rome, March 22, 1866, Maj. Frantzl to FML Crenneville.

3

War plans and mobilization

Prussia's General Staff chief Helmuth von Moltke was no less interested in the Schleswig-Holstein question than Bismarck. By the spring of 1865, he was already advising Prussia's king to annex the duchies, even if annexation entailed war with Austria. "Prussia," Moltke later wrote, "would never have consented to the duchies becoming a sovereign middle state," for an independent Schleswig-Holstein would have opened a hole in Prussia's northern, seaward flank and, once subjected to Augustenburg and joined to the German Confederation, would have served Habsburg rather than Hohenzollern interests.[1]

Hence, Moltke, like Bismarck, was prepared to fight the Austrians for Schleswig-Holstein and political control of Germany. In the pending struggle, the Prussian army would enjoy the crucial advantage of time. Prussia had spent the 1850s and 1860s building railroads while Austria's rural economy slumbered. The result by 1866 was that Austria's sole double-tracked railway north from Vienna to Bohemia – the most probable theater of war with the Prussians – was met by five Prussian lines touching the Austrian frontier along the rim of the salient formed by Silesia, Moravia, Bohemia, and Saxony. For Austrian war planners, this complicated plans for an Austro-Prussian war immensely. Their own mobilization and deployment would take at least twelve weeks, twice the time needed by the Prussians.[2] The time factor weighed no less heavily on the Austrians in Italy. In Venetia, General Benedek warned that the Italians, with their excellent, French-financed double-tracked northern railways, would be able to deploy a formidable invasion force on the Lombard-Venetian frontier in just fourteen days, while the Habsburg Army of Italy, with the bulk of its reserves garrisoned in faraway Galicia and Hungary, would require three *months* to reinforce the Quadrilateral.[3]

1 Grosser Generalstab, *Der Feldzug 1866*, pp. 1–3. Gall, *Bismarck*, vol. 1, p. 265.
2 KA, MKSM-SR 1866, 22/5, Vienna, August 1865, k.k. Evidenz-Bureau, "Berechnung der gegenseitigen Stärke-und-Machtverhältnisse zw. Österreich und Preussen, so wie die Zeit welche beide Armeen brauchen, um operationsfähig zu werden."
3 HHSA, IB, Karton 364, BM 1866, 33, Venice, April 29, 1866, Direzione di Polizia to Belcredi. Schmidt-Brentano, p. 153.

Time, then, was critical to Prussian war plans in 1866. Moltke had to strike fast and hard at Austria in order to activate his ninety-day Italian alliance and break the Habsburg Monarchy's resistance before it had time to mobilize its much larger population, thirty-four millions compared with Prussia's nineteen. It was, however, precisely this factor of time that nearly ruined Moltke in 1866. Prussia's King Wilhelm I was a timid statesman, who hesitated to make war with "brother Austria," Prussia's fellow German Great Power. The king's inconvenient scruples threatened to wreck Moltke's finely tuned mobilization plans, which required a timely Prussian declaration of war that would engage Italy and knock Austria's larger army off balance.

While Berlin hesitated, Vienna began to arm. Worried by Prussian and Italian threats, Austrian Emperor Franz Joseph triggered the mobilizations of 1866 on February 28 by ordering cavalry regiments stationed in Austria's easternmost districts to make themselves "march ready."[4] Two weeks later, the Austrians, mindful of Prussia's faster mobilization schedule, sought to steal a march on Moltke by "prepositioning" twenty infantry battalions and an entire cavalry division on the Austro-Prussian border in Bohemia.[5] Although Bismarck and Moltke, who were impatient to launch a preventive war, interpreted this provocation as an adequate *casus belli*, King Wilhelm would agree to no more than a partial countermobilization of five Prussian divisions, which he strung protectively along Prussia's straggling borders with Austria and Saxony. Moltke deplored the king's moderation, which squandered Prussia's great advantage, its speed of mobilization, and Bismarck insisted, in vain, that "it would be shrewder to bring about [a war] when the situation is favorable to *us* than to wait until Austria starts it in conditions advantageous to herself."[6]

Thwarted again by King Wilhelm's caution, Moltke and Bismarck fretted throughout April as the Austrians continued to move troops – seventy battalions by Moltke's reckoning – into Moravia and Bohemia, while the Prussian king sought merely to negotiate an end to the German crisis.[7] On April 21, King Wilhelm, now decidedly under the influence of pacifists in his entourage like Rudolf Delbrück and Count Fritz Eulenburg, agreed with the Austrian emperor to withdraw and demobilize all troops deployed on the Austro-Prussian frontier. To Bismarck's chagrin, the Austro-Prussian War, a near certainty one month earlier, appeared to have been defused.[8]

4 KA, MKSM-SR 1866, 22/3, Vienna, March 1866, "Vermerkung für die Mobilisierung der Armee 1866."

5 The pretext for this provocative troop movement was the need to bring a wave of pogroms under control. Geoffrey Wawro, "The Habsburg *Flucht nach vorne* in 1866: Domestic-Political Origins of the Austro-Prussian War," *International History Review* 17 (May 1995), pp. 238–40.

6 Carr, *Origins*, p. 127.

7 Grosser Generalstab, *Feldzug 1866*, pp. 5–17, 28.

8 Chester Wells Clark, *Franz Joseph and Bismarck* (Cambridge, Mass.: Harvard University Press, 1934).

Yet even as King Wilhelm poured oil on Germany's troubled waters, Bismarck's Prusso-Italian alliance, designed to snare the Austrian Empire in a two-front war, was taking hold. Throughout March and April, Austrian police agents in Italy had reported the mobilization of the Italian army and fleet and a troubling increase in armaments production at Italian arsenals. In the last week of April, the Italians, worried that Austrian diplomacy might rob them of the chance to annex Habsburg Venetia, began to deploy thousands of troops on Austria's Venetian frontier, a dangerous provocation that forced the Austrian emperor to order a countermobilization in Venetia. After some hesitation, Franz Joseph then made the fateful decision to extend this partial mobilization to Moravia and Bohemia as well. By late April, Vienna was apprised of the Prusso-Italian alliance and had thus to prepare for the worst.[9]

PRUSSIA'S WAR PLANS AND MOBILIZATION

Stung by Franz Joseph's resumption of the Austrian mobilization against Prussia on April 27, Prussia's King Wilhelm responded with a flurry of Prussian mobilization orders in the first week of May, authorizing Prussia's eight army corps and its entire *Landwehr* establishment to embody their reservists and equip themselves for war. As the Prussian, Austrian, and Italian armies began to deploy, French Emperor Napoleon III, prodded by England and Russia, sought to avert the war by calling for a European congress that would peacefully resolve the Schleswig-Holstein and Venetian questions. Once again, Bismarck's aggressive policy seemed to have been thwarted, as the European Great Powers belatedly engaged themselves in the German crisis. Yet once more Bismarck was saved, this time by his Austrian counterpart, Count Alexander Mensdorff, who was an exceedingly unimaginative foreign minister and actually refused even to attend Bonaparte's proposed congress if changes to the status of Venetia were contemplated. Since a European congress convened to settle the German and Italian questions had perforce to treat the question of Venetia, Napoleon III's congress plan had to be abandoned, and King Wilhelm, his patience with the House of Austria exhausted, authorized Moltke to finalize his plans for war.[10]

Although the Austrian army in 1866 was larger than Prussia's, opposing ten corps and a total strength of 400,000 to Prussia's eight corps and 300,000, Moltke knew that the Austrians would have to make big detachments to defend Venetia.[11] Indeed, to parry the attack on the Quadrilateral forts by 200,000 Italian troops, Emperor Franz Joseph would be forced to post three entire infantry corps and two cavalry brigades to Venetia, which would leave him just seven corps

---

9 KA, MKSM 1866, Karton 338, 33–1/8, no. 5, Rome, March–May, 1866, Maj. Frantzl to FML Crenneville.

10 Clark, *Franz Joseph and Bismarck*, pp. 410–41. F. R. Bridge, *The Habsburg Monarchy among the Great Powers, 1815-1918* (New York: Berg, 1990), pp. 74–85.

11 Grosser Generalstab, *Feldzug 1866*, pp. 18–26.

and six cavalry divisions for use against the Prussians in Bohemia. Thus, in Bohemia, the war's decisive theater, an Austrian "North Army" of 245,000 would confront a slightly more numerous Prussian army of 254,000.

Prussia's edge in troop numbers, however, was offset by Austria's strategic advantage of internal lines. In order to subdue the western German states and accelerate an invasion of Saxony and Austria, Moltke was forced to break the Prussian army into four groups small enough to be transported quickly by Prussia's widely separated rail lines to the Austrian, Saxon, and Hanoverian frontiers. Only thus could Moltke recoup the precious time lost to the Prussian king's vacillation in March and April.[12] By mid-June 1866, one of these groups was arrayed on the Hanoverian border; two were deployed around Saxony and Bohemia; the fourth was 500 kilometers to the east, in Upper Silesia, separated from the other three by Bohemia's Giant Mountains. With most of Benedek's North Army massing at Olmütz in Moravia, the Austrians, though slow to mobilize, found themselves in an unexpectedly promising position. Moltke's hasty, fractured deployment meant that, if quick to react, all of North Army could thrust into the gap between the eastern and western halves of the Prussian army and destroy them separately.[13]

For a critical week in mid-June, the four Prussian armies in Germany, Lusatia, and Silesia exchanged worried cables and nervously awaited a declaration of war so that they could begin their descent on the German states and the Austrian province of Bohemia, where Moltke planned to unite three of his four armies. Even the usually unflappable Moltke, who had been forced by Mensdorff's "peace offensive" in April to concede the Austrians three full weeks to begin their mobilization, was tormented by doubt.[14] His three principal armies would need at *least* a week to pass through the Giant Mountains and close to within one march of each other in Bohemia. In mid-June, General Karl Herwarth von Bittenfeld's Elbe Army in Torgau found itself five marches removed from Prince Friedrich Karl's First Army in Görlitz, which was itself seven marches distant from Crown Prince Friedrich Wilhelm's Second Army at Neisse.[15] These yawning gaps between the Prussian armies offered General Benedek, the "Lion of Solferino," now commandant of Austria's North Army at Olmütz, brilliant opportunities, a danger Moltke fully appreciated. "The mere *name* Benedek," he wrote, "means that he will come *quickly*, dealing blows left and right."[16] Although Moltke modified his plan in early June because of doubts about Benedek's intentions, shifting two corps from Görlitz to Neisse to defend Upper Silesia from Austrian

12 Grosser Generalstab, *Feldzug 1866*, pp. 5–17.
13 KA, Nachlässe, B/1109: 1 (Sacken), "Notizen über den Feldzug 1866," p. 4.
14 Clark, *Franz Joseph and Bismarck*, pp. 333–89.
15 Helmuth von Moltke, *Strategy: The Wars for German Unification*, trans. British War Office (1907; Westport: Greenwood Press, 1971), p. 39.
16 Oscar von Lettow-Vorbeck, *Geschichte des Krieges von 1866 in Deutschland*, 3 vols. (Berlin: Mittler, 1896–1902), vol. 2, p. 46.

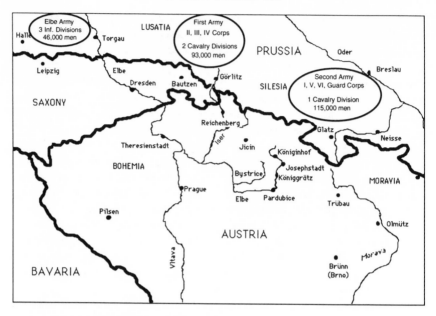

The Prussian mobilization, June 1866

attack, the essence of his bold strategy remained unchanged. He would overrun
Saxony and the other German states, penetrate Bohemia, and there envelop
Benedek's North Army with three *mobile* columns. [17]

   To invade Austria and the German states, Moltke deployed four armies in a
broad arc from west to east. The first of these was West Army – really a strong
corps of 40,000 men – which comprised three Prussian divisions poised first to
overrun Hanover and Hessia-Kassel, then to infiltrate between the numerous but
divided south German armies. Moltke reluctantly agreed to confide this army to
General Eduard Vogel von Falckenstein, a royal favorite who had proven himself
an incompetent soldier in Denmark. Whereas the king viewed western Germany
as a relatively "safe" theater for the discharge of Falckenstein's mediocre talents,
Moltke recognized that the success or failure of West Army's campaign would
weigh heavily on the one in Austria. Though not directly engaged in Bohemia,
West Army played a nonetheless crucial role, for only by beating the German
federal army, which mustered 150,000 men, could Falckenstein secure the lines
of supply and retreat of the three larger Prussian armies operating in Austria.

   On the Austrian front, Moltke deployed three separate armies along the salient
formed by Bohemia. The westernmost and smallest of the three was Elbe Army,
just 46,000 strong. Entrusted to the command of General Karl Herwarth von

17 Albrecht von Blumenthal, *Journals of Field Marshal Count von Blumenthal for 1866 and 1870–71*,
    trans. A. D. Gillespie-Addison (London: Edward Arnold, 1903), pp. 17–30.

Bittenfeld, who vied with Falckenstein for the distinction of most mediocre general in the Prussian army, Elbe Army had a formidable mission. Based at Halle and Torgau, Herwarth's three divisions were to administer a knock-out punch to Saxony in the first days of the war, then, after occupying Dresden, the Saxon capital, to move up the left bank of the Elbe to Bohemia. After passing into Bohemia, Elbe Army would meet with the second of Moltke's three armies on the Austrian front. This was First Army, the central hinge of Moltke's intended envelopment of the Austrian North Army. Command arrangements in First Army were somewhat more promising than in the West and Elbe Armies. Moltke and the king gave First Army – which, containing three infantry corps and two cavalry divisions, was 93,000 strong – to Prince Friedrich Karl, the king's nephew, who had gained a measure of fame by joining with Moltke to rescue the faltering command of Wrangel and Falckenstein in Denmark in 1864. Moltke deployed First Army around Görlitz in Lusatia, the pine-clad northeastern rim of Saxony, annexed by Prussia in 1815. Its task was to push into Bohemia, where it would make contact with Elbe Army and attempt a crossing of the Iser River, a broad, easily defensible water barrier in northern Bohemia that Moltke assumed the Austrians would hold stubbornly.

Once in possession of the Iser bridges at Münchengrätz, Podol, and Turnau, Elbe and First Armies would be free to march eastward to join forces with the third and most vulnerable of Moltke's three armies on the Austrian front: Crown Prince Friedrich Wilhelm's Second Army. Two hundred kilometers east of First Army, astride the Neisse river and only a few marches removed from Benedek's North Army at Olmütz, Second Army had the most difficult mission of all in the war. Though the strongest of the three Prussian armies invading Bohemia – it embodied four infantry corps and a cavalry division for a total of 115,000 men – it had first to repel any Austrian attempt to reconquer Upper Silesia and Breslau – lost by the Habsburgs to the Hohenzollern in 1740 – and then to fight its way through the Giant Mountains to meet Elbe and First Armies debouching from Lusatia and Saxony in Bohemia. Benedek's surprising decision to deploy his northern army not in Bohemia, as expected, but farther east in Moravia, put the Prussian Second Army at considerable risk. Whether Crown Prince Friedrich Wilhelm, a young, untested commander, stood on the defensive against an Austrian drive on Breslau or – if Benedek chose to post westward to hit the Elbe and First Armies in Bohemia – he attempted his own passage of the Giant Mountains to unite with First Army, he would, in either case, find himself heavily outnumbered by the entire Austrian North Army.[18]

Though most Prussian generals and the international press blasted Moltke for the way he seemingly dissipated the strength of the Prussian army, extending eighteen first-rate divisions "like beads on a string," the Prussian *chef* had little choice. He would have preferred to concentrate the Prussian army in the road and

18 Grosser Generalstab, *Feldzug 1866*, pp. 94–9.

rail-rich space between Dresden and Görlitz but was prevented from implementing this plan by diplomatic niceties – chiefly the need to respect Saxon neutrality during Prussia's mobilization – and also by the Prussian king's rather timid insistence that Moltke detach an entire army to defend Upper Silesia and the valley of the Oder. Thus, Moltke later grumbled, he was forced "to disembark the Prussian army [at railheads] on an arc five hundred kilometers in length," from Halle in the west to Neisse in the east. Though Moltke was quite willing to disperse the Prussian army to gain time marching, this was far more dispersal than even he would have liked, for it narrowed his strategic options considerably. After deploying in June, he rued the fact that the scattered deployment forced on him by the king's continual toing and froing had cost him the option of fighting a purely defensive war. Henceforth only a prompt *offensive* into Bohemia by all three Prussian armies could close the vast distances between them.[19] Nevertheless, exhibiting his usual, reassuring phlegm, Moltke advised the king that wherever the Austrians turned, whether against the Prussian Second Army – which had the shortest line to Vienna – or against the Elbe and First Armies – which had Dresden and Prague in their sights – Prussian headquarters would have sufficient time to hurl the neglected armies into Benedek's flank and rear, completing the desired envelopment of the Austrian army.[20]

This was not to say that there were not great, potentially calamitous risks inhered in the Prussian plan. Moltke, who always insisted that "no plan of operations survives the first clash with an enemy force," would have been the first to admit that his plan, like any other, was based upon hopeful assumptions about his subordinates and their ability to march and supply themselves at the fast pace set by Berlin.[21] In the "fog of war," accidents could upset even the best laid plans, and it was this realization that filled Moltke's colleagues with fear. General Karl Steinmetz, the seventy-year-old commandant of Second Army's V Corps, deplored what he called Moltke's needless "attenuation" of Prussia's strength.[22] Even light Austrian resistance in the Bohemian mountains might throw the Prussian invasion out of gear, prevent the three armies from cooperating, and permit Benedek to crush them individually.

Prussian fears were founded on Berlin's reverential assessment of Benedek, "Austria's Blücher."[23] In 1866, the Austrian Feldzeugmeister was an international celebrity. His military exploits were well publicized and had always breathed the offensive spirit. At Mortara in 1849, he had attacked and captured an entire Piedmontese division with a single brigade. In 1859, he had ignored

---

19 Grosser Generalstab, *Feldzug 1866*, pp. 31–2, 44. The gap between Elbe and First Armies was 150 kilometers; between First and Second Armies, 190 kilometers.

20 Dennis E. Showalter, "The Retaming of Bellona: Prussia and the Institutionalization of the Napoleonic Legacy, 1815–76," *Military Affairs* 44 (1980), p. 61. Craig, *Königgrätz*, pp. 45–6.

21 Hajo Holborn, "The Prusso-German School," *Makers of Modern Strategy*, p. 300.

22 Groote, "Moltkes Planungen," *Entscheidung 1866*, pp. 97–8.

23 HHSA, IB, Karton 364, BM 1866, 35, Vienna, May 31, 1866, Belcredi to Mensdorff, Franck.

orders to pull back his wing at Solferino and had instead driven off furious Piedmontese attacks on the Austrian Mincio crossings, covering what would otherwise have been a chaotic Austrian retreat. In 1866, no one, Moltke included, believed that the Feldzeugmeister would delay in carrying an Austro-Prussian war to Prussian soil. This explained Moltke's last minute decision in June to transfer Berlin's Guard Corps and the élite East Prussian I Corps from Friedrich Karl's First Army at Görlitz to Crown Prince Friedrich Wilhelm's Second Army in Silesia. With Benedek's North Army assembling in Moravia, Berlin took for granted an Austrian lunge at Breslau.

AUSTRIA'S WAR PLANS AND MOBILIZATION

What Berlin failed to reckon with was the decline of Benedek as a general and the chaos of his arrangements at Olmütz. Though a good fighting soldier, Benedek had no grasp of strategy. Comfortable with a corps, he was lost with an army, and his frivolous selection of Baron Henikstein to be General Staff chief in 1864 had further complicated matters, for in March 1866 Henikstein insisted on campaigning with Austria's North Army. By that late date, however, Henikstein's incompetence was so widely assumed that the Habsburg army inspector, Archduke Albrecht, felt obliged to assign Benedek an "operations chief," a real strategist who would make Henikstein's dispositions for him. Albrecht's choice was General Gideon Krismanic, a forty-nine-year-old Croat with a formidable reputation. The *sous-chef* of an entire Austrian army at Solferino, a professor of strategy at the Habsburg *Kriegsschule* in Vienna and an expert on the German theater of war, Krismanic exuded confidence and *seemed* a perfect choice. Underneath the confident exterior, however, lurked the soul of a pedant. Krismanic had studied the eighteenth-century campaigns of Generals Daun and Lacy – Frederick the Great's Austrian adversaries – and, in the operations plan he submitted to Benedek in April 1866, he proposed to fight this latest Austro-Prussian war no differently than they had fought theirs, from the safety of Austria's entrenched camp at Olmütz and its forts on the Elbe. Krismanic thus stifled what little remained of Benedek's vaunted "*Offensivgeist*," and refused to exploit Austria's single greatest advantage in the war, its command of the "internal lines" between the invading Prussian armies.

The seventy-page operations plan Krismanic composed for Benedek and Henikstein in April 1866 took for granted the *defensive* concentration of most of the Austrian army at Olmütz in Moravia. Critics, including Benedek, later scolded Krismanic for deploying in Moravia instead of Bohemia, but, as Krismanic assured a court of inquiry convened after the war to review his dispositions, "the basic principles of the plan were established *before* I arrived in Vienna from Italy in March 1866."[24] Indeed, Krismanic's war plan was merely elaborated from a rough draft conceived by another staff college professor, Colonel August

---

24 KA, Nachlässe, B/572: 2 (Nosinic), Wr. Neustadt, January 2, 1869, GM Krismanic to Nosinic.

5. General Gideon Krismanic (1817–76), "operations chief" of the Austrian North
Army in 1866

Neuber, who was a close personal friend of Benedek's and, like Krismanic, a
theoretical disciple of Jomini and Archduke Karl.

  Neuber's rough draft, which was approved by Benedek and Henikstein in
March and presented to Krismanic in April, called for an initial defensive
deployment in Moravia instead of Bohemia in order to remove an Austrian field

army behindhand in its mobilization from the threat of a preemptive Prussian strike.[25] Neuber and Krismanic rightly considered the Moravian fortress of Olmütz – a copy of Austria's entrenched camp at Verona – to be a formidable obstacle that would halt any Prussian advance on Vienna. With its detached forts and entrenchments and its large garrison, Olmütz contrasted favorably with the Elbe forts of Königgrätz and Josephstadt, which were too small to accomodate whole army corps and sited in depressions within gun-range of surrounding hills.[26] Moreover, Krismanic thought it improbable that the Prussians would invade Austria through Saxony and Bohemia because of the difficulties that would be posed by Saxon fortifications at Dresden and Königstein as well as the Austrian forts at Josephstadt, Königgrätz, and Theresienstadt.[27] Krismanic shared this misconception with many contemporaries, including a British war correspondent, who judged Krismanic's initial assumptions "unimpeachable, for the Austrians reckoned on Prussia not attempting to pass the gorges of the Bohemian mountains without extreme caution and circumspection."[28]

In the month before Moltke began massing his three armies on the Austrian frontier, Krismanic assumed that the Prussians would choose the classic Frederician route to Vienna, via Neisse and Olmütz. From Krismanic's traditional perspective, it seemed the obvious choice. It was the shortest operations line to the Austrian capital and it traversed a rich, well-watered plain connected to the Prussian interior by four railroads and a half dozen hardened turnpikes.[29] Austrian intelligence collected in May and June seemed to confirm that the Prussians would come this way. In early May, Austrian spies reported the "pulling together of great troop masses" around Neisse while "reliable sources" in Leipzig described on June 5 "a great migration of the Prussian army from west to east."[30] These shiftings of the Prussian army reflected conflict within the Prussian command itself; Moltke was struggling to deploy the bulk of his army around Saxony while the king and his more cautious generals, preoccupied with the Austrian threat to Silesia, ignored Moltke's orders and tugged the Prussian army back to the east.[31]

25 Neuber's plan has been lost, but its outlines survive in secondary literature. Manfried Rauchensteiner, "Zum operativen Denken in Österreich, 1815–1914," *ÖMZ* 5 (1974), p. 382. Johann Christoph Allmayer-Beck, "Der Feldzug der österreichischen Nord-Armee nach Königgrätz," *Entscheidung 1866*, pp. 112–14, 124–32.
26 Hills that had been well out of range when the forts were constructed in the eighteenth century. KA, AFA 1866, Karton 2274, 13–74, Olmütz, December 1872, Maj. Ripp, "Skizze des Feldzuge 1866."
27 KA, AFA 1866, Karton 2261, Vienna, April 1866, GM Krismanic, "Operationsplan für die k.k. Nordarmee in einem Kriege gegen Preussen, 1866," Abschnitt XIII.
28 Edward Dicey, *The Battlefields of 1866* (London: Tinsley Brothers, 1866), p. 12.
29 A view seconded by Austria's military attaché in Berlin. KA, KM 1866, CK, 47–4/9, Berlin, February 9, 1866, Col. Pelikan to FML Franck.
30 KA, MKSM-SR 1866, 24/3, Vienna, May 2 and Leipzig June 1–5, 1866, "Nachtrag aus dem Kundschaftsberichten."
31 Blumenthal, p. 21. Grosser Generalstab, *Feldzug 1866*, pp. 40–2.

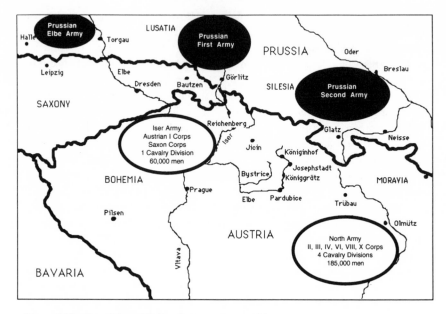

The mobilization of Austria's North Army, June 1866

When Krismanic learned in June that Moltke had transferred two entire corps from Lusatia east to Silesia on the eve of the Prussian invasion, Austria's operations chief was seemingly confirmed in his view that the Prussians would aim for Olmütz, not the Elbe forts and Prague.[32] He cautioned Benedek that henceforth "any Prussian attack toward Josephstadt and Königgrätz would only be a feint, either to draw the Italians into the war, or to lure us toward Bohemia . . . at which point, in the midst of our flank march, the Prussians would shunt their main army to Silesia and pounce on our flank and rear."[33]

Austria's North Army, Krismanic argued, must remain in Olmütz because "based there we can dare far more than the Prussians, who will have the mountain passes in their rear, and will fear for a total catastophe in case of defeat." Krismanic, a military historian, clearly foresaw something akin to the War of the Bavarian Succession in 1788, when one of Frederick the Great's armies had entered Moravia from Upper Silesia and stopped short at Olmütz before retiring to Prussia without battle, reckoning the costs of a siege to be too high. Were this scenario to recur in 1866, Krismanic reasoned that Benedek could first repulse a Prussian attack on Olmütz, then counterattack, wheeling through Neisse and

32 Dennis E. Showalter, "Soldiers into Postmasters: The Electric Telegraph as an Instrument of Command in the Prussian Army," *Military Affairs* 2 (1973), p. 50. HHSA, IB, Karton 374, BM 1866, 2898, Prague, July 21, 1866, Polizeidirektor to Belcredi, vid. Esterházy.
33 KA, Nachlässe, B/572: 1 (Nosinic), Vienna, April 1866, GM Krismanic, "Sammelstellung der Preussen." Vienna, May 2, 1866, GM Krismanic, "Überfall Sachsens."

Cracow to realize what *he* assumed to be Franz Joseph's primary war aim: the reconquest of Breslau and its rich seams of coal, annexed by the Prussians 100 years earlier.[34]

Krismanic further reasoned that were the Prussians simply to bypass Olmütz, overrun the Saxons, and strike into Bohemia, they would *still* have the entire Austrian field army in Moravia on their flank and athwart their communications and would therefore have little choice but to turn east to meet the threat before continuing on to Vienna.[35] The factor of time was also at work. If Franz Joseph allowed the initiative to pass to Prussia, which he did, "the Austrian army would have no choice," Krismanic wrote, "but to relinquish voluntarily the offensive and assume a prepared position in the path of the most likely enemy operations line" in order to complete North Army's mobilization, which involved reeling in regiments from the monarchy's far-flung garrisons.[36] The "guiding principle in North Army headquarters," Krismanic later testified, "was always this: a victory at Olmütz, even if only in a defensive battle, would have been far more advantageous than anything that might have been gained by a risky undertaking in Bohemia, which, for us, was a strategically less advantageous direction."[37] Benedek's adjutant, Colonel Ferdinand Kriz, seconded this view, noting after the war that "in Benedek's headquarters, the talk was *always* of seeking a decision at *Olmütz*. It was said that the army should only abandon the 'concentrated position' there if a truly favorable offensive opportunity presented itself elsewhere. At all events," Kriz concluded, "I often heard it remarked that the wretched condition of our troops arriving from Transylvania and Galicia . . . would have put any Austrian *offensive* at risk."[38]

In May 1866, Franz Joseph, Benedek, Crenneville, Henikstein, Albrecht, and Franck all gave their sanction to Krismanic's eastern deployment. Olmütz was a dozen marches removed from Prussia's jumping-off stations in Saxony and Lusatia; it barred the path of Second Army in Silesia, and it had the added

34 KA, AFA 1866, Karton 2261, Vienna, April 1866, GM Krismanic, "Operationsplan," Abschnitte V and IX. KM 1866, CK, Karton 252, 51–6/49, Vienna, May 29, 1866, FML Franck to FZM Benedek. Vincennes, AAT, MR 83/1606, Vienna, June 21, 1866, Col. Merlin to Randon.

35 KA, AFA 1866, Karton 2261, Vienna, April 1866, GM Krismanic, "Operationsplan," Abschnitte VIII and XIII.

36 In May, the French army attaché in Vienna wrote: "When you consider that many of these [Austrian] regiments have their recruiting depots in far Silesia, eastern Hungary and Transylvania, and that the corresponding railheads are at Lemberg, Grosswardein and Arad, and that troops must often march three weeks to the nearest train station, it is hardly surprising that Austria rejects any offensive while making her preparations." Vincennes, AAT, MR 72/1606, Vienna, May 6, 1866, Col. Merlin to Randon.

37 KA, Nachlässe, B/572: 2 (Nosinic), Wr. Neustadt, July 12, 1866, GM Krismanic to Untersuchungs-Commission. AFA 1866, Karton 2261, Vienna, April 1866, GM Krismanic, "Operationsplan," Abschnitt II, "Freiwillige Verzichtleistung auf die Offensive von Seite Österreichs."

38 KA, AFA 1866, Karton 2270, 8–12aa, Budapest, August 12, 1866, GM Kriz.

advantage of blocking two potentially hostile Russian observation corps deployed in Warsaw and Ukraine, which, owing to Bismarck's shrewd cultivation of the Russians in the years since 1859, Krismanic thought worrisome enough to warrant a large Austrian detachment in Cracow.[39]

In sum, although many Austrian generals, Benedek and the emperor included, sought to distance themselves from the Krismanic plan after its failure, it was undeniably the consensus Austrian plan for 1866. It was in the mainstream of Austria's traditionally defensive thinking; it issued from the staff college and it withstood scrutiny by the entire Austrian high command. Though Krismanic has been harshly judged by historians for removing North Army from the eventual theater of war in Bohemia, most of the criticism has been misplaced, for his April operations plan was only a guideline for Austrian operations and was drafted before Moltke began deploying his armies. More important than the plan itself was how the plan was interpreted and updated by Benedek in light of reconnaissance and espionage findings. In fact, it would be General Benedek's irresolute application of Krismanic's plan, not the plan itself, that would foil Austrian operations in 1866.

In the end, Benedek's irresolution was probably the single greatest defect in Austria's war effort. Rather than question Krismanic, whom he regarded as a bewildering *Shaman* foisted on him by Franz Joseph, Benedek took refuge in a vacuous routine of inspections, reviews, and luncheons at Olmütz.[40] This drift in Austrian headquarters partly explained the amazing, false rumors heard by Moltke in June of a "*secret* plan" taking shape in Benedek's *Kommandantur*. Benedek, Prussian spies (and the Austrian press) alleged, had devised a plan for the invasion of Prussia so ingenious that he would not even share it with his confidants.[41] It was partly this unfounded suspicion that induced Moltke to shift two entire corps to Silesia from Lusatia in June. The reality, however, was that Benedek had no plan other than Krismanic's defensive one, and that he was as uncertain about Moltke's intentions as Moltke was about his. Hence, in June, the Feldzeugmeister detached his I Corps and 1st Light Cavalry Division under General Eduard Clam-Gallas and posted them westward in order to offer some resistance in the event that Moltke's main thrust was at Bohemia, not Moravia. Although Benedek still believed that Moltke intended to strike toward Olmütz and Vienna with everything he had, he instructed Clam to hold the line of the Iser River against a possible Prussian invasion and cover the retreat of Saxony's five brigades, which, by the terms of an Austro-Saxon military convention signed in the second week of June, would withdraw to Bohemia and unite with North

---

39 KA, AFA 1866, Karton 2261, GM Krismanic, "Operationsplan," Abschnitt IV, "Werth von Krakau." HHSA, IB, Karton 364, BM 1866, 35, Vienna, April 16, 1866, Belcredi to Mensdorff, Franck. Karton 366, BM 1866, 228, Cracow, February 17, 1866, Polizeirat to Belcredi.

40 KA, Nachlässe, B/946 (Coudenhove), pp. 9–22. Wilibald Müller, *Geschichte der königlichen Hauptstadt Olmütz* (Vienna: Eduard Hölzel, 1882), pp. 309–11.

41 Müller, *Geschichte Olmütz*, p. 313. Mollinary, vol. 1, pp. 109–13.

Army if Prussia invaded Saxony.[42] Benedek named this Bohemian detachment, which – with the addition of the Saxon Corps and Austria's erstwhile Holstein garrison – would swell to a strength of 60,000, "Iser Army." Its mission was to hold the line of the Iser River against a Prussian invasion of Bohemia long enough for Benedek to finish assembling North Army in Olmütz and march it to Josephstadt and Königgrätz.[43]

Yet even Iser Army was not really Benedek's idea. The Feldzeugmeister, who loathed the liberalism of the German middle states, was perfectly content to leave the Saxon army to its fate and concentrate his *entire* strength at Olmütz.[44] Only Emperor Franz Joseph, fearful of losing the support of Saxony and Bavaria in the war, possessed the good sense and authority to *force* Benedek to detach troops to Bohemia to encourage Dresden and Munich in their resistance to Prussia's aggression. In fact, flummoxed by all the options available to him and urged by Krismanic to fight a purely defensive war, Benedek subsided into a weary fatalism and resolved merely to stand at Olmütz.[45]

It was, however, a private resolve, and one that baffled Benedek's subordinates, whom the Feldzeugmeister ignored as a matter of course. Count Karl Coudenhove, commandant of Benedek's 3rd Reserve Cavalry Division, complained on May 25 that "although my troopers were ordered to Moravia by forced marches, I still haven't the foggiest notion *why*."[46] Coudenhove's daily routine, confided to his diary between his arrival in Olmütz on May 26 and his first meeting with Benedek three weeks later, on June 15, just hours before the Prussian invasion of Saxony, revealed the torpor of Benedek's headquarters. Mornings Coudenhove performed an increasingly perfunctory inspection of his men. Afternoons he went for "lonely walks" around his cantonments and yearned for his wife and chalet in Tyrol. Evenings he repaired to a pub near Olmütz for a glass of wine and a game of cards. On June 2, one day after the Habsburg government turned the matter of Schleswig-Holstein over to the German federal diet, Coudenhove had still not even heard of what would shortly become the *casus belli* in the Austro-Prussian War. He wrote his wife: "As usual I spent the evening in the pub." One week later, on June 9, while Prussian troops invaded Holstein and chased an Austrian brigade out of Kiel and a full fourteen days since Coudenhove's arrival with his division at Olmütz: "I have still heard nothing from Benedek."[47] Coudenhove noted that June 10, the day Austria's ambassador in Berlin demanded his passports and Austria's minister in

42 KA, MKSM 1866, Karton 343, 69–6, Vienna, June 8, 1866, FML Crenneville to Baron Werner. June 12, 1866, Lt-Col. Beck to FML Crenneville.
43 KA, AFA 1866, Karton 2265, 6–515, Prague, June 15, 1866, GdC Clam to FZM Benedek. Olmütz, June 16, 1866, FZM Benedek to GdC Clam. Karton 2280, 13–103, Lemberg, December 19, 1866, Col. Litzelhofen.
44 KA, MKSM 1866, Karton 343, Olmütz, June 8, 1866, FML Henikstein to FML Crenneville.
45 KA, Nachlässe, B/572:1 (Nosinic), Vienna, April 1866, GM Krismanic.
46 KA, Nachlässe, B/946 (Coudenhove), "Tagebuch," pp. 8–22.
47 Ibid.: ". . . wusste auch von der Rede Benedeks in Olmütz kein Wort."

Frankfurt ordered the German federal contingents to mobilize against Prussia, was the occasion in North Army's camp for nothing more momentous than "Sunday lunch. . . . We're all cocking our ears toward Olmütz for a bit of news."[48]

At long last, on June 15, a day after the German middle states had voted for war with Prussia and even as Prussian troops were massing on the borders of Saxony, Hanover, and Kassel, a summons arrived for Coudenhove from Benedek's headquarters. A council of war? No, lunch. "What a lot of guests and hangers-on," Coudenhove, who had no idea that there was a war on in the German states, recorded. "There were forty of us for luncheon. I sat beside the General Staff chief Heniggstein [*sic*], who looks ill, probably from overwork. At six o'clock we stood up from the table and left. Little Prince Holstein [commandant of Benedek's 1st Reserve Cavalry Division] offered us a nice tea in Prossnitz."[49]

The following morning, Prussia's Elbe Army invaded Saxony en route to Bohemia. On June 18 the Prussians were in Dresden, a day later at the Saxon summer palace in Pirna. Nevertheless, the municipal librarian of Olmütz – who appears to have had no trouble breaching security at Benedek's *Kommandantur* – noted that "an unshakable indifference continued to prevail in headquarters. . . . There was only vague talk about marching 'sometime soon,' and hopeful references to a 'secret, *infallible* plan.' "[50]

This lassitude proved too much for Emperor Franz Joseph, who by this late date was being hunted through the corridors of the Hofburg and Schönbrunn by the retired commanders of 1859: Field Marshal Hess and General Karl Grünne. Though bitter enemies, Hess and Grünne agreed that the emperor must *order* Benedek out of Olmütz and over to Bohemia. There was good cause for such a change of plan, for as Moltke marched his corps down to the Austrian and Saxon frontiers, his intentions became less and less mistakable. Already on May 22, Benedek's intelligence bureau had reported no Prussian troops at all east of Neisse and had predicted a Prussian concentration not in Silesia, as originally assumed, but farther west, in Saxony and Lusatia.[51] That same day, Franz Joseph's secret police had advised Vienna that the Prussian General Staff had placed an order in Berlin for 150 linen maps of Saxony and Bohemia. The maps, Austrian agents reported, highlighted a Prussian invasion route through Görlitz and Dresden to *Königgrätz*.[52] This was a truly spectacular intelligence coup, for it revealed in detail Moltke's plan of operation, yet Benedek ignored the report when it was forwarded to him.[53] In short, by June 5 Benedek knew that Moltke had deployed

48 Ibid.: "Wir spitzen alle die Ohren gegen Olmütz, ob denn nicht bald der Alarmschuss von dort zu hören ist."

49 Ibid.

50 Müller, *Geschichte Olmütz*, p. 313.

51 KA, AFA 1866, Karton 2262, 5–160, Vienna, May 22, 1866, Lt.-Col. Tegetthoff.

52 HHSA, IB, Karton 364, BM 1866, 35, Vienna, May 22, 1866, Belcredi to Mensdorff, Franck.

53 KA, KM 1866, CK, Karton 50, 13–4, Frankfurt, May 25, 1866, GM Pakeni to FML Franck. AFA 1866, Karton 2262, 5–245, Frankfurt, May 27, 1866, GM Pakeni to GdC Mensdorff.

in three groups at Torgau, Görlitz, and Neisse, which certainly suggested a three-pronged Prussian invasion of Bohemia via Saxony, Lusatia, and Silesia, yet still the Feldzeugmeister did nothing.[54]

In view of this gathering Prussian storm and Benedek's mystifying failure to fashion a reply, Emperor Franz Joseph's patience snapped in mid-June. By now he had to contend not only with a Prussian conquest of Bohemia, his richest crownland, but also the loss of Austria's best German allies – Bavaria and Saxony – who would be physically riven from North Army by a Prussian drive up the Elbe. With these dangers in mind, Franz Joseph took the highly irregular step of *ordering* Benedek to abandon the position at Olmütz and shift North Army to a new base of operations at Josephstadt.[55] The emperor's order hit Olmütz like a bombshell mere hours before the Prussian invasion of Hanover and Saxony on June 16.[56] Yet Franz Joseph had indulged Benedek too long, for even forced marches would not get North Army to new positions on the Elbe and the Iser before June 26, ten precious days that were all Moltke would need to overrun Saxony, drive the Bavarian-led German federal army *away* from Bohemia, and push his three biggest armies through the Giant Mountains and into Austria.[57]

MOBILIZATION IN ITALY

Benedek's equivocation was in striking contrast to the intelligent, methodical conduct of Austrian headquarters on the Italian front. Emperor Franz Joseph put South Army, a much smaller though no less important command, in the charge of his uncle, forty-nine-year-old Archduke Albrecht Habsburg, the only active field marshal in the Austrian army in 1866 and the eldest son of Archduke Karl, Austria's best general of the Napoleonic era.

Though a serious and scholarly man, Albrecht's only combat experience before 1866 had been a single action in Piedmont seventeen years earlier. In 1859, the Italian War had passed him by as he worked in vain to secure a Prussian alliance in Berlin. Until 1863, Albrecht had commanded a corps at Padua, which was something of a comedown, for Benedek, by then commandant of the Army of Italy, had been one of Albrecht's subordinates during the Austrian invasion of Piedmont in 1849. In 1863, Franz Joseph's political decision to make his uncle a field marshal meant that Albrecht had to be removed from the Army of Italy,

54 KA, MKSM-SR 1866, 24/3, Josephstadt, May 20 and June 2, 1866. AFA 1866, Karton 2273, 13–50, Olmütz, May 28, June 4, 6, 8, 10, 13, 1866, "Mitteilungen des sächsischen Generalstabes."
55 KA, B/572:2 (Nosinic), Wr. Neustadt, January 2, 1869, GM Krismanic to Capt. Nosinic.
56 KA, MKSM 1866, Karton 342, 69–4/18, Olmütz, June 17, 1866, FZM Benedek to FML Crenneville.
57 KA, MKSM 1866, Karton 342, 69–4/18, Olmütz, June 17, 1866, FZM Benedek to FML Crenneville.

6.   Field Marshal-Archduke Albrecht Habsburg (1817–95), commander of the Austrian South Army in 1866

where, techcnically, he outranked Feldzeugmeister Benedek upon his promotion. With or without a marshal's baton, no one thought seriously of giving the comically near-sighted archduke, who was never without his trademark bottle glasses, an important field command. Thus, he was at loose ends in Vienna in the years after 1863. Though Franz Joseph made him "army inspector" in 1864, he simultaneously cut maneuvers from the army's budget, leaving Albrecht little to inspect. Thus the archduke, like Baron Hess, Austria's other "peacetime field marshal," rapidly became the butt of army wisecracks.[58]

With such a lackluster biography, Albrecht was by no means the most likely candidate for South Army command in 1866. Indeed, on the eve of the war there was much uncertainty as to who would replace Benedek when he moved from Verona to Olmütz in May. On April 7, a South Army brigadier predicted that the command would go to an imperial favorite, Count Friedrich Liechtenstein, who, though an ineffectual salon general, was better liked than the priggish archduke.[59] Hence, in mid-April, it was to general astonishment and angry accusations of nepotism that Franz Joseph made his uncle commandant of the Habsburg Army of Italy, renamed "South Army" for the war of 1866.

In the end, Albrecht would prove to be one of the pleasant surprises of the war, for he assumed his new post with that very seriousness of purpose that had made him so many enemies in Benedek's easygoing Army of Italy and that, in 1866, would be so conspicuously lacking in the Feldzeugmeister's North Army. Unlike Benedek, who conferred half his *corps d'armée* on inept protegés and aristocratic mentors and needlessly divided his headquarters into four independent chanceries, Albrecht peremptorily closed South Army to dilettantes and rigorously centralized all his staff and adjutant functions in the hands of a single, talented staff chief: fifty-one-year-old General Franz John.[60] Albrecht then entrusted his three infantry corps and his reserve cavalry to able, non-noble professional soldiers, all with combat experience.[61] These steps distinguished him from Benedek, who divided his staff functions between three uncooperative officers – Henikstein, Krismanic, and Kriz – and, in a self-serving bid for political influence, confided most of his infantry corps to the least qualified aristocrats in the Austrian army.[62]

Once Albrecht's headquarters was in place, the archduke had to grapple with operational problems posed by the Italian theater that were at least as vexing as those faced by Benedek in the north. With its three infantry corps and four fortress garrisons, South Army would not muster more than 130,000 men for the defense of Venetia.[63] Yet this relatively small force would have to repel the entire Italian army, which, in the years since unification in 1861, had quadrupled in

58 Heller, "Benedek und Benedek-Legenden," p. 26. Bartels, *Der Krieg im Jahre 1866*, p. 6. Bartels, *Kritische Beiträge*, p. 70.

59 Franzel, vol. 2, pp. 461–2. Wandruszka, *1866*, p. 223.

60 KA, Nachlässe, B/1109: 2 (Sacken), "Personal-Status des Armee-Hauptquartiers 1866." Josef Benold, "Österreichische Feldtelegraphie 1866" (Vienna Kriegsarchiv Manuscript, 1990), pp. 5–7.

61 Generals Gabriel Rodic, Joseph Maroicic, Ernst Hartung, and Colonel Ludwig Pulz. The Austrian brigade in South Tyrol went to Franz Kuhn. KA, AFA 1866, Karton 2342, 4–38a, Vienna, April 20, 1866, FML Crenneville to FZM Benedek.

62 KA, AFA 1866, Karton 343, 71/62, Vienna, May 17, 1866, FZM Benedek to Franz Joseph. MKSM 1866, Karton 343, 71/62, Vienna, May 17, 1866, FZM Benedek to Franz Joseph, "Geheim: Bestimmung Nachfolger Nordarmee."

63 k.k. Generalstab, *Österreichs Kämpfe*, vol. 2, pp. 1–8.

7.   General Franz John (1815–76), staff chief of Austria's South Army in 1866

strength, from 50,000 to 200,000 bayonets.[64] The addition of General Garibaldi's "volunteer battalions," which had taken their place in all Italian war plans since Garibaldi's successful conquest of Sicily and Naples in 1860, would increase

64 Gooch, *Army, State and Society in Italy*, pp. 7–15. Vincennes, AAT, MR 20/1387, Vienna, May 1866, Col. Merlin, "Aperçu général sur les conditions actuelles des armées italiennes et autrichiennes."

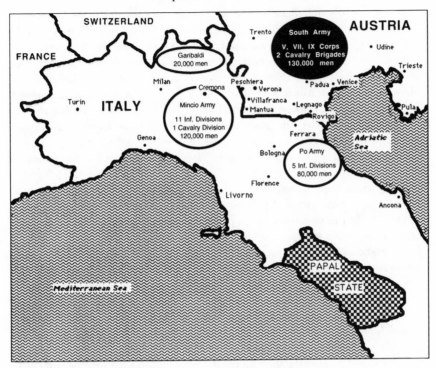

The Italian front, June 1866

total Italian strength to 220,000, an army nearly twice the size of Albrecht's South Army and therefore large enough to infiltrate Austria's Quadrilateral.

Logistics further complicated Albrecht's predicament. His road, rail, and telegraph communications from Venetia to inner Austria were tenuous: northeastward through Slovenia and Styria to Vienna and north up the Adige river valley to Innsbruck. Since 1815 this latter line, easily assailed from Lombardy, had been secured against Italian attack by South Tyrol's inclusion in the German Confederation. Until 1866, any Italian attempt to "redeem" Trentino for national Italy would have triggered an armed German reply, but this security vanished the moment Bismarck dissolved the German Confederation in June 1866 prior to Prussia's invasion of Hanover and Saxony.[65] The demise of the German Confederation also put Austrian Trieste at risk, which was at least as worrisome given Italy's naval superiority in the Adriatic and the fact that Trieste – also included in the German Confederation – had served since 1815 as the *politically* inviolable left wing of the Habsburg Army of Italy.[66]

65 Capt. W. J. Wyatt, *A Political and Military Review of the Austro-Italian War of 1866* (London: Edward Stanford, 1867), pp. 9–12.

66 KA, AFA 1866, Karton 2342, 4–80f., Verona, April 8, 1866, GM John to FM Albrecht. HHSA, IB, Karton 365, BM 1866, 134, Venice, May 16, 1866, Direzione di Polizia to Belcredi.

Whereas in Bohemia Benedek disposed a force roughly equal to the Prussians, Venetia pitted 200,000 Italians grouped in sixteen divisions (four strong corps) against 130,000 Austrians spread thinly across three mobile infantry corps, two light cavalry brigades, and the fortresses. And just as Benedek was in some doubt as to the path Moltke's three armies would eventually take into Bohemia or Moravia, in Venetia Albrecht too faced an Italian army riven into three groups: five divisions under General Enrico Cialdini at Bologna on the lower Po, eleven divisions along the sixty-kilometer course of the Mincio under General Alfonso La Marmora, and twenty battalions of restless volunteers under General Giuseppe Garibaldi in northern Lombardy, menacing Trento and Albrecht's lifeline through the Brenner Pass to Innsbruck.[67]

Given his numerical inferiority and Italy's obscure intentions, Albrecht felt bound to center his defense of Habsburg Venetia upon Austria's entrenched camp at Verona. Yet this cautious decision posed problems, for Verona was not *equidistant* from the twin river arms of the Quadrilateral system, the Mincio and Po. Concentration amid the fortifications of Verona would place South Army just one march from the Mincio, but four or five marches from the lower Po, a gruelling distance in the summer heat. If Albrecht were merely to post an observation corps in southeastern Venetia opposite Cialdini and concentrate the bulk of South Army in Verona, he thought it a certainty that the more numerous Italians would promptly "declare war, simultaneously crossing the Mincio and Po and driving to the Adige." La Marmora would shut up two Austrian corps in Verona, and Cialdini would envelop the third on the Po, reducing Albrecht's meager strength by one-third at a stroke. The archduke also understood that were Cialdini to cross the Po and lodge himself between Verona and Vienna, South Army, in imminent danger of losing its northern supply line to Garibaldi's guerrillas, would lose its only other line of retreat and communication to Cialdini.[68] The Italians "will try to lure us to the Mincio with their stronger army," Albrecht wrote Franz Joseph on June 3. "With their smaller army they will force the Po on the line Ferrara-Padua. . . . These maneuvers will probably be accompanied by marine landings on the Adriatic coast . . . and attacks by [Garibaldi's] irregulars in the Tyrolean passes."[69] Merely to await these attacks inside the Quadrilateral forts was quite out of the question: "South Army would be wedged [*eingekeilt*] between the enemy armies and destroyed."[70]

---

67 HHSA, IB, Karton 365, BM 1866, 134, Venice, May 16, 1866, Direzione di Polizia to Belcredi. KA, AFA 1866, Karton 2343, 5-ad 88c, Venice, May 17, 1866, Direzione di Polizia to FM Albrecht.

68 KA, AFA 1866, Karton 2343, 5-174, Verona, May 1866, FM Albrecht, "Bemerkungen über den Kriegsschauplatz."

69 Belcredi thought that the appointment of a high-ranking Italian admiral to Garibaldi's staff in May augured marine landings in Venice, Trieste, and Rijeka. HHSA, IB, Karton 364, BM 1866, 33, Vienna, May 16, 1866, Belcredi to Mensdorff, Franck.

70 KA, MKSM 1866, Karton 342, 69-5/2, Verona, June 3, 1866, FM Albrecht to Franz Joseph.

To ward off an Italian envelopment and gain themselves some room for maneuver, Albrecht and John deployed their three corps across the waist of Venetia: Gabriel Rodic's V Corps at Verona, Ernst Hartung's IX Corps at Vicenza and Joseph Maroicic's VII Corps at Padua.[71] This deployment permitted South Army to swing west or east depending on the timing of the expected Italian invasion. In June, Albrecht closed up the formation, moving the three corps into the heart of the Quadrilateral, behind the Adige line all within fifty kilometers of Verona.[72] "In this position," Albrecht wrote the emperor, "I can hold both enemy armies in check, for I would require only one forced march in either direction to meet the closer of the two with a reasonable chance of success."[73] Unlike Benedek, Albrecht promptly communicated his plan to his corps generals in scrupulous detail: where to go and what to do if the principal attack came from the west or the southeast. The archduke then posted lookouts with signal rockets up and down the Po and Mincio at thirty kilometer intervals to give early warning of an Italian invasion.[74]

In sharp contrast to North Army, South Army did not blindly conform to an operations plan in the deployment phase of the war. Whereas Krismanic's resolve to keep to the defensive under all conceivable circumstances lulled Benedek's headquarters into complacency, Albrecht posted his army in a central position, then watched enemy movements closely, seeking always for an opportunity to *strike*. Ultimately, he would draft his operations plan in the Napoleonic style, on the eve of battle, when the Italians had committed themselves irrevocably. Something else that distinguished Albrecht from Benedek was his decision to deploy *intelligently*, always validating his position with aggressive reconnaissance and espionage. He took full advantage of the defensive capabilities of the Quadrilateral forts but also looked to exploit South Army's offensive advantage of internal lines, its ability to maneuver *between* the two widely separated Italian armies and concentrate its entire strength against one or the other. Benedek enjoyed the same advantage in the northern theater but, by choosing to remain at Olmütz, voluntarily relinquished it.

For their part, the Italians, despite their advantage in troop numbers, still did not have enough men to attack Albrecht's relatively small field army *and* besiege the Quadrilateral garrisons, which would presumably sally to attack the flanks of Italian divisions attempting to penetrate Venetia. Thus, to squeeze between the Austrian Mincio forts at Peschiera and Mantua and evade their fortress troops, Alfonso La Marmora's eleven divisions would have no choice but to compress

---

71 KA, AFA 1866, Karton 2343, 5–83, Verona, May 16, 1866, FM Albrecht to all corps commandants. 5–174, Verona, May 1866, FM Albrecht, "Bemerkungen."

72 KA, AFA 1866, Karton 2354, 6–40, Verona, June 11, 1866, FM Albrecht to FML Maroicic. Kriegskarten, H IVc, 249, "Skizze Nr. 1: Allgemeine Situation bis zum 22. Juni 1866."

73 KA, AFA 1866, Karton 2344, 6–7, Verona, June 3, 1866, FM Albrecht to Franz Joseph, "Alleruntertänigster Bericht."

74 KA, AFA 1866, Karton 2343, 5–83, Verona, May 16, 1866, FM Albrecht to Corps-Commandants, Brigadiers.

themselves into the narrow twenty kilometer frontage between Salionze and
Goito.[75] Since large numbers could not cross the Mincio at once, Albrecht's three
corps stood a fair chance of hastening down from Verona to surprise the larger
Italian army in the midst of its river crossing.

For General Cialdini, commandant of Italy's five divisions on the lower Po, a
passage over that river barrier would be even more hazardous. Though the Po
wound 120 kilometers east from Mantua to the Adriatic, less than half of this
marshy ground was suitable for a crossing. The middle Po was out of the question
because a river crossing there would have landed Cialdini between the Austrian
forts at Mantua and Legnago. The Po delta was far too wet and pestilential for
operations, which left only the lower Po around Ferrara, precisely where Cialdini
did eventually cross. Yet once over the Po, Cialdini's situation would scarcely
improve. The Polesine, the tract east of the Quadrilateral along the lower Po, was
a hilly, canal-riven marsh seething with mosquitoes. If Cialdini tried to traverse
this ground, it would be at the cost of his tactical unity. Po Army's guns and
reloads would lag far behind the infantry, making opportunities for a concealed,
well-supplied defender.

Once Cialdini floundered, even small Austrian detachments would be able to
destroy his march columns in detail. General Maroicic, posted with the Austrian
VII Corps along the lower Adige, had four defensible water courses across his
front: the Po, the Canal Bianco, the Adigetto, and the Adige. This sector was so
difficult that each of Cialdini's *regiments* would have to carry 300 meters of
bridging equipment, a burden that would slow any Italian invasion to a snail's
pace.[76] "The Italians will be unable to develop their numerical strength in this
broken, irrigated terrain," Maroicic reminded his brigadiers in May. "Remember:
march always to the sound of the guns. If the enemy advances in several columns,
we will fall on the first one with superior force and throw it back into the Po, then
turn on the next, hit it in the rear, and destroy it."[77] In sum, everywhere the
Italian command looked it saw potentially disastrous hazards and pitfalls. This
was the essence of the Quadrilateral: mighty fortresses sited in the only passable
gaps between sucking marshes and broad rivers in full spate. The determination
of Albrecht, John, and their corps generals to make the most of this advantage
and even contemplate an *offensive* against long odds was a revealing contrast to the
extreme pessimism of Benedek and the cloud of ignorance under which his corps
generals functioned in Bohemia.

THE FIRST SHOTS IN GERMANY

To defend themselves against aggression, the states of the German Confederation
had agreed in 1815 to combine their individual armies into a "federal army"

75 KA, AFA 1866, Karton 2344, 6–16, Verona, June 4, 1866, FM Albrecht to GM Moering.
76 J. V. Lemoyne, *Campagne de 1866 en Italie* (Paris: Berger-Levrault, 1875), p. 69.
77 KA, AFA 1866, Karton 2343, 5–81b, Padua, May 8, 1866, FML Maroicic.

whenever German territory was threatened, whether by a fellow German state like Prussia or by a foreign power like France or, as had actually been the case in 1864, Denmark. In 1866, Germany's "federal army," less its big Austrian and Prussian contingents, mustered a wartime strength of 152,000 troops: 65,000 Bavarians, 22,000 Württembergers, 20,000 Saxons, 19,000 Hanoverians, 16,000 Badenese, and 10,000 Hessians.[78] Together the contingents of these German "middle states" were so numerous that France's army attaché in Vienna felt certain that Bismarck would not dare overthrow the German Confederation in 1866, for fear that he would trigger a punitive strike at Prussia by this large *Bundesarmee* arrayed around Prussia's two Rhine provinces and all along the western approaches to Berlin.[79]

The problem, of course, was that Germany's thirty federal contingents did not comprise an "army" at all. None of them had seen sustained action since the Napoleonic Wars and all of them had been maintained at a fraction of their war strength since 1815. Federal war plans were devised not at the federal diet in Frankfurt but in six German capitals by six different General Staffs, each jealous of the other and staffed, as the French amusedly put it, "with nobles and place-men whose grandiose conceptions hardly squared with their limited circumstances."[80] Mobilizing this disorganized *Bundesarmee* would prove an agonizingly slow process. Indeed in the summer of 1865, the Austrian staff calculated that in the event of an Austro-Prussian war, Austria's most likely German allies – Saxony, Bavaria, Württemberg, Hanover, Hessia-Darmstadt and Baden – would have to begin mobilizing *with* Austria and long *before* Prussia if they were to have any chance of actually taking the field in time to affect the outcome of operations.[81]

Politically, however, none of the middle states would contemplate an early mobilization, for even a precautionary deployment would have violated the Confederate constitution of 1815, which forbade the states of Germany to settle their differences by force. Even if only anticipating a Prussian mobilization, a federal one would still have had the appearance of aggression, a precedent the middle states, conscious of their own weakness, were loath to establish. Indeed, Bavaria, which disposed the largest federal contingent – the 65,000 men of the federal VII Corps – advised Austria in early June 1866 that General Benedek could rely on Bavarian support only if the Prussians actually *invaded* a fellow German state, and then only if a majority of the German diet in Frankfurt voted for a "federal reprisal" against Prussia.[82] Austrian spies in Saxony warned Vienna that were

---

78 KA, MKSM 1866, Karton 342, 69–8, Vienna, May 1866, k.k. Generalstab, "Kriegs-Stärke des VII. und VIII. Bundes-Armee Corps und des sächsischen Contingents."

79 Vincennes, AAT, MR 83/1606, Vienna, June 21, 1866, Col. Merlin to Marshal Randon. KA, KM 1866, CK, Karton 251, 50–8/12, Frankfurt, May 29, 1866, GM Pakeni to FML Franck.

80 Vincennes, AAT, MR 32/1537, Paris, 1866, "Coup d'oeil rétrospectif sur la guerre d'Autriche en 1866."

81 KA, MKSM-SR 1866, 22/5, Vienna, August 1865, Evidenz-Bureau des Generalstabs.

82 PRO, FO 9 /174, no. 124, Munich, June 12, 1866, Howard to Clarendon.

Franz Joseph to launch a preventive war to topple Bismarck, "not a single German government would place troops at Austria's disposal."[83]

Bavaria's army comprised the entire federal VII Corps, Saxony most of the IX Corps. Württemberg, Baden, and Hessia-Darmstadt united their contingents to form the federal VIII Corps, whose commandant in 1866 was forty-three-year-old Prince Alexander of Hessia, a general in Austrian service. Though a logical choice for the command – Alexander had actually led troops under fire at Montebello and Solferino in 1859 – none of the German contingents would agree to take orders from him until he formally renounced his oath of allegiance to Emperor Franz Joseph, an abnegation accomplished only on June 17, a day after the Prussian invasion of Hanover and Saxony.[84]

Far from being a cohesive combat unit, VIII Corps was a typical federal army corps in that it contained a host of redundant offices and conflicting attitudes. Prince Alexander, for example, was an Austrophile bent on intervening swiftly in the war to relieve pressure on his comrade Benedek in Bohemia. His staff chief, however, was a more cautious Württemberger under orders from Stuttgart to slow the prince's deployment to a crawl and arrest any movement east in order to conserve Württemberg's regiments for a defense of their own frontiers.[85] Baden's contingent was even less willing to cooperate with Austria. The Badenese dressed in Prussian uniforms, carried Prussian rifles and often sounded like Prussians: "Tell your minister that we will march, but *slowly*," Baden's chancellor warned the Austrian minister in Karlsruhe in June.[86]

Not surprisingly, none of Prince Alexander's contingents would succeed in mobilizing, training and equipping more than a fraction of its strength before war broke out in June. Of Württemberg's three brigades, only one was ready on June 17, a second on June 28, the third on July 5, two full days *after* the climactic battle of Königgrätz in Bohemia.[87] Bavaria's federal VII Corps, the nucleus of the *Bundesarmee*, was at least as inefficient. By May 1866, after a month of mobilization, it had managed to arm and assemble just 10,000 of its 100,000 military-aged men.[88] The Saxons of IX Corps, though direly threatened throughout the spring of 1866 by Bismarck, still found themselves in June with just 6,000 of their 20,000 troops armed and ready. The rest, raw recruits mostly, had to be herded into railroad vans and rolled south to complete their mobilization in

83 KA, MKSM-SR 1866, 24/3, Leipzig, June 7, 1866, "Kundschaftsberichte."

84 KA, MKSM 1866, Karton 342, 69–8, Vienna, June 8, 17, 1866, FML Crenneville to GM Pakeni.

85 KA, MKSM 1866, Karton 342, 69–8, Tügenheim, June 9, 1866, FML Prinz Alexander to FML Crenneville.

86 KA, MKSM 1866, Karton 342, 69–8, Frankfurt, June 9, 1866, Col. Schönfeld to FML Crenneville.

87 KA, AFA 1866, Karton 2274, 13–74, Olmütz, December 1872, Maj. Ripp, "Skizze des Feldzuges."

88 Munich, Bayerisches Kriegsarchiv (BKA), Handschriften-Sammlung (HS) 801, "Beantwortungen der von GL-Lt. von Willisen an Gl-Lt. von der Tann in Bezug auf den Feldzug 1866 gestellten Fragen."

Austria when the Prussian Elbe Army invaded Saxony on June 16.[89] In all, these were not good portents for what, in Frankfurt, was being called the *"Bundeskrieg"* or "federal war" of 1866. Given the tardiness of the German federal mobilization, it appeared that Moltke's little West Army would find time not only to drive the German contingents *away* from Benedek's North Army but to *beat* them in detail, opening the door to vast Prussian annexations in western Germany after the war.

PRUSSIA'S INVASION OF THE GERMAN STATES, JUNE 15–24, 1866

"I feel trapped, like a fox indoors," Prussia's King Wilhelm I grumbled to a Russian envoy in the last week of May 1866. "In the end I will have no choice but to *bite* my way out."[90] He was referring to the way Austria's loose-knit German alliances hemmed Prussia in. Hanover and Hessia-Kassel, both allied with Austria to ensure their survival in the coming war, lay between the eastern Prussian kingdom and the two Rhine provinces Berlin had acquired in 1815. Austria's Saxon ally menaced Prussia from the south and furnished Benedek's North Army with a launch-pad for operations down the Elbe and into the heart of the Hohenzollern kingdom.[91] With these threats in mind, Wilhelm showed his teeth on June 15, gruffly ordering Hanover, Kassel, and Saxony to disarm and repudiate their Austrian alliances. Fearful of Prussian annexation even if they complied, the three states refused and consequently, at sun-up on June 16, King Wilhelm of Prussia, the "fox indoors," began to snap and bite, invading his three neighbors by road and rail. The war of 1866 had begun.

The German federal armies called to halt this Prussian aggression found themselves ill-equipped, untrained, and utterly disorganized in western Germany, the densest, fastest-moving rail net in Europe. As the Austrians had predicted, the north German contingents took ages to get up steam while the Prussian West Army converged quickly on them from all points: westward from Brandenburg, eastward from Westphalia, and south from Holstein. On June 16, King George of Hanover and his army of 19,000, which found itself mobilized only because the Prussian invasion happened to coincide with Hanover's summer maneuvers, barely managed to dodge a powerful Prussian swipe from Minden by racing south to Göttingen on the railroad.[92] Though the Hanoverians broke up the rails behind them, forcing General August Goeben's division at Minden and General Edwin Manteuffel's division, debouching from Holstein, to walk into Hanover, they did so at the cost of most of their supplies and munitions, which they had to leave for

89 KA, MKSM-SR 1866, 22/3, Vienna, March 20, 1866, FML Henikstein, "k. sächsische Armee." 24/3, Vienna, March–June, "Kundschaftsberichte aus Dresden."

90 KA, MKSM 1866, Karton 342, 69–8, Tügenheim, May 31, 1866, Col. Schönfeld to FML Crenneville.

91 Vincennes, AAT, MR 20/1536, Berlin, March 10, 1866, Maj. Clermont-Tonnerre to Marshal Randon.

92 Grosser Generalstab, *Feldzug 1866*, pp. 49–68.

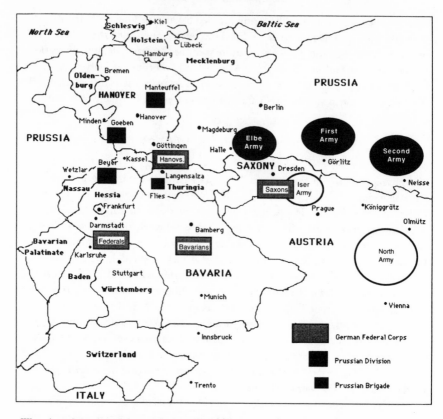

West Army's push to Langensalza, June 1866

the Prussians.[93] The next day jubilant Berlin newspapers itemized the tons of war material captured in Hanover and calculated that the Hanoverians could be fleeing south with no more than three rifle cartridges per man.[94]

Like the Hanoverians, Kassel's brigade narrowly escaped West Army's third and last division, Gustav Beyer's, which invaded Hessia-Kassel from the Hohenzollern enclave around Wetzlar. Kassel's two regiments – descendants of the "Hessians" beaten by George Washington at Trenton in 1776 – retreated south to Fulda on the railway, demolishing the tracks between Kassel and Wetzlar and forcing General Beyer's division, like Goeben's and Manteuffel's, to struggle after them on foot.[95] Like the Hanoverians, however, Kassel's troops had to

93 Theodor Fontane, *Der deutsche Krieg von 1866*, 2 vols. (Berlin: Oberhofbuchdruckerei, 1870–1), vol. 2, pp. 6–9. Lettow-Vorbeck, vol. 1, pp. 185, 201.

94 [Theodor Fontane], *Von der Elbe bis zur Tauber: Der Feldzug der preussischen Main-Armee im Sommer 1866* (Leipzig: Belhagen und Klasing, 1867), p. 49.

95 H. M. Hozier, *The Seven Weeks' War* (Philadelphia: Lippincott, 1867), vol. 1, pp. 163–4. Fontane, *Main-Armee*, p. 39.

abandon most of their supplies (and their princely commandant, who was captured by the Prussians) in the course of this panicky retreat, arriving eventually in the camp of VIII Corps at Frankfurt without even cartridges for their Prussian-made needle rifles.[96]

In Saxony, army engineers foolishly neglected to destroy the kingdom's railroads. Instead of twisting the rails and burning the ties, standard procedure elsewhere in Europe, frugal Saxon engineers merely dismantled the railways, piling the rails and sleepers neatly on their embankments. The Prussians crossed the border, bolted the rails back into place and were in Dresden within forty-eight hours, a veritable *Blitzkrieg*. All of this was revolutionary, a fact remarked upon by a British journalist: "In the course of a few days, three of the most important Middle States of Germany were completely overrun by Prussian troops and their sovereigns driven from their capitals and countries as if by a thunderbolt."[97]

Moltke's decision to mop up the north German contingents before turning against the south Germans assembling below the Main River gave the Bavarians and VIII Corps pause to coordinate their operations. In this, however, they failed egregiously. Although the south German commandants, Prince Karl of Bavaria – a hoary veteran of the Napoleonic Wars – and Prince Alexander of Hessia, knew that they needed Hanover's 19,000 bayonets to beat the Prussian West Army, they hesitated to venture north from their camps in Bamberg and Frankfurt. For them, Germany south of the Main River formed a natural citadel. With the Main across its front, its eastern flank sealed by the Bavarian Woods, and its western flank by the Hessian and Black Forests, southern Germany comprised a remarkably strong defensive theater, particularly for the Bavarians, whose capital was located in the deep south, behind the headwaters of the Danube. Thus, a defensive offered excellent prospects for the South Germans, while an offensive into northern Germany was fraught with danger. Merely to reach the Hanoverian plain, South Germany's two federal corps would have had literally to pick their way through Thuringia, a series of steep, wooded massifs plunging into thickly settled valleys. Preceded by their largely untrained cavalry and light infantry, with rapid-firing West Army fusiliers concealed on their flanks and in every dip in the road, the German federals would have courted disaster.

Therefore, when the various contingents of the federal VIII Corps finally submitted to Prince Alexander of Hessia's command on June 16, the prince responded not by making for Göttingen to rescue the Hanoverians but by declaring that he would not take a single step forward until Frankfurt had been "secured as [his] base on the Main River."[98] The Austrians, who had counted on South German cooperation with Hanover, were crestfallen, yet Prince Alexander had little choice, for his motley corps was still scattered across South Germany.

96 Grosser Generalstab, *Feldzug 1866*, pp. 50–5.
97 Hozier, vol. 1, p. 157. Grosser Generalstab, *Feldzug 1866*, pp. 90–2.
98 KA, MKSM 1866, Karton 342, 69–8, Darmstadt, June 21, 1866, FML Prinz Alexander to FML Crenneville.

Headquarters was at Darmstadt. One Hessian brigade was in Heidelberg; the other had not even mobilized. The Nassauers were in Wiesbaden; Württemberg's two brigades were still in Stuttgart. The Badenese were leaving Karlsruhe but had wired ahead that they would not be ready to fight until July. Austria's Neipperg Brigade – 12,000 garrison troops culled from the German Confederation's Rhine forts and placed under Prince Alexander's command – was resting in Aschaffenburg.[99]

Still, there were glimmers of hope. With the Bavarians camped to the east at Bamberg, the German federals were at least *physically* situated to stop the lower jaw of Moltke's pincers – Beyer's division of 18,000 in Kassel – from closing on the Hanoverians in Göttingen. But everywhere Confederate resolve and organization were lacking. "My head is spinning!" Prince Alexander's Austrian attaché wrote Vienna on June 21. "Since the sixteenth of the month I've been laboring to put this German Tower of Babel in some kind of order, but they cannot even agree on the choice of a General Staff chief! And *nothing* is to be expected of the Bavarian Corps."[100]

The blundering German federals were saved by an unexpected source: the blundering Prussians, who were not all as clever as Moltke. The Prussian king had assigned West Army to sixty-seven-year-old General Eduard Vogel von Falckenstein, a well-connected courtier with vast Silesian estates, who, with Field Marshal Wrangel, had made a hash of Prussia's invasion of Schleswig in 1864.[101] Two years later, in Hanover, Falckenstein was doing little to salvage his reputation. Though Moltke and the king had deliberately given him the war's safest theater, they immediately regretted the decision, for once Falckenstein had entered Hanover and ascertained that King George's army was well and truly gone, he broke off the pursuit and settled down in George's capital to savor the bloodless victory.

Meanwhile, Hanover's twenty battalions were already at Göttingen, one-third of the way to Bavaria. If the Hanoverian and Bavarian armies were allowed to unite, Falckenstein's scattered columns would be outnumbered and outgunned. Yet on June 18, a day after Prussian General August Goeben's division had reached Hanover and made front to the south, Falckenstein ordered a rest day. Moltke was flabbergasted. West Army could rest later, he exploded, but not until the German states were beaten and disarmed and Berlin's lines of communication to Bohemia secured. He curtly ordered Falckenstein after the Hanoverians. Falckenstein, a wealthy seigneur, despised Moltke, a landless *Kammerjunker*, and therefore simply ignored the staff chief's cable, replying to the Prussian king

99 KA, MKSM 1866, Karton 343, 69–9, Vienna, June 21, 1866, FML Crenneville to FZM Benedek. Karton 342, 69–8, Vienna, June 20, 1866, FML Crenneville to Col. Schönfeld. Darmstadt, June 21, 1866, FML Prinz Alexander to FML Crenneville.

100 KA, MKSM 1866, Karton 342, 69–8, Darmstadt, June 21, 1866, Col. Schönfeld to Lt-Col. Beck.

101 Fontane, *Main-Armee*, p. 24.

instead. He had, he reported, discovered so much abandoned food and forage in the Hanoverian capital (700 wagons of it) that he considered it unnecessary to pursue King George's army. It would starve before reaching Bavaria.[102] In fact, the Hanoverians *were* hungry, and poorly supplied, which was why they had decided to waste three critical march days resting and requisitioning around Göttingen.[103] They were sitting ducks, yet Falckenstein would not move, and his lethargy threatened Moltke's entire war plan.

By now Moltke was in a fever of impatience. Prussia's Elbe and First Armies, whose lines of retreat straggled past Bavaria and Hanover, were scheduled to invade Austria on June 23. With this in mind, Moltke wired Falckenstein a fourth order on June 22: Attack the Hanoverians in Göttingen without delay. Yet Falckenstein still would not budge; he needed more time to repair the Hanoverian railways, he replied. The next morning, King Wilhelm himself intervened, personally commanding Falckenstein to march. A day later, West Army began to move south. Falckenstein's cavalry probed ahead only to discover that the Hanoverians were no longer in Göttingen.[104] They had retreated southeast through the Thuringian Forest to a place called Langensalza, which was nearer the Bavarians, who were contemplating a thrust north from Bamberg to reinforce the Hanoverians. Because of Falckenstein's dithering, the Hanoverians were only a few marches from safety. Moltke's trap – sprung on June 16 from Holstein, Westphalia, and Wetzlar – appeared to have grasped thin air.[105]

THE BATTLE OF LANGENSALZA

Moltke would not submit so easily. He realized that by dawdling in their camps, the South German contingents were offering him a golden opportunity to envelop and destroy Hanover's 19,000 men with West Army's combined strength of 40,000. Thus, he and his staff in Berlin labored to undo the damage wrought by Falckenstein. By dint of their efforts and the hard marching of Falckenstein's subordinates, it appeared by June 25 that the Hanoverians, whose prospects had been so bright only a few days earlier, would not escape to Bavaria after all. Prussian engineers had finally repaired the Hanoverian railroads, and Moltke had blocked King George's route south by redeploying 9,000 troops from the Prussian forts to Gotha.[106] Now the Hanoverians at Langensalza were hemmed in on three sides, from the south by General Eduard Flies' fortress troops at Gotha, from the west by General Beyer's vanguard at Eisenach, and from the north by Falckenstein and Goeben descending slowly from Kassel and

102 Lettow-Vorbeck, vol. 1, pp. 187–8, 201, 207–8.
103 PRO, FO 68/144, no. 29, Leipzig, June 28, 1866, Crowe to Clarendon.
104 Fontane, *Main-Armee*, p. 51.
105 k.k. Generalstab, *Österreichs Kämpfe*, vol. 1, pp. 173–84. Lettow-Vorbeck, vol. 1, pp. 185–8, 197–254.
106 Fontane, *Der deutsche Krieg*, vol. 2, pp. 10–11.

Göttingen. King George's only open escape route was to the east, *away* from the Bavarians and into Prussia. Perceiving this with some satisfaction, Moltke ordered Flies at Gotha merely to contain the Hanoverians until the bulk of West Army closed for the kill.[107]

At Langensalza, the Hanoverians waited anxiously for help from the Bavarians and the German VIII Corps, but both federal contingents, still occupied with their own mobilizations, had decided to leave Hanover to its fate.[108] Moltke, aware that further delay might ruin his German campaign, ordered Falckenstein late in the night of June 26 to attack and "put paid once and for all to the Hanoverian episode." He was worried lest King George break camp and lead the Prussian divisions on a time-consuming chase around Thuringia in the *rear* of the Prussian armies invading Saxony and Bohemia. In the daylong interval until Beyer and Goeben came up, Moltke advised Flies to hold Gotha and the Werra valley with his brigade as best he could against the anticipated Hanoverian breakout, which, had King George only hurried, would have matched 19,000 Hanoverians with forty-two guns against Flies's 9,000 Prussians and twenty-two guns.[109]

In what proved to be just one of many instances of Prussian insubordination that periodically threatened to upset Moltke's well-laid plans, Flies, thirsty for glory, exceeded his instructions on June 27 and attacked the Hanoverian army in its fine defensive position at Langensalza.[110] The result was a galling Prussian defeat, as Hanover's superior numbers stormed off their heights and drove Flies' scratch brigade, which embodied just five regular and seven *Landwehr* battalions, back to Gotha in disorder.

For Moltke, the only bright spot in this dreary episode was the ample justication the battle furnished for the "praetorian" army reforms he, Bismarck, and Roon had implemented over stormy parliamentary opposition in the years since 1862. Langensalza was a "black day" for the Prussian *Landwehr*, for not only did Flies' middle-aged battalions of "lawyers and oculists" hesitate to make the supreme sacrifice – taking only 5.3 percent casualties compared with 10.6 percent in the more ingenuous regular army battalions – they also deserted, shammed wounds, and concealed themselves around the field in alarming numbers. No less than 45 percent of Flies's *Landwehr* strength went missing in the course of the battle, a rate of malingering only Austria's mutinous Venetian recruits would surpass in 1866.[111]

107　Grosser Generalstab, *Feldzug 1866*, pp. 62–8.
108　KA, MKSM 1866, Karton 342, 69–8, Darmstadt, June 25, 1866, FML Alexander to FML Crenneville. Karton 342, 69–8, Schweinfurt, June 27, 1866, FML Huyn to FML Crenneville. Munich, BKA, Generalstab, 513, Munich, 1894, Hpt. Höhn, "Geschichte des k. Generalstabes," pp. 157–60. Lettow-Vorbeck, vol. 3, p. 25.
109　Lettow-Vorbeck, vol. 1, pp. 282–5, 301–2.
110　Alexander Malet, *The Overthrow of the Germanic Confederation by Prussia in 1866* (London: Longman's, Green, 1870), p. 237.
111　Lettow-Vorbeck, vol. 1, pp. 305–19, vol. 3, p. 82.

To beat the Hanoverian army, Prussia's *Landwehr* plainly needed help, and it arrived in force the next day, on June 28, when the bulk of Prussia's West Army converged on Langensalza, forcing King George of Hanover to pull off to the east, away from his South German allies.[112] On June 29, with his back to the Harz Mountains, the king surrendered in Nordhausen. Prussia's General Edwin Manteuffel disarmed the Hanoverians, issued them railroad tickets, and sent them home.[113] Berlin's lines of communication to Saxony and Bohemia were finally secure. As the German *Bundeskrieg* petered out, the Austro-Prussian War was just beginning. And down in Venetia, the German Confederation's southern flank, the decisive battle of the Austro-Italian War was nearly a week old, though word of it was only beginning to filter into Germany.

112 k.k. Generalstab, *Österreichs Kämpfe*, vol. 1, pp. 193–209. Grosser Generalstab, *Feldzug 1866*, pp. 68f.
113 Lettow-Vorbeck, vol. 1, pp. 322, 335–6, 347. Fontane, *Main-Armee*, p. 95.

4

Italy declares war

"The Italo-Austrian war seems unavoidable," a German expatriate wrote from Rome in May 1866. "The [Italian] government must conquer or go under. . . . This terrible war will decide the fate of Italy."[1] On June 5, the anniversary of Magenta, Archduke Albrecht's South Army braced itself for an Italian attack on Venetia. Though the *journée* passed peacefully, Italian and Austrian pickets did exchange shots across the Mincio and Albrecht's spies continued to burrow in General Alfonso La Marmora's camp, totting up loaves in Italy's field bakeries, loitering in train stations and telegraph offices, even infiltrating the offices of the Italian General Staff. At night, Austrian agents counted Italian soldiers asleep in churches and public buildings near the front and passed their findings back to South Army headquarters in Verona.[2] On June 12, Austrian police in Verona reported "a growing impatience among [Austrian] officers for things to get started. Everyone is suffering from the summer heat."[3] That same day, Austrian and French officials agreed that, win or lose, Austria would cede Venetia to France after the Austro-Italian War in return, probably, for Prussian Silesia.[4] Napoleon III, partially mobilized and hungry for a foreign policy success after the humiliating collapse of his French-sponsored Mexican Empire, was easing France into the triangular Austro-Prussian-Italian conflict.

From Austria's perspective, with a French army equipping itself in Alsace and Franche-Comté – readying for a swing into Bavaria or Lombardy as circumstances dictated – the cession of Venetia seemed a tolerable price to pay for the French neutrality that would permit Field Marshal Albrecht to deal a knockout blow to the Italian army and reduce the newly united Kingdom of Italy to its relatively

1 Ferdinand Gregorovius, *The Roman Journals of Ferdinand Gregorovius, 1852–74*, ed. Friedrich Althaus, trans. Mrs. G. W. Hamilton (London: George Bell, 1907), p. 252.
2 Pio Calza, *Nuova luce sugli eventi militari del 1866* (Bologna: Nicola Zanichelli, 1924), pp. 10–11, 16–17. KA, AFA 1866, Karton 2343, 5-ad88i, Venice, May 26 and June 12, 1866, Direzione di Polizia to FM Albrecht.
3 HHSA, IB, Karton 364, BM 1866, 33, Vienna, June 14, 1866, Belcredi to Franck.
4 Coppa, *Origins of the Italian Wars of Independence*, pp. 124–5.

harmless, original statelets. The Austrians reasoned that if national Italy disappeared in the storm of 1866, Napoleon III would have little choice but to return Venetia to the Habsburg Monarchy. Indeed, Austrian officials were encouraged in this line of thinking by the pronouncements of Bonaparte's most trusted advisors, Lucien Murat and Eugène Rouher, who viewed Prussia and Italy, not Austria, as the real threat to French interests and actually advised the French emperor to restore Venetia and the Quadrilateral forts to Austria after the war.[5]

PROBLEMS WITH ITALY'S DEPLOYMENT, MAY–JUNE, 1866

In June 1866, 120 of Italy's 400 infantry battalions, some 62,000 troops, were still south of Rome fighting rebels, *mafiosi* and brigands in what, until 1860, had been King Francesco Bourbon's Kingdom of the Two Sicilies.[6] Most of these Italian regiments in the south had to be double-marched up the peninsula through hostile country over primitive roads in time for the war with Austria. Some units had to cover thirty miles a day, a gruelling distance on foot in the Mediterranean heat.[7] Units that rested at midday and marched at night were no better off, for they were ravaged by malarial mosquitoes.[8] At the end of this long march, the Italian command drawn up before the Venetian Quadrilateral had trouble piecing these scattered, fatigued units back together, which prevented the timely formation of divisions and corps and partly explained Italy's poor performance in the war.[9]

There were other problems. Though thirty-five of eighty Italian line regiments were recruited in the Mezzogiorno, Italy's King Vittorio Emanuele II decided to exclude most southern regiments from the war with Austria for fear that they would desert to the enemy. This political decision deprived the Italian army of nearly half its front-line cadres and forced the high command to scrape the bottom of its northern depots for second and third-rate recruits.[10] In June, when the Italian war ministry called 105,000 conscripts for a reserve army, it pointedly

---

5 HHSA, IB, Karton 364, BM 1866, 35, Vienna, May 22, 1866, Belcredi to Mensdorff. KA, AFA 1866, Karton 2272, 13–13, nos. 190, 198, 211, Paris, July 13, 14, 28, 1866, Belcredi to FM Albrecht.

6 KA, MKSM-SR, 1866, 22/3, Vienna, June 15, 1866, k.k. Evidenz Bureau, "Ordre de Bataille der gesammten sardo-italienischen Land-Truppen."

7 KA, AFA 1866, Karton 2343, 5-ad 88i, Venice, May 26, 1866. Direzione di Polizia to Armee Commando Verona, vid. Albrecht, John.

8 Summer was that time of year when Italian peasants warned: "Whoever would live long must see neither the rising nor the setting sun." Norman Douglas, *Old Calabria* (London: Martin Secker, 1915), p. 283.

9 KA, MKSM-SR 1866, 22/3, Verona, February 28, 1866, k.k. Generalstab, Lt. Petrossi to GM John, "Übersicht der sardo-italienischen Streitkräfte." MKSM 1866, Karton 342, 69–5/3, Verona, June 11, 1866, FM Albrecht to Franz Joseph.

10 In Emilia and Lombardy, southern regiments were sent to the rear during the Italian deployment to minimize desertions. KA, AFA 1866, Karton 2344, 6–18, Peschiera, June 5, 1866, k.k. Festungs-Commando Peschiera to Armee-Commando Verona.

excepted all "Neapolitans, Sicilians and Sardinians" from the measure.[11] Ironically, the shaping Austro-Italian War, which King Vittorio Emanuele II insisted on calling the last station in Italian unification, was instead shedding light on the cracks in Italian unity. Beyond the northern middle class, there was little enthusiasm for the Risorgimento in Italy, which peasants identified with taxes, conscription, and war.

Even with southern Italians excluded from his army, General Alfonso La Marmora, Italy's most senior general, still had grave misgivings about the newly formed Italian regiments massing on the Venetian frontier. In a council of war in April, La Marmora admitted that of his 200,000 effectives, "only half might actually be considered 'soldiers.'"[12] Many of the rest were untrained or of uncertain allegiance. In May and June, scores of Italian deserters crossed into Austria, some so hostile to the grasping Kingdom of Italy that Austrian officials in Venetia recommended enlisting them in the Habsburg South Army.[13] When a French officer traveled from Bologna to Milan in May, a journey that took him through the cantonments of three of Italy's four army corps, he noted that "the Italian staff and administration are utterly incompetent."[14] Austrian police spies, who moved freely in and out of the Italian camps, remarked a dire shortage of wagons, horses, bread, forage, and wine and assured Vienna that "chaos reigns along the entire front from Cremona to Bologna. Italian troops have nowhere to sleep and are famished."[15] Their discomfort provoked occasional demonstrations. On May 20, Italy's forty-six-year-old king reviewed his weary regiments in Cremona and rather indelicately warned them against defeatists and turncoats in their midst. Grumbling shot through the ranks and several voices cried: "*Basta che non veniamo traditi noi!*" (And yet *you* are betraying *us*.) An Austrian agent reported the scandal approvingly to South Army headquarters in Verona: "It made a most evil impression; "Italian troops are exhausted and fed up."[16]

In May, Vittorio Emanuele summoned Giuseppe Garibaldi – Italy's great patriot, who had wrested Sicily and Naples from the Bourbons in 1860 – to Florence to begin raising an army of 20,000 irregular troops. A devoted republican and, as such, an enemy of the very royal army he was enlisted in, General Garibaldi immediately met bureaucratic resistance from the king's war ministry,

11 KA, MKSM 1866, Karton 338, 33–1/9–14, Rome, April 2, June 8, 1866, Maj. Frantzl to FML Crenneville. Karton 342, 69–5/3, Verona, June 11, 1866, FM Albrecht to Franz Joseph.
12 KA, MKSM 1866, Karton 338, 33–1/9, Rome, April 3, 1866, Maj. Frantzl to FML Crenneville. Gooch, *Army, State and Society in Italy*, pp. 13–14.
13 Venice, Archivio di Stato, I. R. Presidenza Luogotenenza, Busta 597, Venice, June 15, 1866, Toggenburg to FML Franck.
14 He had visited the corps of Cialdini, Della Rocca, and Cuchiari. Vincennes, AAT, MR 18/1387, Milan, May 12, 1866, Col. Schmitz to Marshal Randon.
15 KA, AFA 1866, Karton 2343, 5-ad 88d, Venice, May 19, 1866, Direzione di Polizia to Armee Commando Verona.
16 KA, AFA 1866, Karton 2343, 5-ad 88j, Venice, May 27, 1866, Direzione di Polizia to Armee-Commando Verona.

8. General Alfonso La Marmora (1804–78), commander of the Italian Mincio Army in 1866

which showed little desire to arm a corps of left-wing zealots. Thus, the royal ministries forced Garibaldi literally to beg, cheat, and steal just to secure rifles, the odd cannon, food, and forage. Even copies of the army newspaper and surplus Austrian rifles captured and put away to rust in 1859 were denied him and his "revolutionary *canaille*," as the king himself called the *Garibaldini* in private. "At Limone, there are eight Austrian rifles," a Garibaldian wrote exasperatedly in June. "But we cannot have them without a signed requisition from the war ministry."[17]

Habsburg agents remarked this infighting at once: "Volunteer regiments are being slowly armed, clothed, and organized against the will of the government, which worries about the creation of an armed proletariat," Franz Joseph's Roman embassy reported. Police in Venice described Garibaldi's volunteers as "boys fifteen to nineteen years old, who've never held a rifle in their hands."[18] Austrian spies watching the formation of volunteer battalions around Lake Como observed rowdiness invariably punished by royal officers with cruel beatings: "Discontent reigns," one agent wrote. "Volunteers suspect that Garibaldi is being used as a tool of the Piedmontese government."[19] Another agent found that "volunteers are handled [by their regular army officers] like pigherds. . . . In Leno there was a mutiny and a royal major was knifed by his own men."[20]

Things were not much better organized in the regular army. Expanding the Italian army to its war strength in May 1866 turned up so many incompetent officers that military cadets with less than two months' instruction had to be sent directly from their classrooms to front-line companies. Few of Italy's divisional generals had any combat experience at all.[21] Some Garibaldian officers – admitted *en masse* to the royal army after the conquest of Naples in 1860 – were entrusted with divisions of 12,000 for political reasons, even though their practical experience had been limited to guerrilla operations in the southern desert.[22] The king placed war ministry desk officers in charge of brigades and had to disqualify a

---

17 Milan, Museo Risorgimento, Archivio Guastalla, Busta 69, Anno 1866, June, "Carteggio della Divisione Volontari Italiani," "Domande al Ministero della Guerra." Vincenzo Gallinari, "I primi quindici anni," *L'Esercito italiano dall'Unità alla Grande Guerra, 1861–1918* (Rome: Ufficio Storico, 1980), p. 67.

18 KA, AFA 1866, Karton 2343, 5-ad 881, Venice, June 1, 1866, Direzione di Polizia to Armee-Commando Verona.

19 HHSA, IB, Karton 364, BM 1866, 33, Trento, June 7, 1866, Commissariato di Polizia to Belcredi.

20 HHSA, IB, Karton 364, BM 1866, 33, Vienna, June 14, 1866, Belcredi to FML Franck. KA, MKSM 1866, Karton 338, 33–1/14, Rome, June 8, 1866, Maj. Frantzl to FML Crenneville.

21 Vincennes, AAT, MR 17/1387, Bologna, May 9, 1866, Col. Schmitz to Randon.

22 Like Giuseppe Sirtori, Garibaldi's staff chief in 1860: Sirtori would dispose badly at Custoza, surrendering the key heights of Santa Lucia to Karl Moering's brigade without a fight. Vincennes, AAT, MR 20/1387, Florence, April 1866, Col. Schmitz to Randon, "Aperçu général sur les conditions actuelles des armées italiennes et autrichiennes." On the mass influx of Garibaldians to the Italian army after 1860, Gooch, *Army, State and Society in Italy*, pp. 9–12.

number of his most senior generals because their ineptitude was so painfully evident.[23] Italy's deployment on the eve of war was thus a bureaucratic and logistical nightmare, which pointed anew to the difficulty of building a single new state from the wreckage of a half dozen old ones in as many years.[24]

PROBLEMS WITH THE ITALIAN COMMAND, JUNE 1866

Italy's high command only abetted the confusion. In May, at the peak of mobilization, France's army attaché in Florence – Italy's capital from 1864–70 – marvelled that "the minister of war [Ignazio Pettinengo] commands an army really commanded by a constitutional monarch whose most senior general [Alfonso La Marmora] continues to toil as prime minister." Even were Pettinengo made chief-of-staff, the French attaché concluded that "he would still not have sufficient authority to impose orders on the two army generals [La Marmora and Cialdini], for his seniority would qualify him only for the post of *sous*-chef of the General Staff."[25] The fact was that since unification in 1861, King Vittorio Emanuele had groomed the Italian army much more for the political management of a fractious peninsula than for war in earnest with a Great Power. Significantly, La Marmora, commander of the field army, would not be relieved of his political functions in Florence until June 18, less than a week before his army was scheduled to invade Venetia. And neither he nor his subordinates would draft an operations plan in time for the war with Austria triggered by Italy's Prussian ally in mid-June.

After June 16, when Prussia invaded Hanover and Saxony and began to descend to the Austrian frontier, Bismarck and Moltke waited impatiently for an Italian declaration of war in the south. The military convention signed in Berlin and Florence in April guaranteed them one, yet none came. The hot season had descended on the Venetian plain, and many Italian officers simply did not believe that Vittorio Emanuele was seriously contemplating a campaign that would have to be fought to a decision in July and August, the hottest months of the year, when the Po basin would be a stew of malaria and typhus.[26]

Throughout the month of June, Theodor Bernhardi, a Prussian envoy in Vittorio Emanuele's camp, submitted alarming reports to Berlin that described an Italian command behindhand in its mobilization, undecided on an operations plan, and attired, even at the front, not in uniform but in cool linen suits and silk

23 Girolamo Ulloa, *L'Esercito italiano e la Battaglia di Custoza* (Florence: Tipografia Gaston, 1866), pp. 15–16. KA, AFA 1866, Karton 2347, 13–16, Verona, January 20, 1866, k.k. Generalstab, "Evidenz Rapport."

24 Geoffrey Wawro, "Austria versus the Risorgimento: A New Look at Austria's Italian Strategy in the 1860s," *European History Quarterly* 26 (January 1996):7–29.

25 Vincennes, AAT, MR 17/1387, Bologna, May 9, 1866, Col. Schmitz to Randon. In 1866, there were no field marshals in the Italian army. *Generale d'Armata* was the next highest rank.

26 Luigi Chiala, *Ancora*, pp. 257, 259.

cravats.[27] From Berlin's perspective, this would not do. By the terms of the Prusso-Italian military alliance, Italy was *obliged* to open a second front against Austria. Thus Bismarck instructed Bernhardi and Count Guido Usedom, Prussia's minister in Florence, to insist upon an immediate Italian assault on Venetia to take pressure off the Prussian army girding to invade Bohemia and the German middle states.

Bernhardi – a military historian – remarked immediately the absence of any war-planning agency in Italy. The General Staff was a bureaucratic backwater.[28] Higher up, Vittorio Emanuele wielded power out of all proportion to his meager talents. His military cabinet, the *Commissione Permanente per la Difesa dello Stato*, was home to the so-called Piedmontese *camorra*: political generals like Petitti, Della Rocca, La Marmora, and Della Rovere, who were always first in line for field commands despite their lackluster performance in the wars of 1848–9 and 1859. Neither the permanent commission nor the royal war ministry took Italian strategy in hand. And little wonder: the ministry had changed ministers six times since unification in 1861.[29] Such organizational problems had hardly mattered in 1859, when French officers had planned for the Piedmontese, enabling young Vittorio Emanuele – *Re galantuomo* – to campaign unfettered by a staff chief.[30] In 1866, however, Italy fought alone and found itself, on the eve of what official papers were calling the "Fourth War of Union," without even a plan to wrest Venetia from the Austrians. "Who directed the war?" an Italian staffer later asked. "No one! While Petitti [the king's adjutant] and La Marmora [the prime minister] organized Italy's deployment, Cialdini [La Marmora's chief rival inside the army] conspired with Pettinengo [the war minister] to secure the best cadres and matériel for Cialdini's sub-command on the lower Po."[31]

Instructed by Moltke to convince the Italians to attack over the Po river into the *rear* of the Quadrilateral (instead of over the Mincio into its *front*), Prussia's Bernhardi spent the critical fortnight before the battle of Custoza shuttling between the unconnected nodes of Vittorio Emanuele's command: the royal palace and war ministry in Florence, General La Marmora's office in the foreign ministry, the principal Italian camp at Piacenza, and Enrico Cialdini's headquarters in

---

27 On June 11, Bernhardi met with General Cialdini in Bologna: "Cialdini, in his headquarters and well aware that war is imminent, received me in *borghese*, not in uniform. . . . It's difficult to imagine that there can be discipline in an army where this sort of thing is permitted." The next day, Bernhardi toured Cialdini's artillery park escorted by a captain also, "as is the custom in this army, in civilian attire: a tropical-weight jacket, linen trousers and a voluptuous necktie." Chiala, *Ancora*, pp. 258–60.

28 The staff *capo*, General Agostino Ricci, would take no part in the coming war. Alberto Pollio, *Custoza 1866* (Città di Castello: Arti Grafiche, 1914), p. 23.

29 Gallinari, p. 52. Lemoyne, pp. 37–8.

30 John Whittam, *The Politics of the Italian Army, 1861–1918* (London: Croom Helm, 1977), p. 51.

31 Corpo di Stato Maggiore, *La Campagna del 1866 in Italia*, 2 vols. (Rome: Carlo Voghera, 1875), vol. 1, p. 130. Pollio, *Custoza 1866*, pp. 23–4.

Bologna. At every stop, Bernhardi reported tension and indecision arising from a fundamental strategic dispute between La Marmora and Cialdini.

There would have been little room for dispute had it been possible for Italy to do the natural thing in 1866 and launch an enveloping attack into Venetia from both sides of the angle where the Po and Mincio rivers touched at Mantua. But Austria's Quadrilateral fortress group had been designed to frustrate precisely this maneuver. The Austrian forts at Mantua and Legnago could be used as offensive bridgeheads into Italy no less than defensive barriers, and thus prevented an Italian concentration at the confluence of Venetia's river frontiers. In view of this fact, the Italians had no choice in 1866 but to concentrate either on the lower Po, 120 kilometers east of Mantua, or on the Mincio, in the narrow, 35 kilometer gap between the Austrian forts at Mantua and Peschiera. A strike at Venetia's Tyrolean lifeline north of Peschiera was – as Garibaldi would shortly discover – virtually impossible owing to the barrier formed by Lake Garda and the Brescian Alps. The lake was patrolled by Austrian gunboats and the three mountain passes – Valsabbia, Stelvio, and Tonale – were defended by Franz Joseph's crack Tyrolean *Jäger*.[32]

A Po crossing could not be attempted anywhere near Mantua because a crossing west of Bologna would have landed the Italian army in the willow swamps between Mantua and Legnago. Farther east, the Po delta was too marshy and pestilential to attempt crossings or marine landings from the Adriatic. Therefore, well before the outbreak of the Austro-Italian War, Austrian headquarters in Verona knew with perfect certainty where Cialdini, chief advocate of the southern invasion route, would eventually cross the Po: on the forty-five kilometer riverfront between Sermide and Cologna. This, in turn, betrayed Cialdini's march route into Venetia: Ferrara–Rovigo–Padua–Vicenza and on to Venice.[33]

Even assuming that Italian "southern" and "western" armies crossed the Po and Mincio unopposed – at least on the Po, the Austrians were unlikely to sally from safe positions behind the Adige to slop through the canals and polders of lower Venetia – they would still find themselves separated by 100 kilometers – a five days' march – and Austria's entire South Army, which, with its flanks and rear secured at all times by the Quadrilateral forts and the Adige river, would have had little difficulty beating the Italians in detail.[34] The problems posed by the geography of the Quadrilateral accounted for its dreadful reputation in military circles. These tactical problems also explained the bifurcation of Italian strategy into "southern" and "western" schools in the years after 1848, a strategic dilemma that

---

32 Lemoyne, pp. 80–1.

33 Corpo di Stato Maggiore, *La Campagna*, vol. 1, p. 121.

34 The Polesine is the twenty kilometer-wide strip between the Po and Adige, described by the Italian staff as "a region that would reduce offensive operations to a continuous passage of water obstacles, one after the other, requiring an enormous quantity of bridging material." And the Adige? "With an enemy in front and on the left flank [at Legnago], a crossing would be extremely difficult." Corpo di Stato Maggiore, *La Campagna*, vol. 1, pp. 122–3.

became pronounced in 1861, when Italy's war minister began constructing entrenched camps at Bologna *and* Piacenza, one, in other words, for the lower Po and one for the Mincio. Thereafter, a French critic remarked, Italy's army "floated between Bologna and Piacenza; no one dared make the decision that would destroy that deadly germ of incertitude."[35] It would be the Italian army's signal misfortune in 1866 that its two most powerful soldiers headed opposing schools, making for irreconcilable strategic problems in the war with Austria.

Sixty-two-year-old Alfonso La Marmora, chief of the western or "Piedmontese" school of Italian strategy, planned to fight the next war exactly as he and his Piedmontese forebears had fought wars with Austria in 1848 and 1859.[36] In 1848, Piedmontese troops had defeated the Austrians at Goito, Peschiera, and Pastrengo to force the Mincio river line before finally being beaten by Radetzky at Custoza in July. It was a war the Piedmontese might have won had they only organized an occupation of Venetia and consolidated their positions once inside the Quadrilateral.[37] In 1859, after their victory at Solferino, the French and Piedmontese had considered whether to invest the Quadrilateral from the Mincio or the Po and had ultimately opted for the Mincio, judging the lower Po too wide, its banks too low, and its waters too high for effective bridging. Whereas an army corps could pass the relatively narrow Mincio in a single day, it would require three to get across the Po, ample time for an Austrian detachment to sally from Rovigo or Legnago to catch it, as an Italian officer put it, *"in flagrante passaggio."*[38] Indeed, prospects for a Po crossing were so bad that Vittorio Emanuele's military cabinet decided in June 1862 that for the next war with Austria, the Italian army would attempt no more than a diversion there.[39]

Nevertheless, Cialdini, backed by the Prussian General Staff, took the opposite view, arguing that Italy ought to make its diversion on the Mincio and its main effort on the Po. Cialdini and Moltke reasoned that a western invasion would only waste time – hence Moltke's lively interest in the debate – and blood reducing Peschiera, Mantua, then Verona. Even were the Mincio Army to capture Verona, Moltke reasoned that it would thus close only one of Austria's two supply lines – the Brenner route – leaving the more important line through Villach open. Under these circumstances, even were Austria to lose Verona, South Army would be able to retire upon its forts at Legnago, Rovigo, and Venice until reinforcements arrived from Vienna, precisely what had happened in the summer of 1848.

A wiser course, Cialdini argued in 1866, would be to lure the Austrians to the Mincio with a diversion, cross the Po in overwhelming force, and make for Padua,

35　Lemoyne, p. 88.

36　Alfonso was the youngest of four La Marmora brothers, all Piedmontese generals of the Risorgimento. *Enciclopedia Italiana* (Rome: Giovanni Tecanni, 1933), vol. 20.

37　Whittam, pp. 34–5.

38　Or simply to flood the left bank of the Po using their watergates at Mantua and Legnago. Pollio, *Custoza 1866*, p. 60. Wandruszka, *1866*, p. 244.

39　Corpo di Stato Maggiore, *La Campagna*, vol. 1, p. 124.

9. General Enrico Cialdini (1811–84), commander of the Italian Po Army in 1866

which was in the *rear* of the Quadrilateral. Once established there, athwart South Army's principal road and rail links to inner Austria, Cialdini's Po Army would crush Venice between land and sea attacks, wheel into the Quadrilateral, and, together with La Marmora's Mincio Army, take Verona, closing the Brenner route and ending the war.[40] Moltke, who had never actually set foot in the wet, trackless region between the lower Po and the Adige, loved this "southern plan" for its beguiling simplicity.[41] He instructed Bernhardi to push hard for its acceptance in Florence over La Marmora's "western school." Moltke assumed throughout that Cialdini would not waste time besieging Verona – "Austria's Sebastopol" – but would merely trap South Army there, detach an observation corps, then hurry with 150,000 men to join the Prussians on the Danube to deal, in Guido Usedom's words, a "stab-in-the-heart" to the Habsburg Monarchy.[42]

The strategic debate between La Marmora and Cialdini dragged into the third week of June, a delay that infuriated Berlin, for even were Vittorio Emanuele ultimately to select Cialdini's plan, most of the Italian army would then have to be redeployed from Cremona to Ferrara, a process that would take additional weeks. In the absence of firm leadership from the king, something had to be done quickly. At last, just days before Italy's declaration of war on Austria, General Agostino Petitti, a royal adjutant on good terms with both Cialdini and La Marmora, brokered a fateful compromise. Petitti, chairman of the king's Permanent Commission for Defense, elected not to choose between the "southern" and "western" schools but to choose them *both*, giving La Marmora eleven divisions – 120,000 men – on the Mincio and Cialdini 5 divisions – 80,000 men – on the lower Po.[43]

Petitti dubbed Cialdini's command a "special mission," a euphemism for complete detachment from La Marmora, the newly appointed Italian staff chief.[44] Since Vittorio Emanuele appointed no one with the authority to coordinate the two armies as well as the 20,000 Garibaldians and the iron fleet swinging at anchor in Ancona, all elements operated independently and were only theoretically united in the king's hand. With La Marmora in Florence, Petitti in Piacenza, Garibaldi at Como, Cialdini in Bologna, Italy's naval minister preparing to take a division with the land army, and the fleet's principal admirals scattered from Florence to Brindisi, the Italian command never settled on a comprehensive, theater-wide operations plan. Indeed, La Marmora did not even think to order the assembly of siege parks at Mantua and Peschiera till June 20, the day Italy declared war on Austria.

On June 22, just two days before the battle of Custoza, 40 percent of Garibaldi's volunteers – mostly impoverished southerners who had enlisted "for the soup" – were still in Apulia on the heel of Italy, far from the Brescian Alps, whence the Garibaldians were supposed to strike toward Riva, relieving pressure

40 Lemoyne, pp. 87–8.
41 Moltke, *Strategy*, pp. 39–40. "An advance upon Padua cuts the enemy's arteries. It compels him to move out, for he would have nothing to eat."
42 Corpo di Stato Maggiore, *La Campagna*, vol. 1, pp. 130–4.
43 Corpo di Stato Maggiore, *La Campagna*, vol. 1, p. 151.
44 Corpo di Stato Maggiore, *La Campagna*, vol. 1, pp. 62–3. Chiala, *Ancora*, pp. 262–4. Lemoyne, p. 103. Whittam, p. 96. Gallinari, *L'Esercito*, p. 64.

on the Mincio Army and diverting the Austrian fortress garrison at Peschiera. The rest of the volunteers were scattered around Lombardy, many of them still un-armed. Overall, less than 25 percent of Garibaldi's "redshirts" – so-called for the rust-colored butcher's smocks they wore to distinguish themselves from regular troops – would be ready in time for La Marmora's declaration of war. The rest would not be mobilized until July, too late to assist the royal army.[45]

Cialdini and La Marmora met on June 17 and *seemed* to agree that Cialdini would cross the Po immediately after La Marmora's passage of the Mincio to unite the two halves of the Italian army on the middle Adige.[46] Yet despite their seeming agreement, both generals, who were chiefly concerned to keep a free hand in the war, refused to commit their plans to paper, leaving both in doubt as to the other's intentions. One Italian historian thought La Marmora's object was really "to occupy the heights between Peschiera and Verona, sever communica-tions between the principal forts of the Quadrilateral and lure the Austrian army to the Mincio," presumably so that Cialdini, after distracting the Austrians on the Po long enough for La Marmora to pass the Mincio, could fall on South Army's rear.[47] For his part, Cialdini clearly believed that his diversionary army would make the main effort, La Marmora's main army the diversion.[48]

Were Cialdini's army of 80,000 really intended to furnish a diversion for the Mincio Army of 120,000, common sense dictated that the Po crossing should have preceded not followed La Marmora's attack across the Mincio. In the end, there was inexplicable confusion on this elementary question. On June 21, Cialdini wired the king asking for a diversion on the Mincio. On June 22, Petitti wired Cialdini promising a "demonstration" on the Mincio on June 24. Yet Petitti knew that La Marmora planned a crossing with ten divisions on June 23, which plainly amounted to much more than a "demonstration." On the twenty-fourth, Cialdini would be literally stunned by the news of Custoza, for he believed all along that he was the hammer, La Marmora the anvil.[49]

When, shortly before the war, a Prussian official asked Petitti how the Italian army proposed to cross the Po and Mincio simultaneously without having its

---

45 KA, AFA 1866, Karton 2344, 6–206, Venice, June 25, 1866, Direzione di Polizia to FM Albrecht. Pollio, *Custoza 1866*, pp. 56–7. Corpo di Stato Maggiore, *La Campagna*, vol. 1, pp. 155–6.

46 Calza, pp. 16–17.

47 The historian in question, Carlo Còrsi, is cited in Gallinari, *L'Esercito*, pp. 65–6.

48 There is no transcript of the meeting of June 17, only this letter from Cialdini to La Marmora dated June 20: "Dearest friend: I write to tell you how happy I am that you found my plan convincing and satisfactory. Nevertheless, it would be foolish to expect too much. Indeed my character inclines me to exaggerate the difficulties of this enterprise as well as the role of chance and unforeseen circumstances (*fortuiti ed imprevedibili*). My intelligence findings are grim. They locate the Austrians . . . at Lonigo [twenty-five kilometers southwest of Vicenza]. It appears that they have discovered our project and will oppose my passage in force. I hope that the day before my crossing, you will succeed in drawing the Austrians toward you." Chiala, *Ancora*, p. 313.

49 Lemoyne, p. 92. Pollio, *Custoza 1866*, pp. 52–3.

unconnected halves beaten piecemeal by Albrecht's centrally positioned South
Army, Petitti assured the Prussian – wrongly as it turned out – that the Austrians would not hazard an attack on either army and would instead yield the lines of
the Po and Mincio and remain behind the more defensible Adige, leaving Cialdini
and La Marmora time and space to join forces. One problem with this assumption
was that the two Italian armies had not agreed on a plan to unite inside Venetia.
The other was that Albrecht intended to maneuver *between* the Italian armies, not
stand rooted on the left bank of the Adige. Clearly no one in the Italian camp had
a clear picture of how the impending war would unfold. A week before Custoza,
one of La Marmora's divisional generals wrote: "It *appears* as though Cialdini will
pass the lower Po and the Adige. *If* this actually happens, things will go splen-
didly."[50] On June 21, La Marmora sent Cialdini a letter that foretold the disaster
ahead: "As commandant of a separate corps, you are free to prosecute operations in
whatever direction seems opportune to you."[51]

Petitti's awkward compromise had cut Italy's mobile army in half. Only
Vittorio Emanuele, as *comandante supremo*, had the authority to issue orders both to
Cialdini and La Marmora. Yet the king refused to impose a single direction on
Italian strategy, probably for political reasons. He relied equally on La Marmora –
boss of the conservative "Piedmontese *camorra*" – and Cialdini – the charismatic
idol of Italy's left-wing Party of Action – and could not afford to spurn either
general. Hence, the king deferred the critical business of planning an invasion of
Venetia until June 18, when La Marmora, under irresistible pressure from Berlin
to strike at Austria, finally relinquished his ministries in Florence and traveled to
army headquarters in Cremona.

On June 20, Vittorio Emanuele officially declared war on Austria "for the
honor of Italy and the rights of the nation."[52] La Marmora dispatched a formal
declaration of hostilities to Archduke Albrecht in Verona and decided to attack
across the Mincio with most of his army on June 23. But "just what exactly La
Marmora had in mind [for the twenty-third and twenty-fourth] is hard to say,"
an Austrian officer later wrote. "Probably La Marmora himself had no idea."[53]
The fact that the Austrians had not demolished their three permanent bridges
over the Mincio should have been a warning to him, but the Italian staff chief
continued to believe that Albrecht would remain behind the Adige. He hoped
that the rapid advance of his army of 120,000 to Verona would prevent Albrecht
from swinging south with his mobile force of 75,000 to oppose Cialdini,
permitting the two Italian armies to join on the Adige. Certainly La Marmora
and the king did not expect the battle they blundered into on June 24 in the
hills above Villafranca. Indeed, La Marmora would cross the Mincio that day

---

50 From one of General Nino Bixio's letters, dated June 17. Chiala, *Ancora*, p. 314.
51 Pollio, *Custoza 1866*, pp. 52, 55.
52 Corpo di Stato Maggiore, *La Campagna*, vol. 1, p. 149.
53 Bartels, *Der Krieg im Jahre 1866*, p. 59.

without his staff, leaving word that he was riding ahead merely "to see how the men marched."[54]

LA MARMORA'S INVASION OF VENETIA AND ALBRECHT'S COUNTERMEASURES, JUNE 21–4, 1866

Archduke Albrecht answered King Vittorio Emanuele's declaration of war with a communiqué to South Army damning Italy's "treachery and arrogance." The field marshal vowed to frustrate the Italian king's plan to "plant his standard on the Brenner and the Karst," Italy's "natural frontiers," which happened to fall well inside Habsburg Tyrol and Slovenia. Despite the onerous odds in Italy – 75,000 mobile Austrian troops with just 168 guns against 200,000 Italians with 370 guns – Albrecht concluded the order with a Radetzkyan taunt: "Remember how often *this* enemy has fled before you."[55]

Until June 21, South Army remained in its central deployment on the left bank of the Adige near Verona, poised to break south or west as circumstances required.[56] Albrecht detached one brigade to the lower Po, but left six railroad trains standing by to move it quickly to Verona in case La Marmora moved before Cialdini.[57] On June 21, Austrian scouts on the Mincio reported that La Marmora would soon cross there in strength. Italian detachments had advanced to hold the bridges left intact by the Austrians, and engineers were busy constructing two additional bridges between Valeggio and Goito. Austrian outposts could see masses of Italian infantry gathering behind the river crossings with the naked eye. Meanwhile, Austrian scouts on the lower Po reported that Cialdini would need at least two additional days to begin a river crossing there.[58]

As Italy's first and heaviest blow descended from the west, Albrecht and his staff chief, General Franz John, quickly planned a reply. They would march west to disrupt La Marmora's crossing, seize the Mincio Army's principal bridges at Valeggio and Goito, then capture or destroy any Italian divisions that managed to get across the river, all the while keeping Cialdini's Po Army under observation. To do all these things at once, John planned to concentrate South Army in the only strategic feature of the Venetian plain, the heights of Sommacampagna, Custoza, and Santa Lucia, part of a chain of hills that extended across the Mincio to Solferino in Lombardy. Positioned on these heights above Villafranca, South Army would be able to change front to the south and descend on La Marmora's left flank as the Mincio Army, which would have to spread itself across a thirty-five kilometer front to cross the river, straggled eastward to the Adige.

General John sent orders to his corps commandants on June 21 to assemble

54 Calza, p. 9.
55 PRO, FO 7/708, no. 370, Vienna, June 26, 1866, Bloomfield to Clarendon.
56 KA, MKSM 1866, Karton 342, 69–5/2, Vienna, June 9, 1866, Franz Joseph to FM Albrecht.
57 KA, Kriegskarten, H IVc 249, "Allgemeine Situation bis zum 22. Juni 1866."
58 k.k. Generalstab, *Österreichs Kämpfe*, vol. 2, pp. 18–19.

under the walls of Verona, on the right bank of the Adige, by sun-up on the 23.[59] Though John scheduled marches only at night, in the early morning, or in the late afternoon, Joseph Maroicic's VII Corps, which had to traverse the twenty kilometers from San Bonifacio to Verona in a blistering heat, barely made it. Maroicic collided with Ernst Hartung's IX Corps en route, forcing his men to stand under a hot sun longer than was healthy. Seventh and IX Corps crossed paths again near Verona, and Albrecht's staff noted uneasily that the final six kilometers of the march from Verona to VII Corps's bivouacs west of the city were littered with sunburnt, dehydrated men. Maroicic's Töply and Welsersheimb Brigades were each reduced to a single *battalion* of effectives by the heat.[60] John worriedly shelved plans for a night attack over the Mincio into La Marmora's rear and presented Albrecht – who now feared that his exhausted army would be unable to march and fight the next day – with orders for an advance to Custoza the following morning: "Your Highness," John insisted, "although we have twenty-four hours till the advance, we have just thirty minutes to expedite the orders." Albrecht promptly signed John's dispositions.[61]

At noon on June 23, Albrecht and John convened a council of war to discuss their plan of operation for the twenty-fourth: a march and change of line by three army corps within striking distance of the enemy on the rolling, ten kilometer-long frontage between Sommacampagna and the Mincio.[62] The maneuver was exceedingly hazardous. Since Italian skirmishers had already pushed Albrecht's pickets back from the Mincio to Verona in the course of the morning, South Army would have no outposts as it moved west and little warning of an Italian advance. At 2:00 P.M., Albrecht received word from Mantua and Peschiera that La Marmora had crossed the Mincio and was assembling in the plain between Valeggio and Villafranca.[63] The archduke knew that he might be sending South Army into a trap: Italian pincers rising north and east from the Mincio bridge-heads. Still, given what he knew of La Marmora's disorganized army, it seemed a risk worth taking.

Thus, while VII and IX Corps subsided gratefully into their bivouacs, Albrecht ordered his "Reserve Division" – thirteen mismatched battalions culled from Austria's Italian forts – and Gabriel Rodic's V Corps, which had been stationed at Verona throughout the deployment, to march west to Sona in the early evening of June 23 to block any attempt by La Marmora to occupy the hills above Villafranca before South Army could concentrate there on the twenty-fourth.[64]

59 k.k. Generalstab, *Österreichs Kämpfe*, vol. 2, pp. 46–9.
60 KA, AFA 1866, Karton 2357, 13–3, Vienna, February 1, 1867, Capt. Wagner.
61 Srbik, *Aus Österreichs Vergangenheit*, pp. 99–100.
62 KA, AFA 1866, Karton 2345, 6–217, Villafranca, July 4, 1866, FML Hartung.
63 KA, MKSM 1866, Karton 343, 69/9, "Operations-Journal Süd-Armee und Dalmatien nebst Flotte." AFA 1866, Karton 2344, 6–204 1/41, Sommacampagna, June 23, 1866, Col. Rüber to Armee-Commando.
64 KA, AFA 1866, Karton 2345, 6–215, Vienna, July 17 1866, FML Rodic.

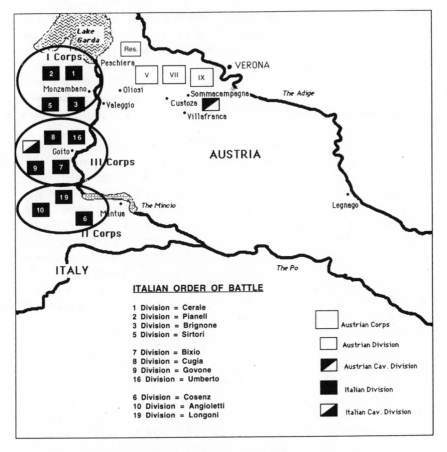

Custoza: La Marmora and Albrecht deploy, June 23, 1866

When the road west had cleared, Albrecht ordered IX Corps's Weckbecker Brigade to march at 2:00 A.M. on the twenty-fourth. Its task was to occupy Sommacampagna, which would serve as the pivot for South Army's wheeling descent south into La Marmora's flank.[65] After the war, Vittorio Emanuele marvelled at Albrecht's audacity, for, as it chanced, this Austrian maneuver was precisely the inverse of the maneuver assigned Giacomo Durando's Italian I Corps on the twenty-fourth, namely to pivot on Valeggio and wheel north into the heights of Custoza and Sommacampagna. And this was hardly an improbable move. Albrecht had to assume that La Marmora, who began crossing the Mincio early on the twenty-third, would send at least a division up to

65 KA, AFA 1866, Karton 2359, 6–40, Villafranca, July 4, 1866, FML Hartung.

Sommacampagna to secure his left flank. "Tell me," the Italian king asked Karl Moering, one of Albrecht's brigadiers, after the war, "why did the archduke risk meeting with my entire army already installed on the Mincio heights?" Vittorio Emanuele correctly judged this "a great strategic error," to which Moering replied: " 'tis true, Sire. We worried the entire march that you would anticipate the maneuver and gain the heights first."[66] Still, long odds required long chances, and, as Albrecht knew, Italy's army was not the threat its numbers alone signified.

The Veronese, who had seen nothing of VII and IX Corps, which crossed the Adige downstream from Verona, were astonished by the sudden apparition of V Corps's march columns in the inner city at 5:00 P.M. on the twenty-third. Though the martial spectacle was prolonged far longer than John would have liked – "Our trains plugged the streets," one of Rodic's staff officers fumed. "The army carried far too much baggage with it!" – V Corps did eventually cross the Adige, touch the right bank, and set off in the direction of Sommacampagna as night and a cold rain began to fall.[67] The rest of South Army ate a hot dinner and bedded down in soggy bivouacs outside Verona. They were scheduled to wake at 2:00 A.M., brew coffee and break camp an hour later unencumbered by trains.[68] At midnight, Albrecht received a disturbing cable from the single regiment he had left in the Polesine that reported Cialdini throwing bridges over the Po much earlier than anticipated. Although Albrecht understood that even were Cialdini to *fly* across the river, he would still need at least two days to unite with La Marmora, the report was nonetheless unsettling, for news from the front was invariably hours late and too sketchy for comfort.[69]

La Marmora spent the night of June 23 at Cerlungo, on the west bank of the Mincio, lulled to sleep by negligent Italian reconnaissance that gave no warning of Rodic's advance.[70] La Marmora thus rose at 4:00 A.M. on the twenty-fourth – the seventh anniversary of the battle of Solferino – and rode into Venetia convinced that there would be no battle that day, a conviction that must have been some comfort to him as he witnessed his army's chaotic river crossing.[71]

The passage La Marmora had ordered on the twenty-third – "to gain a foothold on the left bank of the Mincio" – was not proceeding smoothly. Since he had ordered the construction of only two pontoon bridges to augment permanent bridges in place at Monzambano, Borghetto, and Goito, La Marmora's army, exhausted by the heat, hard marches, and a wet night on the twenty-third,

66 HHSA, PA XL, Karton 124, Venice, December 22, 1866, GM Moering.
67 KA, AFA 1866, Karton 2353, 13–9, Vienna, December 19, 1866, Maj. Wempfling.
68 KA, AFA 1866, Karton 2344, 6–175i, Verona, June 20, 1866, "Disposition zur Conzentrirung der Armee bei Verona für den 23. Juni 1866."
69 KA, AFA 1866, Karton 2344, 6–204 1/4, 1/7, Rovigo, June 23, 1866, Col. Szapary to FM Albrecht. Srbik, *Aus Österreichs Vergangenheit*, p. 100.
70 Corpo di Stato Maggiore, *La Campagna*, vol. 1, p. 159. Calza, pp. 9–11.
71 Lemoyne, pp. 182–3.

trickled slowly into Venetia on the twenty-fourth, stalled by continual traffic jams and foul-ups.[72] Two of Durando's divisional generals, Enrico Cerale (*né* Cérale, a Frenchman of Dieppe) and Giuseppe Sirtori (a former Garibaldian, reviled by the king as a "pompous ass"), had been instructed to occupy the high ground east of the Mincio from Oliosi to Santa Lucia but had bungled their assignment. Cerale strayed from his march route, collided with Sirtori, and debouched into Venetia too late to intercept Austrian troops ascending from Verona and Pastrengo. Elements of Sirtori's division wandered too far east, "smearing I Corps," as the French staff later put it, "over too vast a terrain."[73]

Of course La Marmora should have sent cavalry patrols as far as Verona on the twenty-third, for Austria's entrenched camp was scarcely twenty kilometers east of Valeggio. Yet La Marmora chose instead to leave his fifty cavalry squadrons idle and thus failed to detect Rodic's night march to Sona. He then countenanced a river crossing so slow that by dawn on the twenty-fourth, only half his army was across the river, "weaving," as an Austrian officer put it, "like a drunkard" into the outstretched arms of South Army.[74]

Owing to La Marmora's gross tactical errors, Albrecht now had a chance to emulate his famous father's victory under similiar conditions at Aspern in 1809. The archduke could attack the 65,000 Italians who actually managed to get across the Mincio with South Army's full complement of 75,000.[75] La Marmora's foolish decision to detach Cuchiari's II Corps to mask Mantua needlessly reduced his invasion force by one-third. Up the line at Peschiera, he detached another division to keep the four battalions inside that little fortress under observation.[76] These detachments, added to the five idle divisions of Cialdini's IV Corps on the Po, effectively halved Italy's strength on the critical day of Custoza.

72 Corpo di Stato Maggiore, *La Campagna*, vol. 1, p. 155.

73 Vincennes, AAT, MR 55/1387, Florence, July 1866, "Observations critiques sur les operations de l'armée italienne à la Bataille de Custoza."

74 Bartels, *Kritische Beiträge*, p. 75.

75 At Aspern, on May 21–22, 1809, Archduke Karl defeated Napoleon, who failed to transport his entire strength across the Danube to fight the Austrians.

76 KA, MKSM-SR 1866, 22/3, Vienna, June 1866, "Festungsbesatzungen in Italien." Pollio, *Custoza 1866*, pp. 63–73. Corpo di Stato Maggiore, *La Campagna*, vol. 1, pp. 155–6.

5

Custoza

The Austrian brigades dispatched on June 23 to occupy the heights above Villafranca were assembled on hills north of Custoza and Santa Lucia at 4:00 A.M. on the twenty-fourth. Ninth Corps's Weckbecker Brigade — the pivot of Albrecht's intended envelopment of the Italian Mincio Army — arrived in Sommacampagna at 5:30 A.M., followed by a second brigade at 6:00 and a third at 8:30.[1] Down the line to the west, Rodic's brigadiers were pleasantly surprised to discover their sectors still unoccupied by the Italians. Indeed, the only resistance met by General Moering was offered by an inscrutable troop of Hungarian hussars prowling around in the dark without their German-speaking *Dolmetscher*, and by the adjoining Piret Brigade, which sullenly refused to make front to the south till it had drunk its wine ration.[2] Finally, the maneuver was tipsily executed, and, as day dawned on the twenty-fourth, Eugen Piret's men discovered the all-important ridge above Villafranca — where the pre-Alps touched the Venetian plain and were highest — unoccupied by either side as the bulk of South Army struggled along in column of route from Verona and the Italians, resuming their river crossing and unaware of Albrecht's advance, made slowly for the heights.

Hugo Weckbecker's brigade, which had left Verona at 2:00 A.M., an hour earlier than the rest of the army, arrived in Sommacampagna, keypoint of the Austrian position, at 5:30 A.M. Austrian hussars descended from the hills around Sommacampagna to inform General Weckbecker that the Italians had still not taken the heights above, though rolling dust clouds behind Villafranca did betoken the rapid advance of a large army. An hour later the first shots of battle carried to Weckbecker's position from both ends of the field. On his left, Ludwig Pulz's

1 KA, AFA 1866, Karton 2345, 6–217, Villafranca, July 4, 1866, FML Hartung.
2 "Where have you come from?" Moering demanded of the hussars. " 'To which brigade do you belong?' No answer! . . . I cursed our idiotic system that forces every officer to learn the language of his men, but does not force the men to learn German [the language of their officers]." Wandruszka, *1866*, pp. 246–9. As for Piret's brigade, Moering described the "terrible disorder" caused by the insistent demands of these men for their *Wein-Requisition*. KA, AFA 1866, Karton 2351, 6–102f, San Giorgio in Salice, June 27, 1866, GM Moering to FML Rodic.

10. Custoza and the Belvedere. Photograph by the author.

horse batteries had unlimbered on the outskirts of Villafranca and begun to fire into the town, which was being occupied and fortified by Enrico Della Rocca's Italian III Corps. On the right wing, around Oliosi, in the hills closest to the Mincio, Friedrich Rupprecht's Reserve Division, two weak brigades sent out from Pastrengo the night before by Albrecht to secure the Austrian right, bumped into one of Cerale's brigades at 6:00 A.M. as the two forces converged on the high ground above the bridges at Monzambano and Valeggio.[3]

For Albrecht and John, the battle was taking an unexpected, altogether alarming turn. Instead of marching straight ahead for Verona, La Marmora was wheeling north into the very heights Albrecht was attempting to occupy for a descent on La Marmora's left flank. La Marmora had improvised this change of plan at the last moment. At 5:30 A.M. on the twenty-fourth, he had entered Valeggio and advised Durando, in the process of moving I Corps across the river, that I and III Corps would pause to invest Peschiera while II Corps reduced Mantua, precisely the time-consuming operation Moltke and Cialdini had struggled to avert. Thus by 6:00 A.M., two of Durando's divisions were heading north, not east, toward Peschiera and the Mincio heights, not Verona and the Adige line. But slowly. At Valeggio, Cerale's columns cannoned into Sirtori's, causing a traffic jam that took precious hours to clear, permitting Albrecht's right wing to steal down to Oliosi. Still, despite Cerale's blundering, Durando's I Corps did manage to squirm around to face north, transforming John's artful flank attack into an artless, head-on collision between La Marmora's Mincio Army turning north and Albrecht's South Army changing front to the south.[4]

This turn of events radically altered the nature of the shaping battle. To win, Durando's I Corps had only to defend the crossings at Monzambano and Valeggio while the four divisions of Della Rocca's III Corps and Sonnaz's heavy cavalry crossed the Mincio at Goito and marched through Villafranca to Sommacampagna, turning Albrecht's left wing and severing South Army from its base at Verona. This grand plan, however, would be difficult to accomplish, for La Marmora's reconnaissance was so bad that he had no idea how the Austrians were deployed, and actually supposed that the Austrian *center*, not left, was in Sommacampagna.[5]

For Albrecht to win, it was no longer a question of knifing into La Marmora's unguarded left flank. Instead, with Italy's Mincio Army wheeling to face him, Albrecht had to protract John's original turning maneuver into La Marmora's rear and take Valeggio, cutting La Marmora's principal line of retreat. But with such an imbalance of forces on Albrecht's left — two Austrian brigades against five entire Italian divisions — the archduke would himself be easily flanked if he thrust his right and center too far forward. Moreover, as one of Albrecht's critics later

---

3 KA, AFA 1866, Karton 2349, 13–51, Görz, September 16, 1866, Capt. Weissmann.

4 Lemoyne, pp. 182–3. When La Marmora heard the first shots of the day reverberating from Oliosi around 6:00 A.M., he was unperturbed. Since he had no idea that the Austrians were descending on Valeggio, he assumed that the shots were merely harassing fire from the Austrian garrrison inside Peschiera.

5 Lemoyne, p. 331.

Custoza: La Marmora's passage of the Mincio, June 24, 1866

observed, the imbalance of forces along South Army's own front line – just two men per square meter on the all-important right wing compared with twelve in the center – made it tactically impossible for Albrecht to swing into La Marmora's rear without sacrificing the projected wing to the overwhelming numbers of Italian infantry gathered on the Mincio.[6] Custoza was thus a bloody stalemate in the making. To come to grips with the Italians, South Army would have to abandon its flanking attack and try instead a sledgehammer assault on the Italian center. Yet such was the confusion on both sides as the battle careened out of control, shifting first one way then the other, that it very nearly defied description. Indeed, the battle of Custoza would follow no set plan; it pitted two armies that collided haphazardly and rapidly degenerated into a terrible, inelegant brawl.

6 Only one-seventh of Albrecht's total strength was deployed on the right wing. Bartels, *Kritische Beiträge*, pp. 103–4.

Both the Austrian and Italian headquarters spent the morning of June 24 trying to discover just what was happening on the heights above Villafranca. Neither headquarters had a decent outlook, and neither army performed according to expectations. At 7:00 A.M., after passing through Villafranca and assuring his III Corps brigades that it was safe to stand down and cook breakfast because there could be no Austrians west of Verona, La Marmora rode up to Custoza for a routine scout with a troop of cavalry. He climbed 115 meters to the summit of Monte Croce and was astonished to see Ernst Hartung's Austrian IX Corps moving south in three columns, directly at him. It was La Marmora's first glimpse of the Austrians.[7] And they were close, only a few kilometers distant and closing as quickly as the rolling plowland permitted. Struck with amazement, La Marmora sent gallopers flying off to Durando and Della Rocca for reinforcements. He had only two brigades at Custoza: I Corps's Brignone Division. Brignone alone, however, would not stand against Hartung's entire corps, which threatened to sweep over the Mincio heights and down to La Marmora's bridges.[8]

THE CHARGE OF THE AUSTRIAN LIGHT BRIGADE

While La Marmora slapped together a defense of Custoza, he was startled again, this time by an explosion of heavy fighting *behind* him, in the plain between Sommacampagna and Villafranca. Archduke Albrecht had entrusted his entire "cavalry reserve" — fifteen squadrons of light horse — to Colonel Ludwig Pulz and had deployed him on the road from Sommacampagna to Villafranca to maintain contact with Della Rocca's III Corps and to give early warning of an Italian push toward Albrecht's lightly guarded wing at Sommacampagna.[9] Two of Della Rocca's four divisions had begun crossing the river at 2:00 A.M. with instructions to secure Villafranca, the road junction of western Venetia and then push up to join I Corps on the heights between Custoza and Sommacampagna.[10] Pulz, whose two light brigades had been reconnoitering since 3:00 A.M., watched uneasily as the two Italian divisions — a most unlikely pair: the Piedmontese crown prince, Umberto, to the right, and Nino Bixio, a radical Garibaldian, to the left — deployed in Villafranca, just eight kilometers from the Austrian pivot at Sommacampagana.[11] As if this were not quite menacing enough, Crown Prince Umberto and Bixio were reinforced in the course of the morning by a third division — Sonnaz's heavy brigades — which trotted up on Bixio's left, completing the semicircle round Villafranca.

Thus might matters have rested for the entire day — Pulz and Hartung chewing their nails and Della Rocca sitting on his hands, content to defend Villafranca against an imagined Austrian strike at Goito — had not one of Pulz's more impet-

---

7　Bartels, *Kritische Beiträge*, p. 83.

8　Lemoyne, pp. 186–7.

9　KA, AFA 1866, Karton 2344, 6–204 1/20, Verona, June 23, 1866, GM John.

10　Corpo di Stato Maggiore, *La Campagna*, vol. 1, p. 196.

11　k.k. Generalstab, *Österreichs Kämpfe*, vol. 2, p. 123.

uous officers taken matters into his own hands. At 7:00 A.M., while La Marmora was looking round Custoza and Albrecht and John were peering blindly from their low-lying headquarters in Sona, Colonel Joseph Rodakowksi — every inch the Polish lancer — detached his four squadrons of uhlans from Pulz's division and rode at Bixio's.

Pulz, under orders only to "maintain contact" with Della Rocca, was dumbfounded when, instead of halting on the skirts of Villafranca to reconnoiter the Italians, Rodakowski instead spurred to a gallop and charged them. Only moments earlier, Albrecht had ordered Pulz to conserve his horses for the end of the day. John's revised battle plan — which called for a strike into La Marmora's rear — required that Pulz actually lure Della Rocca *toward* Sommacampagna so that Rodic and Rupprecht could squeeze in between the Mincio Army and its bridges.[12] Rodakowski, however, was too far gone to be recalled, and Bixio's regiments, resting in the morning sun, hurriedly formed squares to repel the unexpected attack. Crown Prince Umberto, out for a stroll, sprinted to the nearest square and dived inside.[13] Alarmed by the sudden movement to their right, the seven squadrons Pulz had assigned to defend the Verona post road also mounted up and cantered through the peach orchards and corn, their brigadier, August Bujanovics, bawling "*Direktion Villafranca! Marsch! Marsch!*"[14]

Near Sommacampagna, Pulz assured a staff officer, who raised an enquiring eyebrow at Rodakowski's decision to commit a single light brigade to battle with two infantry divisions and twenty squadrons of heavy cavalry, that Rodakowski's charge could only be a bluff intended to frighten Della Rocca away from Sommacampagna. Under no circumstances would the attack be driven home. Moments later, Pulz's suite was astonished to hear the thump of guns and the chatter of rifles from Villafranca. Rodakowski's uhlans, three kilometers ahead of Pulz, had fallen on Bixio and Umberto. Pulz, who continued to trust that Rodakowski would not be so stupid as to launch an attack, mistakenly inferred that Della Rocca was finally advancing on Sommacampagna to turn South Army's left flank. Thus, Pulz followed Bujanovics, who had followed Rodakowski, into battle.[15]

It was perhaps as well that John and Albrecht could not actually see this gasconade from their headquarters at Sona, for it killed, wounded, or exhausted one-third of South Army's cavalry and pointed again to the uselessness of cavalry (and cavaliers) in thickly cultivated terrain.[16] Rodakowski thundered into the gap between the two Italian infantry divisions and attacked Umberto's left. His charge was easily thrown back by nine Italian squares deployed among peach trees

12 KA, AFA 1866, Karton 2348, 13–44e, Verona, June 1866, Südarmee-Commando. Karton 2345, 6–223, Sona, June 24, 1866 (7:10 A.M.), GM John to Col. Pulz.

13 Lemoyne, pp. 172, 231.

14 KA, AFA 1866, Karton 2344, 6–204, 1/36, Villach, August 1, 1866, Lt-Col. Krisztiangi.

15 KA, AFA 1866, Karton 2345, 6–218, Sommacampagna, June 30, 1866, Col. Pulz.

16 All John and Albrecht saw were dust clouds rolling from Sommacampagna toward Villafranca. KA, AFA 1866, Karton 2349, 13–54, Vienna, December 20, 1866, Lt-Col. Kröz. And Karton 2348, 13–44e, Verona, June 1866, Südarmee-Commando.

that broke all the momentum Rodakowski's men carried off the Sommacampagna road. As the Austrian uhlans wheeled away to the east to evade the fire of Umberto's riflemen, they fell, one after another, into drainage ditches dug on either side of the Verona post road. Scores of horses turned somersaults spilling their riders. Uhlans who drew up in time were mown down by salvos at point-blank range or pulled from their horses and beaten to death. Pulz's hussars, who trailed Rodakowski's lancers into battle, were also badly shot up as they passed through seven Italian squares before retiring.[17] Some Austrian survivors slid off their horses and gave themselves up. Others followed Rodakowski back to Sommacampagna. In all, Rodakowski lost 260 men, nearly half his strength.[18] Though Pulz would later take credit (and Austria's coveted Maria Theresa Cross) for "paralyzing" Della Rocca's corps with fright, less interested parties viewed the premature cavalry attack as a vainglorious stunt that would literally hobble Albrecht's pursuit in the afternoon.[19]

Still, if Rodakowski's onslaught made little impression on Umberto's steady *bersaglieri*, it undeniably sowed terror *behind* Umberto and Bixio, and this was an important result. Rodakowski's charge frightened Della Rocca's supply train into a panicky flight to the rear, halting for hours the advance of reinforcements that might finally have persuaded the Italian III Corps to test Albrecht's strength at Sommacampagna. Panic washed past Della Rocca's headquarters at Massimbona, ten kilometers behind Villafranca, all the way to Goito, where infantry supports were prevented from crossing into Venetia by a knot of train drivers, riderless horses, and deserters, the last calling "the Germans are coming! We are beaten! Every man for himself!"[20]

An Italian division detached from La Marmora's siege of Mantua to reinforce Della Rocca encountered mass confusion on the bridge at Goito at 8:45 A.M. Assuming III Corps to be beaten and in retreat, General Longoni, the divisional commandant, halted his march to Villafranca and prepared instead to defend Goito, where he remained for two critical hours while Italian staff officers cleared the road to Villafranca of trains and fugitives.[21] Bixio himself, who was with Della Rocca

---

17 KA, AFA 1866, Karton 2344, 6–204 1/36, Villach, August 1, 1866, Lt-Col. Krisztiangi.

18 KA, AFA 1866, Karton 2362, 6–80c, Verona, June 26, 1866, Col. Rodakowski to Col. Pulz. In all, Pulz left 400 dead, wounded, and missing behind – more than four times Italian casualties in the action. Lemoyne, p. 179.

19 One of Pulz's staff officers testified: "I don't agree that our bold attacks broke the enemy's morale. Indeed well into the evening [of the twenty-fourth] I saw ample evidence to the contrary. . . . Anyway, our heavy losses would not have been justified by the mere demoralization of the enemy. . . . It was singularly bad cavalry terrain – trees, ditches – there was simply no way to get at the infantry squares." KA, AFA 1866, Karton 2349, 13-ad 50, Budapest, January 23, 1867, Capt. Kovács.

20 Corpo di Stato Maggiore, *La Campagna*, vol. 1, p. 202. Lemoyne, pp. 328–9.

21 By the time Longoni satisfied himself that Della Rocca was not retreating, around 11:00 A.M., it was too hot to march the fifteen kilometers to Villafranca. Corpo di Stato Maggiore, *La Campagna*, vol. 1, p. 202. Lemoyne, pp. 328–9.

behind the lines when Rodakowski struck, believed that Rodakowski's attack heralded a major Austrian push. Della Rocca agreed and immediately slowed the pace of the battle, ordering Bixio and Umberto merely to stand their ground at Villafranca. This decision, taken without any attempt to discover how things *really* stood behind Austrian lines, relieved pressure on Albrecht's unguarded left wing for the rest of the day and would be a principal cause of Italy's defeat at Custoza.[22]

THE STRUGGLE FOR THE MINCIO HILLS

While Della Rocca's rear echelons ran for their lives and Longoni deployed defensively at Goito, Albrecht and John fretted on a hilltop above Sona, four kilometers north of Sommacampagna, where they had established Austrian head-quarters at 4:00 A.M. Although they could hear the battle well enough, they could not see it. A curious feature of these lush, green pre-Alps was that they were all the same height, making it difficult to obtain an overview of the field. Until 8:30 A.M., Albrecht and John only *heard* the gradual spread of battle along their ten-kilometer front as Pulz attacked in the plain and, west of Sona, Austrian and Italian brigades clashed amid the walled villages above Villafranca. Isolated, bloody fights spread from west to east – in Oliosi, San Rocco, Custoza, and San Giorgio – and through the intervening cornfields, orchards, and vineyards. This heavy fighting on Albrecht's right wing certainly suggested that La Marmora was forsaking his drive on Verona and turning instead into the heights.[23] Thus, Albrecht and John had hastily to rethink their original plan. To envelop La Marmora, it would now be necessary to sink obliquely into his rear. In theory, Rupprecht and Rodic would have to speed their advance on the right, while Hartung and Maroicic proceeded more slowly at the pivot. In practice, however, the battle continued much as it had since 6:00 A.M., a series of violent, uncon-trolled scrimmages through the hills above Villafranca as the Austrian brigades pressed south in obedience to their original instructions.

At Oliosi, on the Austrian right, Enrico Cerale arrived from Valeggio just in time to witness the rout of his division. Bunched up in the narrow defile between the Mincio and the heights, attempting to deflect Rupprecht's Reserve Division marching south toward Valeggio, Cerale's Division blundered through a vineyard and into Eugen Piret's brigade.[24] Cerale himself was shot in the thigh and his entire division disintegrated. With Rupprecht's Croats emerging from the woods on their left and the Piret Brigade deployed in attack columns before them, Cerale's regiments fled back toward Valeggio trampling their officers.[25] Piret then stormed Oliosi in half-battalion masses, taking some of the heaviest casual-ties of the day to root Cerale's infantry out of the village. "I saw the field [at

22 Lemoyne, pp. 174–5.
23 KA, AFA 1866, Karton 2348, 13–44e, Verona, June 1866, Südarmee-Commando.
24 KA, AFA 1866, Karton 2353, 13–11, Lemberg, December 14, 1866, Capt. Schulenburg.
25 KA, AFA 1866, Karton 2353, 13–13, Vienna, December 19, 1866, Capt. Lommer.

Oliosi}," an Austrian critic of shock tactics recalled, "and I do not exaggerate when I say that there were two dead Austrians for every fallen Italian."[26]

At Valeggio, Durando watched Cerale's division dissolve and straggle back to the river. The I Corps commandant personally assembled his reserve – three battalions of *bersaglieri*, twenty guns, and five squadrons of horse – and set off for Monte Vento to block Piret's pursuit. Durando's fourth division – three were already across the river – remained behind in Lombardy to mask Peschiera. Later, apprised of Cerale's rout, this division did nothing, unenterprising conduct that formed the basis of later accusations that the responsible general – Giuseppe Salvator Pianell, a Neapolitan – was really a Bourbon stooge in the pay of the Austrians.[27]

While Cerale was being thrown out of Oliosi, Durando's other division across the river – Giuseppe Sirtori's – was making no headway against Rodic's V Corps, which was moving southwestward from San Rocco to Monte Vento. At 6:30 A.M., Sirtori's vanguard bumped into Rodic's Bauer Brigade, which the Italians mistook for a friendly unit until, too late, they overheard German commands. Bauer, who was himself lost and had just asked an Italian peasant on his way to mass for directions, rode to the front and led the Austrian attack, cruelly sacrificing 660 of his own men and officers in crude bayonet charges to drive Sirtori back. Like Piret, Bauer, weakened by casualties, moved southwest in pursuit as far as the Tione, a stream that bisected the battlefield into western and eastern halves. There Rodic, who worried that he was losing control of his brigades in the lush farmland, halted the advance.[28]

As Sirtori withdrew his bloodied division at 8:00 A.M., King Vittorio Emanuele II awoke on the right bank of the Mincio and ordered his adjutant – General Petitti – up the Cerlungo church steeple to find out how Italy's Fourth War of Union was going. Petitti could see nothing and sent two staff officers across the river to gather information. As he descended to the street, Petitti met with a squad of *carabinieri* bearing Italian deserters off to jail: "We're beaten," the deserters assured Petitti and his startled suite. While Petitti goggled at these men, train drivers careered into town from the east, leaped down, cut their animals out of army harness, and disappeared off to the west. It was 8:30 A.M. Petitti returned to the king with grim tidings.[29]

On Austria's side of the hill, Archduke Albrecht had worries of his own. By 8:30, gaps were opening in the Austrian line as it wended south toward Valeggio and sprawled into Cà del Sol, the sun-bleached plateau between Sommacampagna and Custoza. Frustrated by their isolation, Albrecht and John abandoned Sona and rode four kilometers southwest to San Giorgio to be nearer the action. Still,

26 KA, AFA 1866, Karton 2353, 13–9, Vienna, December 19, 1866, Maj. Wempfling.
27 Calza, p. 19. Lemoyne, pp. 261–3, 276–81, 323.
28 KA, AFA 1866, Karton 2353, 13–10, Vienna, December 19, 1866, Capt. Fiedler.
29 Lemoyne, pp. 300–5.

they could *see* nothing.[30] The only decent "captain's hill" on the field was the aptly-named Belvedere above Custoza, but, by 8:30, it too was in the hands of Durando's Brignone Division, which, en route to Sona from Valeggio, had clashed with Hartung's IX Corps and then taken up defensive positions in and around Custoza.

At San Giorgio, Albrecht and John listened worriedly to the sounds of an uncontrolled battle they knew they were in danger of losing. The Italians held the high ground nearest the plain, had ample reinforcements coming up from Valeggio and Goito, and had three entire divisions in Villafranca, scarcely an hour's march from Albrecht's wing at Sommacampagna. The Austrians had either to fall back on Verona or push their attacks forward. To their credit, Albrecht's corps commandants instinctively chose the latter course, setting to work, often without orders, to dislodge the Italians from the Mincio heights to ensure, at the very least, that South Army would be able to extricate itself from its vulnerable position west of the Adige line.

HARTUNG'S REPULSE ON MONTE CROCE

At 9:00 A.M., Ernst Hartung's IX Corps struck up the Monte Croce from Sommacampagna to drive Brignone's division off the high ground and thus prepare an all-out Austrian counterattack on Durando at Valeggio and Della Rocca at Villafranca.[31] Hartung's Weckbecker and Böck Brigades crossed southwest through the Staffalo — an unshaded depression between Sommacampagna and Custoza — then struggled up the Monte Croce through vineyards and man-high corn toward the Italian division on the summit. This action, like most of the Austrian attacks at Custoza, testified again to the suicidal folly of Habsburg shock tactics against all but the worst infantry. Though their rear echelons dissolved in panic at each Austrian bayonet charge, the men in Brignone's front line coolly poured fire into four consecutive Austrian storm attacks, inflicting grievous casualties.[32] In just thirty minutes, Weckbecker spent his two regiments, plastering the muddy approaches to Custoza with Austrian dead and wounded, who lay groaning in the meridional sun, tortured by heat and thirst.[33] Böck, who was supposed to weigh in on Weckbecker's right, deployed too late to be of any help. The momentum of the battle shifted yet again. With both his regiments crushed by heat and casualties, Weckbecker called for reinforcements, received none, and fell back to Sommacampagna.[34]

By 10:00 A.M., as the heat of the day increased, the Italians seemed to have

30 KA, AFA 1866, Karton 2349, 13–54, Vienna, December 20, 1866, Lt-Col. Kröz.

31 KA, AFA 1866, Karton 2345, 6–217, Villafranca, July 4, 1866, FML Hartung.

32 KA, AFA 1866, Karton 2359, 6–47b, Villafranca, June 27, 1866, Capt. Kaihoe. Hartung lost 77 officers and 2,184 men (including 512 "missing") in these barbarously executed assaults.

33 Lemoyne, pp. 195–9.

34 KA, AFA 1866, Karton 2349, 13–51, Ragusa, January 3, 1867, Capt. Weissman.

overcome their early reverses to control the field. The Austrians were caught, as Vittorio Emanuele later put it, *"sans pied ferme,"* without a foothold, below the commanding heights.[35] Sommacampagna, Austria's left wing and pivot – now shielded by just 2,000 exhausted hussars – was wide open to attack from Della Rocca's two infantry divisions and Sonnaz's heavy cavalry in Villafranca. "In the end," an Austrian staff officer conceded, "South Army would be saved only by the incompetence of Italy's generals."[36]

LA MARMORA'S LINE BEGINS TO CRACK

La Marmora and the king searched for Della Rocca in Villafranca at 10:00 A.M. as an eerie quiet settled over the field. Cerale and Sirtori had been driven back on the left, Brignone was holding in the center, and Umberto and Bixio remained at Villafranca, facing Sommacampagna. La Marmora reviewed Della Rocca's timid dispositions, foolishly approved them, then compounded this error by formally attaching his entire cavalry reserve – Sonnaz's heavy division – to III Corps. Before riding back to Monte Croce to see how Brignone was faring – and to see if he could locate two of Della Rocca's divisions missing since 4:00 A.M. – La Marmora begged Vittorio Emanuele to return to the safety of Valeggio. The battle was going well. La Marmora would join the king later to plot a decisive maneuver.[37] The king agreed, though he was plainly more worried about events on the heights around Custoza than La Marmora was.

Before departing for Valeggio, Vittorio Emanuele took Della Rocca aside and asked whether III Corps could not spare a brigade or two for Brignone, who had suffered 25 percent casualties on Monte Croce. Della Rocca demurred: Villafranca, not Custoza, he assured the king, was the "keypoint of the battle." He would detach troops to the heights only if expressly ordered by the king. Since Vittorio Emanuele too was in doubt as to the placement of Albrecht's corps, he did not insist. He began to have second thoughts as he rode back to Valeggio at 11:00 A.M. and witnessed the moral collapse of Brignone's division, which, after repulsing Weckbecker's storm attacks, began to evacuate the Monte Croce, descending toward the Mincio. The king himself rode in amongst the men and tried in vain to rally them. They had been atop a tall height surveying the field for hours, yet could make no sense of La Marmora's makeshift battle plan. Where was the *front?* There were Austrians all *around* them. Why were Pulz's uhlans lounging in their rear? Infantry dreaded lancers like no other arm, and Brignone's men were no exception to this rule. Thus, hundreds of Italian deserters pushed past their officers and filed by the king – caps off and heads respectfully lowered – but deaf to his appeals.[38]

La Marmora, meanwhile, was returning to the heights when he met with

35 HHSA, PA XL, Karton 124, Venice, December 22, 1866, GM Moering.
36 Bartels, *Kritische Beiträge*, p. 89.
37 Lemoyne, pp. 200–1.
38 Lemoyne, pp. 227–8.

Giuseppe Govone, author of the Italo-Prussian alliance and one of Della Rocca's missing divisional generals, who was supposed to be rushing to the relief of Brignone's tottering division. La Marmora angrily ordered Govone up the Monte Croce, then rode in search of Della Rocca's fourth division – Cugia's – which, like Govone's, was milling around aimlessly in the plain, having made front once to the north (Custoza) and once to the south (Villafranca) in the course of the morning. La Marmora found Cugia and ordered him to advance into line between Bixio and what remained of Brignone's division to complete the semicircular Italian deployment from Villafranca round the heights to the Mincio.[39]

This done, La Marmora considered for a moment that he had the battle finally in hand until Cugia pointed over his shoulder to a flood of disbanded Italian infantry dropping off the Monte Croce. They were Brignone's reserve battalions, frightened by the fourth and final charge of Weckbecker's Hungarians. La Marmora had no way of knowing that Brignone's front line had actually held against Weckbecker. From this panicky flight to the rear, he wrongly deduced that Brignone had yielded the high ground at Custoza and that Weckbecker had burst through his center. To stem this imagined breakthrough, La Marmora himself galloped up the Monte Croce and waded in among Brignone's fugitives, ordering them to turn back and fight. He had another rude shock when he looked over to Custoza, threatened by Hartung's Böck Brigade, which, at long last, was sliding into line beside Weckbecker, and saw no Italian troops there. La Marmora dropped everything on Monte Croce and crossed to Custoza, where he found another of the king's sons, Prince Amadeo, breakfasting below the town. Alarmed by La Marmora, Amadeo – one of Brignone's brigadiers – pushed back from the table, rushed his brigade toward Custoza, and was shot in the chest. Amadeo's Lombard Grenadiers halted beside the wounded infante, and then, like Brignone's other regiments, dissolved, retreating down to the plain at 10:00 A.M., leaving Custoza to Böck and Anton Scudier, a VII Corps brigadier, who had arrived to reinforce Böck with a battalion of Rumanians.[40]

THE ITALIANS CLING TO CUSTOZA

The battle had turned again, this time in Albrecht's favor, yet the Italians had ample reserves to hand. Once Cugia and Govone began moving their fresh divisions up the heights to relieve Brignone, Böck and Scudier were forced to evacuate Custoza, and Weckbecker had to abandon his plans for yet another assault on Monte Croce. Scudier held out briefly in the cemetery at Custoza, calling to Maroicic for reinforcements as Govone's 34th *Bersaglieri* pushed into town from the south. Maroicic's last reserves, however, were his Töply and Welsersheimb Brigades, which Albrecht had designated the army reserve. They could be advanced into line only by order of the archduke himself. Thus, as Govone deployed

39 Lemoyne, pp. 201–2.
40 Lemoyne, p. 206.

his division on the southern rim of Custoza, Scudier retired whence he had come, back to the north. He retreated up and over the highest point on the battlefield, the Belvedere behind Custoza, opening another gap in the Austrian line, which Govone hastened to fill by driving away one of Hartung's regiments, which had ambled over to take possession of the Belvedere. It was 11:30 A.M. Albrecht's wheel had stalled again. Scudier's inglorious flight – for which he would be court-martialed after the war – left just seven Austrian battalions in the gap between Albrecht's VII and IX Corps against an entire Italian division.[41] West of the Tione, Sirtori had reinforced Santa Lucia, stabilizing the Italian left weakened by Cerale's flight in the morning. Rodic, supposed to be spearheading the Austrian descent on Valeggio, had literally lost one of his brigades in the orchards along the Mincio.

After some frightening moments, La Marmora's jerry-built front seemed to be holding and even wearing the Austrians down. In Italy in June one could win merely by forcing the enemy to trudge up a terraced vineyard one time too many, and by 11:00 A.M. most of Albrecht's brigades were dragging their feet, opening vast holes in the Austrian line as it wheeled jerkily south through broken terrain. General Maroicic described his situation as "bad" and noted that the battle was La Marmora's for the taking.[42] Scudier's precipitate retreat to Sona had bared Maroicic's flank, and another hole had opened in the Austrian line between Rupprecht's Reserve Division on the right and Rodic's V Corps in the center.[43]

On the Italian side of the field, the situation appeared at least as grim. King Vittorio Emanuele had just ridden into Valeggio to find the roads from the Mincio heights jammed with retreating troops and wagon trains. The town itself, which had hung out tricolors at dawn and cheered the arrival of the Italian army in Venetia, was now quiet save for the shuffling of thousands of stragglers, who had succeeded in detaching themselves from Cerale, Sirtori, and Brignone in the course of the morning and were making for the west bank of the Mincio without their packs and rifles. Venetians leery of Austrian reprisals had quietly removed Italian flags and bunting from the balconies and shop windows of Valeggio. The king marvelled that two of his divisions had been beaten so thoroughly so quickly.[44]

LA MARMORA LOSES HEART

By 12 noon, the opposing headquarters were in the curious position of both believing that the battle was going badly. Though La Marmora was sure of his

---

41 KA, AFA 1866, Karton 2345, 6–357, Sommacampagna, June 29, 1866, FM Albrecht to FML Franck.

42 KA, AFA 1866, Karton 2357, 13–3a, Maribor, December 15, 1866, Capt. Görger.

43 KA, AFA 1866, Karton 2345, 6–227, Salionze, June 24, 1866, GM Rupprecht to FM Albrecht. Karton 2349, 13–53, Brünn, December 16, 1866, Capt. Döpfner. Lemoyne, pp. 225–6.

44 Lemoyne, p. 326.

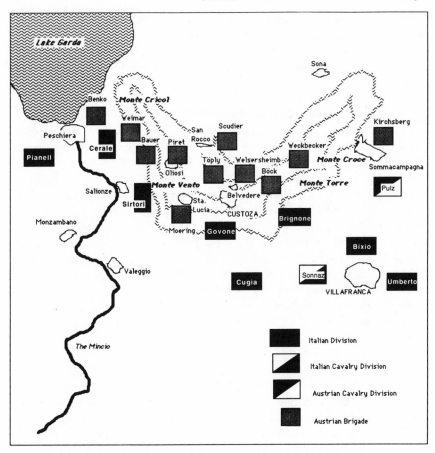

Custoza: The struggle for the Mincio Heights

wings at Villafranca and Santa Lucia, he feared for his center – the hill town of Custoza – where Austrian regiments kept swooping in and out, dislodging Italian brigades sent up from the plain to fasten the center.[45] King Vittorio Emanuele was in even lower spirits than La Marmora. Depressed by news of his son Amadeo's wound, the king quit Valeggio at 12:30, crossed the Mincio, and returned to Cerlungo. There he wired Cialdini on the Po: "Mincio Army in grand battle." This would be news to Cialdini, who would be shocked by the king's telegram ordering him to "disengage" La Marmora in the afternoon.[46] While Vittorio Emanuele thus busied himself in Cerlungo, La Marmora sought in vain

45 Lemoyne, pp. 324–5.
46 "I am desolate," Cialdini wired back. "General La Marmora promised me that he would limit himself to a mere demonstration." Pollio, *Custoza 1866*, p. 54.

for him at Valeggio. At 1:00 P.M., an increasingly distraught La Marmora gave up the search; though no one on the Mincio knew where the king had gone, remnants of Durando's corps streaming west seemed to point the way.

La Marmora, who was ignorant of events on Custoza, where Govone was actually beating the Austrian VII Corps, abruptly decided that the Austrians were too close to his principal bridge at Valeggio for comfort, and that the battle was therefore as good as lost. To assure himself at least one line of retreat, he ordered General Angioletti, Italy's peripatetic naval minister, to turn back from the Mincio heights with his division and secure Goito for a general retreat. Angioletti, whose division had been marching from Mantua since 5:00 A.M., wearily complied. La Marmora then rode down to Goito, pausing only to scribble messages to Petitti in Cerlungo, announcing the retreat, and to Durando in Santa Lucia, instructing I Corps to fall back and defend Valeggio. Petitti, however, had already left Cerlungo and was on his way to Goito. Durando's corps was already broken, its commandant already across the river in Volta. In Villafranca, Della Rocca refused a request for help from Cugia's division near Custoza and resolved instead to cover the Italian retreat he expected at any moment through the crossroads at Villafranca to Goito. All along the line, Italy's generals broke off their attacks and began slouching back to the Mincio. La Marmora observed the collapse from Goito, and burst into tears of rage and frustration.[47]

RODIC STORMS SANTA LUCIA

Albrecht, in the meantime, had problems of his own. Scudier's unwarranted flight from Custoza had ripped a hole in the Austrian center into which elements of Govone's division squeezed in the course of the afternoon. Thus, when Govone finally mounted the Belvedere at 3:30 and observed Scudier withdrawing to the northeast, he gave the Mincio Army's now disconsolate commandant a shock by jubilantly proclaiming an Italian victory and ordering his supply trains up from the plain to cook a celebratory *minestrone*.[48] At Sommacampagna, Pulz's anxious hussars began to despair of an Austrian victory and to whisper of huge Austrian losses in the hills and an impending disaster.[49] Fortunately for Albrecht, Rodic chose this pivotal moment to launch an attack the field marshal had ordered three hours earlier, sending his Piret and Moering Brigades against Monte Vento and the elevated village of Santa Lucia on La Marmora's left.[50] Eugen Piret stormed the Monte Vento at 2:00 P.M. and Karl Moering struck Santa Lucia at 3:00 P.M., just as Govone was celebrating victory in Custoza and Maroicic, Hartung, and Pulz were contemplating a retreat to Verona.

Durando, organizing the defense of Monte Vento, was struck on a finger by a

47 Lemoyne, pp. 256–7, 327, 331, 335–6. Bartels, *Kritische Beiträge*, p. 89.
48 KA, AFA 1866, Karton 2357, 13–3a, Maribor, December 15, 1866, Capt. Görger.
49 KA, AFA 1866, Karton 2349, 13-ad 50, Budapest, January 23, 1867, Capt. Kovács.
50 KA, AFA 1866, Karton 2351, 6–102b, San Ambrogio, July 10, 1866, FML Rodic.

shrapnel ball during Piret's preliminary bombardment. He promptly turned his command over to a subordinate and rode to hospital in Volta, five kilometers behind Valeggio. His troops followed shortly. Across the way in Santa Lucia, Sirtori's division abandoned a hilltop position without resistance, leaving behind 200 unwounded prisoners bawling *"Eviva l'Austria"* and evidence of a horrible atrocity: two Austrian *Jäger* stripped naked, beaten to death, and hung upside down by their canteen straps.[51] As Sirtori gave ground, another torrent of Italian deserters rained on Valeggio, opening a hole in La Marmora's front and threatening his left and rear as Rupprecht's Reserve Division, blundering around for hours, unable to change front in the undergrowth along the Mincio, crept past Salionze, and made for Durando's bridge at Monzambano.[52] In the blink of an eye, Govone's division on Custoza was flanked on every side. Sensing his advantage, Albrecht ordered Pulz at 3:30 P.M. to ride forward and "test the enemy's right wing." The archduke now contemplated a double envelopment of the Mincio Army from both wings. Pulz, resting since midday, rode obediently ahead to Villafranca and was greeted by whole Italian units laying down their arms to surrender without a fight. Behind them, Della Rocca, covered in shame by this inglorious day, began his retreat to Goito.[53]

MAROICIC TAKES CUSTOZA

At 4:00 P.M., Govone, now surrounded by cautiously advancing Austrian brigades, was jolted by a sudden cannonade from the direction of Sommacampagna. Without instructions from Albrecht – who by this late hour had shifted his headquarters farther west to San Rocco, to be closer to Valeggio, where he expected the battle to be decided – Maroicic had decided on his own initiative to commit the 13,000 men of the Töply and Welsersheimb Brigades, resting all day in the shade around Sommacampagna. The two reserve brigades, mostly Hungarians, formed half-battalion masses, hitched their belts, and began to ascend the Belvedere. Army headquarters, which had just ordered Maroicic to use his reserve to stop the hole opened by Scudier between V and VII Corps, belatedly sanctioned this strike at what Moering called the "vital debouchment" linking the Mincio heights and the plain and ordered Rodic to chip in a brigade from Santa Lucia for a flanking attack.[54] Rodic accordingly ordered Moering to gather nine battalions and cross to Custoza. At the same time, Hartung resumed the attack he had begun at 9:00 A.M. and pushed up Monte Torre again, this time driving Cugia's division off the summit, where he discovered six undefended guns, untouched caissons of ammunition, ambulances filled with groaning men, and thousands of

51 KA, AFA 1866, Karton 2353, 13–11, Lemberg, December 14, 1866, Capt. Schulenberg. Karton 2345, 6–215f, San Giorgio, June 27, 1866, GM Moering to FML Rodic.
52 Lemoyne, pp. 290–1, 311–12, 324.
53 KA, AFA 1866, Karton 2345, 6–218, Sommacampagna, June 30, 1866, Col. Pulz.
54 KA, AFA 1866, Karton 2351, 6–102f., San Giorgio, June 27, 1866, GM Moering.

abandoned rifles and backpacks.[55] Some of Cugia's men fled down to the plain, others over to Custoza, where they landed in the path of Maroicic's brigades, which suffered lamentable and altogether unnecessary casualties as they climbed in their thick storm columns through bursts of shrapnel and salvos of rifle fire before breasting the Belvedere and driving the Italians downhill from the cypress heights to the village of Custoza.[56] Maroicic ordered a rest, brought up three reserve batteries, and began to pound Custoza with forty guns, driving the last Italians out at 5:00 P.M. They were the Piedmontese Grenadiers, the crack troops of the Italian army. Taken in front, flank, and rear, they paused to aim a single volley at the Hungarian regiment that carried the village before fleeing in the direction of Goito. Dazed Italian stragglers wandering about Custoza reported that their brigadier and most of their officers were dead.[57] The battle of Custoza, as artless and ineffectual a battle as ever was fought on the north Italian plain, was finally at an end.

ALBRECHT'S FAILURE TO PURSUE

Or was it? "A general who wins a victory, yet doesn't know how to *exploit* that victory, doesn't know his business," Radetzky once said.[58] And when Albrecht humbly wired his thanks to Marshal Hess after securing Custoza – "the grateful pupil thanks his master" – this reproach hovered over South Army's commandant, who was behaving far more like his timid father than the great Radetzky.[59] In its initial boldness, Custoza was indeed a passage of arms worthy of Napoleon, but in its all-important *dénouement*, it just as certainly was not. To inflict a *decisive* defeat on the Italians, Albrecht needed to drive southwest to seize the Mincio Army's bridges at Monzambano, Valeggio, and Goito, which La Marmora had neglected to fortify. An energetic Austrian pursuit would have trapped the disbanded remnants of two Italian corps inside the Quadrilateral and positioned Albrecht for an all-conquering attack across the river like the one in 1849, when Radetzky had crossed the Ticino, routed the Piedmontese army at Novara, and forced King Carlo Alberto to terms in the famous "Hundred Hour War."[60]

All kinds of historical precedents must have occurred to Albrecht, a scholarly man, at 6:00 P.M. on the twenty-fourth, when Maroicic drove Brignone's grenadiers from the southern slopes of Custoza. The situation resembled one faced by Albrecht's father fifty-seven years earlier at Aspern, when Archduke Karl had

55 KA, AFA 1866, Karton 2345, 6–217, Villafranca, July 4, 1866, FML Hartung.

56 Austrian front-line regiments in the attack on Custoza-Belvedere lost 300 to 600 casualties each. KA, MKSM 1866, Karton 343, 69/9, Zerbara, June 24, 1866, FM Albrecht to Franz Joseph.

57 KA, AFA 1866, Karton 2345, 6–216, n.d., FML Maroicic. Karton 2357, 13–3, Vienna, February 1, 1867, Capt. Wagner.

58 Regele, *Radetzky*, p. 433.

59 Heinrich Hess, *Schriften aus dem militärwissenschaftlichen Nachlass*, ed. Manfried Rauchensteiner (Osnäbruck: Biblio Verlag, 1975), p. 30.

60 Vincennes, AAT, MR 27/1537, Paris, September 1866, "La Guerre de 1866."

secured a partial victory over Napoleon but missed the chance to convert it into a decisive one. At Custoza, Albrecht stood on high ground observing the wild flight of a demoralized, largely unarmed Italian army.[61] The fate of the fledgling Italian state was in his hands. What should he have done?

Certainly the temptation – to which Albrecht ultimately succumbed – was to rest on laurels hardly obtained. By 5:00 P.M., Albrecht had committed the last of his reserves, and the men of South Army were marching on their chinstraps. Many of Maroicic's men had died of heat stroke climbing the Belvedere. While some chased the Italians through Custoza and part way down to the plain, Maroicic noted others "slinking away to hide in the vineyards." They plainly had had enough.[62] Colonel Johann Töply, whose brigade had just wrought its way onto the Belvedere, pronounced pursuit "impossible. . . . Some of my men had already died of exhaustion."[63] Still, Töply and Welsersheimb were the brigades that had marched farthest in the sweaty redeployment to Verona on the twenty-second. Other units were fresher. "I cannot speak for VII and IX Corps," one of Rodic's staff officers later wrote, "but I can assure you that V Corps could have pursued the Italians from Monte Vento. . . . Why was no pursuit ordered? A strong push down to Valeggio and Goito would have abetted the confusion in the enemy's ranks and bagged still more prisoners."[64] Another V Corps officer concurred: "The men were willing, and a last effort would have yielded great results. . . . We could even have rested for two hours and then set out. . . . All night long Valeggio was jammed with Italian troops, wagon trains and disbanded stragglers. They would have offered no resistance."[65] One of Pulz's officers judged that even though the colonel had needlessly exhausted Albrecht's reserve cavalry in the morning, the horses could still have been fed, watered, rested, and sent out again in the night. "Darkness would have been to our advantage. For the past three weeks we had been patrolling the Villafranca-Valeggio-Goito region. We knew it; the enemy did not."[66]

Albrecht's hagiographers have cited fatigue and a lack of reserve cavalry as the reasons for the halt ordered by the archduke at 6:00 P.M. on the twenty-fourth when there were still four hours of daylight left.[67] Pulz's horses, which had been saddled since 6:00 P.M. the previous day, attempted a feeble pursuit toward Goito

61 KA, AFA 1866, Karton 2345, 6–216, n.d., FML Maroicic. Karton 2345, 6–258, Salionze, June 25, 1866, Col. Franz.
62 KA, AFA 1866, Karton 2357, 13–3, Vienna, February 1, 1867, Capt. Wagner.
63 KA, AFA 1866, Karton 2354, 6–160, Sona, June 27, 1866, Col. Töply.
64 KA, AFA 1866, Karton 2353, 13–9, Vienna, December 19, 1866, Maj. Wempfling.
65 KA, AFA 1866, Karton 2353, 13–12, Vienna, December 20, 1866, Capt. Schneider.
66 KA, AFA 1866, Karton 2349, 13-ad 50, Budapest, January 23, 1867, Capt. Kovács. Wandruszka, *1866*, pp. 254–5.
67 As did Albrecht himself, who explained to Franz Joseph the reasons for his decision not to pursue La Marmora or interdict Cialdini: "Our losses are great. Not one of my battalions is intact after the battle and the whole army – the only force on hand to defend Venetia – is exhausted." KA, MKSM 1866, Karton 343, 69/9, Verona, June 26, 1866, FM Albrecht to Franz Joseph.

but could not accelerate past a trot.[68] Nevertheless, South Army had a golden opportunity that evening to destroy half the Italian army with little risk to itself. Albrecht himself regarded La Marmora's defeat as merely "a sympton of [Italy's] utter demoralization." Italian prisoners described a broken army on the verge of extinction, and whole Italian units jogged over to the Austrians with their hands up.[69] Thirty-five hundred of 4,500 Italian prisoners taken on the twenty-fourth were unwounded.[70] Most officers on the Austrian side agreed that the Italian artillery – firing singly, not in batteries – had done little harm.[71] "Destroying" the Mincio Army would really have been a matter of pursuing it and accepting its surrender. Radetzky would not have hesitated to descend from the heights of Custoza. Albrecht, his father's son, did, a decision that would haunt him in July, when Cialdini would cross the Po at the head of a reorganized Italian army and march half the way to Vienna while Albrecht, sent north to replace Benedek after Königgrätz, turned to confront the Prussians on the Danube.

Albrecht not only permitted La Marmora to escape on June 24, he failed to take up the chase the next day or see to Cialdini's Po Army, which, after Custoza, marched west to cover Florence.[72] General Moering recorded his "astonishment" when Albrecht did not anticipate Cialdini's flank march past Mantua, summon his entire reserve – the Verona garrison and a brigade at Padua – and hit Cialdini's right as he marched to join the king behind the Oglio. "That would have finished them off," Moering grumbled on the twenty-sixth as Cialdini posted through Modena unharmed.[73]

Instead of invading the Kingdom of Italy after Custoza, Albrecht shifted his headquarters back to Verona on the twenty-sixth and then lost all contact with the Italian army for four days.[74] Were the archduke concerned about a possible French reply to an Austrian invasion of Lombardy, he ought not to have been. Even the official French press egged South Army on, and Franz Joseph advised Albrecht on June 28 to "ignore all political considerations, focus exclusively on military objectives and exploit every favorable opportunity for action."[75] That

68 KA, AFA 1866, Karton 2349, 13-ad 50, Budapest, January 23, 1867, Capt. Kovács. k.k. Generalstab, *Österreichs Kämpfe*, vol. 2, p. 122–3.
69 KA, MKSM 1866, Karton 343, 69/9, Zerbara, June 24, 1866, FM Albrecht to Franz Joseph. AFA 1866, Karton 2345, 6–218, Sommacampagna, June 30, 1866, Col. Pulz. Karton 2345, 6–217, Villafranca, July 4, 1866, FML Hartung: "We took 1,000 prisoners on [the twenty-fourth], and doubled that number in the following days as stragglers came over to us."
70 KA, AFA 1866, Karton 2345, 6–296, Verona, June 26, 1866, FML Jacobs.
71 KA, AFA 1866, Karton 2357, 13–3, Vienna, February 1, 1867, Capt. Wagner.
72 KA, MKSM 1866, Karton 343, 69/9, Verona, June 26, 1866, FM Albrecht to Franz Joseph.
73 Wandruszka, *1866*, pp. 249–50.
74 KA, AFA 1866, Karton 2346, 7–30, Pozzolengo, July 2, 1866, FML Maroicic. HHSA, PA XL, Karton 124, Verona, June 27, July 5, 1866, FM Albrecht to GdC Mensdorff. Vincennes, AAT, MR 27/1537, Paris, September 1866, "La Guerre de 1866 en Allemagne et en Italie."
75 PA XL, Karton 124, Vienna, June 1866, "Instruktionen für dem Erzherzogen Albrecht zugetheilten politischen Kommissar Graf Wimpffen."

same day, General Edgar Ney, Napoleon III's aide-de-camp, hosted a sensational banquet in Paris to *celebrate* Austria's victory at Custoza. In the course of the dinner, another of Bonaparte's adjutants toasted South Army and wished it "even greater victories" in Italy.[76] The French Empire, eager to see the new Great Power forming on its southern flank reduced to the dimensions of a north Italian satellite state, had swung round to Austria's side in the war. Still, Albrecht dared not cross the Mincio until July 1 and then only because the stench of rotting corpses on the Austrian side of the river had become intolerable.[77] Although La Marmora's precipitate retreat had literally marooned General Garibaldi and his corps of volunteers on the rocky ground between South Army and General Franz Kuhn's march-ready corps of 17,000 in Tyrol, Albrecht did nothing to exploit Garibaldi's predicament and permitted him to retire on Brescia without firing a shot.[78]

After crossing into Lombardy on July 1, Albrecht ordered South Army to retrace its steps to Venetia the next day. By July 3, the day of Königgrätz on the northern front, Albrecht was back at Custoza, worried about Cialdini's concentration of a resurrected Italian army around Mantua and the resumption of the siege there at the confluence of the Po and Mincio lines. Strategically, it was as though there had been no Austrian victory ten days earlier. A vast Italian army – La Marmora's eleven divisions combined with Cialdini's five – was rolling east again. Garibaldi was free once more to probe toward Trento and Innsbruck, and Italy's ironclad fleet, still untested, remained master of the Adriatic.[79]

It hardly mattered that Cialdini's new army could have been scattered as easily as La Marmora's old one, for once Benedek was beaten at Königgrätz, there would be no Austrian troops in Venetia to do the scattering. South Army would have to be rushed north to defend Vienna, leaving Cialdini free to pour troops into Tyrol, Venetia, and Slovenia, where they would threaten the rear of the very Danube defense line Albrecht would be summoned to hold against Moltke. Albrecht's failure to finish the job begun at Custoza also aborted a southern insurrection organized by Austrian agents in Papal Rome. Two days before Custoza, Franz Joseph's finance ministry had disbursed one million French francs ($5.4 million) to fund an anti-Italian rising in Naples and Sicily. The money – illegally procured without the consent of Austria's parliament – was delivered to the Habsburg embassy in Rome on the twenty-fourth.[80] In this regard too, Albrecht's

76 KA, AFA 1866, Karton 2272, 13–13, nos. 163, 166, Vienna, June 28 and 29, 1866, Belcredi to FM Albrecht.

77 KA, AFA 1866, Karton 2348, 13–44f., Verona, July 1866, Südarmee-Commando. MKSM 1866, Karton 343, 69/9, Colà, July 5, 1866, FM Albrecht to Franz Joseph.

78 Enrico Guastalla, *Carte*, ed. B. L. Guastalla (Rome: Alfieri, 1921), p. 52.

79 KA, AFA 1866, Karton 2348, 13–44e, Verona, June–July, 1866, Südarmee-Commando, "Begebenheiten."

80 HHSA, PA XI, Karton 208, Vienna, June 22 and 24, 1866, Mensdorff to Hübner. Rome, June 30, 1866, Hübner to Mensdorff. On June 30, Joseph Hübner, Austria's minister in Rome, wrote

excessive caution ensured that Austria would not realize its principal war aim in the southern theater: the smash-up of united Italy.[81]

Albrecht's hesitation after Custoza allowed the Italian army to save itself, regroup, and fight another day, ultimately contributing to the Prussian victory on the Danube in July.[82] Albrecht seemed not to appreciate that the Quadrilateral was as much an offensive bridgehead as a defensive fortress group. "Peschiera," the French staff later wrote, "was an open door through which the Austrians could have assailed La Marmora's flank and rear."[83] Mantua too. An Austrian staff officer later criticized Albrecht's inaction: "Although pursuit of the Italians over the Po or Mincio would have cost the archduke 1,000 men to fever . . . it is remarkable that he not only did not pursue, but, in fact, did nothing at all! The Italians were disbanded, yet he would not finish them off."[84] Early on the twenty-fifth, Albrecht pronounced South Army "in good condition and ready for new undertakings," yet still he would not move.[85] The archduke explained to Franz Joseph that an annihilating drive to Cremona would simply not have been an "appropriate maneuver for a defensive war."[86] But what was appropriate for a "defensive war?" The great Napoleon had never been in doubt on this question, nor Radetzky, who always said: "the best way to defend a province is to attack."[87] Albrecht took the opposite view, and, like his father at Aspern and Wagram, would pay later for his excessive caution.[88]

Mensdorff that Francesco II, the Bourbon pretender lodged in Rome at Austrian expense, would recruit deserters from the Italian army for an insurrection in the south and was in the process of hiring Albanian mercenaries to lead the revolt. He would not have had to look far. South Italy was home to more than 100,000 Albanians. Their most famous son? Francesco Crispi. Douglas, *Old Calabria*, pp. 176–7, 192.

81 Can we infer this grandiose war aim from the amount of field telegraph wire allotted South Army? In 1866, the Austrian army had 205 kilometers of wire. The war ministry gave 106 kilometers (52%) of this commodity to South Army and only 76 kilometers (37%) to North Army. (The rest went to the federal VIII Corps in Germany.) Since the telegraph net inside Venetia was better developed than the one in Bohemia-Moravia, this allotment probably reflected Austrian plans for a drive on Turin or Florence. Benold, "Österreichische Feldtelegraphie 1866," p. 13.

82 In August 1914, while weighing his offensive options, Austria's General Franz Conrad would say: "I do not want a second Custoza." Franzel, vol. 2, p. 488.

83 Vincennes, AAT, MR 55/1387, Florence, July 1866, Col. Schmitz, "Observations Critiques."

84 "He might have pursued to Goito and Valeggio on the 25th, attacked the lower Oglio [where La Marmora was sheltering] on the 26th," or crossed at Mantua to intercept Cialdini marching west to reinforce the Mincio Army. Bartels, *Kritische Beiträge*, pp. 109–11.

85 KA, AFA 1866, 6–220k, Verona, June 25, 1866, FM Albrecht.

86 KA, AFA 1866, Karton 2346, 7-ad 103, Vienna, July 8, 1866, FM Albrecht to Franz Joseph.

87 Regele, *Radetzky*, p. 433.

88 After Aspern in 1809, Archduke Karl refused to pursue Napoleon across the Danube because, as he put it, the Austrian "army [was] the safeguard of the dynasty and could not be risked in battle." He was subsequently crushed at Wagram. After Custoza, Albrecht made a similiar observation, calling South Army "the only force on hand to defend Venetia," jewel of the Habsburg crown. He refused to risk it in operations beyond the Quadrilateral. KA, MKSM 1866, Karton 343, 69/9, Verona, June 26, 1866, FM Albrecht to Franz Joseph.

CONCLUSION

Albrecht's move across the Mincio on July 1 to gather forage and escape bacilli seething on the heights around Custoza may ultimately have explained his other-wise inexplicable decision not to pursue and destroy the Italian army. South Army had marched without trains from Verona to Sommacampagna on June 23–24. The men had carried two-days' rations and left their heavy trains and bridges parked outside the Porta Nuova in Verona. This was one of the luxuries of fighting inside a friendly fortress group, but one Albrecht would not enjoy beyond the Mincio, something he discovered on July 1, when his river crossing was attended by Italianate chaos. Had Albrecht's stumbling passage been opposed by Della Rocca, who was lurking in the vicinity, South Army might have been beaten back before it crossed the Mincio, let alone the Chiese and the Oglio, two Lombard rivers that La Marmora planned to use for cover.[89]

This was unquestionably Albrecht's view of the situation. He preferred to await a second battle inside the Quadrilateral, rather than venture outside to an uncer-tain fate. He informed his corps commandants on July 1 that the war's "decisive battle" would be fought, again, at Custoza, as if Cialdini – the new Italian commandant – had already booked passage across the Mincio for the week ahead.[90] It is interesting to see these defensive tendencies obtruding from a man reckoned by so many admirers – Schlieffen included – to have been a Radetzkyan thruster. Custoza, it must be said, was a rather traditional defense of the Quadri-lateral against reasonable odds that did not require the maneuvering and logistical feats that had made the victories of Napoleon and Radetzky so remarkable. Although La Marmora offered battle with 127,000 men and 282 guns, he man-aged to transport only 65,000 men and 122 guns across the Mincio, conferring the numerical advantage on Albrecht's army – 75,000 men, 160 guns – in the crucial engagement of the Austro-Italian War.[91]

Much criticism of Albrecht's dispositions is justified. The threat from Cialdini in June was slight given the obstacles posed by the Po and the Adige. Indeed, John later claimed that he was prepared to move to the Mincio well before the twenty-fourth, but was restrained by Albrecht's "political considerations."[92] Ar-riving late on the field on the twenty-fourth, the Austrians ceded the command-ing heights to Durando's I Corps and then spent the entire day battering them-selves against positions that, with a bit more foresight, could have been occupied and fortified in advance of La Marmora's crossing. This explained Moering's complaint that the brigadiers of South Army had been forced to wrest a "tactical victory" from Albrecht's "strategically flawed battle plan," at a cost of 5,000

89 KA, AFA 1866, Karton 2353, 13–12, Vienna, December 20, 1866, Capt. Schneider.
90 KA, AFA 1866, Karton 2348, 13–44f., Verona, July 1866, Südarmee-Commando.
91 Alfred Krauss, *Moltke, Benedek und Napoleon* (Vienna: Seidel, 1901), p. 4.
92 Srbik, *Aus Österreichs Vergangenheit*, pp. 99–100.

casualties.[93] Indeed, South Army's sum of dead and wounded, which slightly exceeded Italian losses, formed a powerful indictment of Austrian methods. Witnesses all over the field – from Oliosi east to Sommacampagna – remarked piles of Austrian dead cut down in storm columns and squadron masses as they charged Italian field fortifications and squares.[94] Even Austrian *Jäger* – the army's only trained skirmishers – were frequently sent against Italian positions with the bayonet.

In the end, South Army won because of its excellent artillery, its superior numbers on the left bank of the Mincio, and, as Moering put it, because of the irrational *"Bravour"* of the Austrian infantryman. This was, however, a suicidal instinct that Italy's *bersaglieri* made the most of, and that Prussian needle rifles would hammer away at pitilessly in the north, wiping out whole Austrian battalions with their officers.[95] It was an unintelligent, unsustainable way of war. Whereas Radetzky had swept to victory against a far better disciplined Piedmontese army in 1849 with only 3 percent casualties – allowing him to proceed to Novara after a first, inconclusive victory at Mortara – Albrecht suffered 7 percent casualties at Custoza, heavy, irreplaceable losses that partly explained his decision not to pursue Vittorio Emanuele's stricken army after the battle.[96]

La Marmora's conduct at Custoza was, as the general's French attaché put it, *"une véritable folie."*[97] He invaded the Quadrilateral without an operations plan and failed even to locate South Army or assess its strength before the invasion. On the twenty-fourth, his uncertainty increased as the day wore on and communicated itself like an electric spark to his men, who, all along the line, gave up the fight without resistance.

All of Austria's skepticism about the durability of Piedmont-Italy seemed justified by the result at Custoza. Italians, as the proverb had it, were tough men "created to sing and starve by turns" but few of them would sacrifice themselves willingly for united Italy, a concept that – given Italy's regressive taxes, conscription, and class relations – was anathema to the average peasant. At Custoza, whole Italian brigades simply dissolved on contact with the Austrians and streamed to the rear past their imprecating officers. Indeed, for the Italian line – hot, hungry, and thirsty (some had not been fed for forty-eight hours) – the final straw at Custoza may even have been the sight of these selfsame officers: bearded, bespectacled *ufficiali* of the grasping Piedmontese state. To the peasant conscript,

93 Wandruszka, *1866*, p. 251.

94 KA, AFA 1866, Karton 2353, 13–9, Vienna, December 19, 1866, Maj. Wempfling.

95 Albrecht pronounced officer casualties at Custoza "very great," 68 dead and 215 wounded, 7 percent of total casualties. KA, AFA 1866, Karton 2345, 6–272c, Zerbara, June 25, 1866, FM Albrecht to Franz Joseph.

96 Anton Wagner, "Der Feldzug gegen Italian," *Österreichische Militärische Zeitschrift Sonderheft* 1 (1966), p. 35. Regele, *Radetzky*, p. 295.

97 Vincennes, AAT, MR 33/1387, Cremona, June 25, 1866, Col. Schmitz to Randon.

they must have resembled nothing quite so much as uniformed *avvocati*, the peasant's blood enemy.[98]

Ultimately, *"perseveranza"* was a middle-class word that cut against the grain of peasant instincts. The chief curiosity of Custoza was not that the Italian army was beaten so easily but that it crossed the Mincio at all. After the battle, General John's agents in Lombardy recorded the spread of "chaos" and "despair" – "Peasants are yelling 'long live Austria!' "[99] Even Garibaldi, a godless man, invoked the savior to save Italy: "Please God, send us men who *know* how to lead an army!" The hatred his volunteers felt for the king's army boiled again to the surface after Custoza.[100] As for the king's army itself, a French staff officer mingling with Italian regiments on the retreat from Venetia advised Paris that "morale is very bad since June 24th. The soldiers ask how this could have come to pass."[101] But for Albrecht's forbearance, Austria might have taken back the Po basin. Francesco Bourbon's brigands, Pope Pius IX's Swiss and Irish guards, and the mafia junta in Sicily, which actually launched a rebellion in November, might have seen to the peninsula and islands.

On the field at Custoza, the screaming pain of the ape-and-tiger fight on June 24 devolved from the shady chanceries of corps and army headquarters to the half-starved, dehydrated line troops and regimental officers in the hills. Once hit, the 9,000 Austrian and Italian battle casualties lay unattended for hours. The medical reforms urged by J. Henri Dunant's Red Cross after Solferino made no impression here. The Italians found it difficult to evacuate wounded men across the Mincio and noted a much higher incidence of traumatic lesions and instant death than was the case in 1859, when the Austrians had fought with smooth-bored cannon and been only partially equipped and trained with the Minié rifle.[102] And twelve hours after the last shot had been fired in Custoza, Colonel Otto Welsersheimb, whose shattered brigade was still strewn around the Belvedere, wrote Maroicic: "I have 330 dead and wounded, but as yet not a single surgeon or ambulance has come to attend them."[103]

98 Luigi Chiala, *Cenni storici sui preliminari della Guerrra del 1866 e sulla Battaglia di Custoza*, 2 vols. (Florence: Carlo Voghera, 1870–2), vol. 1, p. viii.

99 KA, AFA 1866, Karton 2348, 13–44f., Verona, July 4, 1866, Südarmee-Commando.

100 Milan, Museo Risorgimento, Archivio Garibaldino, Plico 20, Giuseppe Garibaldi, "Battaglia di Custoza."

101 Vincennes, AAT, MR 40/1387, Cometto, July 3, 1866, Col. Schmitz to Randon.

102 By 1868, 670 more Italians had died in hospital from wounds sustained at Custoza. Vincennes, AAT, MR 24/1388, Paris, September 1, 1868, État-Major, "Guerre de 1866 en Italie."

103 KA, AFA 1866, Karton 2354, 6–182, Custoza, June 25, 1866, Col. Welsersheimb.

6

Podol, Vysokov, and Trautenau

General Benedek had moved North Army headquarters to Olmütz from Vienna on May 27. In early June, an Olmütz official noted his surprise at the unmilitary antics of the Feldzeugmeister's suite: "Pretty boys, mostly. . . . They had a fine time, attending concerts and cavorting round town." Benedek himself made a well-publicized whirl of visits to the villages around Olmütz. In a suburban canton-ment, he paused at the town hall to set down a dramatic line in the visitor's book: "If ever I'm beaten, tear out this page!" Outside of Benedek's circle, however, the mood was less sanguine. Staff officers regretted the Feldzeugmeister's "striving after popularity," his insatiable "appetite for theatrics," and his "impenetrable reserve."[1] Poor leadership merely exacerbated another problem: By mid-June, North Army had exhausted itself with hard marches out of Austria's eastern garri-sons, yet was still barely equipped and thus unprepared to resist Prussian encroach-ments all along the Austrian frontier.[2]

While Benedek dawdled, Moltke invaded Saxony on June 16 with the Prussian Elbe and First Armies. Two days later, while the little Saxon army made for the safety of the Austrian frontier by road and rail, Elbe Army occupied Dresden and installed a Prussian governor there. In Berlin, Moltke savored Prussia's almost bloodless conquest of the north German states but reminded his army command-ers that their principal goal was yet unaccomplished: "The success [in Germany] is real only if we know how to maintain it, and the decision lies in *Bohemia.*"[3]

To win the right to annex Schleswig-Holstein and place the German Confedera-tion under Prussian control, Prussia had first to defeat Austria in battle. Thus, Moltke, who, by mid-June, knew that the bulk of Benedek's army was at Olmütz in Moravia, ordered his Elbe, First, and Second Armies to move up to the Austrian frontier on June 19. His plan was simple: Push into Bohemia and force Benedek to move against one of Prussia's three armies, at which point Moltke

1 Wilibald Müller, *Geschichte Olmütz*, pp. 309–11.
2 KA, AFA 1866, Karton 2287, 13–59, Vienna, December 21, 1866, Capt. Komers.
3 Moltke, *Strategy*, p. 43.

would slam the other two into his flanks.[4] As Moltke's three, still widely separated armies gathered before the Bohemian mountain passes, Emperor Franz Joseph's patience with Benedek finally snapped. On June 16, the emperor *ordered* the Feldzeugmeister to leave his "flanking position" at Olmütz to take up a new position farther west, at Josephstadt and Königgrätz, directly in the path of the Prussian invasion.[5] Thus, Benedek, who preferred to remain as far as possible from the Prussians while he finished outfitting North Army, reluctantly made arrangements for a flank march to Bohemia to begin June 17 and terminate thirteen days later in Josephstadt.[6] To buy time for this tardy move west, the Feldzeugmeister ordered Clam-Gallas' I Corps in Bohemia to unite behind the Iser River line with Prince Albert's Saxon corps and Leopold Edelsheim's 1st Light Cavalry Division to repel the advance of Prince Friedrich Karl's Elbe and First Armies. Only if the Prussians forced the river in earnest was Clam to give ground and retire with Iser Army to the bridge at Königgrätz, where he would join the bulk of North Army behind the Elbe.[7]

North Army quit Olmütz on June 17, not sure where exactly to find Moltke's three armies.[8] Though under orders to march to Bohemia, Benedek still worried that the Prussians were aiming their main blow at Cracow and Olmütz.[9] He thus detached Count Karl Thun's II Corps to shield North Army's flank against this imagined Prussian strike from Silesia and only then began to shunt the rest of his army westward.[10] By June 22, three days after Prince Friedrich Karl invaded Bohemia, North Army was on its way west in three great march columns that kicked up enough dust finally to convince Moltke that Benedek had indeed discarded plans to invade Upper Silesia and was on his way to the Iser. Thus assured of Benedek's direction, Moltke ordered Second Army to leave its defensive positions at Neisse and strike southwest into Bohemia. He advised his three army commanders to march quickly and close to within one march of each other at the Bohemian town of Jicin in order to prevent Benedek from infiltrating *between* the armies to beat them separately.[11] The war had now become a footrace to the Jicin plateau, a fine, open battlefield, where all arms – guns, infantry, and cavalry – could be deployed

---

4 Arthur L. Wagner, *The Campaign of Königgrätz* (1889; Westport: Greenwood, 1972), pp. 25–6. Grosser Generalstab, *Feldzug 1866*, p. 93. Blumenthal, p. 30.

5 KA, MKSM 1866, Karton 342, 69–4/12, Vienna, June 16, 1866, Franz Joseph to FZM Benedek.

6 KA, AFA 1866, Karton 2261, Vienna, April 1866, "Operations-Plan." Karton 2265, 6–691, Olmütz, June 20, 1866, FZM Benedek to corps commandants.

7 KA, AFA 1866, Karton 2265, 6–573a, 6–691 and 691b, Olmütz, June 17 and June 20, 1866, FZM Benedek to GdC Clam-Gallas.

8 Why was Benedek not more aggressive in his reconnaissance? Count Gustav Blome, Austrian minister in Munich, pointed out that "Austria having already been attacked in Holstein [on June 9] . . . it is a mere strategic question when the Austrian military commanders on the Prussian frontiers should respond." PRO, FO 9/174, no. 128, Munich, June 12, 1866, Howard to Clarendon.

9 KA, AFA 1866, Karton 2265, 6–605, Olmütz, June 18, 1866, Col. Tegetthoff.

10 KA, AFA 1866, Karton 2274, 13–74, Olmütz, December 1872, Maj. Ripp.

11 Grosser Generalstab, *Feldzug 1866*, pp. 94–6.

to good effect. Benedek, trusting that Clam-Gallas would hold the Iser line for several days, aimed to get there first. At Jicin, the Feldzeugmeister would fight in the Napoleonic style: first throwing his combined strength of 240,000 against the 140,000 bayonets of Friedrich Karl's Elbe and First Armies, then turning round to confront the 115,000 Prussians of Second Army. For his part, Moltke frankly welcomed such a prospect. He reasoned that any Austrian attack on his two western armies would merely open a path into Benedek's flank and rear for the Prussian Second Army beating down from the northeast. Indeed, before his troops even marched, General Albrecht von Blumenthal, staff chief of the Prussian Second Army, assured his princely commandant that there would be a great "pocket battle" in Bohemia: "If the Austrians accept battle [near Jicin], then, coming in, as we shall, from [Silesia], we shall strike them in flank and rear."[12]

BENEDEK'S FLANK MARCH TO JOSEPHSTADT

While Moltke plotted his *Kesselschlacht*, Benedek planned to thwart it by detaching two or three corps to slow the descent of Second Army from Silesia long enough for North Army to crush the two Prussian armies closing from the west. However, to reach the Iser and join forces with Clam-Gallas and the Saxons, North Army would have to make an extremely arduous flank march. Six Austrian infantry corps and four cavalry divisions – each trailed by 800 supply wagons – had to be moved from Olmütz to Josephstadt on two hardened roads and three dirt tracks.[13] Frequent traffic jams meant that Austria's march battalions were chronically short of hot food and intoxicating drink, the two things that made nineteenth-century soldiering tolerable. Already worn out by mobilization, North Army starved and stumbled most of the way to Bohemia, a wearisome march that depressed morale.[14] On June 23, a typical day, Archduke Leopold's entire VIII Corps – 25,000 hungry souls – went hungry because its supply train stuck in traffic early in the day and never succeeded in overtaking Leopold's famished brigades.[15] Heavy rains in the third week of June washed out three of North Army's five march routes, slowing the redeployment to a crawl.[16] While Moltke's armies hurried through the Bohemian mountain passes, Benedek's haggard brigades inched across the vast space between Olmütz and Josephstadt, some days covering less than twenty kilometers.

12 Blumenthal, pp. 30–1.
13 KA, MKSM 1866, Karton 342, 69–4/18, Olmütz, June 18, 1866, FZM Benedek.
14 KA, AFA 1866, Karton 2282, 13–6, "June 27, 1866, "Operations-Journal der Brigade Thom." Karton 2293, 13–49, Vienna, August 1866, FML Leopold. Karton 2266, 6–970, Josephstadt, June 27, 1866, FZM Benedek.
15 KA, AFA 1866, Karton 2266, 6-ad 923, Nedelist, July 2, 1866, FML Leopold.
16 KA, AFA 1866, Karton 2291, 13–76, Hermannstadt, January 29, 1867, Col. Fröhlich. Karton 2270, 8–121, Pressburg, August 17, 1866, FML Ramming to FM Albrecht.

The physical exertions of the flank march gutted a number of Austrian regiments, the great majority of which were recruited in the poorest, unhealthiest provinces of the Habsburg Monarchy. Throughout the march, alarming numbers of men simply dropped their rifles and rucksacks by the side of the road or fell back among the supply trains to ride atop the commissary wagons. On June 17, North Army's *first* march day, Prince Emerich Taxis, commandant of Benedek's 2nd Light Cavalry Division, reported that he had "already arrested a number of men from General Rothkirch's brigade [Hungarians mostly] for throwing away their rifles and backpacks."[17] Others dropped the heavy bundles of food they were supposed to carry with them to Josephstadt by the wayside. All of them shed their coats and tunics, and gradually assumed the appearance of scarecrows smeared with grime and sweat. An Austrian *Jäger* officer lamented the moral effect of the flank march: "The men looked bad: their grey coats draped over their shirts, tunics balled up inside their backpacks, their haversack and rifle slings crossed on their chest and flapping to either side. My men were fairly crushed under all these dangling appliances; they looked sloppy and were not comfortable."[18] On June 24, one of Ramming's staff officers recorded that "on this, the ninth march day, everyone is exhausted. All anyone talks about is the need for several rest days to restore the men and repair their shoes."[19] Cavalry squadrons – deployed in front of the march columns instead of in the usual position to the side – only added to the squalor. On and on the men trudged, 110 steps to the minute for thirteen restless days, through rolling clouds of dust and steaming clods of horse dung.

Moltke's march proceeded more easily, chiefly because he dispersed the Prussian army in three groups and descended on Bohemia from his railheads by five good march routes.[20] By June 19, Elbe Army was at Dresden; First Army had pushed south from Görlitz through southeastern Saxony to Zittau on the Bohemian frontier, and Second Army was preparing to march southwest from Neisse and Glatz. By June 21, most of the Prussian army was arrayed on the Bohemian border, from the Elbe east to the Oder.[21] An Austrian dragoon scouting around Trautenau in northeastern Bohemia informed headquarters that his "best spies [were] no longer returning from the other side."[22] On the march from Olmütz to

---

17 KA, AFA 1866, Karton 2266, 6–807, Böhmisch-Trübau, June 23, 1866, Col. Tegetthoff. Karton 2270, 12-r, Szenktgotárd, August 10, 1866, FML Thurn und Taxis to FM Albrecht.

18 FML K. von Went., "Erinnerungen eines österreichischen Kriegsmannes 1866," *ÖMZ* 3 (1899), pp. 263–4. Dr. Michaelis, "Die Conservation des Mannes" and "Der Soldat auf dem Marsche," *ÖMZ* 2 (1862), pp. 54–9, 113–15.

19 KA, AFA 1866, Karton 2291, 13–78, Prague, December 1866, Capt. Butterweck.

20 Martin Van Creveld, *Supplying War* (Cambridge University Press, 1977), pp. 81–2. Idem., *Command in War*, p. 105. Moltke described modern armies as "too big either to live or to advance" unless broken into several groups.

21 KA, AFA 1866, Karton 2265, 6–665, Prague, June 19, 1866, GdC Clam to FZM Benedek. Karton 2265, 6–673, Prague, June 19, 1866, Polizeidirektor to FZM Benedek.

22 KA, AFA 1866, Karton 2265, Trautenau, June 21, 1866, Capt. Windisch-Graetz to Col. Appel.

Josephstadt, an Austrian general worriedly noted that "the Prussians seem to be closing from all directions."[23]

FIRST BATTLES ON THE ISER, JUNE 26

Prussia's King Wilhelm I dispatched a formal declaration of war to Benedek's headquarters on June 21.[24] While Benedek weighed his response, Moltke seized the initiative. Prussia's unopposed conquest of Hanover and Saxony had put him in possession of a broad base of operations extending from western Germany to Russian Poland. To exploit this gift and win Crown Prince Friedrich Wilhelm's Second Army time and space to push through the "Three Gates of Bohemia" – the mountain passes at Trautenau, Eipel, and Nachod – Moltke ordered his Elbe and First Armies to drive into Bohemia on June 23, three days before Second Army's invasion from the east.[25]

Prussia's western armies invaded Bohemia on June 23 from opposite ends of Saxony, and closed slowly on the Iser river. Without clear instructions from Benedek, Clam-Gallas and Prince Albert of Saxony yielded the mountain passes into western Bohemia as well as the rich town of Reichenberg without a fight and prepared to fall back on Josephstadt to unite with Benedek and escape the two Prussian armies closing around them. As Iser Army plotted its withdrawal, a shocking telegram arrived from Benedek at 3:00 P.M. on June 26: "Hold the Iser line *at any price*."[26] This inexplicable order contradicted Iser Army's mission in the campaign: a fighting retreat to Königgrätz-Josephstadt to buy time for a grand counter attack by all of North Army. Benedek's choice of the words "at any price" hinted at panic in North Army headquarters and merely compounded the confusion in Clam's. General Leopold Edelsheim, commander of Clam's 1st Light Cavalry Division, believed that Iser Army's task was to delay the Prussian Elbe and First Armies long enough for Benedek to move against the Prussian Second Army at Trautenau, Eipel, and Nachod.[27] The Saxon crown prince, who had only just arrived in Münchengrätz after a week-long march from Dresden, believed – as did Clam's staff – that he was meant merely to slow the advance of the Prussian Elbe and First Armies to give North Army time to reassemble in the fields around Jicin.[28] In short, even as the Prussians invaded Bohemia, none of the Saxon and Austrian generals on the Iser had even an inkling of Benedek's plan for the campaign.

23 KA, Nachlässe, B/946 (Coudenhove), Müglitz, June 23, 1866.
24 KA, AFA 1866, Karton 2265, 6–751, Böhmisch-Trübau, June 22, 1866, GM Krismanic.
25 Grosser Generalstab, *Feldzug 1866*, pp. 95–7.
26 KA, AFA 1866, Karton 2277, 6-ad 383, Josephstadt, June 26, 1866 (3:00 A.M.), FZM Benedek to Crown Prince of Saxony.
27 KA, AFA 1866, Karton 2270, 8–12q, Vienna, August 14, 1866, FML Edelsheim.
28 KA, AFA 1866, Karton 2265, 6–734b, Böhmisch-Trübau, FZM Benedek. Karton 2280, 13–103, Lemberg, December 19, 1866, Col. Litzelhofen.

THE SKIRMISH AT HÜHNERWASSER, JUNE 26

In receipt of Benedek's orders to "hold the Iser line at any price," Clam-Gallas's second-in-command, General Leopold Gondrecourt, decided at 6:00 P.M. on June 26 to cross the Iser with two battalions to make contact with Elbe Army and hurl its outposts back from the Iser crossing at Münchengrätz. While Clam-Gallas and Prince Albert of Saxony prepared to defend the Iser crossings at Podol and Turnau against Friedrich Karl's First Army, Gondrecourt advanced to Hühnerwasser, a village ten kilometers west of Münchengrätz to beat back Elbe Army, which, by the twenty-sixth, had completed a gruelling ten-day march out of Saxony and closed to within a single march of the Iser River.[29]

Count Gondrecourt, whose duties included instructing the emperor's only son, Archduke Rudolf, in the French language, was a fearless man, who delighted in exposing himself to enemy fire. He had done it in Denmark in 1864, and he did it again at Hühnerwasser leading 1,500 men toward the village through thick woods that joined like a roof over the Münchengrätz post road. Hühnerwasser itself was deserted save for two battalions of Herwarth's 31st Brigade, most of them lazing indoors, enjoying beds for the first time since Dresden on the twentieth.

Gondrecourt's troops – Slovakian *Jäger* and a mixed battalion of Hungarian and Rumanian line infantry – stumbled upon a Prussian company posted among trees on the edge of Hühnerwasser. They exhanged shots, alarming the rest of Elbe Army's advanced guard, which formed in skirmish lines and pushed into the wood to repel the Austrian attack.[30] On the Münchengrätz road, Gondrecourt deployed his men in line, met the Prussian counter attack with three salvos, then plunged after them with the bayonet. By now, four Prussian companies had assembled, and they met the charging Austrians with a single aimed volley at 300 meters' range. When the smoke lifted, the Prussian infantry observed Gondrecourt's officers trying in vain to rally their shattered platoons. Dozens of Austrians had been cut down by the accurate Prussian fire, and Gondrecourt's hastily arranged shock columns refused to press on. A second Prussian salvo ripped through the trees and put them to flight. Gondrecourt summoned his reserve companies, but, faced with fresh Prussian platoons racing over from Hühnerwasser and the sight of so many fallen Austrians, he called off the attack and retraced his steps to Münchengrätz. Marveling at the needle rifle's impact, a Prussian witness recalled that "the wood and the road [at Hühnerwasser] were *plastered* with dead and wounded. There were Austrian bodies and backpacks as far as the eye could see. Trees had been stripped of bark by our fire and the cries of the wounded were heart-rending."[31] Whereas the Prussians lost just 4 officers and 46 men in the clash, Gondrecourt lost five times

29 KA, AFA 1866, Karton 2277, 6–392, June 26–7, 1866, GdC Clam-Gallas.
30 Grosser Generalstab, *Feldzug 1866*, pp. 104–8.
31 Hans Wachenhusen, *Tagebuch vom österreichischen Kriegsschauplatz* (Berlin: Lemke, 1806), pp. 46–7.

that number, 13 officers and 264 men, astonishing casualties for an "outpost skirmish," and the first intimation of how this Austro-Prussian War would unfold. One-fourth of Austrian casualties at Hühnerwasser were unwounded prisoners — men panicked by the scything effect of the needle rifle — and this after only two aimed volleys at 300 meters. The Prussians had not even found time to shift over to *Schnellfeuer*, the short-range phase of their fire tactic, when men were ordered to aim and fire as quickly as they could load.[32]

While Herwarth's vanguard sent Gondrecourt reeling back to the Iser, Prince Albert of Saxony and Count Clam-Gallas met in Münchengrätz at 7:00 P.M. to consider how best to implement Benedek's revised orders. A defense of the Iser line would now be difficult, for the key bridges at Podol and Turnau were already in Prussian hands.[33] Though aided by the slow descent of Prince Friedrich Karl's First Army from Lusatia to the Iser and by the time-consuming exertions required of Elbe Army to cross not only Saxony but the best part of Bohemia as well, Clam-Gallas and Prince Albert still had little time to shore up the Iser line, which they had so recently planned to abandon.[34]

THE BATTLE OF PODOL, JUNE 26

The Austrians were acquainted with Prussia's thirty-eight-year-old Prince Friedrich Karl. In the Danish War, the Hohenzollern prince had led so indifferently that the Austrians fervently *hoped* that he would be given an army in 1866. Though credited in 1864 with the flanking maneuver that had prised the Danes out of Schleswig without a fight, the idea had really been Moltke's, and Friedrich Karl had never proven himself adept at Prussia's new fire tactics. As the Prussian assault on the Danish trenches at Dybbøl had demonstrated, the prince preferred shock columns and the bayonet, a system at which the Austrians excelled. Strategically, he distrusted Moltke's plan to unite fast-moving, dispersed columns and, like Benedek, tended to hang back and mass his corps on a single road in the mistaken belief that they could thus be more swiftly concentrated for battle.[35] In the early stages of the Austro-Prussian War, Prince Friedrich Karl did nothing to improve his indifferent reputation; indeed, like Benedek, he allowed his army to be throttled almost immediately by logistics.

After invading Bohemia by three mountain tracks on June 23 and taking Reichenberg without resistance early on the twenty-fourth, Prince Friedrich Karl ignored Moltke's orders to hasten across the Iser to link up with Second Army

32 k.k. Generalstab, *Österreichs Kämpfe*, vol. 3, Beilage 3. Fontane, *Der deutsche Krieg*, vol. 1, pp. 125–30.

33 KA, AFA 1866, Karton 2277, 6–395, Jicin, June 29, 1866, GdC Clam to FZM Benedek. Karton 2266, Münchengrätz, June 27, 1866, GdC Clam to FZM Benedek.

34 Grosser Generalstab, *Feldzug 1866*, p. 103.

35 KA, MKSM-SR 1866, 22/5, Berlin, August 18, 1865, Col. Pelikan to Lt-Col. Beck. Van Creveld, *Command in War*, pp. 123–5. Craig, *Königgrätz*, pp. 50–1.

debouching from Silesia. Instead, like Falckenstein in Hanover, he made himself comfortable in Reichenberg – the fabulously rich center of Austria's textile industry – and began to repair his dire shortages of food, drink, and forage at the town's expense.[36] Farther west, General Herwarth von Bittenfeld, whose famished Elbe Army of 46,000 had invaded Bohemia on a single road without any supply trains at all, was doing much the same thing.[37] These requisitions were elaborate and time-consuming. Indeed, for forty-eight hours, it seemed as though Friedrich Karl's principal aim was not to converge on Jicin, where Moltke planned to unite the three Prussian armies, but merely to devour Reichenberg, where even First Army's lowliest privates could command a pound of freshly slaughtered beef, several loaves of bread, a liter of beer, and ten cheroots each day.[38] Finally, stirred into action by a disapproving telegram from Moltke – "only a vigorous advance of the First Army can disengage the Second" – the Prussian prince reluctantly quit Reichenberg on June 26 and descended to the Iser crossings at Turnau and Podol.[39] Leopold Edelsheim, the Austrian cavalry general assigned to obstruct his progress, marvelled that Friedrich Karl took "four whole days to march just forty-six kilometers," a pace that, even allowing for Edelsheim's intermittent dragonnades, was remarkably sluggish.[40]

Clam-Gallas and Prince Albert had studied their maps in the meantime and decided on a forward defense of the Iser line. Instead of waiting for the Elbe and First Armies to converge on Münchengrätz, Podol, and Turnau, they would cross to the right bank of the Iser and march twenty kilometers north from Münchengrätz to Sichrov, a strong position directly in the path of First Army.[41] Deployed at Sichrov, *between* Herwarth and Friedrich Karl, Iser Army would have been able to turn left or right to face either of the Prussian armies closing from north and west. By June 26, however, the proposed move was injudicious, for the plateau at Sichrov was no longer tenable. With First Army before them, Elbe Army on their flank, and the Iser behind them, the Austro-Saxons would have been easily encircled and annihilated.[42]

Fate – in the form of Friedrich Karl's slow-moving vanguard – intervened. Fattened on the meat and beer of Reichenberg, General Eduard Fransecki's 7th Division made the twenty-kilometer march south to the river crossing at Turnau in two stages on the twenty-fifth and twenty-sixth. General Heinrich Horn's 8th Division moved past Fransecki to take possession of the bridges at Podol, ten

---

36 Schloss Reichenberg was a Clam-Gallas estate. Friedrich Karl quartered 170 men and 235 horses there to Clam's chagrin. A. Jahnel, *Chronik der preussischen Invasion des nördlichen Böhmens im Jahre 1866* (Reichenberg: Selbstverlag, 1867), p. 34.

37 Wachenhusen, pp. 28, 38, 43.

38 Jahnel, pp. 23–5.

39 Moltke, *Strategy*, pp. 48–50.

40 KA, AFA 1866, Karton 2270, 8–12q, Vienna, August 14, 1866, FML Edelsheim.

41 KA, AFA 1866, Karton 2280, 13–117, Schloss Friedland, October 1866, GdC Clam-Gallas.

42 George Glünicke, *The Campaign in Bohemia 1866* (London: Swan Sonnenschein, 1907), p. 80.

11.　General Eduard Clam-Gallas (1805–91), commandant of the Austrian I Corps until Königgrätz. The Prussian staff said of him: "He dines better than he fights."

kilometers further south. The unexpected arrival of Prussian battalions south of Sichrov, at the very Iser crossings Clam and Albert had planned to use the next morning, scotched Albert's plan for a redeployment to the west bank.

He and Clam met again and resolved to secure Podol that very night to shore up the Iser line and gain the Sichrov position before Horn's reinforcements could arrive from Reichenberg on the twenty-seventh. Podol, eight kilometers northwest of Münchengrätz, was the most important Iser crossing, for it was there that both the Reichenberg railway and post road crossed to the east bank of the river on two sturdy bridges. The Prussians needed these bridges to shift First Army's guns, ammunition, and baggage across the river obstacle, and Clam-Gallas, who assumed that Benedek would use the Podol crossings for North Army's pending counteroffensive, dared not destroy them. After deciding to defend Podol, Clam concluded the council of war in Münchengrätz and rode upriver to lead Ferdinand Poschacher's "Iron Brigade" – it had earned the sobriquet in Denmark – against Horn's advanced parties arriving from the north.

Clam entered Podol as night fell, at 9:30 P.M., in the midst of a hot fight. Ninety minutes earlier, Poschacher's brigade, barricaded inside the village, had greeted Prussian skirmishers arriving from the north with a gust of volley fire. The Prussians reinforced themselves with three battalions of line infantry, then came on. A vicious street-fight ensued at close-range, as both sides struggled for control of Podol and its vital bridges. Austrian troops shut in the houses fired into the flanks of the onrushing Prussians, who made short work of Austrian infantrymen deployed in the village lanes. Loading with their ramrods or jabbing with their bayonets, Austrians in the open made easy marks for Prussian riflemen, who, at close quarters, could load and fire their breech-loaders rapidly from the hip. The Prussians pushed deeper into Podol, clearing the houses as they proceeded. The fight climaxed at a pile of chopped-down willow trees, where, as a British journalist observed, "the Prussians pressed up to the barricade, the Austrians stoutly stood their ground behind it, and, three paces distant, assailants and defenders poured their fire into each other's breasts."[43]

While the Prussians in Podol pushed the battle down to the Iser's edge, 400 of their comrades crossed the river downstream on the railroad bridge and attempted the war's first tactical envelopment. But while doubling back to strike Poschacher's flank and rear, they happened upon the brigadier's two reserve battalions, which were sheltered in a stone house between the two bridges. The gory episode that followed testified again to the terrific impact of the Prussian needle rifle and the futility of Austrian shock tactics. General Clam-Gallas, just arrived from Münchengrätz, shook Poschacher's reserve battalions from their cover and hurled them in storm columns at the Prussian rifle companies, which halted, deployed in line, and opened fire. Even in darkness, the Prussian riflemen could not fail to hit the massed Austrian battalions, which slewed around and disintegrated. While Clam-Gallas looked on from the safety of the stone house, scores of his men fell dead and wounded, and hundreds more took to their heels in panicky flight. After repulsing three consecutive frontal attacks, the Prussian companies drew back across the Iser; their ammunition was low and their rifles had become too hot to handle. Here was another sad portent

43 Hozier, *The Seven Weeks' War*, vol. 1, p. 222.

of things to come. In this single action, 400 Prussians had beaten 2,000 Austrians handily.[44]

Across the river in Podol, a Prussian charge up the darkened streets shook the last Austrians from cover and drove them over the Iser. Clam-Gallas, who had wasted Poschacher's reserves in the meantime, admitted defeat at 2:00 A.M. and returned glumly to Münchengrätz, leaving heaps of dead and wounded behind. Prussian casaulties were barely 100. Clam's losses were ten times that: in all, 1,048, 600 of them unwounded prisoners from the mixed Polish and Ukrainian 30th Regiment, which had been routed in the street-fighting.[45] Afterward, some of these prisoners explained to Prussian interrogators that when ordered by their officers to charge the Prussians with the bayonet, they had flatly refused, preferring confinement to the certainty of death or injury. When one of Clam's brigadiers accused these men of cowardice, Clam's staff chief retorted with a marvelous synopsis of the problems that bedeviled Austria's multilingual army: "The regiment fought bravely until nightfall, when the officers could no longer pantomime examples [of what was needed]. As casualties mounted and the Iser valley was obscured by powder smoke and darkness, officers lost sight of their men, who shrank from the fire and sought cover."[46]

Prussian fire tactics had beaten shock twice, once in the woods outside Hühnerwasser, a second time in the night at Podol, where, an Austrian officer later wrote, "although numerically superior and shielded [from the worst effects of the needle rifle] by darkness," the Austrians had still managed to lose the engagement.[47] Austrian infantry, who were provided in peacetime with just one-fifth the practice shots allotted Prussian conscripts, had plainly not improved their notoriously poor marksmanship in the years since 1859. And faced with the choice of death or desertion, hundreds had chosen the latter course, an ominous development. "There is something amiss [etwas faul] in this army," a Prussian officer had observed at Hühnerwasser after chancing upon three Venetian infantrymen sitting out the firefight in the tall corn around the village. At the sight of the Prussian, they had dropped their rifles, covered his hand in kisses, and begged for mercy.[48]

At Podol, the Prussian First Army breached Clam-Gallas's Iser line and captured intact two bridges and the shortest march route to the strategic junction of Jicin, where the best roads in northern Bohemia converged. A few kilometers upstream from Podol, at Turnau, General Fransecki's division seized a third bridge early on the twenty-seventh without resistance. Farther south, Herwarth von Bittenfeld's Elbe Army neared the bridge at Münchengrätz, which, though momentarily defended by the entire Iser Army, had been outflanked by Prince Friedrich Karl's

44　Fontane, Der deutsche Krieg, vol. 1, pp. 156–62.
45　k.k. Generalstab, Österreichs Kämpfe, vol. 3, Beilage 3, p. 12.
46　KA, AFA 1866, Karton 2280, 13–103, Lemberg, December 19, 1866, Col. Litzelhofen.
47　Bartels, Der Krieg im Jahre 1866, pp. 18–19.
48　Wachenhusen, pp. 45, 49. Delbrück, vol. 5, pp. 461–3.

crossing at Podol and would shortly have to be abandoned. Indeed, on his return to Münchengrätz early on the twenty-seventh, Clam-Gallas canceled the move to Sichrov and ordered the bridge at Münchengrätz destroyed.[49] With the principal Iser crossings in hand and Clam and the Saxons in retreat, Moltke's western armies were now effectively united and within a single march of Jicin, where Great Headquarters in Berlin planned to unite the three Prussian armies.[50]

THE BATTLES ON BENEDEK'S FLANK, JUNE 27

By June 26, Benedek's North Army, buoyed by the news of Custoza, had nearly made Josephstadt. There Benedek received a cable from Count Richard Belcredi, Austria's minister of state, informing him that mere rumors of an Austrian victory in Bohemia had provoked wild applause in the French parliament and calls to illuminate Paris. France, belatedly appreciating the threat to its existence posed by Prussia, was coming round to Austria's side in the German war no less amicably than in the Italian one.[51] However, aside from these good political tidings, there was little cause for celebration in the Feldzeugmeister's suite. North Army's flank march – seized from within by its own unruly supply train, described by one staff officer as "the single greatest calamity" to befall the Austrians in the entire war – was faltering.[52] Peasant refugees, streaming out of the Giant Mountains in advance of the Prussian Second Army, crowded on to Benedek's march roads. Austrian officers cursed their outdated maps at every turning.[53] The single corps Benedek had pushed ahead to the Jicin region, where the Feldzeugmeister planned to strike at Prince Friedrich Karl, reported that there was not enough food and fodder there to sustain even a single corps of 30,000, let alone eight of them.[54] While Benedek worriedly drove his men on to an uncertain fate, the Prussian Second Army stole toward his flank through the ravines of Trautenau, Eipel, and Nachod.[55]

Crown Prince Friedrich Wilhelm's four corps had assembled before the Silesian passes on June 25 and begun climbing into Austria in three groups on the twenty-sixth. Each column was divided from its supports by thirty or forty kilometers of rock and forest as it passed through the mountains, a circumstance that posed potentially catastrophic tactical problems, not least because the Prussian king had conferred command of this dangerous passage on his son, thirty-five-year-old

49 KA, AFA 1866, Karton 2266, 6–977c and 980, Münchengrätz, June 27, 1866, Prince Albert to FZM Benedek.

50 Grosser Generalstab, *Feldzug 1866*, pp. 109–16.

51 KA, AFA 1866, Karton 2272, 13–13, 158, Paris, June 24, 1866, Belcredi to FZM Benedek.

52 KA, AFA 1866, Karton 2291, 13–77, Lemberg, December 15, 1866, Maj. Schmedes.

53 KA, AFA 1866, Karton 2285, 13–7c, Brünn, December 16, 1866, Capt. Riedl (III Corps): "During the march from Brünn to Miletin [June 19–27], I often discovered that good driving roads indicated on even the newest maps were really nothing more than dirt tracks."

54 KA, AFA 1866, Karton 2266, 6–943, Miletin, June 26, 1866, FML Ernst to FZM Benedek.

55 KA, AFA 1866, Karton 2266, 6–807, Böhmisch-Trübau, June 23, 1866, Col. Tegetthoff.

Crown Prince Friedrich Wilhelm. Renowned far more for his university studies and liberal politics than for his military prowess, Crown Prince Friedrich Wilhelm had not even been offered a command in the Danish War two years earlier.[56] His reputation was so lackluster that, in mid-June, an Austrian spy reported that Bismarck was insisting that "the inept crown prince be assigned a deputy general with strict instructions not to permit his highness to operate independently."[57]

Friedrich Wilhelm's corps generals inspired still less confidence. Two of them – Louis Mutius and Karl Steinmetz – were septuagenarian veterans of the Wars of Liberation in 1813–14. A third, Adolf Bonin, born in 1803, could not even boast of experience in the Napoleonic Wars, nor could the fourth, fifty-three-year-old Prince August of Württemberg, commandant of the Prussian Guard Corps.[58] In short, Second Army's generals were unimposing, and they ought to have been easily beaten as they struggled, widely separated, through the Giant Mountains on June 26. Each Prussian corps extended fifty kilometers head to tail as it snaked into Bohemia. If Benedek had only thought to attack the heads of the Prussian march columns as they debouched on open ground in Bohemia, the rearmost Prussian units would have needed more than four hours to reinforce the front.[59]

As it chanced, the crown prince's army need not have worried. Determined to make Josephstadt with all possible speed, Benedek left only weak detachments to oppose the Prussian Second Army and thus set his own eventual envelopment in train. Though Benedek had known of Friedrich Wilhelm's advance since the twenty-second, he nevertheless seemed startled by the apparition of four Prussian corps on his right flank.[60] "Headquarters moved to Josephstadt on the 26th," Benedek's adjutant noted after the war. "At the time, it was obvious that the army commandant still had no definite plan and was merely reacting to events."[61] Neither of Benedek's staff chiefs proved much help. Henikstein, who had spent the first week of the flank march battling with Vienna to have a bumptious Polish aristocrat removed from his suite, made no arrangements to stave off the crown prince's immensely threatening *Flügelarmee*.[62] For his part, Operations Chief Krismanic, an old-fashioned tactician, refused even to consider a right turn into the wooded hills of northeastern Bohemia. He preferred the flat country around Jicin and thus drove North Army ahead to the Iser, looking neither left nor right.[63]

56 Fontane, *Der deutsche Krieg*, vol. 1, pp. 257–8.

57 KA, AFA 1866, Karton 2265, 6–523p, Prossnitz, June 15, 1866, Vertrauensmann to Nord-Armee Kommando. PRO, FO 68/144, no. 26, Leipzig, June 5, 1866, Crowe to Clarendon.

58 KA, Nachlässe, B/572: 1 (Nosinic), Verona, March 20, 1866, GM Schönfeld, "Zur Charakteristik der k. preussischen Armee."

59 Blumenthal, p. 37. Hozier, vol. 1, p. 277.

60 KA, AFA 1866, Karton 2266, 6–806, Böhmisch-Trübau, June 23, 1866, Col. Tegetthoff. 6–907, Trautenau, June 25, 1866, Botenjäger Schmidt to FZM Benedek.

61 KA, AFA 1866, Karton 2270, 8–12aa, Budapest, August 12, 1866, GM Kriz.

62 KA, AFA 1866, Karton 2266, 6–836, Böhmisch-Trübau, June 23, 1866, FML Henikstein.

63 KA, Nachlässe, B/572:2 (Nosinic), Timisoara, December 27, 1866, Capt. Woinowitz.

Still, something had to be done lest Friedrich Wilhelm's army of 115,000 descend on North Army's exposed flank and rear. After conferring with Krismanic, Benedek decided to detach two corps northward to shield his right. He sent General Ludwig Gablenz's X Corps to block the passes at Trautenau and Eipel, and General Wilhelm Ramming's VI Corps to stand in the pass at Nachod. Needless to say, had Benedek been plotting an elaborate revenge upon Gablenz and Ramming – his principal rivals in the Habsburg army – he could scarcely have done better than this. By June 27, the northeastern corner of Bohemia was a lost post for two unconnected corps with unguarded flanks operating against twice their number. Indeed, at a meeting with Benedek on the twenty-sixth, Gablenz had requested reinforcements so that, as he prophetically put it, "X Corps would not have to abandon [Trautenau] after taking it in battle." Benedek, determined to seek battle at Jicin, had refused Gablenz the men.[64]

On June 27, X Corps moved wearily up to Trautenau. Gablenz' men had been afoot for nine consecutive days, walking the 215 kilometers from Olmütz in torrid heat on crumbly sidetracks with little food. After resting on the twenty-sixth near Josephstadt, X Corps was rousted from its bivouacs at 8:00 A.M. on the twenty-seventh to march thirty more kilometers, this time north to Trautenau. To make a march of this length and fight in a single day was a tall order, a fact not lost on Gablenz, who later raged to Archduke Albrecht about the hard, debilitating marches ordained by Benedek's increasingly remote headquarters.[65] Gablenz himself, a hero of the Danish War, came in for criticism from one of his brigadiers – Georg Grivicic – who complained that X Corps's brigades marched for Trautenau without instructions and without any idea what Benedek, Gablenz, or the Prussians had in store for them.[66]

On the road to Trautenau, Gablenz received a written order from Benedek: "Attack the enemy with utmost energy wherever he shows himself." It was a curious order, and a source of considerable controversy after the war in view of Benedek's refusal to strengthen Gablenz's corps the previous afternoon.[67] Gablenz's Mondel Brigade, which had preceded the others to Trautenau during the night of the twenty-sixth, made the heights south of Trautenau at 7:45 A.M., where Colonel Mondel beheld the lead battalions of Adolf Bonin's Prussian I Corps entering the market town. Back in Josephstadt, his comrades were only beginning the seven-hour march north. It promised to be a hot morning for

---

64 "There is nothing connecting me [with the main army] on the left," Gablenz testily reminded Benedek as he marched to Trautenau, the Prussian I Corps before him, the Guards on his flank. KA, AFA 1866, Karton 2266, 6–946, Jaromir, June 26, 1866, FML Gablenz to FZM Benedek.

65 KA, AFA 1866, Karton 2270, 8–12p, Floridsdorf, August 16, 1866, FML Gablenz.

66 KA, AFA 1866, Karton 2296, 13–9, Vienna, December 18, 1866, Col. Grivicic.

67 At his court of inquiry after the war, Benedek maintained that he had never issued the order in spite of the fact that the order itself survived as evidence, in Benedek's handwriting. KA, AFA 1866, Karton 2294, 6–105a, Floridsdorf, July 14, 1866, FML Gablenz.

Friedrich Mondel's brigade, alone against the entire right wing of the Prussian Second Army.[68]

Twenty kilometers to the east, General Ramming's VI Corps was hurrying up to Nachod to block the passage of Friedrich Wilhelm's left wing into Bohemia, or trying to hurry. Ramming's two lead brigades left Opocno at 6:00 A.M. and collided twice on the road north to Nachod. Each time they had to be halted and separated one sullen and uncooperative battalion at a time. The men had been marching for ten days without a rest and had lost sleep the night before when, at 1:30 A.M., Benedek's changed orders for an urgent movement north had arrived in Ramming's headquarters after an unconscionable five-and-a-half hour delay.[69] Ramming's staff had been flabbergasted: "From the beginning to the end of the flank march we were told nothing about the Prussian [Second Army]," one of Ramming's aides recalled. "Even when our orders referred to the enemy's presence near Nachod, they never described his strength, so we had no idea where the crown prince was concentrated."[70]

Early on the twenty-seventh, there was no time to investigate this important question. Instead Ramming had to flog his men blindly into the breach. He dispatched some of his units at 3:30 A.M., the rest at 5:00, just as they were lighting their cook fires. Sixth Corps weaved groggily on to the road for a twenty-kilometer march to Nachod without breakfast.[71] Ramming placed his Venetian regiments under surveillance at the rear of the queue. Several days earlier they had scandalized North Army by pausing beside a flooded ditch to empty their cartridge pouches into the water and thus show solidarity with the Kingdom of Italy's Prussian ally.[72]

Meanwhile, in Nachod pass, old General Steinmetz and the Prussian crown prince found themselves trapped between V Corps' caissons, guns, and wagon trains in a narrow, sinuous gorge. They listened helplessly to the sounds of a battle developing ahead as Steinmetz's vanguard emerged in the town of Nachod and came under fire from an Austrian horse battery deployed on the Vysokov plateau, a broad, flat-topped table that blocked the way west.[73] With most of

68 KA, AFA 1866, Karton 2294, 6-ad 108, Hohenmauth, July 4, 1866, Col. Mondel.

69 KA, AFA 1866, Karton 2266, 6–950, Josephstadt, June 26, 1866, FZM Benedek to FML Ramming. The orders, drafted in Josephstadt at 8:00 P.M. on the twenty-sixth and marked "sehr dringend und zuerst expediren" were not delivered to Opocno, only fifteen kilometers away and connected to Josephstadt by telegraph, until 1:30 A.M. on the twenty-seventh, by a dispatch rider: "A clear proof," a British officer concluded drily, "that the proceedings of the Austrian Staff were not very business-like." Glünicke, p. 90. Benold, "Österreichische Feldtelegraphie," p. 34.

70 KA, AFA 1866, Karton 2291, 13–79, Prague, December 1866, Capt. Stanger.

71 KA, AFA 1866, Karton 2291, 13–78, Prague, December 1866, Capt. Butterweck.

72 They were Venetians of the 79th Regiment recruited in Pordenone. The governor of Moravia investigated the incident and reported: "On the 20th, the men of the 79th Regiment threw their cartridges into puddles at Thanowitz declaring that they would not fight the Prussians." KA, AFA 1866, Karton 2266, 6–820a, Brünn, Landes-General-Commando to FZM Benedek.

73 Hozier, vol. 1, p. 278–9.

their division strung out for fifteen kilometers behind them, Steinmetz's lead companies repelled a charge by an Austrian cuirass regiment and then took cover from shells raining down from Vysokov.

As more Prussian infantry squeezed through Nachod, three battalions mounted the Vysokov plateau to clear a way out of the mountains for the rest of V Corps. Incredibly, there was still no Austrian infantry on the high ground. Recalling the five-hour delay in the delivery of Benedek's orders for Ramming on the twenty-seventh, a VI Corps staff captain vented his frustration: "If the orders . . . had arrived only *two* hours earlier, we could have occupied Vysokov *before* the enemy and the battle would have turned to *our* advantage."[74] It was not to be. Three Prussian battalions took the heights without resistance and watched as, too late, Ramming's tired brigades moved through the plain of Skalice and toward the plateau.[75]

THE BATTLE OF VYSOKOV, JUNE 27

Ramming's Hertwek Brigade was first on the scene, arriving obliquely from the south at 9:00 A.M. after a six-hour march. Ramming, who had galloped ahead and was fretfully waiting in the Skalice railway station for the arrival of his brigades and guns, watched dismayed as Hertwek turned right to face east and, after a brief cannonade, sent his 41st Regiment – Ukrainians mostly – up the gently-rising southwestern face of the plateau. Ramming had not planned to attack the height at all after studying Steinmetz's vanguard, which had deployed on the plateau in good positions.[76] The Prussians had made their center in Vaclavice (Wenzelsberg), a walled churchyard, and concealed their left and right wings in woods to either side. A half dozen companies of infantry waited in reserve in the village of Vysokov behind the right wing.[77]

Against several thousand needle rifles trained southwest and five field guns spewing shrapnel and canister, Hertwek's first wave, laboring through high grass and brambles in four battalion masses, did not stand a chance. Ripped by Prussian *Schnellfeuer*, the men retired at the run through the files of Hertwek's second regiment, Poles, who quickly subsided in the tall grass as the Prussian fusilade intensified. Their *Jäger* escorts fared better, swarming round Vaclavice in open order and flushing the Prussian defenders from the churchyard. With his 25th *Jäger* lodged in the Prussian center and Hertwek's Poles under cover, Ramming at least had a foothold on the plateau.

Still, he had no intention of wasting more troops storming Vysokov. He preferred to deploy behind the railway embankment and on the heights around Skalice to await Steinmetz's descent from the plateau. The problem, however, was

74 KA, AFA 1866, Karton 2291, 13–79, Prague, December 1866, Capt. Stanger.
75 Grosser Generalstab, *Feldzug 1866*, pp. 130–2. Craig, *Königgrätz*, pp. 59–60.
76 KA, AFA 1866, Karton 2291, 13–103, Sopron, December 16, 1866, Capt. Handel-Mazzetti.
77 Fontane, *Der deutsche Krieg*, vol. 1, pp. 298–301.

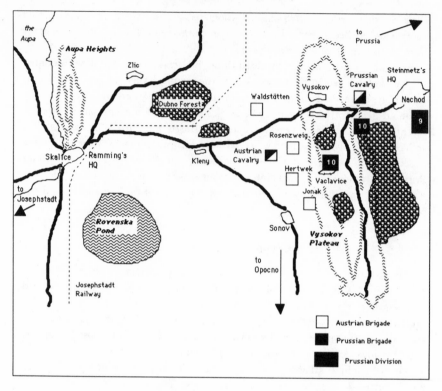

The Battle of Vysokov, June 27, 1866

that as Ramming's brigades shuffled up from the south, they were turning off the road at Sonov, five kilometers short of Ramming's post at Skalice, and attacking directly up the plateau. Thus, at 10:45 A.M., Johann Jonak's brigade, like Hertwek's before it, began to ascend into a withering fire without orders from Ramming, who, again, watched helplessly from Skalice as Jonak moved to support the Austrian *Jäger* at Vaclavice and renew the attack on the Prussian center, while Hertwek — still without orders — emerged from cover to attack the Prussian left.

A sixth Prussian battalion had come up from Nachod in the meantime to enfilade Jonak. Halfway up the Vysokov heights, Jonak stumbled over the demoralized remnants of Hertwek's brigade cowering in a streambed. "I ordered them to join us," one of Jonak's officers recalled, "and they complied, but grudgingly." While Jonak paused to embody Hertwek's stragglers, his own two regiments crossed paths. He ordered them forward but his Hungarians steadfastly refused to advance till their files had been cleansed of Poles.[78] Finally, the brigade made

78 KA, AFA 1866, Karton 2278, 13–78, Prague, December 1866, Capt. Butterweck.

12. The Austrian attack on Vysokov, June 27, 1866

Vaclavice and, ripped by errant fire from its own batteries, passed into the woods on the crest of the plateau as Hertwek's intact battalions attacked on its right. Jonak's Hungarians had already lost half their strength, two-thirds of their officers, and their regimental colonel, Count Alfons Wimpffen, who had been shot down at the head of a storm column.[79]

A ninety-minute brawl ensued in the woods, much of it hand-to-hand. One of Jonak's officers shuddered at the memory: "In the woods atop [Vysokov] our battalions were all mixed up and could not be sorted out. So many Austrian officers had been killed or wounded that there was no effective supervision. Our men fired at anything that moved and many simply ran away."[80] A disciplined Prussian push drove Hertwek's rabble from the woods and back down to Sonov at the southwestern foot of the plateau. Hertwek's *Jäger* panicked, lost their way, and ran toward Jonak's position, prompting an entire battalion of Hungarians to step out of the woods in company columns to cover their flight. It was a brave but suicidal impulse. "Who ordered an advance?" an Austrian officer screamed as his cursing NCOs attempted to drive their bewildered men back under cover while the Prussian rifle companies above aimed and fired as fast as they could load, dropping whole files of Magyar infantry. Here was yet another tragic example of Austrian tactics breaking down for want of a universally comprehensible language of command.[81]

"From Skalice," Ramming wrote, " I could see columns of Prussian troops arriving in Vysokov from Nachod. My principal concern at this moment [11:30 A.M.] was to take the Vysokov plateau to prevent the enemy from pushing down to Skalice from Nachod, isolating Jonak and Hertwek on the heights." With half his corps accidentally committed, Ramming felt he had little choice but to commit the rest.[82] For his part, Steinmetz, now atop the plateau, called angrily for his guns, which were wending their way slowly up the cluttered road from Nachod.[83] While Steinmetz fretted, Ramming launched his Rosenzweig Brigade at the Prussian right, the village of Vysokov. This attack, timed to coincide with a third push on the Prussian left and center by Hertwek, Jonak, and the five squadrons of heavy cavalry Ramming had with him, carried the lower reaches of the plateau.[84] The Prussian battalions pulled back into Vysokov village and hid themselves on the wooded rim of the plateau, where the road up from Nachod opened a broad trench.

Rosenzweig's 4th Regiment – the *Hoch-und-Deutschmeister,* men recruited in

79 KA, AFA 1866, Karton 2266, 6–975uu, Cracow, February 5, 1867, Col. Peinlich.

80 KA, AFA 1866, Karton 2278, 13–78, Prague, December 1866, Capt. Butterweck.

81 "I must attempt to explain how this dreadful catastrophe could have happened," one of Jonak's platoon leaders wrote from his hospital bed two days later. "All I said was ' . . . Prepare to receive the skirmishers' [einige Abteilungen der kette aufzunehmen]." KA, AFA 1866, Karton 2288, 6–228a, Nachod, June 29, 1866, Lieutenant Weber.

82 KA, AFA 1866, Karton 2288, 6–221, July 20, 1866, FML Ramming. Karton 2291, 13–79, Prague, December 1866, Capt. Stanger.

83 Grosser Generalstab, *Feldzug 1866*, p. 134.

84 KA, AFA 1866, Karton 2266, 6–975kk, Nagy-Källo, December 19, 1867, Col. Coburg.

the slums and vineyards of Vienna – tumbled into Vaclavice with heavy losses, joining the three Austrian brigades on the plateau wing-to-wing. At this point – 12 noon – the Austrians had to rest; they were thoroughly blown by their six-hour march from Opocno and four hours of battle under a hot sun. It was, as Ramming later admitted, an ill-advised halt, but the men simply could not go on. They had not eaten since the afternoon of the previous day.[85] Ramming ordered his fourth and last brigade, Georg Waldstätten's, to move up from Skalice to Kleny to cover the flank and rear of the three Austrian brigades catching their breath on the plateau. Sixth Corps, its reserve committed, was now in great danger as Prussian reinforcements continued to push up from Nachod.

Rather than relinquish ground gained at great cost on the Vysokov heights, Ramming decided to escape *forward*. At 1:00 P.M., he ordered Waldstätten, whose Poles and Venetians had just taken heavy casualties dislodging a Prussian flanking column from the woods around Kleny, to storm up on Rosenzweig's left, take the village of Vysokov, turn Steinmetz's right flank, and force the Prussians back down to Nachod. It was a difficult mission for two weary line regiments, one of which – the 79th from Pordenone – had mutinied only a few days earlier. Still, the men ascended bravely to Vysokov in three dense columns.

Steinmetz's artillery advantage at this stage of the battle was decisive, for Ramming's reserve guns, stuck in traffic on the road from Opocno, had still not arrived. Thus, forty-two Prussian guns ranged themselves against Ramming's twenty-four, bringing Waldstätten's brigade under heavy, unanswerable fire. And even as Waldstätten advanced on the left to exploit the gains made by the *Deutschmeister* in the center, an entire Prussian division was deploying on the plateau above him. While a fresh Prussian regiment overran the exhausted *Deutschmeister* battalion holding Vaclavice, another dashed over to Vysokov to hit Waldstätten's storm columns in the flank.[86] Two Austrian columns were flattened by rapid-fire. The third – three companies of German and Czech *Jäger* and a battalion of Venetians – made Vysokov, blazed away for a few, harrowing minutes – killing two Prussian brigadier generals – and then fell back, chased by virtually every Prussian on the plateau. "We ordered our three other brigades to disengage Waldstätten," one of Ramming's aides recorded, "but they would not storm again. They were spent, and they gave up . . . allowing the Prussians to throw everything they had at Waldstätten."[87] Four Austrian brigades had been sucked piecemeal into the Prussian mincing machine, at a cost of 5,719 men, five times Steinmetz's casualties of 1,122.[88] At 2:00 P.M., his reserves expended, Ramming ordered his men back to Skalice, where they took up defensive positions behind the railway embankment. Steinmetz, engaged in bringing the rest of

---

85 Nor would they eat that night. Dinner for VI Corps would not arrive from Josephstadt until 7:00 A.M. on the twenty-eighth. KA, AFA 1866, Karton 2291, 13–103, Sopron, December 16, 1866, Capt. Handel-Mazzetti.

86 Grosser Generalstab, *Feldzug 1866*, pp. 138–40.

87 KA, AFA 1866, Karton 2291, 13–79, Prague, December 1866, Capt. Stanger.

88 Craig, *Königgrätz*, p. 61.

his corps up from Nachod to Vysokov, elected not to pursue, probably wisely, for by now Ramming's reserve batteries had arrived, and the Austrians had eighty rifled guns trained on the slope down from Vysokov.[89]

Ramming sat astride his horse on the crossroads at Kleny and put on a brave face as the *Deutschmeister* filed sadly past him. "Eighth Corps is coming!" he called cheerily. But inwardly he was anything but cheery: "We cannot resist another attack," he warned Benedek. "We must be relieved immediately."[90] Although Benedek had already sent Archduke Leopold's VIII Corps to relieve Ramming, it too was poorly supplied and worn out by marching.[91] Later Ramming would rationalize his defeat at Vysokov thus: "The result was satisfactory. Still in possession of Skalice, I was able to cover North Army's concentration at Josephstadt."[92] Yet this minimal result came at the cost of 232 officer casualties and 5,487 men, so many dead, wounded, and missing that Benedek would have to detach two entire fortress battalions from his Josephstadt garrison to replenish VI Corps.[93] Krismanic, who shared Benedek's dislike of Ramming, lamented the general's "brainless dispositions" and crippling losses.[94]

Yet Krismanic himself bore a large measure of responsibility for the débacle. He and Benedek had ordered Ramming up to Vysokov too late, imposing a wearisome forced march on the men of VI Corps and ceding the commanding heights to Steinmetz. This made for a battle under the worst possible conditions and led to the otherwise inexplicable result that, by mid-morning, twenty-one Austrian battalions had been beaten and nearly disbanded by half their number.[95] As an Austrian witness angrily noted: "Our men were sent through tall grass over broken ground after a six hour march under a burning sun. They were pushed to their limits before the battle even *began*."[96]

Tactics saw to the rest. Ramming, respectfully described by the Prussian General Staff before the war as a "military genius," operated shrewdly enough once he gained control of his brigadiers after 11:00 A.M., yet each of his operative strokes was defeated by the Austrian line's clumsy tactics, which made no headway against Prussian rapid-fire. As Field Marshal Schlieffen observed in later years, Vysokov "was a battle of open order against closed, of lines against columns, of rested men against exhausted ones, of breech-loaders against muzzle-

89 Grosser Generalstab, *Feldzug 1866*, pp. 139–44. Glünicke, p. 93. Fontane, *Der deutsche Krieg*, vol. 1, pp. 305–15.

90 KA, AFA 1866, Karton 2266, 6–975, Skalice, June 27, 1866 (5:45 P.M.), FML Ramming to FZM Benedek. Karton 2288, 6–228, Vienna, n.d., "Anteil des Infanterie-Regiments Hoch-und-Deutschmeister Nr. 4 am Treffen von Wisokow."

91 After an eleven-hour march on the twenty-seventh, Leopold's VIII Corps would rise at 3:00 A.M. on the 28th to march north from Dolan to relieve Ramming. KA, AFA 1866, Karton 2288, 6–167, Zaslavek, June 27, 1866 (9:00 P.M.), FML Leopold to FML Ramming.

92 KA, AFA 1866, Karton 2288, 6–221, July 20, 1866, FML Ramming.

93 KA, AFA 1866, Karton 2288, 6–174, Josephstadt, June 28, 1866, FZM Benedek.

94 KA, Nachlässe, B/572: 2 (Nosinic), Wr. Neustadt, January 2, 1869, GM Krismanic.

95 Delbrück, vol. 5, p. 492. Grosser Generalstab, *Feldzug 1866*, p. 138.

96 KA, AFA 1866, Karton 2266, 6–975nn, Cracow, February 5, 1867, Col. Peinlich.

loaders, of marksmen against targets."[97] The outcome was never in doubt. Austrian tactics that had worked in similiar terrain at Custoza against skittish Italian troops armed with muzzle-loaders clearly did *not* work against steady Prussians armed with breech-loaders.

Strategically, the consequences of Vysokov were far reaching. Benedek lost a powerful position that, if carried and linked to Gablenz's corps at Trautenau by the nearby brigades of II and IV Corps – both within a march of Skalice – would have put at least one Austrian corps on either flank of the two Prussian Guard divisions pushing up the central Eipel pass. But this thrilling scenario was not to be. Instead, Gablenz was left "in the air" at Trautenau, while Steinmetz and the Prussian crown prince were free to push down from Nachod to Josephstadt, transforming Benedek's relatively orderly flank march into a rout.

THE BATTLE OF TRAUTENAU, JUNE 27

With Ramming beaten, Nachod pass open, and Steinmetz's V Corps arrayed on the Vysokov plateau, the Prussian Guard Corps continued to struggle through the central Eipel defile ten kilometers west of Nachod, thankful that Benedek had chosen not to oppose *them*. Ten kilometers further west, at Trautenau, Adolf Bonin's Prussian I Corps was also finding the going difficult. Indeed, the battle at Vysokov was nearly over before Bonin's vanguard emerged from the mountains and entered Trautenau at 10:00 A.M. on June 27. Spent by an eight-hour march over rough ground, Bonin's advanced parties gave Trautenau a perfunctory once-over and merely noted the existence of three great heights, which ramped steeply up from the town's edge, blocking the view south to Josephstadt.[98]

Gablenz's Mondel Brigade had been on the heights behind Trautenau since 7:45 A.M. As the first of Bonin's footsore divisions slumped gratefully in the shade of Trautenau's arcaded square, Mondel's *Jäger* stole down from the hills and opened fire on them. Startled Prussian infantry leaped to their feet and returned fire while others broke into the houses around the square, climbed to the upper storeys, and fired up the tree-clad heights, where many of their own comrades were scrambling in pursuit of Mondel's light infantry. It was a bloody free-for-all. Tasting battle for the first time, the excited Prussians banged away, dropping as many of their own men as Mondel's and ignoring repeated orders from their officers to cease firing.

Ordered by Gablenz to operate cautiously until most of X Corps was on the scene, Mondel pulled his regiments back to evade the Prussian 1st Brigade ascending from Trautenau. Leaving two battalions on the central height, the Johannesberg, Mondel descended one kilometer south to Hohenbruck. His rearguard, untroubled by Bonin's vanguard, which had lost itself in the maze of

---

97 Cited in Johann Allmayer-Beck, "Der Feldzug der österreichischen Nordarmee nach Königgrätz," in Groote and Gersdorff, eds. *Entscheidung 1866*, p. 111.
98 Lettow-Vorbeck, vol. 2, pp. 313–15. Fontane, *Der deutsche Krieg*, vol. 1, pp. 364–85.

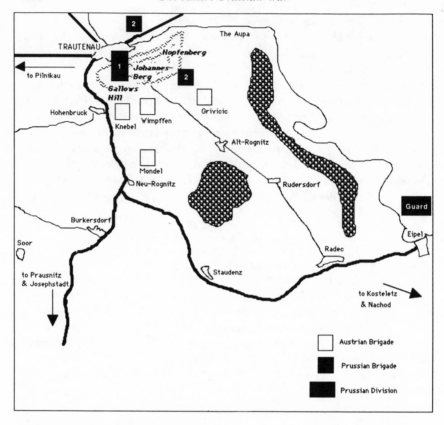

The Battle of Trautenau, June 27, 1866

ravines below the heights, held the Prussians up for an hour and gave way only after a vicious fight for the chapel on the summit. When a company of Prussian fusiliers broke into the west end, the Poles and Ukrainians inside fought backward, pew by pew, until, pinned in the choir, they finally surrendered.[99]

By 12 noon, as Ramming's last reserves were being mown down at Vysokov, Bonin's I Corps seemed to have secured the Trautenau end of the great Landshut Pass with considerably less effort than had been required of Steinmetz at Nachod. Bonin's 1st Division had driven off Mondel, and pushed all the way down to Neu-Rognitz in the course of the morning. Bonin's 2nd Division had taken the Hopfenberg, and scouted as far as Alt-Rognitz. The town, heights, and hinterland of Trautenau, a sort of beachhead in Bohemia, were in Bonin's hands, and for three hours Prussian infantry, guns, and supplies rolled in from the mountains. Gablenz, who had arrived outside Trautenau at 10:30 A.M., watched Bonin's

99 KA, AFA 1866, Karton 2296, 13–11, Vienna, December 20, 1866, Lt-Col. Bastendorff. Karton 2294, 6-ad 108, Hohenmauth, July 4, 1866, Col. Mondel.

advance with mounting frustration. Mondel's were the only troops he had with him. His three other brigades were still plodding up from Josephstadt and would not arrive until the afternoon. Bonin, convinced that he had seen the last of the Austrians, assured an adjutant from the 1st Guard Division, who rode over from Eipel at midday to offer assistance, that his pass was secure.[100]

As the Guard adjutant returned to Second Army headquarters at Eipel with the news that Bonin's corps was safely through the mountains, two of Gablenz's brigades hove in to Neu-Rognitz from Josephstadt. Gablenz, who had commanded the Austrian expedition to Denmark in 1864, set to work at once. Earlier he had noted the vulnerable location of Trautenau and the critical importance of the heights behind it: Gallows Hill, Johannesberg, and Hopfenberg. In possession of these commanding heights, Gablenz knew that he would be able to press the Prussians down into the low-lying town and drive them back into the mountains with plunging fire from his seventy-two guns. To accomplish this plan, Gablenz ordered his Wimpffen Brigade to march past Mondel and storm the central Johannesberg while his Grivicic Brigade passed to the right of Mondel, worked round the left flank of the Prussian position, and stormed the Hopfenberg, taking the heights between two fires. Gablenz's fourth brigade, Albert Knebel's, had not yet arrived from Josephstadt. To prepare the Austrian assault, Gablenz deployed forty guns at Hohenbruck and pounded the heights at close range. The Prussian artillery, which had been able to tow just ten guns up the steep slope from Trautenau, hardly responded to an hour-long cannonade the like of which Bonin, a greenhorn, had never seen or heard.[101] Realizing that this Austrian bombardment portended a major push by the second most famous general in the Habsburg army, Bonin resolved not to hold Trautenau and the heights after all but to turn tail and escape back to Landshut.

Grivicic's storm columns brushed past a weak Prussian detachment at Alt-Rognitz, then struck up the Hopfenberg at 4:00 P.M., while Adolf Wimpffen's men, exhausted by the long march from Josephstadt, shrugged off their backpacks and made for the Johannesberg in half-battalion masses, cutting through a screen of Prussian skirmishers at Hohenbruck with the bayonet. This two-pronged Austrian attack broke down immediately as the prongs stumbled and lost time in thick cover while Gablenz galloped back and forth between them. Grivicic hit the Prussian left well ahead of Wimpffen and made no progress against the needle rifle. Split by fire, his columns tumbled down the hill leaving scores of dead and wounded behind them. Grivicic's Hungarians, who had whooped excitedly during the approach, fell silent. "My 23rd and 2nd Regiments were decimated," Grivicic recalled sadly. "Losses in this single episode exceeded

---

100 Grosser Generalstab, *Feldzug 1866*, p. 123.
101 One of Gablenz's batteries later discovered that it had fired no less than 2,360 shells on the twenty-seventh, more evidence of the expanding role of field artillery in modern combat. KA, AFA 1866, Karton 2266, 6–975, n.d., k.k. Artillerie-Regt. Nr. 3. Karton 2294, 6–105a, Floridsdorf, July 14, 1866, FML Gablenz to FM Albrecht.

the worst I had experienced in three previous wars."[102] Wimpffen's attack, conducted across the broken, wooded reverse slope of the Johannesberg, staggered on the final, very steep ascent to the chapel and was torn apart by the steady, accurate fire of Bonin's rearguard, two battalions of the East Prussian 43rd Regiment.[103]

General Bonin — a royal adjutant and courtier, who had never been in battle — was now in the embarrassing position of being in headlong retreat with the royal army's élite East Prussian corps while just four of his battalions were busy beating the entire Austrian X Corps from formidable defensive positions. Yet since the roads in and out of Trautenau were blocked with Prussian baggage and guns, Bonin could not move reinforcements to the heights. This explained why fourteen of his infantry battalions and most of his artillery retired from the battle without firing a shot. Bonin's loss of control at Trautenau threatened Moltke's entire war plan, for his was the corps Moltke had designated to cover the passage of the Guard Corps and Second Army headquarters through Eipel and then to race across Bohemia to make contact with Friedrich Karl's First Army near Jicin.[104] Bismarck, stunned by the repulse at Trautenau, called it "a slap that rocked the whole Prussian army."[105] Bonin himself was disgraced. "We cannot *all* be heroes," one of his disgusted subordinates spat as I Corps scrambled away to the north.[106] Meanwhile the two doughty Prussian battalions left stranded on the Johannesberg were fairly choking in their own gunsmoke. It was a still day and powder smoke clung to the hills, concealing the advance of Gablenz's fourth and last brigade.

Arriving in Neu-Rognitz from Josephstadt at 5:00 P.M. and ordered by Gablenz to wait in reserve beside Mondel, Colonel Albert Knebel took stock of the situation at Trautenau. Grivicic had been driven back to Alt-Rognitz by the Prussian 4th Brigade. Wimpffen — who had just dispatched an urgent summons to Knebel — was collecting the remnants of his largely Ukrainian 58th Regiment from the south face of the Johannesberg, where they, like Wimpffen's Venetians before them, had been cut up by the two Prussian battalions deployed round the chapel. Knebel decided to ignore Gablenz's order to wait in reserve and resolved to attack the Johannesberg instead. "I considered that the enemy had to be fatigued, and that repeated storms by my brigade would break him," Knebel later wrote to justify his insubordination. He passed to the left of Wimpffen, who tried one last frontal assault on the chapel. Knebel's half-battalion masses clambered toward the Prussian right, losing 43 officers and 859 men in the process. Together, Wimpffen and Knebel lumbered onto the summit, cleared the church with their bayonets, and drove Bonin's rearguard down to Trautenau, where they

102 KA, AFA 1866, Karton 2296, 13–9, Vienna, December 18, 1866, Col. Grivicic: "This attack convinced me that storm tactics will never work against Prussians on the defensive. Instead, we ought to emphasize the firefight and try to go around their flank."
103 Grosser Generalstab, *Feldzug 1866*, pp. 124–5.
104 Moltke, *Strategy*, p. 45. Fontane, *Der deutsche Krieg*, vol. 1, p. 385.
105 Craig, *Königgrätz*, pp. 62–4.
106 Lettow-Vorbeck, vol. 2, pp. 314–16. (Lettow was a staff officer with Bonin's I Corps.)

Das 1. Infanterie-Regiment „Kaiser Franz Josef I." beim Sturm auf den Kapellenberg bei Trautenau, 27. Juni 1866

13. The final Austrian assault at Trautenau, June 27, 1866

followed the rest of the Prussian I Corps up the Aupa river valley shadowed by Grivicic.[107]

Victory! But to what end? Even as his men assembled on the three heights at 7:00 P.M. to watch Bonin's retreat, Gablenz knew that the Prussian Guard Corps was emerging from the mountains at Eipel and working across his rear.[108] Since Krismanic had agreed to detach only two Austrian *battalions* to cover X Corps' exposed flank, Gablenz knew that he would have to abandon the hard-won heights of Trautenau and hurry back to Josephstadt to avoid being cut off from the rest of North Army and crushed between the Guard Corps and a resurgent Bonin the next day. His tactical victory at Trautenau, in short, was without strategic significance. Indeed, earlier in the day, on the march from Josephstadt, Grivicic had asked why Gablenz was even bothering to advance as far as Trautenau. Would it not have been wiser simply to retract Mondel and take up a position farther south, where X Corps would have been in contact with Ramming's VI Corps and positioned to stop not only Bonin but the Prussian Guard Corps as well?[109]

Ultimately, Trautenau proved a Pyrrhic victory for the Austrians. Despite overwhelming artillery superiority, Gablenz's brigades suffered 5,000 casualties, nearly four times Prussian losses of 1,300. And whereas the Prussians lost just 56 officers, the Austrians saw 191 of theirs cut down, losses that would weigh heavily in subsequent operations, when more and more Austrian combat units would have to be entrusted to inexperienced cadets and desk officers sent up from Vienna.[110]

After the battle, Trautenau and the hills around it were strewn with dead and wounded. Three generations later, in 1936, a German historian visited the town and reported that "old people here *still* speak in awe of the rows and heaps of Austrian corpses that day."[111] Neither side had made any provision for casualties, and the anguished cries of the wounded must have detracted from the elation felt by survivors. As at Custoza, most of the men injured in this and other battles in Bohemia were simply left to die from shock and bleeding. Less fortunate ones were removed to a bowling alley in Trautenau to have their wounds scoured with petroleum and creosote, and their injured limbs sawn off. Others were loaded into springless carts and borne off to nearby monasteries by charitable monks and nuns.[112]

Austrian troops who emerged unscathed from the battle waited expectantly for a hot dinner, a flask of wine, and a tot of brandy – the soldier's reward for a hard-

107 KA, AFA 1866, Karton 2294, 6–119, n.d., GM Knebel.

108 KA, AFA 1866, Karton 2296, 13–10, Vienna, December 19, 1866, Capt. Schulz.

109 "It seemed to me," Grivicic wrote, "that such an operation would not only have secured our sector, but would also have cohered strategically with the battles being waged at Skalice." KA, AFA 1866, Karton 2296, 13–9, Vienna, December 18, 1866, Col. Grivicic.

110 Grosser Generalstab, *Feldzug 1866*, pp. 126–7.

111 "Trautenau," *Die Freiheit* (Teplice), June 28, 1936. In KA, AFA 1866, Karton 2275.

112 Edward Wondrák, "Die Wahrheit vom Trauerspiel 1866: Das Leid und Elend in sogenannten deutschen Krieg" (Private manuscript, Olomouc, 1990), p. 20.

fought action. But, true to form, the Austrian supply service disappointed them. Tenth Corps bedded down hungry, for Gablenz's food trains had been forgotten on the crowded road at Josephstadt. When the wagons did finally arrive in Trautenau the next day, Gablenz's famished battalions smelt them a long way off, for they contained nothing but grey-green carcasses of rotten meat.[113] This did not bode well for the day ahead; Austrian troops were accustomed to flesh and wine. Without nourishment, these men would have difficulty outrunning the Prussian Guards closing from Eipel.[114]

ARMY HEADQUARTERS, BERLIN AND JOSEPHSTADT, JUNE 27

In Berlin, Moltke followed operations in Bohemia anxiously. He had hoped that Prussia's superb telegraph net would enable him to transmit orders instantly to the front, yet his cables were taking an average of twelve hours to reach the Prussian armies operating in Bohemia. This was because the Austrians were tearing down their telegraph wires as they retreated, forcing Moltke's orders to be carried on horseback beyond the Prussian border. Thus, the critical telegram Moltke sent from Berlin on June 23 ordering Prince Friedrich Karl to attack across the Iser to disengage Second Army took three full *days* to wend its way to Reichenberg.[115] Return telegrams to Moltke from the front moved no faster. Prussian headquarters in Berlin would not be informed of the battles at Vysokov and Trautenau until June 28, when Moltke also discovered, to his astonishment, that Prince Friedrich Karl, instead of following orders and hastening east to support Crown Prince Friedrich Wilhelm's passage through Nachod, Eipel, and Trautenau, was turning south, to envelop the Austro-Saxon Iser Army at Münchengrätz. First Army was, in short, steering away from Benedek in order to win a relatively insignificant tactical victory over Clam-Gallas. Hell-bent on glory, Friedrich Karl was reviving Benedek's advantage of internal lines, offering him the chance to throw all of North Army against the isolated Prussian Second Army.[116] Before the war, Moltke had insisted that the railroad and the telegraph would permit modern generals to conduct distant campaigns from their capitals. Idle hope: how Moltke must now have envied Benedek, who, lodged at Josephstadt on the twenty-seventh, was in the thick of his army.

In Josephstadt, Benedek, Henikstein, and Krismanic spent much of June 27 on the ramparts of the fortress observing the funnels of gunsmoke rising from Vysokov and Trautenau. The contrast these men made with Moltke's increasingly remote command could not have been more vivid. Yet the Austrian commanders

---

113 KA, AFA 1866, Karton 2266, 6–1033a, Neu-Rognitz, June 28, 1866, FML Gablenz to FZM Benedek.

114 "Meat extends the time between meals, relieves exhaustion, restores health and gives men a reserve of strength. The meat ration must be maintained in wartime." – "Über Feldverpflegung: Das Fleisch," *ÖMZ* 3 (1860), p. 319.

115 Van Creveld, *Command in War*, pp. 124–6.

116 Moltke, *Strategy*, p. 51. Craig, *Königgrätz*, pp. 54–5.

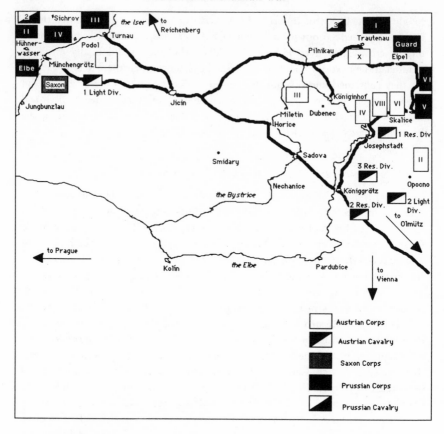

The strategic situation on June 27, 1866

were no more easy in their thoughts than was the Prussian *chef*. Though alarmed by the size and ferocity of the battles on their northern flank, they felt constrained to continue their march *west* to the Iser.[117] Benedek, prodded by Krismanic, wanted desperately to throw his entire strength against the five corps of the Prussian Elbe and First Armies by marching to join Clam's Iser Army at Jicin on the twenty-ninth. He worried that a turn northward to confront Second Army would throw his entire war effort out of gear. Thus, earlier in the day, while the Prussian Second Army hammered on Benedek's flank at Vysokov and Trautenau, the Feldzeugmeister ignored the threat, drafting plans instead for an Austrian concentration at Jicin and Königgrätz.[118]

117 KA, Nachlässe, B/572: 2 (Nosinic), Wr. Neustadt, July 12, 1866, GM Krismanic.
118 KA, AFA 1866, Karton 2266, 6–982, Josephstadt, June 27, 1866, FZM Benedek to corps
     commandants. MKSM, Karton 343, 69/9, Josephstadt, June 27, 1866, FZM Benedek to FML
     Crenneville.

The ink was not dry on Benedek's march tables before news of the Austrian defeats at Vysokov and Trautenau spoilt them and forced Benedek suddenly to confront enemies on both flanks. Though by the evening of June 27 the Feldzeugmeister knew that Moltke's planned envelopment of North Army was in motion, he nevertheless elected *not* to move against Second Army on the twenty-eighth with the four infantry corps and three cavalry divisions he had with him at Josephstadt. Why? Because Benedek and Krismanic were concerned above all to execute the plan agreed upon earlier in the day, the march to Jicin. They therefore strove to minimize the number of detachments sent north. This explained their rather pedantic refusal to divert troops passing within earshot of the battles at Skalice and Trautenau from their march routes and their notorious rebuffs to the parade of messengers sent down by Ramming and Gablenz in the night to request reinforcements. When, late on the twenty-seventh, the staff officer dispatched by Krismanic to observe the battle of Vysokov recommended massive reinforcements for Skalice, Krismanic checked his maps, checked his march tables, checked his watch, and muttered: "*Ei was, es ist zu spät. Nun, soll es dorthin* [Josephstadt] *marschieren*" (What can I do? It's too late. Everyone should just carry on to Josephstadt).

From Krismanic's viewpoint, it was quite enough that he had agreed to detour Archduke Leopold's entire VIII Corps, which had been scheduled to march to Königgrätz on the twenty-eighth, to Skalice instead.[119] He and Benedek were determined to make their main thrust at Jicin on the thirtieth. It was a major crossroads and a much more favorable battlefield from Krismanic's classical perspective, for it was flat, open ground buttressed by "reply points" – forts and bridges – at Josephstadt, Königgrätz, and Pardubice.[120] The clinching argument, as far as Krismanic was concerned, was that it would have been logistically impossible to reroute North Army to Trautenau and Skalice. In the first place, there were not enough roads. That was why Gablenz and Ramming had proceeded single-file to their battles, with ruinous results, when their brigades had stormed individually, not collectively, into action. Moreover, Bonin's easy escape from Trautenau suggested just how dangerous it would be to pursue Second Army into Silesia while Prince Friedrich Karl's greedy cohorts ravaged the Prague basin and cut eastward across Benedek's own lines of retreat to Olmütz and Vienna.

With all of these considerations in mind, Krismanic and Benedek agreed to leave Gablenz behind at Josephstadt on the twenty-eighth with two corps to obstruct Second Army's advance while the bulk of North Army resumed its flank march westward.[121] At Trautenau, Krismanic later wrote, "we only intended that Gablenz make contact with [Second Army]. After the battle, his job was done."

119 KA, AFA 1866, Karton 2293, 13–49, Vienna, August 1866, Maj. Rheinländer. Nachlässe, B/572: 2 (Nosinic), Wr. Neustadt, January 2, 1869, GM Krismanic.

120 Benedeks, *Benedeks nachgelassene Papiere*, p. 368.

121 KA, AFA 1866, Karton 2266, 6–982, Josephstadt, June 27, 1866, FZM Benedek to corps commandants.

He ought to have disengaged and hurried back to Josephstadt, removing his corps from danger and obviating the need for a time-consuming rescue operation the next day. "If Gablenz remains [at Trautenau]," Krismanic had warned Gablenz's galloper, who arrived in Josephstadt at 2:00 A.M. on the twenty-eighth, "then the Prussians will envelop him."[122] For all his many faults, Krismanic could read maps and project operations with certainty. The fate he predicted for Gablenz early on the twenty-eighth came to pass later in the day.

Clearly, however, Krismanic and Benedek were also to blame. They might have warned Gablenz not to go all the way up to Trautenau during their meeting on the twenty-sixth. After all, Gablenz was a notorious thruster. He had been criticized in 1864 for pushing the pursuit of the Danish army to Oeversee too aggressively and thus was the last person Benedek should have enjoined to "attack the Prussians with utmost energy."[123] As for Ramming, Krismanic deplored his "brainless dipositions" at Vysokov and wondered how the pride of the Austrian staff could have dashed an entire corps against an impregnable position. Yet it was Krismanic's own five-hour delay in transmitting orders to Ramming that permitted the Prussians to consolidate that hilltop position between Nachod and Skalice. Thus, the torpor of Benedek's headquarters contributed at least as much to the Austrian defeat at Vysokov as Ramming's failure to take his brigades in hand.

On the Iser front, the bloody clash at Podol left I Corps badly shaken. Clam-Gallas's staff chief, Colonel Eduard Litzelhofen, noted the steep odds before Hühnerwasser and Podol – 140,000 Prussians against just 60,000 Austrians and Saxons – and recalled that "my understanding was that I Corps was to linger in the exposed Iser position only until the Saxons arrived. We were then to withdraw immediately to form the left wing of North Army" at Josephstadt and Königgrätz. Litzelhofen and Clam were therefore flabbergasted by Benedek's order of June 21 to "hold the Iser line at any price." Litzelhofen bitterly recorded that "the strategic aim intended by this deployment was never specified." Indeed, Litzelhofen continued, "it was not until July 1st that General Krismanic explained it to me thus: 'North Army did not want to surrender Prague without firing a shot!' " – "Why," Litzelhofen concluded, "did [Benedek] abandon the original plan, the speedy concentration of the entire Austrian army, for this extremely dubious enterprise," the cordon on the Iser?[124] It was a valid question underscored by the useless, costly battles at Hühnerwasser and Podol on the twenty-seventh, and at Münchengrätz on the twenty-eighth.

Still, despite these setbacks, Benedek had reasonably good prospects as he retired to his bed on the twenty-seventh. Archduke Leopold's corps had moved up to Skalice to relieve Ramming and bar Steinmetz's way west. The rest of North Army was moving toward a junction with Iser Army at Jicin on seven parallel roads.

122　KA, Nachlässe, B/572: 2 (Nosinic), Wr. Neustadt, January 2, 1869, GM Krismanic.
123　"Die Österreicher im schleswig-holsteinischen Krieg," *ÖMZ* 3 (1864), p. 342.
124　KA, AFA 1866, Karton 2280, 13–103, Lemberg, December 19, 1866, Col. Litzelhofen.

North Army's munitions park — the tons of shell and shrapnel needed to counterbalance the needle rifle — was being shuttled up from Brno and dumped at Pardubice, twenty kilometers south of Königgrätz. Gablenz was expected to return victorious from Trautenau in the night after driving Bonin's East Prussians out of Bohemia. As for the Iser front, ignorance fostered by Clam's slow-moving postal wagons was bliss. Incredibly, Clam-Gallas — a reactionary in all things — had still not deployed the field telegraph he had with him. Hence, Krismanic actually believed that far from being beaten on the Iser, I Corps and the Saxons were victorious and girding for a push toward Reichenberg. [125] This hoped-for diversion would buy Benedek the two precious days he needed to concentrate his infantry corps and cavalry divisions at Jicin for what he called North Army's "*Hauptstoss*" (main thrust) — "Our situation *seemed* extremely favorable," Benedek's adjutant recalled, "for *we*, at least, were united, while the Prussians were still far apart." [126] To make sure of his flank and rear while he made front to the west, Benedek planned a staff ride to Skalice the next morning to supervise Archduke Leopold's relief of Ramming. While the Feldzeugmeister slept, an Austrian staff officer sat up in North Army's operations room scribbling in his diary: "Tomorrow Benedek intends to throw the entire army at Prince Friedrich Karl, who is at Münchengrätz. But now we have Prussians on our *heels*, at Skalice. No one here *really* knows what's happened to Gablenz at Trautenau. Oh dear God, how will this business end?" [127]

125 KA, MKSM 1866, Karton 343, 69/9, Josephstadt, June 27, 1866, FZM Benedek.
126 KA, AFA 1866, Karton 2270, 8–12aa, Budapest, August 12, 1866, GM Kriz.
127 KA, AFA 1866, Karton 2275, 13–166, Josephstadt, June 27, 1866, Capt. Stransky, "Tagebuch."

7

Münchengrätz, Burkersdorf, and Skalice

While Benedek planned his march to Jicin, the Prussian Elbe and First Armies stepped up their requisitions in western Bohemia and contemplated a descent on Prague. "The damage is great," a French observer wrote. "The Prussians are handling Bohemia, the most industrialized region in the Austrian Monarchy, like a conquered land, and are plundering it to pay their war costs. A quick Austrian victory is needed."[1] Indeed, so alluring were the riches of Bohemia that Prince Friedrich Karl was tempted to postpone the crucial march Moltke had assigned him: eastward to Jicin, to disengage Second Army at Skalice and Trautenau.[2] Instead, the prince strove to score the war's first great *Kesselschlacht* victory. Erroneous Prussian intelligence informed him that he had not only the Saxons and the Austrian I Corps at bay in Münchengrätz but the Austrian II Corps as well. With such a big prize so close at hand, the First Army commandant planned a detour south on June 28 to envelop Iser Army before swerving back to the east to aid the now hard-pressed Prussian Second Army.[3] In Berlin, Moltke, who relied entirely on his three field armies for information about events in Bohemia, knew nothing about this time-consuming and insubordinate maneuver laid on by Prince Friedrich Karl. He would therefore be unable to countermand it in time to prevent the loss of a valuable, perhaps critical, march day. Indeed, for the next three days, the three Prussian armies would operate more or less independently, with little or no coordination from Great Headquarters in Berlin.[4]

Clam-Gallas's headquarters in Münchengrätz was more cheerful and assured, but only on account of the copious amounts of champagne drunk throughout the campaign. Austrian prisoners captured by the Prussians on June 28 swore they had seen Count Clam-Gallas mount the left side of his horse that morning only to

---

1 Vincennes, AAT, MR 89/1606, Vienna, July 3, 1866, Col. Merlin to Marshal Randon. Jahnel, pp. 25–8.
2 Moltke, *Strategy*, p. 51.
3 Grosser Generalstab, *Feldzug 1866*, pp. 152–4.
4 Van Creveld, *Command in War*, pp. 124–6.

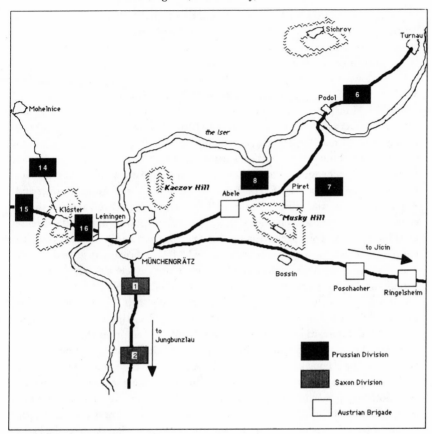

The Battle of Münchengrätz, June 28, 1866

glide across the saddle and fall to the ground on the right.[5] He would have to sober up quickly. Though Clam was tucked inside a naturally strong position at Münchengrätz, Herwarth von Bittenfeld's Elbe Army was nearing his front, while two of Friedrich Karl's three infantry corps turned south from Podol to hit his flank and cut across his lines of retreat to Jicin.[6]

THE BATTLE OF MÜNCHENGRÄTZ, JUNE 28

Clam-Gallas and Prince Albert of Saxony decided to abandon their exposed position at Münchengrätz, though on divergent lines of retreat, a tactical error that

---

5 Wachenhusen, p. 57.
6 Craig, *Königgrätz*, p. 55. Glünicke, p. 96.

would figure mightily in the next day's fighting at Jicin. While three of Clam's brigades remained in Münchengrätz to slow the Prussian pursuit, the two others – Joseph Ringelsheim's and Ferdinand Poschacher's – marched east to Jicin. Instead of waiting for the Jicin road to clear, Albert sent his five Saxon brigades down the south road to Jungbunzlau, a lengthy, exhausting detour that would cost the Saxon prince half his strength at the battle of Jicin.

To reach Münchengrätz, Friedrich Karl's divisions descending from Podol would have to pass between two mounts, Musky Hill east of town and Kaczov Hill one kilometer to the north. Herwarth, continuing eastward from Hühnerwasser, would have to fight through two obstacles before coming to grips with the Austrian brigades in Münchengrätz: first Kláster, an elevated monastery on the west bank of the river, then the Iser itself. The Austrian left was Kláster; Münchengrätz and Kaczov Hill were the center, Musky Hill the right wing. Clam, busy with the retreat to Jicin, entrusted one of his brigadiers, Count Leiningen, with the defense of Münchengrätz. Leiningen deployed his *Jäger* in town and posted his two line regiments across the river in Kláster. Ludwig Piret's brigade deployed on the crumbly sandstone slopes of Musky Hill while Clam's Abele Brigade drew up in battalion columns below them and faced the road from Podol.

All was apparently set for the arrival of Herwarth's 16th Division, leading the Prussian Elbe Army in from Hühnerwasser after an exhausting eight-hour march. The Prussian vanguard – still under General Schöler – comprised the seven battalions of the Prussia 31st Brigade, which had repulsed Gondrecourt at Hühnerwasser two days earlier. Four kilometers west of the Iser, they came under fire from the Austrian batteries mounted on the hill at Kláster and in the Jewish cemetery behind it. Schöler deployed his own batteries, shook out two flanking columns, and rose toward Kláster. Leiningen's 38th Regiment, Italians from Venetia, scarcely bothered to defend the height. When the sounds of fighting behind them on the Podol road carried across the river, they abandoned Kláster, retired across the Iser to Münchengrätz, and torched the bridge.[7]

Prince Friedrich Karl and his staff chief, Konstantin Voigts-Rhetz, watched the battle from Podol. They saw the flashes and white puffs of Herwarth's batteries pushing closer to Kláster, then the sudden eruption of black smoke as the Iser bridge caught fire at 10:00 A.M. The Prussian prince, who had observed an Austrian general's suite on Musky Hill through his telescope, thought for a thrilling hour or two that he must have bagged the entire Iser Army between the pincers of Elbe and First Armies.[8] Meanwhile Friedrich Karl's advanced brigades – Horn's 8th Division – attacked the north face of Musky Hill, engaging Piret and Abele, while Fransecki's 7th Division – guided by an obliging German peasant – slopped through the morass behind the hill to sever its communications to Münchengrätz and Jicin. It appeared that all three Austrian brigades at Münchengrätz would be

7 Grosser Generalstab, *Feldzug 1866*, pp. 154–7.
8 Hozier, pp. 233–7. Craig, *Königgrätz*, pp. 71–2.

caught in Friedrick Karl's closing trap. Recognizing this, the Austrian gunners shelling Horn's column from Musky Hill limbered up and departed as Fransecki moved across their rear. They retired as quickly as they could through Musky village, where whole platoons of Piret's 45th Regiment — Venetians from Verona — were observed throwing away their rifles and descending gratefully toward Fransecki's flanking column with their hands in the air.

In Münchengrätz, General Leiningen had begun retreating east to Sobotka, leaving the deserted town to Herwarth and the Prussian Elbe Army. Schöler's regiments, half mad with thirst and hunger, removed their shoes, rolled up their trousers, and impatiently awaited orders to wade across the Iser to the promise of food and drink. The Prussians were in an ugly mood, for their march from Hühnerwasser had been extremely taxing. As usual, Herwarth's supply trains had lagged hours behind the men, and at every roadhouse the Prussian march battalions had discovered bare larders and poisoned wells. By the time Schöler's vanguard took Kláster, his men were delirious with thirst and hunger. Finding nothing to eat on the west bank of the Iser, they splashed across to Münchengrätz, smashed down the doors of the Wallenstein Palace, and descended to the ducal brewery, a cool underground labyrinth stocked with beer. Kegs were carried above ground and tapped. The men gathered round and drank deeply.[9]

Were there a moment for Leiningen to counterattack, this was certainly it. But the Austrian brigadier was well out of it, on the outskirts of Münchengrätz heading east to Jicin. He had eluded Prince Friedrich Karl's flanking column thanks to Abele's Czechs and Hungarians, who held the pitted, overgrown south slope of Musky Hill and Bossin long enough for Leiningen and Piret to escape to the east. Prince Friedrich Karl barreled through the gap between the Kaczov and Musky Hills and struck thin air. Iser Army had eluded him; Friedrich Karl's detour south had been in vain, or nearly in vain. The Elbe and First Armies were now side-by-side, and the 1,400 prisoners made by the Prussians were some consolation, as was Wallenstein's famous beer. The five Prussian divisions bivouaced in Münchengrätz drank the whole night through. They had lost only 300 comrades in the battle, and there was cause for celebration in this.[10] Kláster and Musky Hill were redoubtable positions, yet fourteen Prussian battalions had sufficed to take them. Though Friedrich Karl's left wing was still fifty kilometers from Friedrich Wilhelm's right — with the entire Austrian North Army united between them — that did not seem to matter as the Elbe and First Armies filled their cups with beer and rollicked through the night.[11]

9 Fontane, *Der deutsche Krieg*, vol. 1, p. 180–3. Wachenhusen, pp. 66–70.

10 KA, AFA 1866, Karton 2274, 13–74, Olmütz, December 1872, Maj. Ripp, "Skizze." Of 732 unwounded Austrian prisoners at Münchengrätz, 487 were Italians. In all, the Prussians lost 8 officers and 333 men at Münchengrätz, the Austrians 20 officers and 1,634 men.

11 Grosser Generalstab, *Feldzug 1866*, pp. 158–9, 195.

THE BATTLE OF BURKERSDORF, JUNE 28

The Prussian crown prince had been with Steinmetz at Vysokov on the twenty-seventh. In the afternoon, he had shifted his headquarters to Eipel Pass, where, early on the twenty-eighth, he anxiously listened to the sounds of battle from left and right. He had intended to send one of his two Guard divisions to Skalice on the twenty-eighth to help Steinmetz over the Aupa river line, but Bonin's repulse on the twenty-seventh had forced him to send the entire Guard Corps northwest to clear Gablenz out of Trautenau, open the only mountain pass still closed to the Prussians, and begin securing the strategically vital Trautenau-Königinhof-Jicin road, which would ultimately link the western and eastern halves of Moltke's army.

Kosteletz, eight kilometers southeast of Eipel, where Friedrich Wilhelm sat among the rear echelons of the 2nd Guard Division on the twenty-eighth, offered no view of Bohemia, and this merely compounded the crown prince's nervousness. Both of his flanks were now threatened – one by Bonin's panicky flight from Trautenau, the other by the three Austrian corps he knew were in the vicinity of Skalice – and the crown prince felt, as he himself put it, like a "helpless spectator." In Berlin, Moltke felt even less useful. He would receive no detailed reports of the defeat at Trautenau until June 29, two days after the battle, and would exert no influence over the hard fighting on the twenty-eighth.[12]

Burkersdorf, a battle that the Prussians called Soor, was essentially the second battle of Trautenau. It nearly did not happen thanks to the hesitation of Prince August of Württemberg, commandant of the Prussian Guard Corps, who resolved to give the feisty Gablenz a wide berth till Bonin showed himself again in Trautenau. "The connection with I Corps is *still* not established," Prince August complained to the crown prince early on the twenty-eighth, seeking a postponement of his scheduled advance. At 9:00 A.M., however, the prince's hussar patrols returned from scouting Gablenz with the news that the Austrian X Corps was decamping from the heights around Trautenau and retreating slowly toward Josephstadt, offering the Prussian Guards their left flank. Throwing his earlier caution to the wind, Prince August began the march assigned him by Second Army headquarters: to Deutsch-Prausnitz, south of Trautenau, where Grivicic had advised Gablenz to stand on the twenty-seventh.[13]

Gablenz meanwhile was trying to escape from Trautenau with his corps intact. By marching all the way to the mountains on the twenty-seventh, he had over-reached himself and now had to recover his balance in a hurry. Tenth Corps's instructions for the twenty-eighth were to retire south to Prausnitz – half-way home to Josephstadt – and to stand there against the Prussian Guard. Although

12 Lettow-Vorbeck, vol. 2, p. 278. Van Creveld, *Command in War*, pp. 129–30.
13 Glünicke, p. 103. Fontane, *Der deutsche Krieg*, vol. 1, pp. 390–400.

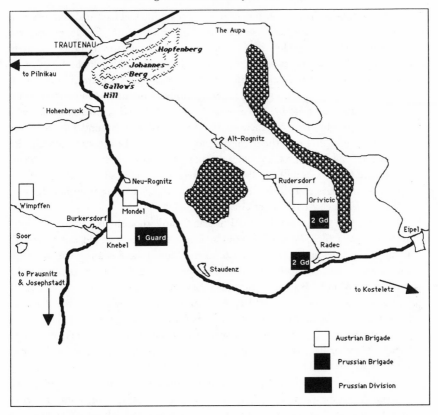

The Battles of Burkersdorf and Rudersdorf, June 28, 1866

Krismanic dictated these orders at 2:00 A.M. on the twenty-eighth, they some-how did not reach Gablenz in Trautenau – a two-and-one-half-hour gallop from Josephstadt – until 7:00 A.M., yet another instance of execrable Austrian staff work.[14] Once in possession of his late-arriving orders, Gablenz proceeded to make some poor decisions. Though in danger of encirclement by the Guard Corps cutting across his rear and I Corps reemerging in Trautenau, he could not resist a parting shot at the Prussians. Pugnacious as ever, Gablenz sent Grivicic's brigade southeast to Radec to hit the unsuspecting Guards in the flank as they marched northwest from Eipel to envelop X Corps. Gablenz's staff raised an eyebrow at this incautious riposte through rolling, forested terrain, for it would almost certainly end up matching Grivicic's lone brigade against an entire Prussian *division*.[15]

14 KA, AFA 1866, Karton 2270, 8–12p, Floridsdorf, August 16, 1866, FML Gablenz.
15 KA, AFA 1866, Karton 2296, 13–10, Vienna, December 19, 1866, Capt. Schulz.

By camping at Trautenau on the twenty-seventh, Gablenz had lost precious time. He did not really need orders for the twenty-eighth, for, in view of the successful passage of the Prussian Guard, V, and VI Corps through the mountains to his right, he had no choice but to pull back to the safety of the Elbe line at Josephstadt. Still, it took him hours to begin his escape. Gablenz did not get his trains on the road till 5:00 A.M. They were followed by his corps gun reserve, his uhlan regiment, and the 17,000 men of the Wimpffen and Knebel Brigades, who lost more time hunting for their backpacks in the fields around Neu-Rognitz, where they had dropped them the previous afternoon before storming the Johannesberg. By the time Gablenz himself left Trautenau at 8:00 A.M., the Prussian Guard Corps was on him. Five kilometers down the road at Burkersdorf, his march column was sighted by the 2nd Guard Brigade closing from Staudenz, at the head of Prince August's 1st Guard Division.[16]

Gablenz had been expecting the Prussian Guard, though not so soon. Luckily, he had already placed three batteries at Burkersdorf and trained them east. To secure his last remaining escape route to the Elbe – the roads from Burkersdorf and Hohenbruck west to Pilnikau – he lurched around to the left, deploying the Knebel and Mondel Brigades, previously headed south, in a protective half-circle facing east – Mondel on the left at Neu-Rognitz, Knebel on the right at Burkersdorf. Gablenz then took eight more batteries from his corps reserve and placed them at Burkersdorf. It was fast work and before the Prussian Guards could engage, Gablenz had sixty-four guns pointed at them. Although the steady fire of X Corps's guns held the Prussians in check for an hour, the 2nd Guard Brigade broke through to Burkersdorf at 9:30 A.M., storming up rising ground to the village. In the meantime, Gablenz had shunted most of his corps onto the road west to Pilnikau, leaving a single regiment behind in Burkersdorf to slow the Prussian pursuit. These men – Germans and Czechs of the Lower Silesian 1st Regiment – inflicted heavy casualties on the Prussian Guards, who had to cross 400 meters of open ground to gain the village. On this final approach, they absorbed more shellfire and several aimed salvos that carried away dozens of guardsmen and every company captain in the Prussian charge.[17] While Austria's 1st Regiment gave ground in Burkersdorf, Gablenz's Knebel and Mondel Brigades scattered through the fields to Pilnikau, leaving hundreds of unwounded prisoners in their wake. As the Austrian fire slackened, more and more Prussian Guards staggered into Burkersdorf, lungs heaving, most of them covered with dirt and blasted sod. In their reckless haste to envelop Gablenz, they had hazarded an Austrian-style frontal attack with the bayonet and had taken Austrian-style casualties as a result: eighteen officers and 478 men laid on the field. It was 10:00 A.M.[18]

16 KA, AFA 1866, Karton 2294, 6–107a, Floridsdorf, July 14, 1866, FML Gablenz.
17 Fontane, *Der deutsche Krieg*, vol. 1, pp. 396–400. Grosser Generalstab, *Feldzug 1866*, pp. 162–7.
18 In all, however, the Prussians maintained their 1:5 ratio in casualties. There were 3,719 Austrian
   dead, wounded, and missing at Burkersdorf, 713 Prussian. Bartels, *Kritische Beiträge*, p. 205.

Knebel's 1st Regiment yielded Burkersdorf and followed Gablenz toward Pilnikau. Under Prince August of Württemberg's cautious leadership, an energetic Prussian pursuit was quite out of the question, for most of the Guard Corps was still on the road from Eipel, and Bonin, to everyone's amazement, would not return to Trautenau until the following day. Satisfied that Gablenz was beaten, the 1st Guard Division halted in the fields between Burkersdorf and Soor and lit their cook fires. Physically they were shattered; the Guard Corps had marched fifty kilometers in two days, and the approach to Burkersdorf from Eipel, first down a narrow dirt track, then through standing corn had been exhausting.[19]

To while away the afternoon, curious guardsmen picked over booty abandoned by the panic-stricken Austrians on the Josephstadt road: caissons, food wagons, and Gablenz's entire cash reserve – 10,000 silver florins ($135,000). "We had no idea the Prussians were so near," the war ministry official responsible for the lost cash explained after the battle. "I was among the commissary wagons when the enemy materialized 'out of the blue.' There was no going back or forward."[20] Indeed, had Prince August not delayed the advance of the Guard Corps from Eipel that morning, he might have bagged much more of X Corps at Burkersdorf. As it was, Gablenz had to renounce his retreat south on a good hardened road and lurch into the soft fields behind him. Incredibly, he lost only two guns in the course of this steeplechase and conducted the three brigades he had with him – Knebel, Mondel, and Wimpffen – to safety.[21]

Colonel Grivicic's brigade, however, was doomed by Gablenz's hasty retreat, for just as X Corps was yielding the last of its wooded positions west of Burkersdorf, Grivicic was wheeling south from the Aupa and marching his regiments into the rear of the Guard division at Burkersdorf and Soor. Although Gablenz had cancelled this risky maneuver earlier in the day, his messengers had failed to locate Grivicic.[22] At 12 noon, Grivicic, alone in the wilderness southeast of Trautenau and oblivious to the outcome at Burkersdorf, reached Rudersdorf. He was poised, albeit unwittingly, to wedge himself between the 1st and 2nd Guard Divisions. Clearly this would have been desirable had Gablenz won at Burkersdorf. As things stood, however, Grivicic would have been wise to double back to Trautenau and escape to the southwest. But the terrain around Rudersdorf gave no prospect in any direction. Waves of corn and hops mounted rolling, wooded hillocks as far as the eye could see.

"[Gablenz] deprived me of my cavalry in the morning," Grivicic later complained. "Though I heard cannon fire off to the right, I did not know what was going on." So Grivicic followed his original orders, which were to continue three kilometers south to Radec, make front to the northeast, and hit whatever Prussians were coming down the road from Eipel. He wrongly assumed that the guns hammering away at Burkersdorf were batteries of the Austrian IV Corps arriving to reinforce Gablenz. Lost in this fog of ignorance, Colonel Grivicic blundered into a trap with his 5,000 hungry men.[23]

THE BATTLE OF RUDERSDORF, JUNE 28

Grivicic was spared a massacre only by the chance arrival of a single Prussian battalion at Rudersdorf, where he was resting with his troops on the way south. These four Prussian rifle companies had been routinely detached from the 2nd Guard Division's march column for flank protection. Plowing through the corn at Rudersdorf, they literally bumped into Grivicic. At first they took his brigade for an advanced party of Bonin's I Corps, but then the lieutenant-colonel in charge of the Guard flankers called to his adjutant: "I see white tunics; it's the enemy. Report that [Rudersdorf] is occupied by the enemy and that we will take it."[24] The hour-long action that followed pitted four Prussian rifle companies against an entire Austrian brigade and testified again to the extraordinary defensive potential of the breech-loading rifle in the hands of good troops with "bottom."

Without the detailed information on enemy movements that cavalry scouts would have supplied, Grivicic could only assume that he had met with an entire Prussian division. So instead of brusquely shoving the Prussian battalion out of his path and continuing on, he took up defensive positions in Rudersdorf to draw the brunt of the Guard attack down on himself and thereby, as he put it, "buy time for Gablenz and the rest of X Corps to move south to [Josephstadt]." Unfortunately, Grivicic had no idea that Gablenz had been bumped off the Josephstadt road and Gablenz had no idea that Grivicic was at Rudersdorf. The hapless brigadier communicated a front change to his scattered regiments by horn and drum signals, drove the Prussian battalion away from Rudersdorf, and shut himself in the village's sturdy farm buildings with seven battalions of Hungarian, Polish, and German infantry. Only when the single battalion of Prussian Guards opposite him refused to attack did Grivicic begin to realize that he had encountered not a full division, but a weak reconnoitering party.

At 1:00 P.M., the rather abashed Grivicic Brigade resumed its cautious advance. By now, the hard-pressed Prussian battalion before it had been reinforced by a second battalion, which had come up to investigate the sounds of fighting at Rudersdorf. As Grivicic's skirmishers combed through the high corn south of Rudersdorf, they were set upon by 2,000 Prussians and overrun. As the Austrian *Jäger* raced back to Rudersdorf, advanced elements of the 4th Guard Brigade pursued and brought Grivicic's line infantry under fire. Though he still outnumbered the Prussians around him two-to-one, Grivicic could make no headway against the needle rifle and thus ordered his men back to the safety of Rudersdorf,

23 KA, AFA 1866, Karton 2294, 6–115, Vienna, September 10, 1866, Col. Grivicic.
24 Hozier, vol. 1, p. 273. Fontane, *Der deutsche Krieg*, vol. 1, p. 406.

where the battle continued house-to-house. "I needed desperately to communicate with Gablenz," Grivicic later wrote, "but I had no cavalry; my adjutants were all wounded, and I had lost most of my staff officers at Trautenau the previous day." Things shortly went from bad to worse for him. Three more Guard battalions came up and turned Grivicic's right flank, panicking his Polish 23rd Regiment. Grivicic praised his Hungarian and German battalions, who fought on stoically while the Poles quit: "I rode into their midst to restore order," he recalled. "We had to retire, but with so much confusion behind us, it was impossible. Unable to sound the 'retreat' [because of the crush of unruly Poles], I signalled 'rally,' over and over, but it was no use. Then I too was shot and fell from my horse."[25] Now leaderless and surrounded by the Prussian Guard Corps, Grivicic's demoralized brigade gave up. Hundreds of men fell, hundreds surrendered, and hundreds more hid themselves between the rows of grain or fled into the nearby woods. Only 1,600 Austrian stragglers, stealing through the night – speeded by their fear of a long detention in Prussia's Baltic prison camps – would eventually rejoin North Army. Of these traumatized survivors, only 600 would be judged fit to fight in the battle of Königgrätz one week later.[26]

THE BATTLE OF SKALICE, JUNE 28

While Prussian cavalry patrols hunted through the woods around Rudersdorf for Grivicic's stragglers, a much more momentous battle was beginning thirty kilo-meters to the east, at Skalice, the market town at the foot of the Vysokov plateau.

For Benedek and Krismanic, Friedrich Karl's fruitless detour to Münchengrätz earlier in the day was all that they could have hoped for. It gave North Army time to reinforce Clam-Gallas and the Saxons at Jicin while Gablenz, joined to Archduke Leopold's VIII Corps at Skalice, slowed or halted the advance of the Prussian Second Army from defensive positions at Jo-sephstadt, Prausnitz, and Königinhof.[27] To see that this was done, Benedek and Krismanic rode up to Skalice at 10:30 A.M. on the twenty-eighth and met first with Ramming, in VI Corps's reserve position at Trebisov, then with Archduke Leopold on the Aupa heights at Skalice.

Skalice, one of Krismanic's deputies approvingly noted, was a "famous re-doubt" of the eighteenth century. Indeed, Nachod, Vysokov, and Skalice had been choke points of the Silesian Wars, where the Giant Mountains, the highest

25 Austrian officers in 1859 remarked that it was always thus: Troops deployed in reserve, with nothing to do but dodge stray shots and carry back wounded comrades, always broke first. KA, AFA 1866, Karton 2294, 6–115, Vienna, September 10, 1866, Col. Grivicic.

26 Total Austrian casualties at Burkersdorf-Rudersdorf were 123 officers and 3,696 men, including 2,225 unwounded prisoners. Seventy-eight officer casualties and 2,434 men were missing from the Grivicic Brigade alone. The Prussians lost 28 officers and 685 men. Lettow-Vorbeck, vol. 2, pp. 310–12. Grosser Generalstab, *Feldzug 1866*, pp. 167–72.

27 KA, AFA 1866, Karton 2271, 13–1, n.d., Maj. Sacken, "Bericht."

ground in Central Europe, touched the Bohemian plain. Austrian armies had stood here each time Frederick the Great descended the valley of the Oder – "nursing mother of the Prussian army" – to invade Austria.[28] Having already fumbled away Nachod and Vysokov, Ramming was for reinforcing Skalice forthwith. He wanted to move up on Leopold's left and summon Count Tassilo Festetics's IV Corps from Schweinschädel to extend the position on the right. Prussian infantry masses had been forming on both sides of the road down from Vysokov since 6:00 A.M., and Prussian shells had been falling on the Austrians since 10:00 A.M. Ramming thought the time ripe to bring up three Austrian corps to blunt Steinmetz's attack and drive him from the Vysokov plateau. Benedek seemed to like Ramming's idea, but Krismanic, envisioning the logistical pitfalls of such a daring counterstroke, opposed it.[29]

Benedek and his staff left Ramming at Trebisov and continued on to Skalice, where they arrived at 11:00 A.M. There Benedek began to appreciate the difficulties posed by Ramming's proposed counterattack. Valuable time would be lost for North Army's all-important march west, and what would the Austrians do if Steinmetz chose not to descend from the plateau and fight? Would they storm the Vysokov heights a second time? With General Louis Mutius's Prussian VI Corps coming up from Nachod to reinforce Steinmetz, there was little point in repeating the previous day's folly across 6,000 meters of open ground already ranged by the Prussian artillery. Ramming, of all people, should have known better. Moreover, the Skalice position, though famous in the eighteenth century – when armies were small and cannonballs did not carry six kilometers – was vulnerable in the nineteenth and easily turned, as an Austrian staff officer with an eye for terrain observed: "Completely dominated by Vysokov, only 600 meters wide, with the high, steep banks of the Aupa river *behind* it and both flanks exposed, Skalice was scarcely defensible."[30]

A decision had to be made promptly and Benedek, viewing the ground between himself and Vysokov for the first time, chose not to interrupt the march to Jicin for a costly and questionable prize. While Krismanic made notes and briefed staff officers in Skalice, Benedek toured the position. "There were some Prussians on the move," one of his aides recalled, "but it seemed as though they were only trying to lure us from cover."[31] Though Steinmetz had thrown six battalions down toward Skalice, the bulk of his corps remained high atop the

28　KA, AFA 1866, Karton 2275, 13–166, Capt. Stransky, Josephstadt, June 28, 1866, "Tagebuch." Christopher Duffy, *The Military Life of Frederick the Great* (New York: Atheneum, 1985), pp. 95–8.
29　One of Ramming's staff officers reconstructed the meeting thus: "Arrival of Benedek and his entire staff [ca. 10:00 A.M.]. A short conversation followed which was audible to all of us. Ramming argued hotly for a resumption of yesterday's battle and the commitment of IV Corps as well. Benedek then rode ahead to the battlefield, seeming to agree with General Ramming's arguments." KA, AFA 1866, Karton 2291, 13–103, Sopron, December 16, 1866, Capt. Handel-Mazzetti.
30　KA, AFA 1866, Karton 2291, 13–78, Prague, December 1866, Capt. Butterweck.
31　KA, AFA 1866, Karton 2275, 13–166, Capt. Stransky, Josephstadt, June 28, 1866, "Tagebuch."

plateau, for Steinmetz knew that three Austrian corps were in the vicinity and he worried that Benedek was preparing a counterthrust to recover ground lost the previous day.[32]

Benedek rejoined Krismanic at noon and was overheard saying that there would be no "serious fighting" at Skalice that day. "Anyway," he loudly exclaimed, "I've no intention of offering battle *here.*" He and Krismanic assumed that Steinmetz would spend the day covering Mutius's ascent from Nachod and trying to make contact with the Guard Corps in Eipel. Gazing up at Vysokov, Benedek announced that he would carry out the plan decided on the day before: a junction with Clam-Gallas's Iser Army at Jicin.[33] He asked Krismanic to write out the order: "If a serious battle has not developed [at Skalice] by 2 o'clock," the Feldzeugmeister began to dictate. "And whatever shall do we do if a serious battle *has* developed?" an VIII Corps officer queried. "What are you getting at?" Benedek shot back. Silence. Benedek continued: "If a serious battle has not developed by 2:00 P.M., Archduke Leopold, preceded by Ramming, will abandon Skalice and begin his scheduled march west toward Königinhof and the army's [new position] at Jicin."[34]

After dictating the order, Benedek rather recklessly decided to speed its execution by ordering Leopold's right wing, the Schulz Brigade, to start its march west. Skalice was a cramped town with only one bridge over the Aupa, and Benedek worried that it might take an entire day to move three brigades through the bottleneck. After revising his orders, Benedek, ever the solicitous courtier, invited Archduke Leopold to join him in Josephstadt for luncheon. Leopold declined with thanks, for shells from Vysokov had begun to fall in the Austrian position, and assault columns of the Prussian 9th Division were beginning to descend on Skalice. Benedek continued to insist that this portended nothing more than a skirmish. Shortly after 12 noon, he returned in the direction of Josephstadt convinced that Steinmetz was bluffing. No more than fifteen minutes after his departure from the front, the battle of Skalice erupted.[35]

While Benedek had conferred with Leopold, Steinmetz had made some calculations of his own. Although the march objective assigned him by Second Army headquarters was Gradlice, a village behind Skalice, nearer the Elbe, he doubted whether he could reach it on the twenty-eighth against opposition by the three Austrian corps he had before him. Behind him, the Prussian VI Corps would be little help, for it would need the entire day to pass through Nachod and gain the Vysokov plateau. Here again, Bonin's failure to break through at Trautenau the previous day and his failure to reemerge on the twenty-eighth weighed heavily on

32 Grosser Generalstab, *Feldzug 1866*, pp. 173–5.
33 KA, Nachlässe, B/572: 2 (Nosinic), Wr. Neustadt, August 24, 1866, GM Krismanic to Untersuchungs-Commission.
34 *"Was haben Sie d'rein zu reden?"* KA, AFA 1866, Karton 2293, Vienna, August 1866, Maj. Reinländer. Krismanic's actual order, *eindiktirt* and signed by Benedek in Karton 2266, 6–983h.
35 KA, AFA 1866, Karton 2292, 6–75a, Neustift, July 14, 1866, FML Leopold.

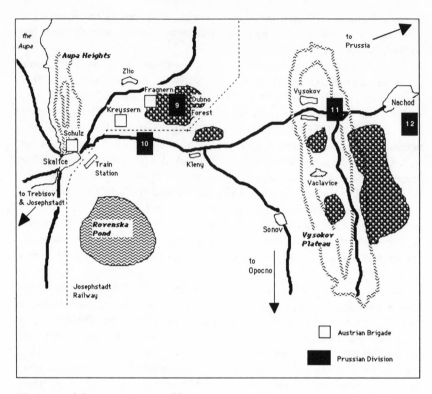

The Battle of Skalice, June 28, 1866

events, for Benedek could now turn a large fraction of his army against Steinmetz alone with little risk to his flank.

Undaunted by the long odds against him, Steinmetz – the very image of old Blücher with his shock of white hair and his oilskin infantryman's cap – decided to press the attack he had begun the day before. He would ask Mutius and the Guards at Burkersdorf for support, push down to the Aupa, and try to punch through Benedek's line at Skalice. Though not overly confident of his chances, he knew that he had put the worst of the campaign behind him on the twenty-seventh by fighting clear of the Nachod defile. At this late date, Benedek could do no more than throw him sideways into the arms of the Guard Corps, or back to Vysokov, where Mutius could come forward with the Prussian VI Corps to disengage him.[36]

At 8:30 A.M., Steinmetz had thrown half his 9th Division – eight infantry battalions and three gun batteries – down toward Skalice to test the left flank of VIII Corps's compact position. While his 9th Division turned Leopold's left,

36 Grosser Generalstab, *Feldzug 1866*, pp. 176–7.

Steinmetz planned to lead his 10th Division straight into Skalice to pin Leopold's brigades in their positions and permit the 9th Division to roll them up from the flank and rear. Benedek had actually witnessed the opening moves of this envelopment but, after consulting with Krismanic, had decided not to sidetrack three entire corps to defeat Steinmetz. Already the road and bridge behind Skalice were clogged with troops, and this was with just one Austrian corps on the scene. It would have been physically impossible for Benedek and Krismanic to deploy two additional corps on short notice.[37]

Ramming later charged that Benedek passed through his reserve position at Trebisov, three kilometers west of Skalice, at 1:30 P.M., when the fighting at Skalice was heaviest. The single shots of skirmishers had been replaced by rolling salvos. Leopold's supply trains rattled through Trebisov at high speed making for the rear to clear the front line at Skalice for battle. One of Ramming's staffers described the "feverish impatience and tension" in Trebisov as Benedek alighted from his carriage for a last word with Ramming before continuing on his way to Josephstadt. General Tassilo Festetics, commandant of the Austrian IV Corps, had come up in the meantime from Schweinschädel to recommend an immediate march to the front by his corps and Ramming's.[38] Benedek and Krismanic vetoed the idea, assuring the two corps commandants that VIII Corps would suffice to secure North Army's flank and rear against a Prussian breakthrough. Benedek then ordered Ramming and Festetics to begin their marches west. Ramming protested that the battle before them at Skalice was "in full flux" (*heftig im Gange*) and again requested permission to engage. Benedek again refused: "I am," he told Ramming, "motivated by more important considerations than the battle *here*."[39] He and Krismanic then took their leave of the stupefied VI Corps commandant and returned to Josephstadt to supervise North Army's march to Jicin.

Steinmetz might have been held had Benedek not entrusted the defense of Skalice to Archduke Leopold. Though Ramming had not led particularly well at Vysokov the day before, Benedek's decision to subordinate him to the Habsburg archduke in this vitally important follow-on battle was an abomination. Forty-three-year-old Archduke Leopold had never been under fire. He was fat, sick in the kidneys, half blind, and despised by his men. With an entire Prussian corps closing on him and his men packed eight men to the square meter inside a narrow position with a deep river at their backs, Leopold, who served in peacetime as the Habsburg navy inspector, neglected to issue even a single order to his brigadiers. All along the

---

37 KA, AFA 1866, Karton 2291, 13–78, Prague, December 1866, Capt. Butterweck.

38 KA, MKSM 1866, Karton 343, 69/9, Josephstadt, June 28, 1866, FZM Benedek to FML Crenneville.

39 ". . . wichtige und höhere Gründe." – "I have no idea what reasons could have dictated that the battle of Skalice was fought with only VIII Corps when there were three army corps and a cavalry division at hand," Ramming replied. KA, AFA 1866, Karton 2291, 13–78, Prague, December 1866, Capt. Butterweck.

line, his troops looked about anxiously. The archduke's left wing was in the air and woods approached to within 500 meters of his front, affording excellent cover to Steinmetz's advance. Retreat was desirable under the circumstances, but difficult given the dense concentration of Austrian troops and the single bridge behind it. When, early in the battle, one of Leopold's subordinates worriedly indicated the Prussian brigade probing the archduke's left, Leopold, the officer recalled, "gave one of his sarcastic snorts and declared that I was seeing things."[40]

Up on the Vysokov plateau, Steinmetz, having by now reconnoitered the road south to Opocno and assured himself that nothing threatened his left flank, ordered a general advance on Skalice, entrusting his base at Vysokov to a single brigade of Mutius's 11th Division.[41] By 11:00 A.M., Steinmetz's 9th Division had approached to within 3,000 meters of VIII Corps's Fragnern Brigade on Leopold's left wing. Although some of Leopold's gunners trained their fire on this Prussian flanking column, most of the shells bored harmlessly into the soft ground before exploding. At noon, Steinmetz learned from a staff rider that he could expect no assistance from the Guards that day, for both Guard divisions were engaged against Gablenz at Burkersdorf and Rudersdorf. Undeterred, Steinmetz ordered his 9th Division to infiltrate the tactically vital Dubno Forest, which covered the approach to Leopold's unsecured left wing, while his 10th Division stormed Leopold's heavily fortified center. Inside the Dubno Forest, the Prussian 9th Division encountered a single battalion of Slovaks, who threw down their rifles and ran for their lives back toward Skalice. Racing ahead, calling *"schnell avancieren"* – a cry Austrian infantry would learn to dread – the Prussians deployed at the edge of the wood, took aim, and fired after the Slovaks. Half the Austrian battalion was killed or wounded in the time it took the men to lope 1,400 meters through standing corn.[42]

Up on the Aupa heights, which formed the left wing of Leopold's position, General Gustav Fragnern watched all this uncertainly. He was still without instructions from Leopold and worried that the Prussian 9th Division would shortly cross through the Dubno Forest to Zlic, turn his left flank, and break into VIII Corps's rear. Fragnern decided to unhinge this attempted envelopment by storming with his two regiments down to the Dubno Forest to throw back the Prussian flanking column. At 12:30 P.M., Fragnern struck up his bands, ordered his men forward, and left his formidable hilltop position; by 1:00 he was dead, his brigade badly shot up.[43] His staff later claimed that the unauthorized attack had not really been a case of insubordination, for Benedek's visit to the front, the presence of Ramming's corps at Trebisov, and the rising volume of the cannonade had convinced Fragnern that a major Austrian push toward Nachod was beginning.

40 KA, AFA 1866, Karton 2292, 6–75c, Kronna, July 5, 1866, Col. Roth. Lettow-Vorbeck, vol. 2, pp. 273–4.
41 Grosser Generalstab, *Feldzug 1866*, pp. 178–9. Glünicke, pp. 106–7.
42 KA, AFA 1866, Karton 2292, 6–75p, Josephstadt, July 1, 1866, Infanterie-Regiment Nr. 75.
43 KA, AFA 1866, Karton 2292, 6–75a, Neustift, July 14, 1866, FML Leopold.

Company commanders in the Fragnern Brigade later recalled that their troops could not have been restrained anyway. Even the brigade artillery limbered up and joined the charge, trundling down the steep slope behind the infantry columns, which ran at the Prussians with the bayonet in a kind of ecstasy. Most of the Austrian officers and half the men in Fragnern's first wave were knocked down by the first Prussian salvo. Fourteen horses crashed heavily to the ground at a stroke. The Ukrainians and Poles of Fragnern's 15th Regiment, deployed in reserve, were so eager to have at the Prussians that they actually overtook Fragnern's first wave and had to be sent back. Six thousand Austrians crowded into Dubno Forest only to be cut down by the converging Prussians, who opened *Schnellfeuer* at 400 meters. Fragnern, moving among his men, was struck and killed by three bullets. A search for the eldest surviving colonel in the brigade turned up no one. All the other officers either had been struck down or had dismounted and taken cover in the woods. Within an hour, Fragnern's mixed-up regiments had lost 3,000 men and six guns.[44]

Austrian survivors – hotly pursued by Prussian riflemen bawling *"Marsch! Marsch!"* – put as much distance between themselves and Dubno Forest as they could manage. A wild-eyed battalion of Ukrainians fled toward Skalice, overran the fortified railroad station, and burst into General Karl Schulz's sector on the right wing of the Austrian position: "I asked them what the devil they were doing on *my* wing," Schulz later testified. "Their officers replied that the men refused to obey orders and could no longer be controlled. I had no choice," Schulz wrote, "but to order some of my men to fix bayonets and march them back to their assigned places in line."[45]

In the Austrian center, between Fragnern and Schulz, General Leopold Kreyssern was sucked into Fragnern's ill-conceived offensive. Still without orders from Archduke Leopold, Kreyssern felt compelled to launch five of his battalions at the southwest corner of Dubno Forest to rescue Fragnern's shattered brigade. Between Kreyssern and the wood, the Skalice railway curved north to east on a high embankment, affording excellent cover, but Kreyssern's battalions started toward it too late. A regiment of Prussian grenadiers, turning to shield 9th Division's left flank from this unexpected attack, made the railway first, flung themselves behind it, and poured rapid-fire into Kreyssern's half-battalion masses, which arrived at the run. Kreyssern's first wave crumpled; the second struggled ahead to the embankment with steep losses, while an entire brigade of the Prussian 10th Division sprinted down the railway and along the road beside it to oppose them. Here the fighting intensified and casualties mounted. Austrian batteries posted at the entrance to Skalice fired shrapnel and canister at the embankment from close range. Steinmetz's corps batteries, which had descended from Vysokov to masked positions inside Kleny Wood, fired back.[46] Leopold, as

44 KA, AFA 1866, Karton 2293, 13–50, Graz, December 25, 1866, Capt. Samonigg.
45 KA, AFA 1866, Karton 2292, 6–75d, Nedelist, July 2, 1866, GM Schulz.
46 Grosser Generalstab, *Feldzug 1866*, p. 179.

14.   The Austrians storm the railway embankment at Skalice, June 28, 1866

startled by Kreyssern's attack as by Fragnern's, sent a staff major hurrying through no-man's-land to the railway embankment to order Kreyssern back to Skalice. Kreyssern, however, like Fragnern before him, was dead, his corpse riddled with bullets. Leopold's messenger arrived safely at the embankment and crabbed through the grass and gravel seeking the eldest surviving officer. The message clutched in his hand read: "It is not our intention to permit ourselves to be drawn into a serious battle."[47]

While Schulz's brigade looked on in horror from Skalice, Kreyssern's regiments, massed in half battalions, were cut to pieces in the clearing below them. When the survivors tried to regain the safety of the Aupa heights, two Prussian battalions came on in hot pursuit, firing on the run and penetrating as far as the Skalice railway station, the heart of VIII Corps' position, directly beneath the Schulz Brigade.[48] At 1:00 P.M., an adjutant arrived in Schulz's position with the retreat order Benedek had dictated an hour earlier. Staff officers carried the order down to the men, who were formed in attack columns above and to the right of the beleagured railway station. At first the Schulz Brigade — Czechs and Germans of the 8th and 74th Regiments — refused to retire. The men had been standing in the position since 6:00 A.M. and were spoiling for a fight. Leopold's staff messengers repeated the retreat order again and again at the top of their lungs. Each time the men drowned it out with cries of *"Hurra! Hurra!"* All along the line, in every brigade, Austrian infantry wanted to have at the Prussians that day. Some officers attributed it to pluck, others to rage at the needle rifle and the sight of so many dead and wounded comrades, others to the double wine ration decanted at 11:45 A.M.[49] Four hundred drunken Ukrainians of the 15th Regiment, who had somehow managed to cross through enemy fire to the east end of the Dubno Forest, took off across open ground in mad pursuit of some astonished Prussian fusiliers. Their officers called them back, to no avail.[50]

Needless to say, these reckless, uncoordinated attacks by Leopold's brigadiers were the opposite of what Benedek and Krismanic had intended. Steinmetz had torn a gaping hole in the defensive cordon at Skalice, and Ramming's VI Corps, already heading west, could do nothing at this late hour to plug it. Meanwhile, Steinmetz's 10th Division was swarming around Skalice railway station, pouring fire into Leopold's center and right, while the Prussian 9th Division busied itself turning the archduke's left flank at Zlic. Two Prussian regiments breasted the Aupa heights and advanced on VIII Corps' only bridge. It was 2:00 P.M. In the center, Steinmetz himself rode to the front to lead the West Prussian 47th Regiment's assault on the railway station. Only bucketloads of shrapnel and case

47 KA, AFA 1866, Karton 2292, 6–75a, Neustift, July 14, 1866, FML Leopold. Karton 2293, 13–49, Vienna, August 1866, Maj. Reinländer.

48 Grosser Generalstab, *Feldzug 1866*, pp. 183–4

49 KA, AFA 1866, Karton 2292, 6–75c, Kronna, July 5, 1866, Col. Roth.

50 KA, AFA 1866, Karton 2293, 13–51, Budapest, November 23, 1866, Capt. Bilimek. Karton 2293, 13–50, Graz, December 25, 1866, Capt. Samonigg.

shot from Leopold's reserve batteries and the valiant efforts of a hastily-assembled Austrian rearguard held up the Prussian attacks on front and flank long enough for the leaderless brigades of Kreyssern and Fragnern to retire.[51] Belatedly recognizing that he was being swallowed in a "pocket battle" of Steinmetz's making, Archduke Leopold sounded the retreat at 2:15 P.M. His disbanded units, enfiladed by the Prussian brigade closing from Zlic, surged backward through the town borne on a wave of panic. "The streets were clogged with stragglers, wounded men, wagons and guns," a staff officer recalled.[52] Two regiments – Fragnern's 15th and Kreyssern's 32nd – had dissolved completely, complicating what was already an exceedingly difficult withdrawal over a single bridge.[53] Many Austrian troops drowned attempting to swim across the Aupa to the safety of the right bank. Others were incinerated in the burning houses of Skalice, where they took cover from the angry Prussian pursuit. The Prussians, Steinmetz in their midst, took nearly 3,000 prisoners when they finally secured the town at 3:00 P.M.[54]

Once clear of Skalice, VIII Corps, sped by panic, overtook Ramming's more orderly march columns and forced them off the Josephstadt road and into the fields alongside. Sixth Corps would have to find its way to the Elbe that night cross-country.[55] At Skalice, the Austrians had felt the full impact of the Prussian needle rifle. Kreyssern's brigade lost 2,000 dead, wounded, and missing; Fragnern's, 3,200 men and 100 officers. In all, VIII Corps yielded six guns and 6,000 casualties, a sum that included 3,000 prisoners, 1,300 of them unwounded. With only two brigades under fire in the course of the day, this amounted to one-third Leopold's effective strength at Skalice. Steinmetz had shaken the Austrians from an elevated position and passed the Aupa with just one-quarter Leopold's losses.[56] The battle attested again to the laxness of Austrian leadership, the unsuitability of shock tactics, and the murderous efficiency of the Prussian rifle.

ARMY HEADQUARTERS, BERLIN AND JOSEPHSTADT, JUNE 28

In Berlin, the triumphal events of June 28 were no comfort to Moltke, who late in the day still knew little about the battles at Podol, Vysokov, and Trautenau, and much less about Burkersdorf and Skalice. This was because the three Prussian

---

51 Grosser Generalstab, *Feldzug 1866*, pp. 182–9.

52 KA, AFA 1866, Karton 2291, 13–78, Prague, December 1866, Capt. Butterweck.

53 KA, AFA 1866, Karton 2293, 13–51, Budapest, November 23, 1866, Capt. Bilimek.

54 Total Austrian casualties at Skalice were 205 officers and 5,372 men, including 1,287 unwounded prisoners. The Prussians lost 62 officers and 1,305 men. KA, AFA 1866, Karton 2292, 6–75a, Neustift, July 14, 1866, FML Leopold. Lettow-Vorbeck, vol. 2, p. 294. Grosser Generalstab, *Feldzug 1866*, p. 189.

55 KA, AFA 1866, Karton 2291, 13–78, Prague, December 1866, Capt. Butterweck. Karton 2293, 13–49, Vienna, August 1866, Maj. Reinländer.

56 KA, AFA 1866, Karton 2292, 6–75c, Kronna, July 5, 1866, Col. Roth. Karton 2270, 8–12m, Vienna, August 16, 1866, FML Leopold to FM Albrecht.

armies operating in Bohemia were still not linked by field telegraphs to Berlin. Their correspondence with Moltke had thus to be carried by dispatch riders to the nearest telegraph station, which, for First Army, was Reichenberg, for Second Army, Libau in Silesia. So long and frustrating were the delays that by June 28, Moltke, who lingered on in Berlin only to oversee the armistice with Hanover — signed on June 29 — resolved to shift royal headquarters to Bohemia at the earliest possible date in order to lead and follow events more closely.

On the ground in Bohemia, communications between the principal Prussian armies were even sketchier than contacts with Berlin. Although Moltke's strategy called for the First and Second Armies to cooperate closely, direct communication between them would not be established until July 2, the eve of Königgrätz.[57] Thus, the two principal Prussian armies advanced and fought their battles independently. Until Königgrätz, when Moltke finally arrived on the scene in Bohemia, the General Staff chief's influence was slight and, for a willful subordinate like Prince Friedrich Karl, easily defied.

Nevertheless, Moltke remained sanguine. Though annoyed with his army commandants, who, in their efforts to keep a free hand and minimize Berlin's meddling, were far less forthcoming than they might have been, Moltke knew just enough about the battles in Bohemia to deduce that his armies were everywhere through the mountains and, in the west, over the Iser. He was, in short, closing the jaws of his envelopment on Benedek and could only hope that the Feldzeugmeister would not choose the twenty-ninth to hit with everything he had at either of Prussia's two great armies, for they were still too far apart to cooperate.[58]

In Josephstadt, Benedek, just returned from Skalice, had his lunch shortly after 2:00 P.M. in the commandant's lodge. His situation was radically altered, though he did not know it at the time. Like the Prussian generals, he preferred to campaign without a field telegraph and would thus remain ignorant of events at Skalice for several more hours.[59] He had heard the sounds of battle at Burkersdorf and Rudersdorf in the morning and on the way back from Skalice had heard the guns there and declared to an officer beside him: "It seems that the Prussians are attacking again."[60] Still, none of this seemed very worrisome at the time. Indeed, the first thing Benedek did upon his return to Josephstadt at 2:00 P.M. was make sure North Army was en route to Jicin.[61] Defensive arrangements had been made to contain the Prussian Guards and Steinmetz. What Benedek could not know at the time was that his staff had committed yet another terrible error, which jeopardized the outcome at Burkersdorf. As for Skalice, Benedek was still unaware that Archduke Leopold, one of his less reputable protegés, was overseeing a catastrophe there.

57 Van Creveld, *Command in War*, pp. 124–32.
58 Grosser Generalstab, *Feldzug 1866*, pp. 195–6.
59 Benold, "Österreichische Feldtelegraphie," pp. 36–7.
60 Lettow-Vorbeck, vol. 2, pp. 273–4.
61 KA, AFA 1866, Karton 2270, 12–7, Vienna, December 16, 1866, Capt. Pohl.

Gablenz had plotted his retreat to the Elbe on the assumption that there would be at least a regiment from IV Corps waiting for him at Deutsch-Prausnitz, ten kilometers south of his bivouacs at Trautenau. Since he had known that there was a Guard division at Eipel on the twenty-seventh, he had asked for the IV Corps detachment to secure his left flank and reinforce Grivicic's drive on Radec from Rudersdorf.[62] North Army headquarters, however, had sent the troops not to Deutsch-Prausnitz but to Ceska-Prausnice. The two places were quite different and were twenty kilometers apart. When Gablenz frantically signaled Deutsch-Prausnitz for reinforcements early on the twenty-eighth, there were no Austrian troops there. Confounded by their own maps, Benedek's staff had unwittingly left Grivicic alone against four times his strength and bared Gablenz's left flank in the process, permitting the Prussian Guards to ram into it at Burkersdorf.[63]

The defeat at Skalice was owed chiefly to Archduke Leopold's incompetence abetted by Benedek's sycophantic indulgence of it. Indeed, just exactly why in May Benedek had designated this sickly war ministry bureaucrat to be the vice-commandant of North Army remains an intriguing mystery.[64] On June 28, a feckless Archduke Leopold and his impulsive brigadiers did for the Prussians in sixty minutes what Steinmetz would otherwise have needed one or two days to accomplish: the evacuation of Skalice and the Aupa line. Many historians have suggested that the outcome of the entire war hinged on this battle. Had Benedek only brought up the two corps he had in reserve behind Skalice and driven Count Karl Thun's II Corps, arriving from the south, into Steinmetz's left flank, what then? Might not Benedek have dealt a deadly blow to Second Army, then crushed Elbe and First Armies at his leisure? More than one historian has suggested that "time stood still" at 12 noon on June 28, 1866.[65] Others have claimed that Benedek actually quarreled with Krismanic for the implementation of (yet another) "secret plan," this time to move against Steinmetz and Mutius at Skalice.[66] Others suggest that Benedek might have returned to Skalice and led the battle there with three or four army corps had not a freak thunder storm drowned out the noises of battle as he jogged home through the rain to Josephstadt.[67] This "thunder of Skalice," however, like the "fog of Chlum" later conjured by Benedek's apologists to explain the defeat at Königgrätz, was really a fanciful attempt to ascribe a humiliating Austrian defeat to an invisible hand. Ramming would testify that Benedek in fact heard the noises of battle at Skalice quite

62 Bartels, *Der Krieg im Jahre 1866*, pp. 22–3.
63 KA, AFA 1866, Karton 2294, 6–107a, Floridsdorf, July 14, 1866, FML Gablenz. Karton 2270, 8–12p, Floridsdorf, August 16, 1866, FML Gablenz. Karton 2296, 13–9, Vienna, December 18, 1866, Col. Grivicic.
64 KA, MKSM 1866, Karton 343, 71/62, Vienna, May 17, 1866, FZM Benedek to Franz Joseph, "Geheim: Bestimmung Nachfolger Nordarmee."
65 Franzel, vol. 2, p. 576.
66 John Presland, *Vae Victis* (London: Hodder and Stoughton, 1934), pp. 233, 240.
67 Friedjung, *Struggle for Supremacy*. Craig, *Königgrätz*, pp. 66–7.

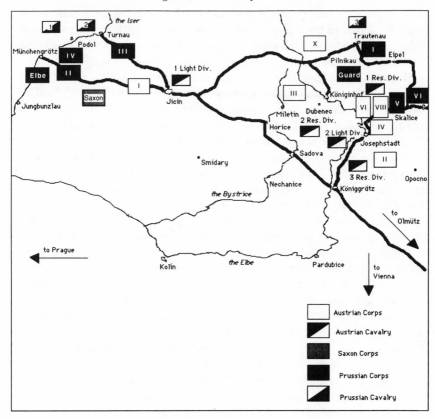

The strategic situation on June 28, 1866

clearly while he was still in Trebisov, only three kilometers west of the fighting front. It was therefore not weather conditions but rather Benedek's own predispositions that prevented him from countermanding the withdrawal from Skalice.

From his vantage point among the batteries at Skalice in the morning, Benedek had seen quite clearly that a renewed Austrian attack on the beech-clad heights of Vysokov would have been a suicide mission. Moreover, Count Thun's II Corps was in fact not fit even to approach Steinmetz's flank, let alone turn it and pursue down to Nachod, where, presumably, it would have been greeted by Louis Mutius's entire Prussian VI Corps. Resting at Opocno on the twenty-eighth, the Austrian II Corps covered just half the distance to Skalice before Leopold's guns fell silent. One of Thun's brigadiers, Michael Thom, noted that a large part of his brigade did not even make it that far. The Austrian infantrymen collapsed from exhaustion and lay prone in the middle of the road, raindrops splashing on their upturned faces. Hundreds of men from Thun's Saffran and Henriquez Brigades keeled over beside them. Second Corps had been marching without a rest since

June 17, had not slept the night before, and had not eaten in more than twelve hours.[68] Thun's shattered corps, worn out by the flank march from Olmütz, was living proof of Moltke's aphorism that "an error in the *original* concentration of armies can hardly be corrected during the whole course of a campaign."[69]

On June 28, Benedek had to move against one of two Prussian armies in one of two quite different theaters, and he settled upon the theater that favored Austrian arms and did not require a time-consuming change of line. Only to turn round to face Steinmetz at Skalice, to say nothing of actually fighting him on a narrow front, Benedek would have had to halt North Army's flank march, sidetrack its supply convoys, gun reserve, ammunition park, and field hospitals, and spend an entire day wheeling round to face north. Moltke called just such a *changement de ligne* one of the most perplexing and bothersome aspects of war.[70] It was therefore understandable that Benedek chose merely to parry the Prussian thrust at Skalice while continuing on to Jicin. Still, as he posted west with the bulk of North Army, Benedek did have to make sure that *someone* parried Steinmetz and kept the converging Prussian armies apart. Hence, the significance of the Feldzeugmeister's morning visit to Skalice on the twenty-eighth, where he failed to organize a stout, lasting defense of the Aupa river line with the three corps he had to hand. Archduke Leopold's altogether predictable collapse in the afternoon then threatened North Army with disaster.[71] At Josephstadt, one of Benedek's aides expressed shock at the sudden strategic reversal: "Gablenz is surrounded; Skalice is lost!" Moltke's vise was closing much sooner than anticipated.[72] Now more than ever, Benedek needed to speed the march west, to escape the closing Prussian pincers and crush Prince Friedrich Karl's First Army before the Prussian Second Army, strung out between Skalice and Trautenau, could converge on his flank and rear. Instead, Benedek, his confidence destroyed, chose the worst possible course. He turned at bay.

At 9:30 P.M. on June 28, Benedek issued revised orders to his corps commandants. In view of the defeats at Skalice and Burkersdorf, North Army would "suspend" the march west and assume a "central position" at Königinhof on the

---

68 So much for critics of Krismanic who would have had him commit four "fresh" corps at Skalice on the twenty-eighth. KA, AFA 1866, Karton 2282, 13–6, "Operations-Journal der Brigade Thom."

69 Hajo Holborn, "The Prusso-German School," in *Makers of Modern Strategy*, p. 289.

70 "For all operative plans and administrative work must be abandoned and re-done. A general contemplating a change of line must first consider whether it can really be done." Vincennes, AAT, MR 6/1536, Helmuth von Moltke, "De l'influence des armes perfectionées sur le combat," *Militär-Wochenblatt*, July 8, 1865.

71 Staff critics later ridiculed Leopold's first cable, from Trebisov at 2:00 P.M., for its unjustified and misleading note of panic: "The Prussians are already west of Skalice and are pursuing us quickly." His second cable, at 5:15 P.M., read by Benedek at 6:45, included the wild exaggeration that "the Prussians hit us in the Skalice position with at *least* two army corps." KA, AFA 1866, Karton 2266, 6–1004 and -ad 1004, Trebisov and Caslawek, June 28, 1866, FML Leopold to FZM Benedek. Lettow-Vorbeck, vol. 2, p. 294.

72 "*Gablenz ist abgeschnitten! Skalitz ist verloren!*" KA, AFA 1866, Karton 2275, 13–166, Josephstadt, June 28, 1866, Capt. Karl Stransky, "Tagebuch."

Elbe. Positioned between the oncoming Prussian armies, Benedek would swivel to face the nearer of the two: Steinmetz and the rest of Second Army descending from the north.[73] Confusion, however, muddied Benedek's new dispositions from the start. The Feldzeugmeister did not manage to dispatch the new orders until the following morning at 8:00 A.M. Even officers in Krismanic's Operations Chancery went to bed on the twenty-eighth unsure of what was planned for the next day.[74] Benedek's own adjutant asserted that he was under the impression that Königinhof was merely the first halt on a continuing march to Jicin.[75] When it finally became clear the next day what Benedek intended, nearly everyone in North Army was baffled.[76] The staff chief of III Corps, which had planned to probe toward the Iser on the twenty-ninth alongside IV Corps, recalled that "we still considered the news from Skalice to be exaggerated and none of us believed that [Benedek] would *really* commit himself in that direction. Furthermore, we had *no* information on the battles at Vysokov, Skalice and Trautenau, or the whereabouts of IV Corps."[77] By developing his plans secretly and haphazardly, Benedek ran his officers in the field ragged on the twenty-ninth. General Coudenhove's 3rd Reserve Cavalry Division covered half its scheduled march to Jicin before Benedek's counterorders finally overtook it: "Right turn and advance to Königinhof."[78] While Coudenhove raged, cooler heads in North Army head-quarters noted the futility of Benedek's abrupt change of line: "Redeploy the *entire army* merely to rescue Gablenz??!!" an officer in the Operations Chancery scrib-bled in his diary. "What this *really* means is that *now* the Prussians can hit us from *three* directions: Trautenau, Skalice *and* Jicin. What a stupid idea."[79]

In sum, the critical mistake in Benedek's war was committed *after*, not before, the battle of Skalice. Instead of seeing his original plan through, the Feldzeug-meister pulled up at Königinhof, made front to the north, and sat down to await the Prussian Second Army on the right bank of the Elbe. He stopped six Austrian infantry corps in their tracks to await one: Gablenz's X Corps, whose connection with the rest of North Army was threatened by the rapid advance of Steinmetz and the Prussian Guards. The Feldzeugmeister was plainly rattled by Gablenz's

73 KA, AFA 1866, Karton 2286, 6-ad 90, Vienna, August 22, 1866, FML Festetics and Capt. Sembratowicz, "Rélation über die Aufstellung am 28. Juni." Karton 2285, 13–7, Graz, February 5, 1867, Col. Catty.

74 KA, AFA 1866, Karton 2270, 12–7, Vienna, December 16, 1866, Capt. Pohl, "Darstellung der im Hauptquartier der k.k. Nordarmee mitgemachten Kriegsereignisse."

75 KA, AFA 1866, Karton 2270, 8–12aa, Budapest, August 12, 1866, Col. Kriz.

76 KA, AFA 1866, Karton 2286, 6-ad 90, Vienna, August 22, 1866, FML Festetics.

77 KA, AFA 1866, Karton 2285, 13–7, Graz, February 5, 1867, Col. Catty. Ramming marveled that the "projected offensive to Jicin had been abandoned" so abruptly. Karton 2270, 8–121, Pressburg, August 17, 1866, FML Ramming to FM Albrecht.

78 KA, Nachlässe, B/946 (Coudenhove), Smiritz, June 29, 1866, FML Coudenhove, "Tagebuch."

79 He was referring to Benedek's description of Königinhof as an "*Aufnahme-Stellung*": North Army would pause there to "pick up" Gablenz, confront Second Army, and then carry on to the west. KA, AFA 1866, Karton 2275, 13–166, Josephstadt, June 28, 1866, Capt. Stransky, "Tagebuch."

mysterious disappearance after Burkersdorf and Leopold's defeat at Skalice. A staff officer recalled that late on June 28 Benedek sent him over the Elbe to find Gablenz. When the officer asked Benedek what orders he should give Gablenz once he located him, Benedek merely shrugged.[80] While the North Army commandant waited in his new position for Steinmetz, Mutius, Bonin, and Prince August to make their separate ways down from the northern passes, the whole Austrian war effort rather absurdly came to depend upon Clam-Gallas's little Iser Army backpedalling from Münchengrätz to Jicin. Would Clam and the Saxons hold long enough for Benedek to repulse Second Army at Königinhof and then resume his march west?

80 KA, AFA 1866, Karton 2296, 13–10, Vienna, December 19, 1866, Capt. Schulz.

8

Jicin and Benedek's flight to Königgrätz

"Had Benedek not altered his *original* march plan," Count Karl Coudenhove fretted on June 29, "my division would have arrived at Jicin in time to reinforce" Iser Army in its decisive engagement with the Prussian First Army.[1] Indeed, half of North Army would have. Archduke Ernst's III Corps was already at Miletin on the twenty-ninth, Leopold's VIII Corps scheduled to arrive there the same day. Festetics's IV Corps, Ramming's VI Corps, and Prince Thurn und Taxis's 2nd Light Cavalry Division were all supposed to arrive near Jicin on June 29.[2] Hours before Iser Army's battle there, Archduke Ernst received an appeal from Clam-Gallas for reinforcements. He might have marched to Jicin in plenty of time to shore up Clam's right flank and center had the archduke – every bit as ineffectual as his cousin Leopold – not refused the assistance, lamely explaining "that such a move would have frustrated the purpose of Benedek's revised plans for the concentration of the army" at Königinhof.[3]

Benedek himself was stuck in the jumble of wagon trains trying to negotiate the muddy tracks between Josephstadt and Dubenec, a village at the heart of the new North Army position above Königinhof.[4] Since Benedek had forbidden units still east of the Elbe to cross to the right bank on the bridges at Josephstadt (for fear Steinmetz would materialize in mid-crossing to take the fortress by surprise), three Austrian corps had to construct pontoon bridges and skirt the best roads to Königinhof.[5] "How hungry the poor devils look," one of Benedek's staffers observed when Leopold's weary corps passed through Josephstadt from Skalice. "I'm

1 KA, Nachlässe, B/946 (Coudenhove), Smiritz, June 29, 1866, "Tagebuch." AFA 1866, Karton 2270, 8–12y, Sopron, August 12, 1866, FML Coudenhove.

2 KA, AFA 1866, Karton 2280, 13–104, Vienna, December 1866, Col. Pelikan. Karton 2291, 13–103, Sopron, December 16, 1866, Capt. Handel-Mazzetti.

3 KA, AFA 1866, Karton 2285, 13–7, Graz, February 5, 1867, Col. Catty.

4 "Headquarters moved to Dubenec from Josephstadt. All roads jammed with wagons. None of them knew where they were supposed to go." KA, AFA 1866, Karton 2270, 12–7, Vienna, December 16, 1866, Capt. Pohl.

5 KA, AFA 1866, Karton 2270, 8–12l, Pressburg, August 17, 1866, FML Ramming. Nachlässe, B/572: 2 (Nosinic), Vienna, January 6, 1867, Capt. Sembratowicz.

afraid that we're pushing and pulling them in and out like drawers."[6] A VI Corps officer wending his way to Dubenec found that this march, like the ones before it, "was calculated without consideration for the factors of time, space or the waning stamina of the men." Whereas supply had begun to be regulated on the routes west, "there would be no food on *these* roads till the 30th." Traffic to Königinhof was so congested that some Austrian brigades needed sixteen hours to march just eleven kilometers.[7] The stage was rather dismally set for the battle of Jicin. Twelve hours earlier it had been the focal point of Benedek's war effort. Now it was a neglected sideshow in the hands of two demonstrably inept generals: Count Eduard Clam-Gallas and Prince Albert of Saxony.

FIRST ARMY MOVES EAST, JUNE 29

Early on June 29, in receipt of two importuning cables from Moltke ordering him eastward to prevent Benedek from turning the five corps he had at Josephstadt against Second Army, Prince Friedrich Karl finally bestirred himself at München-grätz and ordered General August Werder, commandant of the Prussian 3rd Division, to probe toward Jicin and reestablish contact with the Austrians.[8] This was all rather late and undertaken only after Moltke had persuaded the Prussian king himself to order his nephew eastward in no uncertain terms. Prince Friedrich Karl, who was proving a great disappointment to Great Headquarters in Berlin, complied reluctantly. His campaign, so promising at the outset, was wilting from hunger, thirst, and long marches. Whereas Reichenberg and its environs had furnished inexhaustible quantities of food and drink, Friedrich Karl's regiments were finding the Iser valley a desert by comparison. Wells were poisoned and farms stripped bare. "There is," the prince wired Berlin on the twenty-eighth, "nothing to eat here. With hungry, exhausted men and horses, we cannot possibly fight. Send wagons of bread and hay immediately." Elbe and First Armies were literally starving. Though Austrian logistics were bad, Prussia's were much worse. The lightning offensive planned by Moltke and supplied by Roon was moving forward too swiftly and was stretching its lines of supply to the breaking point.[9]

These formidable, nearly incapacitating supply problems notwithstanding, Moltke – still snugly ensconced in Berlin – considered that Prince Friedrich Karl was conducting a slack and witless campaign. From the prince's unauthorized detour south with 60,000 troops on the twenty-eighth – which had the calamitous logistical effect of concentrating 100,000 hungry Prussians in the barren town of Münchengrätz – Moltke inferred that Friedrich Karl was more interested in claim-

6 KA, AFA 1866, Karton 2275, 13–166, Dubenec, June 29, 1866, Capt. Stransky, "Tagebuch."
7 KA, AFA 1866, Karton 2291, 13–103, Sopron, December 16, 1866, Capt. Handel-Mazzetti. Karton 2293, 13–49. Karton 2291, 13–79, Prague, December 1866, Capt. Stanger.
8 Grosser Generalstab, *Feldzug 1866*, pp. 195–8. Van Creveld, *Command in War*, pp. 126–7.
9 Lettow-Vorbeck, vol. 2, pp. 263–5.

ing credit for the capture of Prague than in uniting with Second Army at Jicin.[10] When the Prussian staff chief finally persuaded the prince to resume his march east on the twenty-ninth, the orders were distributed so late that the Prussian divisions did not set off until midday, under a hot sun.[11] Herwarth von Bittenfeld's Elbe Army turned south toward Jungbunzlau and followed the route taken by the Saxons the day before. Both Prussian armies were footsore, famished, and noting an ever higher incidence of illness and malingering. Prince Friedrich Karl remained behind on the Iser, damning Moltke's eyes and pleading with Berlin for more food and drink.[12] He would thus exert no control over the pivotal battle at Jicin, which, though audible in Münchengrätz, would be fought to a conclusion before the prince could negotiate the crowded route east to Jicin and the Elbe.

THE BATTLE OF JICIN, JUNE 29

On their midday march to Jicin, dozens of General Werder's sunburnt and thirsty men collapsed from heat stroke. Marching songs petered out after a listless bar or two.[13] As Werder's 3rd Division neared Jicin at 6:00 P.M., they heard shots northeast of them. Ludwig Tümpling's Prussian 5th Division – descending the Turnau to Jicin road on Werder's left – had struck the center of Clam-Gallas's position west of town.

Clam-Gallas's mission to "hold the Iser line at any price" had been superseded on the twenty-seventh by Benedek's plan to concentrate North Army at Jicin, the former seat of Wallenstein's Duchy of Friedland and the most important crossroads between the Elbe and the Iser. Clam settled down before Jicin on the twenty-ninth confident that he would be relieved that evening by Archduke Ernst's III Corps, and reinforced by three others the next day.[14] Though he had no idea what was going on at Königinhof, nor even where North Army headquarters was, things seemed to be looking up.[15] Jicin was a naturally strong position and only needed bodies to fill it. These, Clam believed, were on the way.[16] Nevertheless, he was deeply troubled. Prussian skirmishers had fired on his pickets late on the twenty-eighth. Clam knew that an attack from the west could come at any hour, yet he had absolutely no idea how he fit into Benedek's larger scheme, whether or not, as he put it, "he ought still to regard himself as a link in the chain of [Benedek's] strategic combinations."[17]

10 Grosser Generalstab, *Feldzug 1866*, p. 159.
11 Moltke, *Strategy*, pp. 51–2.
12 Lettow-Vorbeck, vol. 2, p. 350. Wachenhusen, pp. 95–112.
13 Fontane, *Der deutsche Krieg*, vol. 1, pp. 189–91.
14 KA, MKSM 1866, 69/6, Josephstadt, June 27, 1866, FZM Benedek to GdC Clam.
15 KA, AFA 1866, Karton 2280, 13–103, Lemberg, December 19, 1866, Col. Litzelhofen.
16 KA, AFA 1866, Karton 2280, 13–104, Vienna, December 1866, Col. Pelikan.
17 KA, AFA 1866, Karton 2280, 13–117, Schloss Friedland, October 1866, GdC Clam-Gallas, "Meine Erlebnisse im Feldzuge 1866." Fontane, *Der deutsche Krieg*, vol. 1, p. 203.

Had Clam been able to deploy the Saxons at Jicin, his front to north and west would have been much stronger. But instead of taking the shortest route to Jicin, the Saxon retreat from Münchengrätz had described a long detour south: to Jungbunzlau on the twenty-seventh, west to Jicineves on the twenty-eighth, and finally north toward Jicin on the twenty-ninth, where the Saxon 2nd Division arrived exhausted in the afternoon. The Saxon 1st Division remained behind in Jicineves and would play no part in Iser Army's most important battle.[18] This Saxon long march had been hotly debated at Münchengrätz, where Clam's staff had volunteered to cover the Saxon retreat on the direct route to Jicin, which was the one the Austrians took. But Saxony's quarrelsome staff chief, General Georg Fabrice, had insisted on the southerly route, a long, exhausting loop that left half the Saxon army *hors de combat* on the day of Jicin.[19]

On the twenty-ninth, the two Saxon brigades bound for Jicin had risen at 3:00 A.M. and marched for seven hours. When Prince Albert arrived on the edge of Jicin at Podhrad, ten kilometers south of Clam's position at Brada-Dilec, he decided that there would be no battle that day. Instead of moving his division into line, which would have required more hours of marching and maneuvering in the midday heat, he pitched camp more than an hour south of the sector he was supposed to occupy, unintentionally opening a lethal gap in Iser Army's Jicin front.[20]

Without the Saxons, Clam-Gallas's I Corps and 1st Light Cavalry Division mustered just 40,000 of Iser Army's 60,000 bayonets, yet now Clam had before him the possibility that the Prussians would try to envelop Jicin with two armies from Turnau and Münchengrätz. Another "strategic withdrawal" was quite out of the question, for, as far as Clam knew, Jicin figured to be the crucial road hub for North Army in the days ahead. Three march routes converged on the town from the east, making it the hinge of Benedek's redeployment from Josephstadt and the most likely spot for the Feldzeugmeister's first big battle with the Prussian Elbe and First Armies. To secure the town against Prussian attacks from the west, Clam selected a famous position — extolled by generations of Austrian staff mappers — north and west of Jicin on either side of the Privysin, a forested cliff rising from the plain that rolled in from the Iser. The right wing of this position was Eisenstadtl, an elevated village that flanked the road in from Turnau. The left wing was Lochov, on the road from Münchengrätz. Clam placed a brigade in both of these places, a third on the east face of the Privysin, above the Turnau road, a fourth on the south face, above the Münchengrätz road, and a fifth in reserve, behind the Privysin.

Leopold Gondrecourt, Clam's second-in-command, supervised the Austrian deployment and had high hopes for this naturally strong frontage of interlocking

---

18 KA, AFA 1866, Karton 2266, 6–1080, Dubenec, June 29, 1866, GM Krismanic to FML Crenneville.

19 KA, AFA 1866, Karton 2280, 13–103, Lemberg, December 19, 1866, Col. Litzelhofen. Grosser Generalstab, *Feldzug 1866*, p. 220.

20 KA, AFA 1866, Karton 2280, 13–104, Vienna, December 1866, Col. Pelikan.

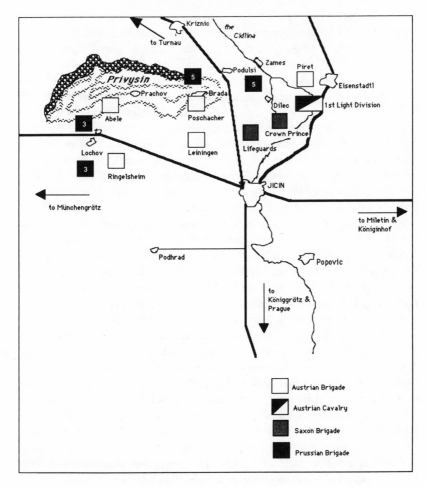

The Battle of Jicin, June 29, 1866

Flügelpunkte. Eisenstadtl and Brada Hill enfiladed the Turnau road, and the two brigades at Lochov and Prachov Hill barred the road from Münchengrätz to Jicin.[21] The center of the position, Dilec, was a sunken village with the swampy Cidlina brook coursing behind it. This was the Saxon sector, foolishly left unoccupied by Prince Albert throughout the afternoon of the twenty-ninth. Here Gondrecourt deployed fifty-six of his ninety-six guns as well as Leopold Edelsheim's 1st Light Cavalry Division. Forty more guns were divided between the Privysin and Piret's position at Eisenstadtl.

By June 29, Ludwig Tümpling's Prussian 5th Division, which had not joined

21 KA, AFA 1866, Karton 2270, 8–12a, St. Pölten, August 7, 1866, FML Gondrecourt.

in the battle of Münchengrätz the day before, was already half way to Jicin from Turnau. After a twelve-hour rest, the division resumed its march at 1:30 P.M. and arrived before the Privysin two hours later. Though outnumbered by the Austro-Saxon force before him, Tümpling, who had learned from Prince Friedrich Karl that the Austrian III Corps was probably on its way to Jicin, resolved to attack Iser Army before it could be reinforced. He thus rolled his brigade batteries into line and began softening up the Austrian position with eight-pound shells.[22] In Podhrad, a startled Crown Prince Albert sounded the alarm and spent a frustrating ninety minutes getting the Saxon 2nd Division on the road to its assigned place in line at Dilec. The first brigade in Albert's march column, the Saxon Lifeguards, did not even reach Jicin, still four kilometers south of Dilec, until 6:00 P.M., leaving the Saxons and the Prussians equidistant from the keypoint of the Austrian position as the two sides came to grips.[23]

Failed by the Saxons, Clam-Gallas considered refusing battle and retiring to the Elbe but clung to the hope that Archduke Ernst's III Corps would arrive shortly to fall on Tümpling's flank and line of retreat.[24] After an hour-long cannonade (throughout which Clam, Gondrecourt, and Litzelhofen begged Prince Albert to move his brigades faster to Dilec), Tümpling attacked at 5:00 P.M., hurling his 9th Brigade along the Cidlina to Zames and Dilec, his 10th Brigade at the mammoth bulk of the Privysin.

Both Prussian brigades came under fire from Clam's twelve batteries, but Tümpling, who was wounded in the fight, pushed the attack restlessly forward. A single Prussian company cleared Podulsi with rapid firing, putting two of Ferdinand Poschacher's battalions to flight. Poschacher regrouped his regiments in Brada, the next village up from Podulsi on the Privysin. To offset the Prussian rifle's superior rate-of-fire, Poschacher ordered his line troops to do nothing but load rifles and pass them forward to his sharpshooting *Jäger*. In this way, three Prussian companies storming Brada were blown back with heavy casualties at 6:00 P.M., just as August Werder's 3rd Division arrived from the direction of Münchengrätz and began its attack on Lochov, Clam's left wing.

Tümpling's left-hand column, five battalions strong, struck up the north face of the Privysin. With his 9th Brigade halted, Tümpling sought to regain the initiative by pushing his 10th Brigade up and into the flank and rear of Poschacher's brigade at Brada. However, on the boulder-strewn, overgrown slope Tümpling met unexpectedly with Vincenz Abele's brigade, which rushed forward in storm columns to repel Tümplings flanking attack. After a hand-to-hand struggle, the Prussian 10th Brigade fell back, moved west through the trees, exchanged shots with Poschacher's skirmishers, and then retired. To Abele's left, on the Münchengrätz road, Joseph Ringelsheim's brigade was pushing back the

22 Grosser Generalstab, *Feldzug 1866*, pp. 199–200.

23 One and a half to two hours' march time. KA, AFA 1866, Karton 2280, 13–104, Vienna, December 1866, Col. Pelikan. Lettow-Vorbeck, vol. 2, p. 353.

24 KA, AFA 1866, Karton 2280, 13–117, Schloss Friedland, October 1866, GdC Clam-Gallas.

Prussian battalion leading Werder's 3rd Division into the fight. Even without the Saxons, Clam's front seemed to be holding.[25]

Not for long: on the Austrian right, Tümpling's 9th Brigade renewed its attack. Two fusilier battalions followed the Cidlina brook as far as Zames, where they met with an Austrian line battalion hurriedly pushed into their path from the Austrian wing at Eisenstadtl by General Ludwig Piret. Prussian eyewitnesses claimed that these Austrian troops – Italians of the Veronese 45th Regiment – actually had to be driven into the fight with loaded revolvers leveled at their backs.[26] Not surprisingly, a well-aimed Prussian salvo drove them off, allowing Tümpling to advance three batteries. By this opportunistic, probing advance, small Prussian firing parties found every soft spot in Gondrecourt's sprawling position, stealing undetected through the heavily-defended *Flügelpunkte* toward the center, trailed by their guns. It was hard to believe that two Prussian battalions could install themselves in Zames, near the heart of the Austrian position, and not immediately be crushed by the massive force arrayed around them. Yet Leiningen's brigade, deployed in reserve only two kilometers away, did not even stir, and Piret's regiments sullenly refused to storm the needle rifle. Saber cavalry proved useless against this disciplined Prussian infantry. General Edelsheim, who had lobbied unsuccessfully in the interwar period for carbines, sent several squadrons of Austrian hussars against Zames only to see them blown back by rapid-fire, leaving fifty casualties strewn in their wake. "Our infantry did this in line," a Prussian officer recalled. "We did not even bother to form squares."[27] Only the Austrian batteries on Privsyin and around Eisenstadtl offered effective resistance to Tümpling's push. They brought Zames under fire and ignited the village. The Prussian battalions resting there escaped forward, racing toward Dilec, keypoint of the Austro-Saxon defense of Jicin.[28]

The Prussian capture of Dilec at Jicin was like a dress rehearsal for a similiar *coup de main* at Chlum, which would decide the battle of Königgrätz four days later. Looking south to Jicin, the Prussians could see a Saxon brigade hurrying north to occupy Dilec. Though the village was a wretched, low-lying place exposed to plunging fire from all around, it flanked the Privysin massif and straddled the Cidlina. If the Prussians could take and hold Dilec, Clam-Gallas would have no choice but to fold up his whole position and abandon Jicin. This easy Prussian success was so astounding that Clam maintained to the end of his days that he had been up against two Prussian corps at Jicin, when in fact he had been fighting only two unconnected divisions.[29] The Prussian rifle, a terrific

25 Fontane, *Der deutsche Krieg*, vol. 1, pp. 193–215. Grosser Generalstab, *Feldzug 1866*, pp. 200–4.

26 Wachenhusen, p. 87.

27 KA, AFA 1866, Karton 2280, 13–103, Lemberg, December 19, 1866, Col. Litzelhofen. Wachenhusen, p. 85.

28 Grosser Generalstab, *Feldzug 1866*, pp. 204–6.

29 KA, AFA 1866, Karton 2280, 13–103, Lemberg, December 19, 1866, Col. Litzelhofen. Karton 2280, 13–117, Schloss Friedland, October 1866, GdC Clam-Gallas.

force-multiplier, explained this partly, but the Austrians were also repeating errors observed time and again in Italy in 1859. Masses of their infantry were standing idly by while others were chased away by faster moving enemy columns.

Tümpling scented blood. He summoned a reserve battalion and sent it forward to support the attack on Dilec. Fifteen Prussian rifle companies swarmed into the town from all sides at 7:30 P.M., loading and firing their breech-loaders as quickly as they could, driving the late-arriving Saxons back across the Cidlina. Another battalion of Piret's Venetians, closing on Dilec from the right wing, mistook the Saxon Crown Prince Brigade for Prussians and hit them broadside with a volley. Saxon officers danced along the muddy streambed waving white handkerchiefs, signaling their Austrian comrades on the other side not to fire again. Prussians pursuing from Dilec in the lowering darkness observed this apparent Saxon surrender with glee and jogged over to accept it. The Saxon infantry, unaware of what their officers were doing behind them, received the Prussians with a salvo at point-blank range, waded the Cidlina, and headed south, stumbling through ditches, bogs, and water courses toward Jicin with the furious Prussian infantry hot on their heels.[30]

Up at Eisenstadtl, on the Austrian right wing opposite Dilec, Ludwig Piret, without orders from Clam or Prince Albert, decided on his own initiative to disengage the luckless Saxons by pinching off the salient Tümpling's 9th Brigade had pushed deep into the Austrian position. He struck up his marching bands, deployed his entire brigade in battalion columns, and conducted them down to the Cidlina. Though outnumbered, the Prussians calmly put their rifle sights up to 250 meters and opened fire. Piret's first column broke and ran after three aimed volleys. He sent two more columns, three battalions in all, up to Zames to take Dilec from behind. Recognizing the danger of this maneuver, Tümpling shook out his last reserve battalion and sent it at the run from Podulsi to Zames, where it greeted Piret's storm columns with rapid-fire.[31] An Austrian private who survived this bayonet charge into withering fire recalled the sensation: "I shudder to think how many balls flew past me, less than a hand's breadth too wide. One actually hit me, ripping the sleeve off my coat." His company advanced too far and found a Prussian flanking column in its rear. "I was nearly taken prisoner. My company turned around and we ran back toward Eisenstadtl, every man for himself. I was among the last ones and couldn't take another step." An Austrian stretcher-bearer pulled him to his feet and dragged him away to the south. "Although it was dark, the Prussians kept up the pursuit," he remembered.[32]

Six Prussian companies had beaten four battalions of the Piret Brigade, which suffered 25 percent casualties and then disbanded. Cut off from the rest of I Corps, Piret's men fled into the night. And so it went for their comrades all along

---

30 Fontane, *Der deutsche Krieg*, vol. 1, p. 222.
31 Grosser Generalstab, *Feldzug 1866*, p. 208.
32 KA, Nachlässe, B/1453 (Lebeda), Lauterbach, November 13, 1866, Pvt. Lebeda.

the line. Austrian troops spilled from the Privysin and bolted for the rear, desperate to escape the exhausted Prussian companies wandering round the center of Clam's crumbling position. The seven battalions of Leiningen's brigade and Poschacher's reserves could have reached Dilec in under thirty minutes, yet they did not budge throughout the entire battle. Now they took to their heels.

Dilec, the keypoint of the Austrian position, was lost to the Prussian 5th Division. On the Münchengrätz post road, Werder's Prussian 6th Brigade had reinforced the 5th, and was presently striking into the cornfields south of the Austrian left wing, attempting to outflank Ringelsheim's brigade at Lochov and complete the envelopment of Iser Army begun by Tümpling. An attack along the road by Werder's 42nd Fusiliers had been halted in Lochov by Abele's brigade, which descended a second time from the Privysin. The entire left wing of the Austrian position was obscured by powder smoke. Many Prussian units had used up their ammunition and had to be sent back to reload. While his light infantry fell back in confusion, Werder sent a battalion of grenadiers through their files. Advancing straight up the road, they pushed Abele and Ringelsheim back toward Jicin with rapid-fire, exhausting all *their* ammunition in the process. As the Prussians passed through Lochov to exploit the victory, they saw two of Abele's battalions on the Privysin gazing down at them but making no effort to hit their offered flank. Now nothing stood between Werder and the strategically vital town of Jicin.[33]

At this moment, roughly 8:00 P.M., when Clam-Gallas and Prince Albert of Saxony had managed to lose a battle despite their excellent position and superior numbers, new orders arrived from Benedek in Josephstadt: "I have suspended the move to the Iser. Today the army will take up the new position described in the appendix. Continue your movement to join with the grand army. Until the junction is complete, avoid all major battles."[34] General Gondrecourt seized the order, turned it over, and back again. Where was the promised appendix or *Beilage* describing the new position of North Army? *"Lag nicht bei!"* he thundered. Had not so many men been dying in the fields west of town as a consequence of this sort of bungling, the situation would have been comical. Benedek's order had been drafted at 12 noon in Josephstadt and transmitted not by telegraph but on horseback, and only after a seven-hour delay owed to General Henikstein's forgetfulness.[35] Though Benedek ordered Iser Army to rejoin North Army, he did not specify a meeting place.

Crown Prince Albert – Iser Army's supreme commander – brusquely ordered a retreat. This touched off another quarrel in headquarters. Gondrecourt was

---

33 Fontane, *Der deutsche Krieg*, vol. 1, p. 196–7. Grosser Generalstab, *Feldzug 1866*, pp. 209–20.

34 KA, AFA 1866, Karton 2266, 6–1091, Josephstadt, June 29, 1866, FZM Benedek to Crown Prince Albert. Karton 2280, 13–104, Vienna, December 1866, Col. Pelikan.

35 Benedek's Byzantine headquarters required that General Henikstein, as "headquarters president," handpick the courier for important messages. He did not hit upon Count Sternberg until late in the day. Benold, "Österreichische Feldtelgraphie," p. 43. KA, AFA 1866, Karton 2270, 8–12a, St. Pölten, August 7, 1866, FML Gondrecourt.

angry with the Saxons for arriving late and with only a fraction of their strength at Dilec. The battle of Jicin was in full swing. Clam still had uncommitted reserves to hand. Crown Prince Albert's second brigade was just beginning to trickle into action from its bivouacs south of Jicin. Colonel Joseph Pelikan, Austria's military attaché in Berlin before the war, urged Albert to stand his ground. First drive back the Prussians, he argued, *then* withdraw. Pelikan's sensible recommendation fell on deaf ears; Crown Prince Albert and General Fabrice were adamant. Orders were orders, they said.

In fact, Prince Albert probably viewed Benedek's poorly timed retreat order as a heaven-sent opportunity to disengage from the mess before him. Thirty-three Austro-Saxon infantry battalions with ninety-six guns had been dislodged from a strong position by twenty-four Prussian battalions with just thirty-six guns.[36] And there would assuredly be many more Prussian divisions advancing behind these two. Prince Albert therefore decided to cut his losses, "dictating the retreat order not in his usual jolly style, but in a most decided fashion that brooked no argument," Colonel Pelikan recalled.[37] Both staffs had long since given up peering toward Eisenstadtl, where Archduke Ernst's III Corps was *supposed* to have appeared hours earlier. And everyone was worn out by the arduous retreat from the Iser. Though Clam and Albert did not know it, they were still three long marches from North Army. Had Prince Friedrich Karl's hungry army only been faster on its feet, Iser Army could easily have been encircled and destroyed.[38] Clam-Gallas's left wing on the Münchengrätz road would not hold for long, for the Ringelsheim Brigade, like so many others, had been run ragged by Iser Army's chaotic retreat. Ringelsheim's men had not seen their supply trains since the twenty-seventh and many of them were fighting barefoot.[39] To Joseph Ringelsheim, who had been in Austrian headquarters throughout the calamitous war of 1859, all of this must have struck a familiar chord.

While Ringelsheim's regiments made a last stand at Lochov and Piret's brigade reeled back from Dilec, the Austro-Saxon retreat surged through Jicin. Though Clam-Gallas and the crown prince had reserved the south road to Königgrätz for the Saxons and the east road to Königinhof for the Austrians, their attempts to enforce this arrangement were spoilt by Werder's capture of Jicin at 10:30 P.M., which scattered Austro-Saxon headquarters in all directions. Thereafter, it was every man for himself in Iser Army.[40] Since four Austrian brigades had to be evacuated along a single road, the withdrawal foundered immediately amid confusion and panic. Guns, trains, ambulances, and troop columns blocked the Königinhof road. "All the [Austrian] troops we met were out of ammunition,"

36 Fontane, *Der deutsche Krieg*, vol. 1, p. 238. Grosser Generalstab, *Feldzug 1866*, pp. 206, 220.
37 KA, AFA 1866, Karton 2280, 13–104, Vienna, December 1866, Col. Pelikan.
38 KA, AFA 1866, Karton 2280, 13–103, Lemberg, December 19, 1866, Col. Litzelhofen. [FML Nagy], "Bemerkungen über den Feldzug der k.k. Nordarmee 1866," *ÖMZ* 2 (1867), p. 161.
39 KA, AFA 1866, Karton 2278, 7–6, Hotischt, July 2, 1866, GM Ringelsheim.
40 Grosser Generalstab, *Feldzug 1866*, pp. 214–17.

Gondrecourt later testified. The battle, so promising at the outset, was irretrievably lost.[41]

Poschacher and Leiningen passed through Jicin without any idea how the battle had been lost. One minute they had been holding up a solid fighting front, the next there had been Prussians in their rear. Utterly demoralized, their men slouched through the darkened town mute and resigned. Two entire Hungarian battalions lost their way in the dark and were captured by the Prussians. Two hundred leaderless stragglers from Piret's brigade climbed out of the Cidlina depression and set off for Josephstadt, perhaps anticipating Svejk's meandering anabasis in the Great War. Edelsheim's hussars rattled through Jicin and mistakenly took the south road behind the Saxons.[42] Had Prince Friedrich Karl only thought to provide Tümpling and Werder with some reserve cavalry, they could easily have ridden Clam-Gallas's unguarded I Corps into the ground that night.[43]

Spared a vigorous Prussian pursuit, most of I Corps reunited in the course of the night at Miletin, where Archduke Ernst's III Corps, which had been sitting uselessly on its hands for three entire days, at first fired on Clam's stragglers, then let them pass. As the beaten men of I Corps shuffled past Ernst's 46th Regiment, an officer noted that they "described the Prussian needle rifle in the most dreadful terms. Tales of bloody murder flowed from the mouths of the demoralized troops."[44]

First Corps crossed the Bystrice river at Horice, paused to cook a hot meal, and then continued on its way south to the Elbe fort at Königgrätz. Clam-Gallas's staff chief remarked that only the absence of a stern Prussian pursuit had saved his brigades, which were "too tired and jumbled to resist even a cavalry attack." Only one regiment in all of I Corps remained intact. The other seven had been broken up by desertion and intermingling.[45] This motley crew marched till dawn on the thirtieth, arriving on the heights of Dub with a good prospect of Königgrätz far in the distance. Some of the men descended through the village of Sadova to the Bystrice to bathe and fill their canteens. Others staked out bivouacs on the heights. Count Clam-Gallas rode ahead to refresh himself in Königgrätz while Gondrecourt and Litzelhofen remained behind at Sadova to begin sorting out Clam's rabble. In four badly conceived, badly executed battles, I Corps had lost nearly 5,000 men – the strength of a brigade – and 184 officers. It arrived on the Elbe disbanded.[46] A private soldier in Piret's brigade reflected on what he had

41 KA, AFA 1866, Karton 2270, 8–12a, St. Pölten, August 7, 1866, FML Gondrecourt.

42 KA, AFA 1866, Karton 2270, 8–12a, St. Pölten, August 7, 1866, FML Gondrecourt. Fontane, *Der deutsche Krieg*, vol. 1, pp. 231–2, 240. Lettow-Vorbeck, vol. 2, pp. 374–6.

43 KA, AFA 1866, Karton 2280, 13–104, Vienna, December 1866, Col. Pelikan. Van Creveld, *Command in War*, p. 127.

44 Capt. Cristofek, "Meiningen Nr. 46 in Feldzuge 1866," *ÖMZ* 4 (1867), p. 217.

45 KA, AFA 1866, Karton 2272, 13–19, Sadova, June 30, 1866, Col. Nádösy. Karton 2280, 13–103, Lemberg, December 19, 1866, Col. Litzelhofen.

46 Lettow-Vorbeck, vol. 2, p. 368. Bartels, *Der Krieg im Jahre 1866*, pp. 18–20. In all, 4,704 Austrian casualties, including 1,832 unwounded prisoners, more than three times Prussian losses. The Saxons lost 25 officers and 566 men, the Prussians 71 officers and 1,482 men.

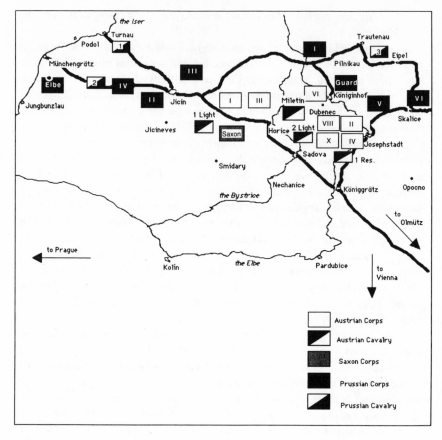

The strategic situation on June 29, 1866

been through at Jicin: "It was a Friday, an unlucky day," he wrote, "but thank God a lucky one for me and the others who survived."[47] Later, a North Army adjutant rode up to Gondrecourt at Sadova and handed him a message dictated by Benedek at Josephstadt two days earlier. It said: "Third Corps will arrive at Jicin on June 29th. My offensive toward Turnau with at least four army corps will commence from Jicin on June 30th."[48]

AUSTRIAN ARMY HEADQUARTERS, DUBENEC AND KÖNIGGRÄTZ, JUNE 29 – JULY 1

When the French newspapers, which mostly sided with Austria in the war, heard the news of Jicin, they were crestfallen. One judged Austria *"une puissance en*

47 KA, Nachlässe, B/1453 (Lebeda), Lauterbach, November 13, 1866, Pvt. Lebeda.
48 AFA 1866, Karton 2280, 13–103, Lemberg, December 19, 1866, Col. Litzelhofen.

décadence; qu'il n'y a plus rien à espérer, que c'est fini."[49] And indeed there was something hopelessly decadent about the way Benedek had squandered the only advantage he had begun the campaign with, that of the central position: his ability to turn North Army's entire strength against one of the three Prussian armies without exposing his rear or flank to the others. And he had done this willingly. On June 29, while Clam-Gallas's Iser Army was being thrashed at Jicin, Benedek offered only token resistance to the advance of Steinmetz, the Guards, and Bonin to the banks of the Elbe, which meant that the Prussian Second Army had closed at last to within a single march of the Elbe and First Armies. Someone in Austrian headquarters put a brave face on events and explained – with truly Svejkian discernment – to Vienna that Clam's headlong retreat from Jicin had actually been a *good* thing, for it had "completed the concentrical concentration" of North Army.[50]

On June 30, Feldzeugmeister Benedek installed himself in new headquarters on the Dubenec plateau behind Königinhof, beyond all bounds the most awesome position catalogued in the Austrian General Staff's survey of the Habsburg Monarchy. Viewed from the north, it looked like a pine forest turned on its side and driven into the right bank of the Elbe. Frederick the Great had come this way with an army in 1778, taken one look at the obstacle, and retired to Prussia.[51] Holed up at Dubenec, Benedek succeeded finally in retrieving Gablenz's shattered corps on the twenty-ninth. All of X Corps's brigades, including some of Grivicic's men, straggled through Königinhof, crossed the Elbe, and climbed to Dubenec during the day and night. They had made three marches and fought two battles without food.[52] Benedek sacrificed a regiment to cover this retreat, leaving a large part of Festetics's 6th Regiment down in Königinhof to be overwhelmed and captured by the Prussian 1st Guard Division pursuing from Burkersdorf. He sacrificed another regiment to hold up Steinmetz's pursuit at Schweinschädel, a village by the Trebisov crossroads, where Ramming and Benedek had debated the battle of Skalice on the twenty-eighth. North Army suffered more than 2,000 casualties in these rearguard actions, the Prussians just 400.[53] By sundown on the twenty-ninth, three Prussian corps were resting on the Elbe and Bonin, westernmost of the three, had closed to within a single march of Friedrich Karl's First Army. Benedek's withdrawal to Dubenec left the strategically vital Trautenau-Jicin post road in Prussian hands. Moltke's Elbe, First, and Second Armies could now unite at their leisure. There were no more obstacles between them.[54]

What had Benedek gained by his front change at Dubenec and the interruption

49 KA, AFA 1866, Karton 2272, 13–113, Vienna, July 4, 1866, Belcredi to FZM Benedek.
50 HHSA, PA XL, Karton 124, Pardubice, June 30, 1866, Count Chotek to Mensdorff.
51 During the War of the Bavarian Succession. Wandruszka, *1866*, p. 168.
52 KA, AFA 1866, Karton 2296, 13–10, Vienna, December 19, 1866, Capt. Schulz.
53 KA, AFA 1866, Karton 2266, 6–1082, Dolan, June 29, 1866, FML Festetics to FZM Benedek. Karton 2286, 6-ad 90, Vienna, August 22, 1866, FML Festetics. Lettow-Vorbeck, vol. 2, pp. 329, 337–40.
54 Grosser Generalstab, *Feldzug 1866*, pp. 223–35.

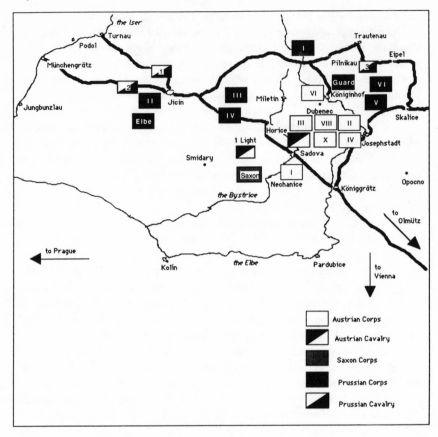

Benedek's Dubenec position, June 30, 1866

of his march west? Only trouble. His Jominian tendency to seek battle from prepared, central positions had, in this case, backfired, for by June 29 Dubenec was a trap. Second Army's advance to the Elbe and First Army's passage of the Iser endangered both of its flanks, as well as its rearward communications to Josephstadt and Vienna.[55] And the Dubenec plateau itself, so daunting and picturesque from without, was scarcely defensible from within. "The steep wooded slopes down to the Elbe were too broad to defend," a VI Corps staff officer noted. "Only to cross the gap between us and VIII Corps took fifteen minutes!" As for the Austrian skirmishers hidden among the pines waiting to snipe at a Prussian attack: "We could not have reinforced them. The slope was too steep and muddy,

---

55 "The so-called Königinhof-Dubenec redoubt," one of Benedek's subordinates snarled, "where we packed the army on rolling, broken ground bereft of communications and *pretended* to make a stand." KA, Nachlässe, B/1109: 1 (Sacken), pp. 6–7. Grosser Generalstab, *Feldzug 1866*, p. 239.

and there were too many trees." Retreat to a more suitable position was called for, yet "there were no proper roads, only washed-out tracks and gullies." Five Austrian infantry corps, three cavalry divisions, dozens of gun batteries, and hordes of peasants fleeing before Second Army's rapid advance became hopelessly tangled on the plateau. Supply trains could not pass and many units went hungry as a result.[56] "The troops," an Austrian staff officer wrote, "were physically and morally crushed." Men from different corps mingled, swapping dispiriting stories about the Prussian rifle, the chain of Austrian defeats, and their 30,000 missing comrades. So many officers had been killed and wounded in the battles of the week gone by that the bonds of discipline snapped. With the Prussians so near at hand, the night of June 29 passed fitfully; weary Austrian regiments awoke time and again to false alarms. All across the Königinhof position, friendly units exchanged fire, mistaking their comrades for Prussians.[57]

On the thirtieth, General Ramming reconnoitered the Dubenec plateau, took note of the obvious – that Second Army's capture of several Elbe crossings above Josephstadt had bored a hole in one flank of the position, Friedrich Karl's passage of the Iser the other – and reported this to Benedek's headquarters in Dubenec, which had secluded itself since Skalice. "The *Feldherr* was nowhere to be seen," one of Ramming's aides recalled. "He made no attempt to rally the men or regain their trust." Nor did he confer with his corps generals gathered on the plateau around him. Throughout that critical day of the campaign, Benedek brooded.[58] As for Krismanic, Karl Stransky, a captain in North Army's Operations Chancery, marvelled that "the operations chief still refuses to acknowledge that we are in a *cul de sac*. He seems utterly indifferent. He smokes his cigars, eats and drinks, but does little else." Staff chief Henikstein, like Benedek, crept around "like a scalded cat," doing nothing. August Neuber, Krismanic's *sous-chef*, "was his usual voluble self, but no one was listening." In sum, Stransky recorded, Austrian headquarters "presented a wretched aspect."[59] Early on the twenty-ninth, Benedek had ordered his army to make front to the north to engage Second Army. That night, while the battle of Jicin was in full spate, he had received Gablenz's reports of the battles at Trautenau and Burkersdorf, passed them along to Henikstein and Krismanic without comment, and sat down to write the emperor a doleful letter.[60]

The Feldzeugmeister's first draft began with the now legendary phrase "*ich*

56 KA, AFA 1866, Karton 2272, 13–19, July 1866, Col. Nádosÿ, "Tägliche Vorfallenheiten des Train-Commandos der Nord-Armee 1866." Karton 2291, 13–78, Prague, December 1866, Capt. Butterweck.
57 KA, AFA, Karton 2270, 8–12v, Altenburg, August 14, 1866, FML Taxis to FM Albrecht. Karton 2291, 13–103, Sopron, December 16, 1866, Capt. Handel-Mazzetti. Karton 2282, 13–6, Kukus, June 29, 30, 1866, "Operations-Journal der Brigade Thom." Karton 2282, 13-10, Hermannstadt, December 20, 1866, Capt. Prybila.
58 Ramming later judged this "frivolity in the extreme." KA, AFA, Karton 2291, 13–103, Sopron, December 16, 1866, Capt. Handel-Mazzetti.
59 KA, AFA 1866, Karton 2275, 13–166, Dubenec, June 29, 1866, Capt. Stransky, "Tagebuch."
60 KA, AFA 1866, Karton 2296, 13–10, Vienna, December 19, 1866, Capt. Schulz.

will Rechenschaft ablegen über die bisherigen Ereignisse" (I want to make an accounting of events thus far). The letter listed the sins of Austria's politicians, diplomats, and allies, and then, on military matters, broke down in a hopeless muddle that proved Benedek had little understanding of the elements of strategy, or even of events around him. "The Prussians have the internal lines now," he ventured. No, that was impossible, for the Prussian Second Army was off to his right, the Elbe and First Armies away to the left. He gave up and summoned Krismanic to attempt a second draft, the one that would reach Emperor Franz Joseph the next day. This one included all of Benedek's political excuses, but cleaned up the military bits. No, the Prussians did not have the internal lines *yet*. North Army still had them, "but could no longer use them decisively." How had that come to pass? Prussia had more railroads. Anything else? Benedek added a complaint about Austria's military intelligence. "We received our allowance for espionage too late." The Feldzeugmeister closed with brave assurances that "once I have the army in hand, I will consider landing a decisive blow, the success of which will depend entirely on God and my old soldier's luck."[61]

This was what the Viennese called *"Schmäh"*: a scarcely relevant outpouring of excuses that reflected Benedek's increasing isolation and frustration at not being able simply to wash his hands of the whole Austro-Prussian War. He was at odds with his staff and best generals and seemed to be giving up on the campaign before him, occupying himself instead with briefs for posterity. This was especially ironic because down in Königinhof, Prussian Guard officers were talking fearfully of a "second Hochkirch," a reference to the bloody battle in 1758, when Austria's Marshal Daun had stolen down from a high position in the night to slaughter the Prussian army camped beneath him.[62] Instead of acting, Benedek was subsiding into a mortal funk. The next day, he was still in seclusion when word of Jicin reached headquarters. Again he cast himself as the blameless victim of incompetent subordinates: "Débacle of Iser Army *forces* me to retreat in the direction of Königgrätz," he wired the emperor.[63]

BENEDEK'S FLIGHT TO KÖNIGGRÄTZ

In truth, Benedek would have had to abandon his position above Königinhof anyway. Already on June 28, one of Benedek's aides had described Dubenec as a "mouse trap," where North Army "offered both of its flanks to the enemy."[64] By the twenty-ninth, Steinmetz and the Guard Corps were situated either to maneu-

61 KA, MKSM 1866, Karton 343, Dubenec, June 29, 1866, FZM Benedek to Franz Joseph.
62 Lettow-Vorbeck, vol. 2, p. 381.
63 KA, MKSM 1866, Karton 343, 69/9, Dubenec, June 30, 1866 (6:00 P.M.), FZM Benedek to FML Crenneville.
64 KA, AFA 1866, Karton 2275, 13–166, Josephstadt, June 28, 1866, Capt. Stransky, "Tagebuch."
    Eduard Bartels, *Österreich und sein Heer* (Leipzig: Otto Wigand, 1866), pp. 8–9.

ver Benedek out of the position or to shut him up inside it. The extended front above Königinhof was full of holes, and Dubenec itself was an impassable quagmire of trains and refugees. It was merely convenient for Benedek to blame Clam-Gallas, called – like Daun before him – "Gallas the Army Drum, heard only when he's beaten."[65] After dinner on the thirtieth, Benedek voided the orders he had distributed on the twenty-ninth and decided upon yet *another* change of line, this time to the southeast. North Army would yield all of Bohemia to the Prussians and return to Olmütz in Moravia to restore itself. The first halt on this morale-crushing countermarch would be Königgrätz.[66] March columns were to be packed and ready by nightfall.[67]

North Army and its 100 kilometer-long supply train slithered through the night toward the Elbe bridge at Königgrätz. As Austrian headquarters moved out at 2:00 A.M., a staff captain put aside his diary: "The Prussian armies are free to join. We have failed to grasp the advantage freely offered us by the enemy. *Adieu.*"[68] For some Austrian units, this was the third consecutive night without sleep, and it was stop-and-go over third-rate roads in rainy weather.[69] General Karl Thun's II Corps, one of the last to leave Dubenec, needed twenty miserable hours to walk just fifteen kilometers.[70] All through the day and night of July 1, Austrian brigades, trains, and batteries arrived at bivouacs on either side of the Bystrice among the hills occupied by Clam-Gallas's I Corps on the thirtieth. Benedek ordered trains to deposit essential supplies with their corps and then continue down to Königgrätz, where they were to cross to the left bank of the Elbe and continue on their way to Olmütz.[71] Krismanic recalled that in the course of this demoralizing retreat from Dubenec, Benedek "turned against him," and ceased confiding in North Army's operations chief altogether.

Thus, Krismanic may or may not have had a say in Benedek's rather odd choice

---

65 Yet as a I Corps staffer later charged: "Responsibility for the defeat at Jicin resides with the army command, for its vacillating telegrams and contradictory orders revealed uncertainty in the plans and aims of the supreme army leadership. They alone bear the guilt for the casualties, exhaustion, discouragement, defeatism and sacrifice of both [the I and Saxon] Corps." KA, AFA 1866, Karton 2280, 13–104, Vienna, December 1866, Col. Pelikan.

66 KA, Nachlässe, B/572: 1 (Nosinic), Wr. Neustadt, August 10, 1866, GM Krismanic to Untersuchungs-Commission: "At Dubenec we decided to retreat to Olmütz after learning of the mishap at Jicin. The move to Königgrätz was only the first march in this new direction."

67 Again, staff officers were taken by surprise. There were no hardened roads between Dubenec and Königgrätz. KA, AFA 1866, Karton 2266, 6–1109, Dubenec, June 30, 1866, FZM Benedek to all corps commandants. Karton 2270, 12–7, Vienna, December 16, 1866, Capt. Pohl.

68 KA, AFA 1866, Karton 2275, 13–166, Prager Vorstadt, July 1, 1866, Capt. Stransky, "Tagebuch."

69 KA, AFA 1866, Karton 2270, 8–12L, Pressburg, August 17, 1866, FML Ramming to FM Albrecht. Karton 2271, 13–1, n.d., Maj. Sacken.

70 It took Festetics's IV Corps just as long. KA, AFA 1866, Karton 2287, 13–59, Vienna, December 21, 1866, Capt. Komers. Karton 2267, 7–177 1/2, Vienna, August 12, 1866, FML Mollinary.

71 KA, AFA 1866, Karton 2270, 12–7, Vienna, December 16, 1866, Capt. Pohl.

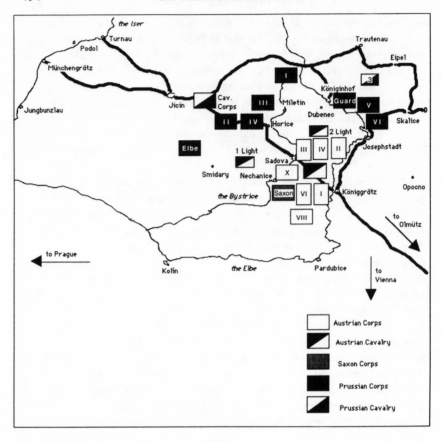

Benedek's flight to Königgrätz, July 1, 1866

of campsite at Königgrätz, an exposed position in *front* of the fort on the *wrong* side of the Elbe.[72] Basic tactical doctrine required that Benedek cross the river without delay to place the water obstacle between himself and the pursuing Prussian armies. As usual, the Feldzeugmeister did not consult with his corps commandants. Indeed, they did not even know that they were en route to Olmütz; they knew only what was in their orders: "*Richtung Königgrätz.*"[73] Prince Wilhelm Holstein, commandant of the Austrian 1st Reserve Cavalry Division, actually believed that Benedek had been ordered by Franz Joseph to give ground "for political reasons." Prince Taxis, another Austrian cavalry general, thought

---

72 KA, Nachlässe, B/572: 2 (Nosinic), Wr. Neustadt, July 12 and 20, 1866, GM Krismanic to Untersuchungs-Commission.

73 An officer in the *Operationskanzlei* thought it odd that Benedek refused to describe the march as a "*Rückzug*," which would have given the corps generals some inkling of what was going on. KA, AFA 1866, Karton 2275, 13–166, Dubenec, June 30, 1866, Capt. Stransky, "Tagebuch."

that North Army was dipping south to Königgrätz in order to resume its offensive toward the Iser on a new line.[74] General Gablenz noted that he was "baffled" by Benedek's "constant modification and cancellation of half-completed combinations."[75] Ramming, who had observed the rout of Leopold's VIII Corps at Skalice when it had unwisely offered battle with a river at *its* back, was for getting across the Elbe as quickly as possible. North Army, he later testified, plainly needed two or three days' rest "behind a natural obstacle that would prevent the Prussians from hitting it with their combined strength."[76]

Benedek, however, was dazed by the hurly-burly of trains and straggling brigades all along the approaches to Königgrätz. He thus collapsed wearily on the Elbe's right bank, judging an immediate river crossing impossible.[77] As North Army settled at last around Clam's I Corps and the Saxons on the Bystrice, an infantryman in the Piret Brigade observed its progress and jotted a disapproving note to his brother: "You always said that you wanted to see an army in its cantonments. If only you could see *this* one! What an awful confusion of men and wagons."[78]

PRUSSIAN ARMY HEADQUARTERS, JICIN AND KÖNIGINHOF, JUNE 30 – JULY 2, 1866

With Hanover beaten and the Bavarian army banished south of the Main River, Moltke and the Prussian king felt secure enough to move Great Headquarters in Berlin to Bohemia to be nearer the war's decisive action. Accompanied by Bismarck, Roon, and six carriages of courtiers, officials, and foreign attachés, they journeyed by rail on June 30 from Berlin to Reichenberg, and on to Jicin the next day. There Moltke was disappointed to learn that his three army commandants had somehow managed to lose all contact with the Austrians and had not the foggiest notion where to find Benedek's North Army. After Jicin, Herwarth and Prince Friedrich Karl had not pushed their cavalry forward to pursue Clam-Gallas, and Crown Prince Friedrich Wilhelm had failed even to detect Benedek's midnight withdrawal from the Dubenec plateau.[79] Thus, July 1–2 passed anxiously in Moltke's headquarters as Prussian mounted patrols scoured both banks of the Elbe in search of North Army.

Moltke knew that Benedek had retreated toward Königgrätz, but beyond that

74 KA, AFA 1866, Karton 2270, 8–12s, Eisenstadt, August 15, 1866, FML Holstein. Karton 2270, 8–12r, Szenktgotárd, August 10, 1866, FML Taxis.

75 KA, AFA, Karton 2270, 8–12o, Floridsdorf, August 16, 1866, FML Gablenz.

76 KA, AFA, Karton 2270, 8–12l, Pressburg, August 17, 1866, FML Ramming.

77 Colonel Kriz, Benedek's adjutant, remarked the Feldzeugmeister's "depression" on the first and second of July: "Every road, path, bridge, defile and crossroads traveled by the army and its trains was jammed with columns as far as the eye could see." KA, AFA 1866, Karton 2270, 8–12aa, Budapest, August 12, 1866, GM Kriz to FM Albrecht.

78 KA, Nachlässe, B/1453 (Lebeda), Lauterbach, November 13, 1866, Pvt. Lebeda.

79 Grosser Generalstab, *Feldzug 1866*, p. 237.

had no definite information. His best guess was that the Feldzeugmeister had taken refuge *behind* the Elbe, planting his right wing on Josephstadt, his left on Königgrätz, and resting his flanks and rear on the Aupa and Adler river lines. He assumed, in short, that Benedek would use the Elbe fortress group for the very purpose for which it had been constructed and maintained at colossal expense for 120 years: to defend Austria against a Prussian invasion.[80] For this reason Moltke ordered Second Army *not* to cross to the right bank of the Elbe to join First Army. Were Benedek behind the Elbe, Moltke wanted to be able to attack him from either side of the river. The two principal Prussian armies took three rest days in succession (June 30–July 2) while their cavalry searched along North Army's march routes. Moltke, prodded by Bismarck, who had just learned that a French envoy would shortly arrive in Prussian headquarters to insist upon an immediate end to the Austro-Prussian War, planned a reconnaissance-in-force along both banks of the Elbe to find Benedek and prepare a knock-out blow. Both Bismarck and Moltke wanted desperately to locate and defeat the Austrian army before an armed French intervention denied them the chance to smash and reorganize the German Confederation along Prussian lines.[81]

Though at rest after a hard week of marching and fighting, there was little joy in the Prussian camp. It had been raining since the thirtieth and a war correspondent noted that Elbe and First Armies were "plagued with hunger and physically exhausted." They had lost hundreds of men to fatigue on the march from the Iser and, in their exhausted state, were susceptible to dysentery and typhus, epidemic diseases that might decimate their remaining effective strength. Morally, Prussia's vaunted troop discipline had also begun to erode. Royal officers no longer bothered to intervene when their men ransacked palaces, farms, shops, and breweries in search of food and drink. First Army's meager supplies, already exhausted at Münchengrätz, had not been replenished, and the supply situation was even worse in the Elbe and Second Armies.[82] Quartermasters in the field deplored Berlin's inability to move supplies overland from Prussia's rail terminals in Saxony, Lusatia, and Silesia to the three armies in Bohemia. When General Albrecht von Blumenthal, staff chief of the Prussian Second Army, traveled to Jicin on July 2 to meet with Moltke and Roon, he confided his resentment of these well-fed, "long-faced loafers" to his diary. Berlin headquarters transplanted to Jicin was, in Blumenthal's eyes, "an odious sight."[83] Communication between the Prussian armies continued to be tenuous despite the approach of royal headquarters and Bonin's capture of the Trautenau-Jicin road. Throughout the day on June 30, Crown Prince Friedrich Wilhelm in Königinhof received no news at all of the battle at Jicin. Indeed, so slack was Prussia's reconnaissance that he actually

80 KA, AFA 1866, Karton 2274, 13–74, Vienna, 1872, Maj. Ripp.
81 Moltke, *Strategy*, pp. 52–4. Lettow-Vorbeck, vol. 2, p. 317. Grosser Generalstab, *Feldzug 1866*, p. 241.
82 Wachenhusen, pp. 102–14. Lettow-Vorbeck, vol. 2, pp. 314–16, 402–4.
83 Blumenthal, p. 39.

believed that the Elbe and First Armies were still at Münchengrätz and Podol, and that Benedek remained in force on the plateau above him.[84]

On July 2, Moltke held a staff conference to plot the Prussian army's next move, summoning the staff chiefs of the First and Second Armies — Generals Voigts-Rhetz and Blumenthal — to royal headquarters in Jicin. Still ignorant of Benedek's whereabouts, Moltke ordered Second Army to remain at Königinhof on the left bank of the Elbe, while the Elbe and First Armies pressed ahead to Königgrätz on the right bank.[85] The Prussian *chef* was, in short, still determined to envelop Benedek, even if the Feldzeugmeister had taken refuge behind the Elbe. Were that the case, Moltke would throw pontoon bridges across the river, attack North Army frontally with the Elbe and First Armies, and then slide Second Army down the left bank into Benedek's flank and rear.

The Prussian staff conference was remarkable for the lack of agreement among the Prussian generals on Moltke's plan. The previous day, Blumenthal had pushed Bonin's corps over the Elbe to the right bank in order to join forces with First Army. Only a last minute rebuke from Moltke prevented the crown prince from crossing the river with Steinmetz and the Guards on the second. While Second Army thus endeavored to push westward, Prince Friedrich Karl planned to post eastward with First Army, dragging Elbe Army with him on his right. This too was in defiance of Moltke's orders, which called for Elbe and First Armies to advance south to Königgrätz. Instead, Friedrich Karl took First Army to Miletin and Horice on June 30, where he hoped to rendezvous with Crown Prince Friedrich Wilhelm on the first of July.[86] Second and First Armies were, in short, striving, in a conventionally Jominian way, to combine in order to deny Benedek once and for all the chance to maneuver between them on internal lines to beat them separately.

Moltke, however, saw in this excess of caution the defeat of his bold plan to envelop North Army. Were the Prussian army commandants to unite on the right bank of the Elbe, leaving Benedek alone on the left, nothing would impede the Feldzeugmeister's escape to Vienna and the even more defensible line of the Danube. Furthermore, though he had lost touch with North Army for the moment, Moltke felt certain that the Austrians were near at hand. If they were, the three Prussian armies were *already* close enough to cooperate. As Moltke himself explained after the war, from June 30 onward, the dispersal of the Prussian army into three groups had great tactical *advantages*, for now they could outflank any position selected by Benedek, while Benedek would be unable to fall upon any of the three Prussian armies without finding the other two on his flanks or in his rear.[87] With these considerations in mind, Moltke ordered his field armies to rest

84 Grosser Generalstab, *Feldzug 1866*, p. 238. Van Creveld, *Command in War*, pp. 131–40. Lettow-Vorbeck, vol. 2, pp. 389, 430.
85 Grosser Generalstab, *Feldzug 1866*, pp. 235–6.
86 Grosser Generalstab, *Feldzug 1866*, pp. 235–8.
87 Grosser Generalstab, *Feldzug 1866*, p. 240.

on July 2, while Prussian cavalry patrols continued to probe toward Königgrätz and Josephstadt on both banks of the Elbe.[88]

NORTH ARMY AT REST, JULY 1 – 2

Massed in his new position on the Bystrice River between Sadova and Königgrätz, Benedek's supply problems worsened. Whereas Moltke deliberately scattered his armies across a frontage of forty-five kilometers to facilitate magazine supply and requisitioning, Benedek crowded his entire army onto a line barely eight kilometers in length, thwarting all efforts to deliver adequate quantities of food, drink, and ammunition.[89] At wit's end, the Feldzeugmeister stunned Emperor Franz Joseph on July 1 by demanding an immediate armistice. "A catastrophe of the army is inevitable," Benedek wired the Hofburg. This "catastrophe telegram" struck Vienna like a bolt from the blue; Franz Joseph recoiled in amazement. If North Army truly were on the brink of disaster, why did Benedek not march it over the Elbe and into the heart of Austria's "northern Quadrilateral?"[90] Why was Benedek not straddling the broad river behind him like a horse and changing banks on the bridgeheads at Josephstadt, Königgrätz, and Pardubice in order to menace Moltke's flanks and force the Prussian *chef* to detach "observation corps" that would substantially weaken his three armies?[91] Instead, Benedek was loitering on the *threshhold* of the fortress group, on the very spot where, once apprised of his whereabouts, the three Prussian armies would inevitably converge. He had, in short, backed himself into a corner. The Aupa River had disorganized Leopold's flight from Skalice; the Elbe could do far worse to Benedek's withdrawal from Sadova.[92]

All of this was obvious from a passing glance at the map, yet Benedek would not act. He occupied himself throughout July 1 with trivial camp business, prompting a staff officer to register his disgust: "Is it really possible that we will remain here with the Elbe and the fortress at our *back?* Clearly there is no limit to the blundering of army headquarters, for it appears that we will *remain* here tomorrow!"[93] On July 2, General Edelsheim rode to Count Festetics's bivouacs and asked him whether he thought Benedek was still fit to command North

88 Van Creveld, *Command in War*, pp. 132–4. Craig, *Königgrätz*, pp. 81–3. Grosser Generalstab, *Feldzug 1866*, pp. 195–8, 241–3.

89 KA, AFA 1866, Karton 2274, 13–59, Vienna, 1868, FML Nagy, "Randbemerkungen." Grosser Generalstab, *Feldzug 1866*, p. 251.

90 KA, KM 1866, CK, Karton 242, 14–5/33, Wr. Neustadt, September 27, 1866, FZM Nobili.

91 Soldiers called this operating *à cheval* of a river line. "Benedek ought to have used the curve of the Elbe at Pardubice, which offered excellent offensive prospects against an enemy attempting to pass above or below it, as well as a natural line of retreat well supplied with magazines." KA, AFA 1866, Karton 2274, 13–72, Olmütz, December 29, 1872, Maj. Ripp, "Kritisches Resumé."

92 KA, Nachlässe, B/1109: 1 (Sacken), Maj. Sacken, p. 8.

93 KA, AFA 1866, Karton 2275, 13–166, Prager Vorstadt von Königgrätz, July 1, 1866, Capt. Stransky, "Tagebuch."

Army: "I felt it my duty to note that the Feldzeugmeister was physically and morally a broken man," Edelsheim later testified. Festetics, though a close friend of Benedek's, agreed.[94] The Feldzeugmeister's staff appeared as haggard and demoralized as Benedek himself. On July 2, an Austrian officer noted "the terrible confusion in headquarters, where the senior men are utterly helpless." The knot of Austrian supply trains blocking the Elbe bridges at Königgrätz and Pardubice only complicated the situation. Benedek had directed his entire army south on a single line of march and was now paying the price. His march columns were so disorganized that the Königgrätz fortress commandant threatened to seal his fortress and deprive North Army of its principal bridge if Benedek could not restore discipline to his regiments.[95]

The seven Austrian corps and five cavalry divisions camped along the Bystrice felt this confusion keenly. None had eaten a square meal since Dubenec, and without adequate food, clothing, or tents, they were suffering grievously from a cold front and steady rain that had settled over Bohemia on the last day of June. An officer in III Corps recalled that Benedek's campsite above Sadova offered "nothing to eat, not even bread. All our wagons were gone; there were no sutlers or peasants selling food, and we had to sleep on wet ground covered with excrement."[96] Things were no better in I Corps. Its train had crossed to the left bank of the Elbe without leaving anything for the men on the right: "Men and wagons everywhere," a war-weary private scoffed, "why, then, do we have nothing?"[97] In view of all this, General Ringelsheim, a knowing veteran of 1859, predicted a major defeat: "My men are without money, shoes, essential supplies or meat. All the corps are mixed up. We cannot find *anyone* from army headquarters. . . . North Army faces a disaster."[98]

Needless to say, such evidence of helplessness on the Austrian side belies the conventional view that Benedek *deliberately* remained on the right bank of the Elbe so that he could more easily launch a counteroffensive after repelling Moltke's attack.[99] In fact, Benedek was on the brink of nervous collapse by July 1, as his rather hysterical "catastrophe telegram" to the emperor amply testified: "Pray conclude a peace at any price . . . a catastrophe of the army is inevitable."[100] For Benedek, Königgrätz was nothing more than the first halting place on North Army's retreat to Olmütz.[101] When Lieutenant-Colonel Friedrich

---

94 KA, AFA 1866, Karton 2270, 8–12q, Vienna, August 14, 1866, FML Edelsheim.

95 KA, AFA 1866, Karton 2275, 13–166, Prager Vorstadt, July 1, 1866, Capt. Stransky, "Tagebuch." KM 1866, CK, Karton 254, 67–50, Königgrätz, August 18, 1866, GM Wigl.

96 Vincenz Cristofek, "Meiningen Nr. 46 im Feldzuge 1866," *ÖMZ* 4 (1867), p. 218. K. von Went., "Erinnerungen eines österreichischen Kriegsmannes 1866," *ÖMZ* 3 (1899), p. 265.

97 KA, Nachlässe, B/1453 (Lebeda), Lauterbach, November 13, 1866, Pvt. Lebeda.

98 KA, AFA 1866, Karton 2278, 7–6, Hotischt, July 2, 1866, GM Ringelsheim.

99 Craig, *Königgrätz*, pp. 81, 87–9.

100 KA, MKSM 1866, Karton 343, 69/9, Königgrätz, July 1, 1866, FZM Benedek to Franz Joseph.

101 KA, Nachlässe, B/572 (Nosinic), Wr. Neustadt, August 10, 1866, GM Krismanic to Untersuchungs-Commission.

Beck – sent by Franz Joseph after Jicin to gather information in North Army headquarters – visited Benedek on July 1–2, he described the sad state of North Army to the Hofburg and made no mention of plans to fight a battle on the Bystrice.[102] Indeed, an officer in Krismanic's Operations Chancery noted that July 1–2 "passed idly. . . . There was no discussion whatsoever of converting our campsites on the right bank of the Elbe into a *real* position, where one could fight a battle."[103] This damnable negligence at the top of North Army was never more apparent than in the staff conference convened by Benedek on July 2.

BENEDEK'S "COUNCIL OF WAR," JULY 2

In May, Benedek had assured the French army attaché in Vienna that he would permit no foreign princes or staff officers to accompany his headquarters in the field because, as the Feldzengmeister put it, "every army makes mistakes that must quickly be rectified *en famille*."[104] Now was his chance. There was a great deal to rectify, beginning with North Army's loss of four casualties to every Prussian one in the week before Königgrätz: in all, 31,000 Austrian casualties, including 1,000 officers. Having consistently underestimated the danger posed by Prussia's breech-loading rifle before the war, Benedek had now to meet the challenge head-on. Ferdinand Poschacher's defensive *Etagenfeuer* at Jicin and Ludwig Gablenz's early, massive commitment of his gun reserve at Burkersdorf were possible solutions to North Army's plight.

There were, of course, other problems. North Army command had to deliver orders more quickly and stop beginning each day with a change of line and operations object. Austrian corps generals had to be told what the Feldzeugmeister was planning. Generals like Clam-Gallas had to be made to use Bohemia's excellent telegraph net. Generals like Benedek had to be made to use the *field* telegraphs they kept uselessly packed in their trains. Logistical wrinkles had to be ironed out. And the authority of the Austrian corps had to be reestablished. Reckless brigadiers had hastened the defeats at Vysokov and Skalice. Gustav Fragnern had abandoned a good position and dashed his brigade against a wood bristling with Prussian rifles at Skalice. Albert Knebel had attacked a hilltop position without orders at Trautenau and needlessly decimated his regiments. Ludwig Piret had smashed *his* brigade to pieces at Jicin. In theory at least, Franz Joseph had eliminated the army division from the Austrian order-of-battle after 1859 in order to solidify operations around a small number of demonstrably competent corps commandants. Yet the new model army was functioning in practice as unreliably as had the old.[105]

102 KA, MKSM-SR 1866, 24/1, Pardubice, July 1, 1866, Lt-Col. Beck to FML Crenneville.
103 KA, Nachlässe, B/1109: 1 (Sacken), Maj. Sacken, p. 7.
104 Vincennes, AAT, MR 76/1606, Vienna, May 26, 1866, Col. Merlin to Marshal Randon.
105 Arno, vol. 7, pp. 14–15. Bartels, *Kritische Beiträge*, p. 71. Toilow, *Die österreichische Nordarmee*, p. 31.

When Benedek's generals arrived in army headquarters at 1:00 P.M. on July 2, most of them expected a thoroughgoing critique of Austria's lackluster war effort and a debate on the wisdom of prolonging North Army's stay in the exposed Bystrice position.[106] What they got was something altogether different. "All [Benedek] asked us," General Gondrecourt recalled, "was whether or not we had sufficient drinking water in our campsites. Then he decided, unilaterally, without *any* discussion of strategic or tactical questions, that we would remain in the position before Königgrätz."[107] Count Thun, commandant of II Corps, had the same recollection: "The possibility of a battle never came up. [Benedek] spoke only of disciplinary matters, nothing about operations."[108] Ramming reported that although Benedek raised the issue of "timely and clear march dispositions," he refused to describe the *new* aim of Austrian operations now that the push to the Iser had been called off, or to consider the possibility that North Army might be attacked on the Bystrice.[109] When, after the war, Benedek attempted to characterize this toothless conference as a full-blown "council of war," Gablenz and most of his colleagues angrily dissented. "That was no *Kriegsrat*," Gablenz protested. "At three o'clock on July 2nd, when we returned from headquarters to our bivouacs, it was plain that the army commandant still had *no* information on the enemy's position, strength or movements and had *no* intention of fighting a battle on the 3rd." General Coudenhove agreed: "Do you *really* suppose," he wrote Archduke Albrecht after Königgrätz, "that a *proper* council of war would have resolved to make a stand with the Elbe *behind* us?"[110]

At 3:00 P.M., Benedek adjourned the meeting, peremptorily declaring that North Army would extend its rest on the Bystrice "several days." He did not even hint at the possibility of a battle, nor did he take the elementary precaution of instructing his generals to study the Prim-Chlum-Nedelist position they were camped in with an eye toward defending it. This lapse would explain all the fumbling the next day, when Austrian generals would try to make sense of their late-arriving orders through a low-lying fog and a driving rain.[111] As the generals got up to leave, General Edelsheim, whose hussars had been skirmishing with Prussian mounted patrols since the previous day, reminded Benedek that the enemy was near at hand. An attack could be expected that very evening or the following morning at the *latest*. "And when did *you* become a prophet?" Benedek

106 As a VI Corps staff officer put it: We expected "some discussion of the life-or-death situation faced by the army and the Austrian state." KA, AFA 1866, Karton 2291, 13–103, Sopron, December 16, 1866, Capt. Handel-Mazzetti.

107 KA, AFA 1866, Karton 2270, 8–12a, St. Pölten, August 7, 1866, FML Gondrecourt.

108 KA, AFA 1866, Karton 2270, 8–12e, Graz, August 21, 1866, FML Thun.

109 KA, AFA 1866, Karton 2270, 8–12l, Pressburg, August 17, 1866, FML Ramming.

110 KA, AFA 1866, Karton 2270, 8–12p, Floridsdorf, August 16, 1866, FML Gablenz. Karton 2270, 8–12y, Sopron, August 12, 1866, FML Coudenhove. Krismanic later affirmed that "we had no intention of fighting a major battle (*Hauptschlacht*) at Königgrätz." Nachlässe, B/572: 1 (Nosinic), Wr. Neustadt, July 20, 1866, GM Krismanic to Untersuchungs-Commission.

111 KA, AFA 1866, Karton 2274, 13–67, n.d, FML Weber.

15. General Leopold Edelsheim (1826–93) and the staff of Austria's 1st Light Cavalry Division in 1866

laughed. "You youngsters *always* have ideas."[112] Ramming, who was ill, missed the conference. When presented with a transcript in the afternoon, an aide recalled that Ramming "could not believe that [Benedek] still assumed there would be no battle." The VI Corps commandant considered North Army's predicament "drastic."[113]

The Austrian corps commandants returned to their units past army engineers digging battery positions on Chlum, Lipa, Masloved, and Nedelist, the central and right-hand heights of the Bystrice position overlooking Sadova.[114] Since this work was not accompanied by any activity on the much more vulnerable left wing and since no roads were widened, no trees felled, and no field telegraphs installed anywhere in the position, it was clear that the small number of trenches dug on July 2 were intended not for a decisive battle but merely to give cover to a rearguard during North Army's forthcoming passage to the left bank of the Elbe.[115] Though Krismanic was at Königgrätz for two full days before the battle, he did not scout the position once, an astounding lapse given his predicament. Even more astounding was the recollection of a VI Corps staff captain detailed to accompany Benedek's artillery and engineering chiefs on a tour of Chlum and Lipa on July 2; he reported that "neither alluded even to the *possibility* of a battle" the next day.[116]

112 *"Wo haben Sie denn das Prophezeien gelernt ?"* – *"Junge Leute pflegen immer Ansichten zu haben."* KA, AFA 1866, Karton 2270, 8–12q, Vienna, August 14, 1866, FML Edelsheim. Karton 2274, 13–75, *Neue Freie Presse*, July 3, 1886. Bartels, *Kritische Beiträge*, p. 249.

113 KA, AFA 1866, Karton 2291, 13–103, Sopron, December 16, 1866, Capt. Handel-Mazzetti.

114 KA, AFA 1866, Karton 2267, 7–86 3/4, Zwittau, July 6, 1866, "Rélation Genie-Abteilung." Grosser Generalstab, *Feldzug 1866*, p. 255.

115 Engineers would not be sent to Prim-Problus on the unguarded left wing until 10:00 A.M. on July 3, three hours after the battle had begun! KA, AFA 1866, Karton 2273, 13–31 1/2, Linz, November 10, 1866, Maj. Ghyzy. Lettow-Vorbeck, vol. 2, pp. 396, 416.

116 KA, AFA 1866, Karton 2291, 13–103, Sopron, December 16, 1866, Capt. Handel-Mazzetti. Karton 2272, 13–19 1/2, Olmütz, July 10, 1866, Genie-Regiment Nr. 1.

9

Königgrätz: Benedek's stand in the "Bystrice pocket"

Had Benedek expected a great battle at Königgrätz, he would never have stood at Sadova on the line of the Bystrice River. An officer in headquarters considered the position "abominable." The right wing was placed on "sunken ground completely dominated by heights [1,500 meters] to the north."[1] The left wing was even more vulnerable. Anchored by no natural obstacle, it dangled "in the air" atop the lonely heights of Prim and Problus. General Herwarth von Bittenfeld had only to assemble his Elbe Army divisions and march toward Königgrätz leaving these hills on his left and, an Austrian staff officer bitterly recalled, the Prussians "would have had [North Army's] left flank and the battle as well."[2] Together, the Prim and Nedelist wings of Benedek's position joined to form a salient angle at Chlum. Any staff college cadet could have told the Feldzeugmeister that the resultant "half-moon front" was the worst of all possible deployments, for it compressed North Army's reserves and lines of retreat inside a narrow, inverted "V" and, by refusing both wings and projecting the center, prevented the two halves of the Austrian battle line from supporting one another. In this singularly uneconomical configuration, Benedek's center would be every bit as vulnerable as his wings during a flanking attack. Since the wings fell away from the out-thrust center – instead of rising around it – a Prussian attack on either face of the Austrian salient would be able to turn into Chlum – "keypoint of the position" – as easily as if it were a flank.[3]

In sum, Prim-Chlum-Nedelist was an antique eighteenth century position that had been listed in the Austrian army's geographic survey during Empress Maria

---

1 KA, Nachlässe, B/572: 2 (Nosinic), Vienna, January 6, 1867, Capt. Sembratowicz: "We were standing in a hole . . . a flat, uncovered plateau . . . completely dominated by heights with excellent gun positions only 2,000 paces distant . . . Army Command must never have *seen* this terrain."

2 KA, AFA 1866, Karton 2270, 8–12dd, Hetzendorf, July 31, 1866, Col. Pelikan. Karton 2274, 13–72, Olmütz, December 29, 1872, Maj. Ripp, "Kritisches Résumé."

3 KA, AFA, Karton 2274, 13–61, Berlin, August 1867, "Brief von einem preussischen Offizier." Nachlässe, B/208 (Fischer), "Über den Angriff und die Verteidigung." Hamley, pp. 309–10.

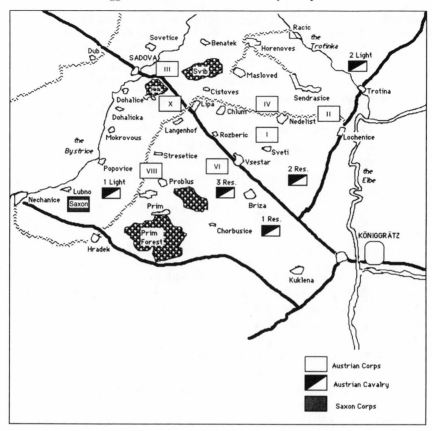

Königgrätz: Benedek's position on the Bystrice, July 2, 1866

Theresa's reign: with eighteenth-century gun ranges and army strengths in mind. Like the position at Skalice, it was hardly defensible in the mid-nineteenth century. From Masloved, a plateau 1.5 kilometers north of Chlum, Frederick the Great and his Prussian musketeers would never have been able to hit Lipa or Nedelist in the 1760s. Armed with *rifles*, however, they would have found themselves well within range in the 1860s. Rifled *artillery*, which could fire accurately to a range of several kilometers, would do even more damage. Packed into the narrow space behind Chlum, Benedek's reserves would have to absorb everything Prussian gunners threw at them, including every single projectile that overshot its target in the front line.[4]

There were still more problems with Benedek's position before Königgrätz. It lacked a decent "captain's hill," which made command and control of a battle

4 Grosser Generalstab, *Feldzug 1866*, p. 277.

difficult. Though the central heights of Chlum and Lipa commanded the Bystrice crossing at Sadova, they offered only a partial view of North Army's left and right wings, and were overshadowed by the heights of Dub and Horenoves, high ground to the north which the Prussians would not hesitate to occupy. Chlum itself, the highest point in the Austrian position, would be difficult to defend. Four sunken roads approached the village hidden from view by their mud ramparts and by peasant huts, fruit trees, and standing corn. To defend Chlum against an enemy *coup de main*, Austrian sappers would have had to raze it to the ground, something no one had the time or stomach for. Overall, General Alois Baumgarten, the officer who would replace Krismanic as operations chief on July 3, thought it odd that Benedek had selected a position "far more easily compassed *from without* than from within," conferring a formidable advantage on the Prussians before the battle of Königgrätz had even begun.[5]

MOLTKE AND KRISMANIC DISPOSE FOR BATTLE, JULY 2 AND 3

Austrian light cavalry had been skirmishing with Prussian patrols on the Jicin plateau since July 1. The Saxons had discovered the Prussian IV Corps at Horice, halfway to Königgrätz from Jicin, early on the 2nd. In the hours after Benedek's staff conference, Austrian mounted patrols returned from the west describing more skirmishes and large camps of Prussian troops within a march of the Bystrice. The Prussian First Army was camped around Horice and Miletin, Elbe Army southeast of Jicin at Smidary. Earlier in the day, Benedek had actually rushed III Corps to its battle stations on Lipa after Prussian troops were spotted on North Army's right wing. Army headquarters had dropped everything in Königgrätz and galloped up to Chlum to mill about in nervous expectation of a battle until lunchtime, when the sighting proved to be a false alarm.[6]

At 7:30 P.M. on July 2, Saxon outposts skirmished with advanced parties of the Prussian Elbe Army, which were reconnoitering the Bystrice river crossing at Nechanice. Crown Prince Albert of Saxony reported this keen Prussian interest in the exact placement of Benedek's left wing and warned Austrian headquarters that North Army could expect "an enveloping attack in the early morning hours." Thirty minutes later, General Edelsheim warned *again* of the "rapid Prussian advance from the northwest." Austrian dragoons, watching the Jicin-Königgrätz road, returned late on July 2 with prisoners from First Army, who confirmed that Prince Friedrich Karl was marching through the night to reach the Bystrice.[7]

5 KA, AFA 1866, Karton 2270, 8–12bb, Vienna, August 15, 1866, FML Baumgarten. Gustav Treuenfest, *Geschichte des k.u.k. Infanterie-Regimentes Nr. 46 FZM Féjerváry* (Vienna: Verlag des Regiments, 1890), pp. 448–50.

6 KA, AFA 1866, Karton 2270, 8–12aa, Budapest, August 12, 1866, GM Kriz. Karton 2274, 13–74, Vienna, 1872, Maj. Ripp, "Skizze." Capt. Cristofek, "Meiningen Nr. 46 im Feldzuge 1866," *ÖMZ* 4 (1867), p. 218. Lettow-Vorbeck, vol. 2, p. 398.

7 KA, Nachlässe, B/572: 2 (Nosinic), Timisoara, December 27, 1866, Capt. Woinowitz.

Only then, at 11:00 P.M. on July 2, after letting vital days and hours slip idly by, did General Krismanic finally sit down to dispose North Army for battle. When the clock in Austrian headquarters struck twelve midnight, he ordered his subordinates to back-date everthing they wrote to the second. This eleventh hour response to *predictable* Prussian movements was just too embarrassing and, in the event of a court martial, too incriminating.[8]

Though Prussia's camp was better organized than Austria's, Moltke had problems of his own by the evening of July 2. His scouts had still not located the Austrian army, and the Prussian *chef* was beginning to have doubts about the orders he had issued since arriving in Bohemia. Although his orders for July 3 had his two largest armies probing again toward Königgrätz – Second Army on the left bank of the Elbe, First Army on the right – Prussian supply problems and impending French intervention in the Austro-Prussian War made a quick end to the conflict desirable. Yet if Benedek had successfully entrenched *behind* the fortified bridges at Josephstadt, Königgrätz, and Pardubice, it would be difficult – even with armies on both sides of the Elbe – to dislodge and crush him. Thus, Moltke had now to consider a change of plan. On the second, he pondered pushing Second Army over the Elbe after all, to march past Königgrätz to Pardubice to prevent Benedek sallying from that bridgehead to hit the exposed flank and rearward communications of the Elbe and First Armies once they began their assault on the fortress works at Königgrätz. Though disappointed at the turn events had taken since Jicin, Moltke felt reasonably sure that once he moved Second Army to Pardubice, Benedek, his line of retreat to Vienna threatened by this large Prussian army *beneath* him, would have no choice but to yield the line of the Elbe and its forts.[9] Nevertheless, such an operation would take more precious days, permitting Benedek to rest and restore North Army and giving Napoleon III time to dictate mild terms for the Austrians, who, for obvious reasons, he now viewed as far less dangerous to French interests than the Prussians.

Even as Moltke weighed his thorny options, a lone Prussian uhlan patrol, searching the right bank of the Elbe late on July 2, made a startling discovery. Advancing carefully to avoid ambush by the superior Austrian numbers they suspected were in the vicinity, the Prussian uhlans, who Austrian sentries posted atop the heights of Dub mistook for Saxons, passed through an Austrian picket line in broad daylight and had a long look at North Army's vast concentration of tents and cook fires in the Bystrice valley.[10] By 6:30 P.M., the Prussian uhlans were back in First Army headquarters at Horice with the news. By 9:00 P.M., Prince Friedrich Karl and his staff chief, Konstantin Voigts-Rhetz, had distributed orders for a general advance by the Elbe and First Armies to the Bystrice. The prince, hell-bent on glory, deliberately neglected to include the four infantry

---

8 KA, AFA 1866, Karton 2270, 12–6, Vienna, December 15, 1866, Capt. Hoffmeister. Karton 2271, 13–1, n.d., Maj. Sacken, "Bericht."

9 Grosser Generalstab, *Feldzug 1866*, pp. 242–3.

10 Fontane, *Der deutsche Krieg*, vol. 1, pp. 460–2.

corps of Second Army in his plan. He asked only that Crown Prince Friedrich Wilhelm send a corps across the Elbe to keep Josephstadt under observation and prevent a sally into First Army's flank by the Austrian garrison there.[11]

In accordance with what had by now become standard operating procedure in Prussian headquarters, Friedrich Karl ignored Moltke altogether, put finishing touches to his plan, transmitted it directly to Herwarth von Bittenfeld and Crown Prince Friedrich Wilhelm, and only then roused the king, informing him that he and Herwarth would force the Bystrice at Sadova and Nechanice the next morning. Moltke, awakened by Voigts-Rhetz, rose with a start. The Austrians were on the *right* bank of the Elbe? "Thank God!" he cried. Who would have thought that Benedek would voluntarily back himself into such a perfect *Kessel* or "pocket?"[12] Prussian staff officers learnt early in their careers never to deploy for battle with their backs to a river. Indeed, so improbable was Benedek's deployment on the ground before Königgrätz that Moltke would assume until mid-morning the next day that the Feldzeugmeister had left but a rearguard there and was busy transporting the bulk of his army across the bridge behind him.

His sleep interrupted, Moltke read Friedrich Karl's plan and noted its principal defect, the fact that it did not involve Second Army. He corrected the error by dispatching two staff riders at midnight with revised orders for the crown prince: cross immediately to the right bank of the Elbe and march against the right flank of the Austrians.[13] This done, an aide turned back Moltke's bedclothes and wondered aloud if the Prussian plan had not perhaps been conceived in too great haste. Might not this attempted combination of three armies in the face of a concentrated enemy be dangerous? "In war," Moltke replied with a shrug of his pyjamaed shoulder, "*everything* is dangerous."[14]

Things were not nearly so serene in Austrian headquarters. While most of North Army's staff officers were at work on Krismanic's battle plan, Benedek and staff chief Henikstein – later condemned by Krismanic as a "vapid, lazy dawdler" – were at war with Vienna.[15] Earlier in the day, after seeing off a deeply disturbed Lieutenant-Colonel Beck, Henikstein had telegraphed the emperor's first adjutant, General Franz Crenneville, to explain that Beck had caught North Army headquarters "in an unhappy moment," but that "things [were] fast improving." Franz Joseph, who, in the meantime, had begun to receive details of Benedek's ruinous

---

11 Grosser Generalstab, *Feldzug 1866*, pp. 244–9.

12 In 1867, a Prussian veteran of 1866 described the "astonishment" felt by all three Prussian army commandants when they discovered that Benedek had deployed with his back to the Elbe. KA, AFA 1866, Karton 2274, 13–61, Berlin, August 1867, "Brief von einem preussischen Offizier."

13 Moltke, *Strategy*, p. 55. Grosser Generalstab, *Feldzug 1866*, pp. 249–50. Van Creveld, *Command*, pp. 134–6. Craig, *Königgrätz*, pp. 84–6.

14 The French General Staff was much impressed by Moltke's *sang-froid*, noting that "on July 2nd, Moltke had only a few hours to revise his crude operations plan to take account of the [newly discovered] Austrian concentration between Josephstadt and the Elbe." Vincennes, AAT, MR 32/1537, Paris, October 1866, "Coup d'oeil rétrospectif."

15 KA, Nachlässe, B/572: 2 (Nosinic), Wr. Neustadt, January 2, 1869, GM Krismanic.

leadership on the northern front, refused to be duped again. He angrily seized Henikstein's telegram, scrawled "*Miserabel*" on it with a red crayon, and curtly recalled Henikstein to Vienna for questioning.[16]

Henikstein's recall, however, was easier ordered than done. Besides being chief of the Austrian General Staff, Alfred Henikstein was Benedek's cosset, and the Feldzeugmeister flatly refused to part with him: "It cuts me to the heart to see a brave man like Baron Henikstein stripped naked and indicted beneath the gaze of the public," Benedek wrote the emperor on the second. Instead of Henikstein's head, Benedek offered the emperor Krismanic's. Was the "operations chief" not the *real* culprit in North Army's débacle? There would be a great battle the next day, and Benedek would need Henikstein at his side.[17]

To these untimely, rather grotesque efforts on Henikstein's behalf, Benedek added a much longer letter to the emperor that night, again blaming his predicament on the Bavarians, parliament, the foreign ministry, and his unworthy subordinates.[18] It was a rehash of the exculpatory letter posted from Dubenec on the twenty-ninth, and Henikstein appended some special pleading of his own. "I am," Henikstein wrote Crenneville at the Hofburg, "in the tragic position of being held responsible before the whole world for errors and mishaps that are not *my* fault . . . I am the General Staff chief *in name alone.* . . . Will there *really* be a court martial? Please do not convene it in Vienna. Could we not hold it in a provincial fortress instead? Will I no longer be allowed to wear my uniform? Will I be cashiered? If only I could shoot myself." He laid the letter aside, then took it up again and queried in the margin: "My pension?"[19] Henikstein, who would have been more gainfully employed in the Operations Chancery, finished this apologia at 3:15 A.M. on July 3, while Austrian staff riders were thundering off to all points with Krismanic's hastily scribbled battle dispositions. Owing perhaps to the shameful absence of Benedek and Henikstein from the operations room, they had not been completed till 3:00 A.M.[20] That the two most senior officers in North Army headquarters were thus engaged on the eve of the battle of Königgrätz may, in some measure, explain the sketchiness of Krismanic's dispositions, which left all Austrian generals in the field guessing as to the purpose and direction of the battle before them.

Krismanic began work on North Army's battle plan so late that none of the Austro-Saxon corps could be moved from their original campsites chosen on July 1. This explained why Benedek refused a request from Prince Albert to shift the Saxon divisions southwest to Hradek, where they could have mounted guns and opposed

---

16 KA, MKSM-SR 1866, 24/1, Königgrätz, July 2, 1866, FML Henikstein to FML Crenneville.

17 KA, MKSM 1866, Karton 343, 69/9, Königgrätz, July 2, 1866, FZM Benedek to Franz Joseph.

18 GM Eduard Steinitz, "Aus den Tagen vor Königgrätz," *Militärwissenschaftliche und technische Mitteilungen* 7/8 (1926), pp. 393–401.

19 KA, MKSM 1866, Karton 343, 71/62, Prager Vorstadt von Königgrätz, July 2, 1866, FML Henikstein to FML Crenneville.

20 KA, AFA 1866, Karton 2270, 8–12aa, Budapest, August 12, 1866, GM Kriz.

Herwarth's Bystrice crossing at Nechanice from a formidable height.[21] Because time was so short, North Army's left wing would have to be Edelsheim's 1st Light Cavalry Division — deployed in a wood at Prim — with the Saxons and VIII Corps in reserve. Gablenz's X Corps on the ridge at Langenhof and Archduke Ernst's III Corps at Chlum-Lipa would be the Austrian center. The right wing extended from Chlum to Nedelist and on to Trotina; it was held by Festetics's IV Corps, Thun's II Corps and Prince Taxis's 2nd Light Cavalry Division. This wing *should* have been swung forward from Nedelist to the high ground at Masloved, an essential tactical adjustment overlooked by Benedek that IV Corps would have to attempt under fire early in the battle. In reserve, Benedek held Ramming's VI Corps, Clam-Gallas's I Corps, his three heavy cavalry divisions, and sixteen batteries of guns.

An obvious flaw in Krismanic's disposition was that it contained no guidelines for an eventual *retreat* from the Bystrice position. Though the two corps and the cavalry division on the right wing would be able to slip sideways over the Elbe on pontoons, most of North Army would have to retire through the overcrowded interior of the Bystrice salient to the fortress and bridge at Königgrätz. Austrian corps commandants thought it odd that although ordered "not to disturb the fortress" — the only fixed crossing in their rear — they were provided with no information on alternate bridges or lines of flight. Detailed retreat dispositions were promised "for the next day." What Krismanic meant, of course, was later the *same* day. To dissemble his tardiness in disposing for battle, Krismanic had back-dated his disposition for the third to the second. But this sleight of hand merely confounded most officers, who did not receive their incomplete dispositions until 4:30 A.M. on the third, two hours before the Prussians attacked.[22] As a result, North Army faced an enveloping attack by three Prussian armies with no delineated lines of retreat and no bridges over the river behind it.[23] This was a recipe for disaster, and a North Army adjutant who proofread Krismanic's disposition in the early hours of July 3 was frankly aghast: "At first *I couldn't believe it.* We were offering battle *with a river behind us* and only one line of retreat!! And this beautiful piece of work did not even specify *the direction* for an eventual retreat, let alone intervening localities or bridges!! *Was this really possible?*"[24]

There was another problem with Krismanic's disposition. It furnished no information on North Army's general situation or the aim of the battle ahead, two areas in which Benedek himself was clearly at a loss.[25] Krismanic later testified

21 KA, AFA 1866, Karton 2280, 13–104, Vienna, December 1866, Col. Pelikan.

22 KA, AFA 1866, Karton 2267, 7–58, Königgrätz, July 2, 1866, FZM Benedek to corps commandants. Karton 2296, 13–10, Vienna, December 19, 1866, Capt. Schulz. Nachlässe, B/1109: 1 (Sacken), p. 8. Bartels, "Der Nebel von Chlum," pp. 27–8.

23 Later, the Prussian staff noted: "General Benedek does not seem to have considered that by not [preparing lines of retreat or] standing behind the Elbe, he would suffer not a simple defeat but a panic-stricken rout." AFA, Karton 2274, 13–61, Berlin, August 1867, "Offener Brief von einem preussischen Offizier." Hamley, pp. 415–16.

24 KA, AFA 1866, Karton 2275, 13–166, Hohenmauth, July 4, 1866, Capt. Stransky.

25 KA, AFA 1866, Karton 2270, 8–12r, Szenktgotárd, August 16, 1866, FML Taxis.

that on July 2 the Feldzeugmeister had instructed him to prepare only for a localized attack on the Austrian left wing, and that he, Krismanic, had "drafted dispositions for the eventuality of a bigger battle on [his] own initiative."[26] Yet even Krismanic's draft emphasized the attack from the northwest by Elbe and First Armies, alluding only to the *possibility* that the battle might "extend through the center to the right wing" as well. Because Benedek had not discussed the location and probable objectives of the three Prussian armies at his staff conference on July 2, Austrian corps commandants were, as General Coudenhove put it, "utterly ignorant" of Prussian movements on the third.[27] Some Austrian generals assumed that Prussia's Second Army had crossed the Elbe and moved westward to unite with First Army. Others thought that it remained on the left bank at Josephstadt. An Austrian officer whose regiment was installed on Chlum, in the heart of the Austrian position, recalled that "none of us suspected even the *existence*, much less the *advance* of a second enemy [flanking] army" on July 3.[28]

Krismanic should have considered the fact that he was disposing for battle generals accustomed to "march to the sound of the guns." Since North Army was arrayed on a salient angle, it needed only one excited general to do this for the whole Austrian front to buckle. "The disposition was superficial, imprecise and incomplete," a staff major who helped write it later testified. "Contact between the individual corps should have been encouraged, established and maintained with utmost care."[29] Instead, the Austrian *corps d'armée* would deploy for battle singly and in great haste, without reference to an overarching operations plan, or even contact with the masses of troops to either side of them. This explained the muddle that developed in the course of the afternoon and the ease with which Prussian units would slip through gaps in the Austrian line. By not putting his generals in the picture on the second, Benedek invited disaster on the third.

THE PRUSSIAN MARCH TO THE BYSTRICE

The three divisions of the Prussian Elbe Army rose at 2:30 A.M. on July 3 and began marching to the Bystrice in a pelting rain. To General Herwarth's left, the six divisions of the Prussian First Army moved most of the way from Horice to Dub in the course of the night and at 4:00 A.M. were arrayed in fields of corn an hour's march from the Bystrice. Few men in either army had eaten a square meal in more than a week, and their guns lagged far behind them on the muddy roads.

Further east at Königinhof, Prussian Second Army headquarters passed a sleepless night, jerked one way then the other by conflicting orders. Friedrich

26 KA, Nachlässe, B/572: 2 (Nosinic), Wr. Neustadt, July 12, 1866, GM Krismanic to Unter-suchungs-Commission.

27 KA, AFA, Karton 2270, 8–12y, Sopron, August 12, 1866, FML Coudenhove.

28 Treuenfest, pp. 448–50. KA, Nachlässe, B/1109: 1 (Sacken), p. 7.

29 KA, Nachlässe, B/1109: 1 (Sacken), p 8.

Karl's request for an armed demonstration at Josephstadt arrived at 2:00 A.M. No sooner had Crown Prince Friedrich Wilhelm and Blumenthal directed their VI Corps to Josephstadt than Moltke's revised orders, calling for an immediate descent by all of Second Army to the Bystrice, arrived at 4:00 A.M. Moltke's new instructions required another time-consuming change of plan and direction. Thus, when Friedrich Karl and Herwarth began descending to the Bystrice valley at 5:00 A.M., Crown Prince Friedrich Wilhelm was only *drafting* march tables for *his* units, canceling the demonstration at Josephstadt and directing three of his infantry corps and his cavalry division down the right bank of the Elbe to Königgrätz instead. While Steinmetz's V Corps stood guard against Austria's Josephstadt garrison, the rest of Second Army would, time permitting, bury itself in Benedek's right flank. However, the looming battle of Königgrätz would be a near-run thing, for the nine divisions of Second Army were all twenty kilometers from Sadova, a hard day's march. Because of Friedrich Karl's midnight machinations, Second Army did not get its marching orders until long after sun-up on July 3. Would it arrive in time to hurl its weight against Benedek's flank?[30] Would the eastern jaw of Moltke's envelopment close on North Army in time, or would Benedek find time to dodge backward across the Elbe or, much worse, throw everything he had at Prince Friedrich Karl and Herwarth von Bittenfeld?

At 6:30 A.M., Herwarth's vanguard, after wallowing down the muddy tracks to Nechanice from Smidary, pushed pickets of the Saxon 1st Division over the Bystrice to the Austrian position on the left bank, pausing only to wonder why Benedek had placed his left wing at Problus, not Hradek. If the Austrians had only extended this wing and actually *defended* the Bystrice line, "they could have made things very bloody for us," a journalist in Herwarth's suite observed.[31] Although the bridge at Nechanice – the only fixed crossing on Benedek's left wing – was absolutely essential to Moltke's planned envelopment of North Army, last minute Saxon attempts to burn it sputtered out in the rain. As Saxon engineers tore up the floorboards and attempted to set fire to the wooden trestles, they were driven off by fusiliers of the Prussian 28th Regiment, who cleared the bridge with rifle fire and seized it intact.[32] The battle of Königgrätz had only begun and the Prussians already had their first river crossing and unopposed access to the commanding heights on Benedek's left. This explosion of fighting on North Army's left wing spoilt breakfast for most of Benedek's regiments, which had to fall into line clutching uncooked rations, or nothing at all.[33]

In the Prussian center, really the Prussian center and *left* for most of the day in the absence of Crown Prince Friedrich Wilhelm's late-arriving Second Army, the light infantry of General Heinrich Horn's 8th Division breasted the heights of

30 Grosser Generalstab, *Feldzug 1866*, pp. 258–61.
31 Wachenhusen, pp. 116–18. Grosser Generalstab, *Feldzug 1866*, p. 264.
32 Craig, *Königgrätz*, p. 98.
33 KA, AFA 1866, Karton 2282, 13–13, Vienna, December 21, 1866, Lt-Col. Matschenko.

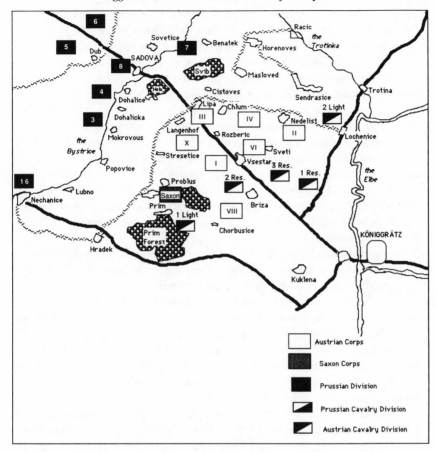

Königgrätz: Attack of the Prussian Elbe and First Armies, July 3, 1866

Dub and drove the Austrian cavalry screen there down to the village of Sadova, which was lightly held by Archduke Ernst's Prohaska Brigade. At this stage, Prince Friedrich Karl was uncertain what to do. It made sense to await the arrival of the Prussian Second Army, which was still twenty kilometers up the line at Josephstadt and Königinhof. But if the Austrian North Army really were in the midst of a crossing to the left bank of the Elbe – as Moltke and the Prussian army commanders assumed it had to be – every minute lost improved Benedek's chances of getting cleanly away to dig in *behind* the river barrier.

While Friedrich Karl pondered this dilemma in a thick fog that hid Benedek's eight corps from view, King Wilhelm arrived on the heights of Dub with Moltke and Bismarck at 7:45 A.M. Bismarck was clad for battle in his *Landwehr* major's uniform. He too believed that Benedek was in the process of crossing the Elbe to the safety of Austria's "northern Quadrilateral," for he rode directly to Moltke and asked him: "How *long* is this towel whose corner we've grabbed here?" Peering blindly into the murk that enclosed the Bystrice valley, Moltke replied: "We don't know exactly. It's at least three corps, perhaps the whole Austrian army."[34] Though Second Army was still hours away, Moltke decided promptly upon a course of action. He would attack Benedek's Bystrice line from Sadova round to Nechanice and pin what units of Benedek's North Army remained on the right bank of the Elbe long enough for Second Army to envelop them. The danger that the Feldzeugmeister might still have his *entire* force of 240,000 on the right bank of the Elbe, and that he might turn it against the 135,000 men of Elbe and First Armies, had to be faced squarely. Moltke reasoned, however, that even if Benedek did have all of North Army with him before Königgrätz, once Elbe and First Armies controlled the Bystrice, they would be able to shelter behind the water obstacle and fend off Benedek's attacks long enough for Crown Prince Friedrich Wilhelm to engage with his flanking army of 110,000 from the northeast.[35]

To begin the battle, Moltke ordered the small Prussian gun line on Dub – most of the Prussian batteries were still rolling up the soft roads from Horice and Smidary – to open fire on the Austrian position across the Bystrice. For the next several hours, the river valley shook with the detonations of an ever louder, more potent cannonade. Whenever Prussian troops positioned a new gun, an Austrian gun across the river would drop its mask and open devastatingly accurate counterbattery fire. When Prussia's King Wilhelm appeared on Dub with Bismarck, two Austrian shells bracketed him at once, carrying away the king's uhlan escort on a spout of mud. By 8:30 A.M., 300 cannon were trading fire, heralding the world's biggest battle since Leipzig in 1813.

Shortly before 9:00 A.M., still hours before even the advanced formations of the Prussian Second Army could be expected from the north, the Prussian First Army was ready to descend to the Bystrice in force to seize the fords and bridges at Sovetice, Sadova, Dohalice, Dohalicka, and Mokrovous. Most of Friedrich Karl's regiments had been sheltering from the cannonade on the reverse slope of Dub. They went into action, a British correspondent observed, "as if by the utterance of a magician's spell, one hundred thousand Prussian warriors springing into sight from the bowels of an armed earth."[36] While Horn's 8th Division followed the Jicin-Königgrätz road down to Sadova in company columns, the 3rd and 4th Divisions of the Pomeranian II Corps struck the Bystrice to Horn's right at Dohalice, Dohalicka, and Mokrovous, while Eduard Fransecki's 7th Division passed to the left of Horn, waded the Bystrice at Sovetice, cleared Benatek of defenders, and entered the Svib Forest, a tactically vital wood that overlooked Benedek's right wing and secured Friedrich Karl's left.[37] Though Moltke con-

34 Craig, *Königgrätz*, pp. 96–7.
35 Grosser Generalstab, *Feldzug 1866*, pp. 269–70.
36 Hozier, vol. 1, pp. 312–17.
37 Craig, *Königgrätz*, pp. 100–1.

ceived of these movements as mere containing attacks to buy time for the arrival of Second Army on Benedek's flank, Prince Friedrich Karl, thirsty for glory, fervently hoped that they would be the *decisive* ones.

General Benedek missed most of the cannonade, as well as the first Prussian attacks on the Bystrice line. He, Henikstein, and Krismanic passed the early morning hours in a hotel on the outskirts of Königgrätz frantically briefing Alois Baumgarten, Krismanic's successor as operations chief.[38] Though Emperor Franz Joseph had appointed Baumgarten – headmaster, in peacetime, of the Theresan Military Academy in Wiener Neustadt – to replace Krismanic at 9:15 the previous night, Benedek had not invited him to headquarters till 5:00 A.M. on the third, an hour before the first Prussian attacks on Nechanice.[39] A farcical scene ensued as Benedek, Henikstein, and Krismanic, who had no intention of returning to Vienna until *after* the battle that was exploding around him, all sat with Baumgarten and described the situation on the Bystrice, while Prussian shells burst atop the vacant captain's hill at Chlum-Lipa.[40] At 7:30 A.M., ninety minutes after the first shots on the left wing, Benedek finally quit the *Gasthof zur Stadt Prag* and began riding the ten kilometers to Lipa.

While the Feldzeugmeister rode to the front, Prince Friedrich Karl's divisions fought their way across the Bystrice. At Sadova, Horn's 15th Brigade crossed the river and rather easily put Prohaska's regiment of Rumanian borderers to flight. To Horn's right, August Werder's 3rd Division – the Pomeranian unit which had landed the decisive blow at Jicin on June 29 – waded the Bystrice and drove Gablenz's Wimpffen Brigade – detached from the heights of Langenhof and Stresetice – out of the villages of Dohalice, Dohalicka, and Mokrovous. As the Prussians emerged dripping from the Bystrice and sprinted into the villages, firing on the run, Wimpffen's men – mostly Venetians of the 13th Regiment – shucked off their packs, dropped their rifles, and fled back up the heights behind them. Downstream at Mokrovous, Werder's 54th Regiment attempted, in the usual Prussian style, to pursue and envelop the disordered Wimpffen Brigade but was immediately thrown back by a curtain of shell and shrapnel laid down by Gablenz's vigilant gunners at Langenhof. Sixty Prussians were struck down by this brief barrage alone, and Werder's attempts to move his brigade guns over the Bystrice to provide counterbattery fire were all thwarted by the concentrated fire of Gablenz's gun line. To Werder's left, the Prussian 4th Division – assailing the Hola Forest between Sadova and Langenhof – also tried to mount its guns on the left bank of the Bystrice, but they too were shattered by shell fire from the

38 KA, Nachlässe, B/2: 97 (Beck), "Rangsliste des k.k. Generalstabes." Bartels, *Der Krieg im Jahre 1866*, p. 34.

39 KA, MKSM, Karton 342, 69–4/38, Vienna, July 2, 1866 (11:30 A.M. and 9:15 P.M.), FML Crenneville to FZM Benedek. AFA 1866, Karton 2270, 8–12bb, Vienna, August 15, 1866, FML Baumgarten.

40 KA, AFA 1866, Karton 2274, 13–61, Berlin, August 1867, "Offener Brief von einem preussischen Offizier."

heights, their crews wiped out.[41] Some of the Prussian guns – antique twelve-pound smoothbores – had to be transported across the Bystrice just to get within range of the Austrians. These guns – one-third of Prussia's outmoded artillery establishment in 1866 – were instantly silenced by Austria's more modern rifled pieces, which, everywhere in the Bystrice valley, were firing down marked ranges.[42]

At 9:00 A.M., Benedek hove finally into Chlum, passed forward to Lipa, and began, belatedly, to orient himself. He and Archduke Ernst, whose III Corps was posted on Lipa and Chlum, watched as the Prussians first gained control of the villages along the Bystrice, then plunged ahead to the woods beyond them to seek cover from the accurate fire of Benedek's massed guns. As III Corps's seventy-two cannon rained shell on the scrambling Prussians, Benedek and Ernst paused to admire the spectacle. Across the Königgrätz road to their left, Gablenz' nine batteries were also deployed and firing steadily, preventing the three Prussian divisions beneath them from pushing their attacks up the Bystrice heights to Lipa, Chlum, or Langenhof. Though Moltke had accomplished his modest aim of seizing the line of the Bystrice early in the day, Prince Friedrich Karl had been thwarted in his much grander plan to break Benedek's center before the arrival of Second Army. Yet even as Benedek's powerful center rebuffed these first attacks by the Prussian First Army, his right wing had begun to creep forward, disturbing the Feldzeugmeister's original deployment and, unwittingly, opening a path for the Prussian Second Army into his flank and rear.

Benedek first noticed this unauthorized advance when he arrived at Lipa. While the Prussians established themselves in the Bystrice villages, two Austrian brigades launched themselves at the southeastern corner of the Svib Forest. One of them was Archduke Ernst's own Appiano Brigade, sallying from its forward position in Cistoves. The other was a IV Corps brigade, followed by another. This was puzzling. Krismanic's disposition showed the Appiano Brigade on Chlum and located IV Corps in the gap between Chlum and Nedelist.[43] Benedek wondered what was happening.

There had been a foul-up. Ernst had sent his Prohaska Brigade down to Sadova at 6:30 in the morning after the first alarms of Friedrich Karl's advance. This had been a foolish move, immediately regretted by the young archduke's staff chief, for Sadova was the one place Austrian troops should never have been. It was at the foot of the Prussian base on Dub and indefensible. To provide cover for Prohaska's inevitable retreat from the Bystrice, Archduke Ernst then compounded his original error by advancing Karl Appiano's brigade from Chlum down to Cistoves. All of this muddling had a familiar look. Benedek instructed Ernst to undo what he had wrought and pull the 12,000 men of the Appiano

41 Grosser Generalstab, *Feldzug 1866*, pp. 296–302.
42 Craig, *Königgrätz*, pp. 103–4.
43 KA, AFA 1866, Karton 2270, 12–6, Vienna, December 15, 1866, Capt. Hoffmeister.

and Prohaska Brigades back to the relative safety of Lipa and Chlum.[44] Even as Benedek attended to III Corps, however, Count Tassilo Festetics's IV Corps – assigned the Austrian center-right – was busy making even more radical revisions to Krismanic's battle disposition.

FESTETICS AND MOLLINARY ATTACK SVIB FOREST

Count Festetics was an uncomplicated soldier. When he ordered IV Corps to leave its place in line and march west at 8:00 A.M., he was marching to the sound of guns hammering away to his left at Lipa, Langenhof, and Nechanice. Krismanic's disposition, not delivered to Festetics' sector till 5:00 A.M., suggested that the battle might be confined to the Austrian left wing. Therefore, to Festetics, a hard-charging Hungarian hussar, Eduard Fransecki's Prussian 7th Division, crossing the 300 meters from Benatek to the Svib Forest, appeared to be the left wing of Moltke's combined army. Without the cover that Second Army would provide him later in the day, Fransecki had an exposed flank, was on the move, and had just engaged Festetics' outposts on the Bystrice. Like any self-respecting corps commandant, Festetics wanted to have at him.

At 7:30 A.M., Festetics rode ahead to Masloved, verified the size of the Prussian force attacking his Brandenstein Brigade in the Svib Forest, and summoned his reserve batteries. He would rake the Prussian columns coming up from Benatek with his seventy guns, and perhaps take things a step further. He ordered his second-in-command, General Anton Mollinary, to turn IV Corps round to the left and march it into the Svib Forest to hit Fransecki's flank. General Mollinary, a high-ranking staff officer who had been placed at Count Festetics's side to restrain precisely this sort of impulse, could not help but see the *wisdom* of the move. Benedek had placed North Army's IV and II Corps and Taxis's light cavalry division in a bowl on the right of the Austrian position, where they would be exceedingly vulnerable to fire from the still unoccupied high ground north of them. Since Benedek had not constructed sufficient entrenchments on Lipa and Nedelist, there was nowhere to shelter most of these men. The Austrians had dug just four battery emplacements and four battalion trenches on North Army's right wing: "What were we supposed to do with the *other* eighteen batteries, fifty-four battalions and twenty-eight squadrons" in the sector, a IV Corps staff captain wondered? "The needle rifle was unanswerable. The only way we could win was with artillery, but our gun emplacements were [too few] and too low-lying. . . . To deploy large numbers of guns in dominant positions, we *needed* the plateau of Masloved and the heights of Sendrasice and

---

44 "The Bistritz line at Sadova was completely exposed to fire from Prussian guns on the heights of Dub. Defending this line was in absolute contradiction of the disposition." KA, AFA 1866, Karton 2285, 13–7, Graz, February 5, 1866, Col. Catty. Karton 2285, 13–7b, Alt-Arad, December 19, 1866, Capt. Hegedus.

Horenoves."[45] To get them, Festetics had first to root Fransecki out of his flanking position in Svib Forest.

Although Benedek would later blame Festetics and Mollinary for Austria's defeat at Königgrätz, the fault was entirely the Feldzeugmeister's. He had unaccountably left a number of key points in his position unoccupied: Hradek on the left wing and Svib Forest and Masloved on the right. These places were not, as Benedek seemed to think, equivalent to Sadova, Dohalice, and Dohalicka – forward posts to be lightly held with skirmishers and then abandoned. With field guns devastatingly accurate to five kilometers, it was self-defeating to cede Horenoves, Masloved and Sendrasice to the Prussians. As for Svib Forest, it was one and a half kilometers long and 700 meters deep and grew right up the side of the Masloved plateau, providing excellent cover for Prussian columns approaching from the north or west.

General Mollinary, a senior staff officer with a fine eye for terrain, recognized this at once. He saw that the vital part of the field was not – as Benedek assumed – the heights of Chlum and Lipa, but rather the rising ground from Cistoves to Racic, which included the eastern tract of Svib Forest. Count Karl Thun, commandant of the Austrian II Corps, which was wedged in on low-lying ground between Nedelist and the Elbe, readily agreed.[46] From a forward position at Masloved and Horenoves, the Austrian right wing could either have stood on the defensive, deflecting the blow aimed by Crown Prince Friedrich Wilhelm's Second Army, or could have taken the offensive, northwestward into Prince Friedrich Karl's left flank, which, in the absence of the crown prince, was exposed for most of the battle. There was space for batteries at Masloved and a clear field of fire extending three kilometers down the Bystrice to Sadova and Dub. Peering through his telescope, Mollinary calculated that were the Austrian right wing to *advance* to the Masloved plateau, turning in on Fransecki at Horenoves and Masloved like the horns of the moon, Benedek's faulty position would actually be *improved*, and the battle, in all likelihood, won. With this in mind, Festetics, prodded by Mollinary, rode out at the head of his guns at 8:30 A.M. to occupy the village of Masloved and reposition Benedek's right wing.[47]

Fransecki's two brigades were striking into the northern reaches of the Svib Forest at the same hour, driving Festetics's Brandenstein Brigade before them. Prussia's flexible tactics, which permitted rifle companies to subdivide into platoons and sections, made short work of Brandenstein – who fell dead in the skirmishing – as well as his unwieldy half battalion masses, which lumbered

45 KA, AFA 1866, Karton 2287, 13–60, Vienna, December 20, 1866, Capt. Moser. Karton 2287, 13–59, Vienna, December 21, 1866, Capt. Komers.

46 KA, AFA 1866, Karton 2267, 7–177 1/2, Vienna, August 12, 1866, FML Mollinary: "Around Maslowed the wood mounts to its highest point, and should have been used as a buttress for our *Hauptschlachtlinie*. It was a critical area, whether for an offensive or a defensive." Karton 2282, 7–16b, Vienna, December 26, 1866, Col. Döpfner.

47 KA, Nachlässe, B/572: 2 (Nosinic), Vienna, January 6, 1867, Capt. Sembratowicz.

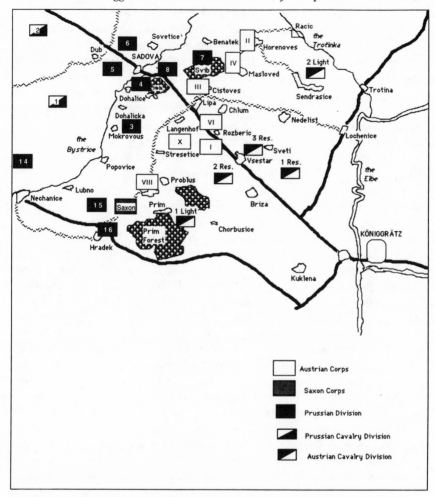

Königgrätz: Mollinary's bid to envelop the Prussian First Army, July 3, 1866

backward through the trees in close-order driven by the more nimble Prussians.[48] Like Prince Friedrich Karl, Fransecki assumed that the Austrian troops before him were only a rearguard covering North Army's passage to the left bank of the Elbe. Thus, two of his battalions passed quickly through the Svib Forest, abandoning the slow-moving cannon they had with them in their haste, emerged on the south side, and set off for Chlum-Lipa. They were in for a surprise at Cistoves, where Archduke Ernst's entire Appiano Brigade, deployed on the valley floor to cover Prohaska's retreat from Sadova, did not miss this opportunity to overpower

48 Fontane, *Der deutsche Krieg*, vol. 1, pp. 522–4, 530–1.

Fransecki's fusiliers and chase them back into the wood just as IV Corps's Fleischhacker Brigade, turned inward by Festetics and Mollinary, materialized from the east and joined the attack, searching for Fransecki's flank. The two Prussian battalions, their regimental colonel — Franz von Zychlinski — in their midst, were routed in this accidental but none the less effective Austrian envelopment. Zychlinski, who must have rued his decision to leave his guns behind, and the panic-stricken remains of his detachment were rescued only by rapid firing from two battalions behind them, which came up to break Fleischhacker's charge and train their rifles on General Mollinary's suite, killing IV Corps's staff chief and bringing Mollinary himself to the ground astride a dead horse. The Prussians pulled back into Svib Forest licking their wounds.[49]

As Fransecki moved the rest of his 14th Brigade into Svib Forest to reinforce Zychlinski's wilting attack, Mollinary, recognizing that Fransecki had overextended his division, ordered Fleischhacker's 61st Regiment into the wood to resume the assault on Fransecki's flank. The 61st were Hungarians, and they flatly refused to attack. A glance at the fringes of the wood strewn with Austrian casualties seemed to confirm the pre-war actuarial predictions of the Austrian war ministry, which held that during a firefight half the men in any given Austrian storm column would be struck by one sort of missile or another, and that most of the wounded would die of traumatic lesions and infection.[50] "The [Hungarians] hung back and refused to relieve the first wave," Mollinary reported. "Their officers could not budge them."[51] It was a critical moment and Mollinary resorted to a cynical ruse to impel his Magyars into the Svib Forest. He ordered the Hungarian hussar squadrons attached to his corps for reconnaissance to come up and hack their way into the wood. Only when the 61st saw their own countrymen being mown down without infantry cover did they finally agree to attack.[52]

Fourth Corps's commandant, General Festetics, had a foot torn off by a shell fragment while he watched this mutinous scene from Masloved at 9:30 A.M. As his tearful batman cleaned the mangled limb, Festetics made light of the pain: "Look at this hypocrite, whining like a mutt, yet he'll have only *one* boot to polish from now on."[53] Inside the Svib Forest, Fleischhacker's Hungarians struggled no less manfully to maintain their formations in the thick cover but were speedily outflanked and thrown back by just two battalions of Fransecki's 26th Regiment. As Fransecki began committing his reserves to the wood in a desperate attempt to hold it against Mollinary's bitter attacks, an Austrian officer vented his frustration with Prussian fire tactics: "We attempted a bayonet attack first on the

49 KA, AFA 1866, Karton 2287, 13–60, Vienna, December 20, 1866, Capt. Moser. Grosser Generalstab, *Feldzug 1866*, p. 283.
50 "Der Sanitätsdienst während des Gefechtes," *ÖMZ* 3 (1860), p. 54. Vincennes, AAT, MR 24/1388, Paris, September 1, 1868, État-Major, "Guerre de 1866."
51 KA, AFA 1866, Karton 2266, 7–177 1/2, Vienna, August 12, 1866, FML Mollinary.
52 KA, AFA 1866, Karton 2266, 7–177 1/2, Vienna, August 12, 1866, FML Mollinary.
53 KA, AFA 1866, Karton 2274, 13–75, *Neue Freie Presse*, July 3, 1886.

northeastern edge of the wood, and then several times inside. Each time the enemy refused to stand his ground. Instead he kept up a steady fire until we had closed to eighty paces, then dropped back using the terrain for cover." Untrained in skirmishing and open-order combat, the exhausted survivors of Fleischhacker's brigade yielded the wood and retired on Cistoves.[54]

Mollinary, meanwhile, had taken command of IV Corps from the wounded Festetics and was improvising a remarkable operation with elements of three Austrian corps, no mean feat. He was attacking Svib Forest on its front and flank from Cistoves and Masloved with the III and IV Corps, while Thun's II Corps attempted to cut Fransecki's lines of retreat at Benatek and fold back Prince Friedrich Karl's dangling left wing. Once taken, Svib Forest would furnish an excellent base for an enveloping attack on First Army's front and flank by all of North Army.[55] While Mollinary's Pöckh Brigade infiltrated the southern face of the wood, Mollinary sent two II Corps brigades, Saffran and Württemberg, against the eastern and northeastern edges. Neither Mollinary nor Thun suspected that the Prussian Second Army was closing on their *own* flank from Josephstadt. Benedek had not even *mooted* this possibility at the staff conference the previous day. Thus they were doing what they had been trained to do: using the terrain and their superior numbers to outflank the enemy before them.[56]

Karl Pöckh's brigade plunged into the Svib Forest at 10:00 A.M. and met only weak resistance from Fransecki's battered infantry. Pöckh immediately struck northwest in closed half-battalion masses without skirmishers. Since his men could not maintain their formations in the forest, all contact between Pöckh's battalions was gradually lost as they ventured deeper into the wood harassed at every step by resourceful Prussian rifle sections, which, as one Austrian officer observed, darted in and out of cover and "peppered our flanks with rapid-fire as our intervals widened." This, he added with heroic understatement, "tended to depress morale." Still, Pöckh, the spearhead of Mollinary's attempted envelopment of the Prussian First Army, drove restlessly ahead toward Sadova.[57]

By this time, 10:30 A.M., Fransecki's ten battalions crouched inside the Svib Forest had endured an hour's bombardment by fifty guns from Lipa, Chlum and Masloved. Though aimed with no kind of precision – Austrian shells were as likely to hit Pöckh's men as Fransecki's in the thick cover – Austrian gunfire combined with sweeps by three Austrian brigades made the wood untenable for Fransecki. With his line of retreat to the Bystrice threatened by the two II Corps brigades breaking into the northeastern end of the wood, Fransecki and his staff – all on foot after having their horses shot out from under them – fell back toward

---

54 KA, AFA 1866, Karton 2270, 9–11, Bruck, September 16, 1866, Maj. Villa: "At Königgrätz we attacked [Cistoves] in echeloned half-battalion masses. The enemy abandoned his position each time we closed for a collision."

55 KA, AFA 1866, Karton 2282, 7–16, "Brigade Württemberg in der Schlacht."

56 KA, AFA 1866, Karton 2282, 7–16, n.d., FML Philippovic, "Rélation."

57 KA, AFA 1866, Karton 2267, 7–96b, Olmütz, January 13, 1868, Col. Moritz.

their base at Benatek.[58] Thun's men, who had charged into the trees in such close order that they had not even been able to fire their rifles, rested briefly and examined the piles of Prussian dead and wounded. Two Prussian battalions remained in the northeastern corner of the wood, which Count Thun pronounced Fransecki's last hold on the left bank of the Bystrice. He resolved to take it at once and force Fransecki back on Dub.[59]

Pöckh, meanwhile, was ambushed in the western end of Svib Forest by two battalions of General Horn's Prussian 8th Division detached from Sadova to stiffen Fransecki's battered wing. They appeared from behind a fold in the ground and opened rapid-fire into Pöckh's startled flank and rear. One of Pöckh's regiments eluded the trap, the other was completely broken up. Pöckh himself was killed as were most of the officers of the 51st Regiment and hundreds of men. Hundreds more played dead, surrendered, or fled in confusion. The Austrian 51st was a Transylvanian regiment, embodying a mixed bag of Rumanians, Magyars, Germans, and Gypsies. An Austrian staff officer who survived the massacre described the tragicomic exertions of these disbanded men of various nationalities trying to tackle Prussian infantry in their midst. They staggered after them, jabbing ineffectually with their empty muzzle-loaders. The Prussian riflemen skipped out of reach, reloaded, and kept firing: "Our troop columns had lost their tactical cohesion; it began to resemble a blood sport."[60] An entire battalion of the broken 51st ran right past Horn's startled fusiliers and emerged on the Prussian side of the wood by mistake. Catching sight of this bedraggled group, a squadron of Prussian hussars trotted over from Benatek and rounded up all 700 of them.[61]

Still, despite Pöckh's costly error, Mollinary controlled Svib Forest, and Fransecki, having absorbed thirteen Austrian storm attacks, was on his last legs. At 11:00 A.M., a Prussian messenger rode out of the wood, crossed the Bystrice, and described the situation to Moltke and the king. King Wilhelm, a mediocre strategist, promptly proposed committing his only reserve divisions to the battle for Masloved. Moltke, the king's minder, promptly interrupted: "I must seriously advise Your Majesty *not* to send General Fransecki a single man of infantry support." Alluding to the *Kesselschlacht* that was already in train, he continued: "Until the Crown Prince has begun his attack, which is the only thing that can bring help to [Fransecki], we must be on our guard against an Austrian offensive." To repel the Austrian counterattack that Mollinary's assault on Svib Forest seemed to portend, Moltke insisted on keeping the Prussian 5th and 6th Divisions in reserve; the king, though urged by Prince Friedrich Karl to let fly with everything he had, wisely left the direction of the battle to Moltke.[62]

Through the gunsmoke and morning fog that clung to the Bystrice valley,

58 Grosser Generalstab, *Feldzug 1866*, pp. 285–8.
59 KA, AFA 1866, Karton 2282, 7–16, n.d., FML Philippovic.
60 KA, AFA 1866, Karton 2267, 7–96b, Olmütz, January 13, 1868, Col. Moritz.
61 Fontane, *Der deutsche Krieg*, vol. 1, p. 532. Grosser Generalstab, *Feldzug 1866*, p. 343.
62 Craig, *Königgrätz*, p. 109. Grosser Generalstab, *Feldzug 1866*, pp. 344–6.

Moltke perceived something that the Prussian king did not. The Austrian North Army, massed before Königgrätz in much greater strength than Moltke had expected, was positioned to deal an annihilating blow to the relatively weak Prussian Elbe and First Armies. Though Benedek, plagued as usual by doubt and caution, did not grasp this fact, his bolder, more imaginative subordinates did. At 11:00 A.M., Mollinary proposed an attack on Fransecki's base in Benatek. He wanted to round Friedrich Karl's flank and push up to Dub in concert with a frontal attack on Sadova and the other riverfront villages by the four Austrian corps and three reserve cavalry divisions arrayed on and behind Lipa, Langenhof, and Stresetice. "There I was, standing before the extreme left wing of the Prussian army," Mollinary later wrote. He had already committed his own brigades and II Corps to the operation. "A determined attack would have snapped off the enemy's left wing and put us on the road to victory."[63] Third Corps liked Mollinary's chances, and Archduke Ernst asked Benedek for permission to join the attack. After the war, Benedek's court of inquiry judged this to have been a pivotal moment. Mollinary's "unauthorized offensive" had taken a "positive turn" but could not be driven home without support from Benedek's reserve. The battle hinged for the next three hours on the Feldzeugmeister's willingness to *maneuver*. If he chose instead to remain on the defensive, Mollinary's gains would be squandered.[64]

BENEDEK'S REFUSAL TO COUNTERATTACK

Colonel Adolf Catty, Archduke Ernst's staff chief, reminded Benedek at 11:00 that Mollinary's brigades now stood ahead and to the right of III Corps, "like a troop echelon in oblique order." This, of course, was the optimal way to assail an enemy flank. Catty wondered why Benedek refused to press the attack. "The Prussians were so shaken that we could have thrown them over the Bystrice. It was not as if there were not enough Austrian *reserve* formations to replace us [on the front line.]" Though Fransecki's division had been reduced to three intact battalions by the morning's *engrenage* – which had pitted nineteen Prussian battalions against fifty Austrian battalions successively committed to the wood by Festetics and Thun – Benedek still would not strike.[65] Mollinary, meanwhile, had applied to Prince Taxis on his right for some light horse squadrons. He was aiming a final blow at the tottering Prussian 7th Division and would need cavalry to run down Fransecki's survivors. When Benedek angrily countermanded these preparations at 11:00, Mollinary dropped everything at Masloved and rode up to Lipa to explain the operation to the Feldzeugmeister. Although Benedek would not receive notification of Second Army's advance for another hour, he still,

63 KA, AFA 1866, Karton 2267, 7–177 1/2, Vienna, August 12, 1866, FML Mollinary.
64 KA, KM 1866, CK, Karton 242, 14–5/33, Wr. Neustadt, September 27, 1866, FZM Nobili.
65 KA, AFA 1866, Karton 2285, 13–7, Graz, February 5, 1866, Col. Catty. Grosser Generalstab, *Feldzug 1866*, pp. 288–94, 339–46. Craig, *Königgrätz*, p. 110.

mysteriously, refused to commit his massive, well-rested reserves to the battle beneath him.[66]

Mollinary considered the hour between 11 A.M. and noon the most critical phase of the battle of Königgrätz. He, Count Thun, and Prince Taxis could have thrown everything they had at Fransecki, crossed to Dub, and, as a IV Corps staff officer put it, "rolled up the Prussian position" from the flank while Benedek slammed through Sadova with four infantry corps and three cavalry divisions.[67] Prussia's First Army was breaking under the fire of 250 Austrian guns, and Herwarth's refusal to press Elbe Army's attack on Benedek's left wing while Friedrich Karl was so obviously weakening in the center meant that Moltke's flanking attack was itself in the process of being flanked from Masloved.[68] As Mollinary thrust into the gap between the First and Second Armies, it became possible for him to envelop Moltke from the east. All he needed was a determined push by Benedek in the center.

Mollinary would later be criticized for his excessive zeal at Königgrätz, but he was plainly on the verge of carrying the day. By 12 noon, the Prussians had managed to mount just forty guns on the left bank of the Bystrice, providing scant artillery cover for the demoralized remnants of their 3rd and 4th Divisions, who flattened themselves against the valley floor and prayed for deliverance as shells screamed in at them from the Bystrice heights. In the Svib Forest, Fransecki's 7th Division, pummeled in front and flank by Austrian cannon, did the same. Fransecki himself, who, by 12:00, had lost 84 officers, 2,100 men, and most of his twenty-four guns, peered anxiously to the northeast for a sign of Second Army. Feeling Mollinary's noose tightening around him, he quoted Wellington's desperate line at Waterloo: "I wish the night would come, or Blücher."[69]

Even when (belatedly) informed by Benedek of the approach of the Prussian Second Army at 12 noon, Mollinary argued no less urgently for an offensive, for only an Austrian *attack* could drive a wedge between First and Second Armies and prevent them from combining. Indeed after the battle, Moltke would praise Mollinary's initiative in the Svib Forest for precisely this reason. Since Benedek had elected not to retreat over the Elbe in the days after Jicin, only an "escape forward" offered him a way out of the "Bystrice pocket."[70] Mollinary, in short, desperately wanted Benedek to *use* North Army's superior strength instead of passively awaiting the arrival of the Prussian Second Army, which would tip the scales in Moltke's

---

66 Prince Taxis also approved of Mollinary's operation: "At 11:00 A.M., II Corps was making remarkable progress at [Benatek]. I thought the moment to introduce cavalry was near." KA, AFA 1866, Karton 2300, 7–29, Wamberg, July 5, 1866, FML Taxis.

67 KA, AFA 1866, Karton 2287, 13–59, Vienna, December 21, 1866, Capt. Komers. Nachlässe, B/572: 2 (Nosinic), Vienna, January 6, 1867, Capt. Sembratowicz.

68 Craig, *Königgrätz*, pp. 98–100.

69 Grosser Generalstab, *Feldzug 1866*, pp. 294, 304, 339-42, 348–52. Craig, *Königgrätz*, pp. 100–10.

70 *Moltke on the Art of War*, ed. Hughes, pp. 136–7. Grosser Generalstab, *Feldzug 1866*, pp. 313–14.

favor and make an Austrian victory impossible. "I went up to Chlum and explained all of this to [Benedek] in person," Mollinary later testified.[71]

Benedek, however, was mesmerized by his own powerful cannonade. He was a cautious soldier and he saw North Army holding its position cheaply with its guns. Why come to grips with the needle rifle at all? The Feldzeugmeister's finest hour had been Solferino seven years earlier, where he had done precisely what he was doing now: stood atop a height and beaten back enemy attacks. Had Benedek only taken a long view of his position – his left and right wings were extremely vulnerable – he would have realized that the morning's state of affairs could not be prolonged into the evening.[72] For the moment, however, four Prussian divisions were pinned on the Bystrice without any prospect of mounting to Benedek's position. For Benedek, this was enough. He was content merely to repulse the Prussians and thus ordered Mollinary and Thun to break off their attacks on Fransecki, change front back to the south and return to their original positions in line at Nedelist.[73]

General Gablenz, defending the Austrian center, was struck with amazement. He too was for an immediate offensive and, at 11:00 A.M., reminded Benedek of the "enormous losses" sustained by the Prussian regiments along the Bystrice. Gablenz sent a messenger to Lipa to enquire *when* exactly the Feldzeugmeister intended to unleash his reserves. An artillery duel, after all, was not an end in itself. More and more Prussians were recrossing the Bystrice and staggering back to Dub pursued by Austrian shellfire so rapid that by mid-morning several of Gablenz's batteries had exhausted their ammunition and crews. On the right bank of the Bystrice, King Wilhelm himself was engaged rallying terrified Prussian line troops. After attempting without success to return some shell-shocked fugitives from Horn's 15th Brigade to the Hola Forest, the king rode disconsolately back to his suite. "Moltke, Moltke," he groaned at midday, "we are *losing* this battle."[74] Gablenz sensed this too and asked Benedek to supply him with more shells and four additional batteries from the army gun reserve. Benedek, who thought Gablenz far too profligate with ammunition – yet had not thought to recall North Army's munitions park from the left bank of the Elbe before the battle – reluctantly complied.[75]

BENEDEK'S LEFT WING IN TROUBLE

The Austrian left too was holding, though no thanks to its terrible position. The fact was that the Saxons, Edelsheim, and VIII Corps could hardly lose in the

71 KA, AFA 1866, Karton 2267, 7–177 1/2, Vienna, August 12, 1866, FML Mollinary.
72 KA, AFA 1866, Karton 2282, 7–16b, Vienna, December 26, 1866, Col. Döpfner.
73 KA, AFA 1866, Karton 2282, 7–16, n.d., FML Philippovic.
74 Van Creveld, *Command*, pp. 137–8. Craig, *Königgrätz*, pp. 101–3.
75 KA, AFA 1866, Karton 2295, 7–13, Floridsdorf, July 17, 1866, FML Gablenz. Karton 2270, 8–12p, Floridsdorf, August 16, 1866, FML Gablenz.

morning, for together they mustered thirty-eight infantry battalions and thirty cavalry squadrons against the six battalions of infantry and ten squadrons of hussars in the van of Herwarth's Elbe Army. Because of the heavy weather and poor roads separating Herwarth's main body and Nechanice, this Elbe Army brigade, the same assortment of light infantry and horse that had won Hühnerwasser and borne the brunt of the battle of Münchengrätz, would do most of the fighting at Königgrätz as well, preventing Moltke from rounding the Austrian left flank until after 3:00 P.M., when the battle had already been decided in the Austrian center.

The first of three supporting divisions trailing Herwarth's 31st Brigade into action did not arrive on the field until 11:00 A.M., and Herwarth, a torpid and unimaginative general, feared to send it across the Bystrice while the First Army divisions to his left were in such obvious danger. Given the ferocity of Benedek's cannonade and the intensity of the battle between Langenhof and Masloved, Herwarth wrongly assumed that Benedek was in the process of launching a counteroffensive from Chlum-Lipa. If this happened, Herwarth had no intention of stranding himself on the left bank of the Bystrice while Prince Friedrich Karl recrossed to the right.[76]

Though seventy-year-old Herwarth, a veteran of the Napoleonic Wars, was unquestionably the wrong general to have in charge of Moltke's right hand flanking column, at Nechanice, as elsewhere in the war, Prussia's fire tactics developed a powerful momentum of their own. As the Saxon Lifeguard Brigade pressed Elbe Army's 16th Division back to the Bystrice at midday, advanced battalions of General Philipp von Canstein's Prussian 15th Division finally reached the river and drove the Saxons, who had wrought their way almost to Hradek with heavy casualties, back to Prim.[77] Austrian sappers, who did not arrive on the left wing until 10:00, hastily abandoned their field works after just an hour's work, managing to scrape only a couple of shallow trenches before being driven back to Chlum by Prussian shellfire.[78] Threatened now by enveloping attacks from Hradek and Nechanice, Prince Albert of Saxony had to renounce his counterattack and retire on Problus. His heavy losses had been for nothing. Since July 1, he had been trying without success to persuade Benedek to chop down the Prim Forest, fortify Nechanice, and extend the Saxon wing to Hradek. General Edelsheim watched the Saxons retreat, noting that their columns were torn by cannon fire from Hradek the whole way.[79]

The Austrian VIII Corps, drawn up behind the Saxons, proved no help at all. General Joseph Weber, hastily promoted VIII Corps commandant after Archduke Leopold's shipwreck at Skalice, rued Benedek's lack of preparation for the battle. "We were trying to deploy on unfamiliar ground in a heavy downpour," he later wrote. Weber's repeated appeals to Benedek for instructions on how to respond to

76 Craig, *Königgrätz*, p. 99. Grosser Generalstab, *Feldzug 1866*, pp. 280–1, 357–9.
77 Fontane, *Der deutsche Krieg*, vol. 1, p. 482.
78 KA, AFA 1866, Karton 2272, 13–19 1/2, Olmütz, July 10, 1866, 1. Genie-Regt.
79 KA, AFA 1866, Karton 2298, 7–8, Schloss Saar, July 7, 1866, GM Edelsheim.

Saxon demands for reinforcement went unanswered. This was not a question of initiative, for the Saxons were attempting the very maneuver – an extension of their wing to Hradek – that Benedek had expressly forbidden that morning. Eighth Corps, reduced to just eighteen battalions by Skalice, was unsure even of its function. Was it a link in the front line or a part of Benedek's general reserve?[80] Weber wondered why there had been "no discussion of *any* operational questions" at the staff conference the previous day. Why had Benedek made "no definite plans for the conduct of the battle?"[81]

It was a valid question, yet for the moment the trouble brewing on Benedek's left wing was only potential. The bulk of Elbe Army's 14th and 15th Divisions would not engage until 1:30 P.M.; 16th Division's 30th Brigade was still far away, mired in the wet roads from the west. Partially entrenched at Problus, the Saxons and VIII Corps stood *between* the Prussian Elbe and First Armies, which explained Herwarth's reluctance to cross the Bystrice in force in the morning.[82]

PRUSSIAN TROUBLES ON THE BYSTRICE

In the center, the four divisions Moltke and Prince Friedrich Karl had pushed over the Bystrice were still pinned on the left bank, subjected to a flailing bombardment in Mokrovous, Dohalicka, Dohalice, Sadova, and the Hola and Svib Forests. Each Prussian attempt to cross the intervening ground to Benedek's battery positions on Nedelist, Lipa, and Langenhof disintegrated in a rain of shrapnel. Prussian counterbattery fire was practically useless, for most of the guns Moltke had sent down to Sadova and Dohalice had been destroyed or withdrawn in the course of the morning. On the heights of Dub, many of Friedrich Karl's 100 guns – less than half the total caliber deployed by Benedek at Lipa-Langenhof – were out of ammunition, their reserve caissons still on the road from Jicin.[83] A foolhardy attempt by Prince Friedrich Karl to launch his only two reserve divisions – Tümpling's 5th and Albrecht von Manstein's 6th – at Benedek's elevated position *before* the arrival of Second Army was detected and postponed at the

80 KA, Nachlässe, B/572: 2 (Nosinic), Wr. Neustadt, September 8, 1866, GM Krismanic to Untersuchungs-Commission: "Benedek was constantly moving around throughout the battle. He usually gave orders out of earshot of the suite. At 11 A.M., I overheard him receiving a Saxon messenger from the left wing. I gathered that VIII Corps was being pushed into the battle line for an attack. I thought this dangerous. My disposition put VIII Corps at the disposal of the Saxons only in the event that the Prussians turned our left wing. Otherwise, it was to form part of the general reserve with I and VI Corps." None of the generals on the front line was made aware of this distinction by either Benedek, Krismanic, or Baumgarten before or during the battle.
81 "The army commandant never appeared on the left wing. Officers sent to find him could not find him." KA, AFA 1866, Karton 2274, 13–67, n.d., FML Weber. After the war, Benedek's court of inquiry deplored this "failure to block [Elbe Army's] advance with a unified leadership." KM 1866, CK, Karton 242, 14-5/33, Wr. Neustadt, FZM Nobili.
82 Grosser Generalstab, *Feldzug 1866*, pp. 357–9
83 Grosser Generalstab, *Feldzug 1866*, pp. 347–50.

last moment by Moltke, but not before Friedrich Karl had marched them all the way down to Dohalice and Sadova, where they idled, needlessly exposed to shell fire, for several more hours.[84] This was the occasion for Manstein's celebrated gaffe, when handed the order from Moltke to suspend the offensive ordered by Prince Friedrich Karl, Manstein replied: "This is all quite correct, but who is General *Moltke?*"[85] Needless to say, the Prussian staff *chef* was not enjoying this crude, disjointed assault on the Austrian center and was by now yearning for Second Army's arrival. After the war he would find it necessary to remind Prince Friedrich Karl – in the Prussian General Staff's official history – that "a frontal attack can succeed only in conjunction with an attack on the flank."[86]

Gablenz was hugely enjoying Moltke's plight. The Prussian divisions beneath him had spared no effort to reach his gun line. They had sent skirmishers, cavalry charges, even storm columns, and each time had been blown back by Austrian gunners firing down ranges marked with colored poles and barked trees. Indeed, the Prussians' only chance to hit back at the Austrians arrived quite unexpectedly in the early afternoon, when one of Archduke Ernst's regimental colonels, hell-bent on a decoration, ordered a storm attack against Dohalice and the Hola Forest from Lipa. He took everyone by surprise, including his own brigadier, and was gone before he could be recalled, leaving half of Ernst's 49th Regiment and much of his light infantry strewn dead or wounded in no-man's-land.[87]

After absorbing this useless tragedy, Gablenz's gunners resumed their fire, supplied by a stream of caissons flowing in and out of the Langenhof artillery position. Gablenz had already broached his corps munitions reserve and had begun dunning shells from Ramming, who was deployed in reserve behind him. At noon, having despaired of ever prodding Benedek into action, Gablenz sent his staff chief to invite Ramming to join an offensive down to the Bystrice with VI Corps. A generals' *fronde* was in the making and Ramming wanted in. His brigades had just eaten a hot lunch washed down with wine and brandy rations and moved up to Langenhof. They were, as the Good Soldier Svejk's Quartermaster Sergeant Vanek would have said, "ready to fight *anybody*."[88] Ramming too, though after considering Gablenz's proposal, he replied that he, like I Corps and North Army's cuirass regiments, could not take so much as a step without orders from Benedek.[89]

On the heights of Dub, Moltke and the Prussian king peered nervously across

84 Craig, *Königgrätz*, p. 111. Grosser Generalstab, *Feldzug 1866*, pp. 303, 346–7.
85 Lettow-Vorbeck, vol. 2, pp. 418–19.
86 Lettow-Vorbeck, vol. 2, p. 464–8. Grosser Generalstab, *Feldzug 1866*, p. 356.
87 KA, Nachlässe, B/1003: 1 (Hirsch), p. 39.
88 "For half a mess tin of wine and a quarter liter of rum, people will fight anybody." Jaroslav Hasek, *The Good Soldier Svejk and his Fortunes in the World War*, trans. Cecil Parrott (1923; New York: Penguin Books, 1981), p. 402. KA, AFA 1866, Karton 2291, 13–78, Prague, December 1866, Capt. Butterweck. Karton 2270, 12–8, Innsbruck, December 28, 1866, Capt. Adrowski.
89 KA, AFA 1866, Karton 2295, 7–13, Floridsdorf, July 17, 1866, FML Gablenz.

the Bystrice. By now the morning fog had lifted and, through a pall of gunsmoke, they could discern Ramming's march to the front. This was the lowest point of Moltke's fortunes in the entire war. Prodded by Prince Friedrich Karl, Moltke had, apparently, initiated what ought to have been the war's decisive envelopment too *soon*, before Second Army had closed to within striking distance. Benedek could now plunge into the gap between the Prussian armies and beat them separately. Moltke's fear throughout the campaign, that Benedek might use his "internal lines" to rupture the connection between the converging Prussian armies, had taken concrete form. Toward noon, as more First Army units abandoned their shell-torn posts on the Bystrice and Benedek's seventy squadrons of reserve cavalry girded to run them down, Moltke, perhaps with an eye on the smooth cavalry country behind him, warned the king: "Here there will be no *retreat*. Here we are fighting for the very *existence* of Prussia."[90]

At Austrian headquarters on Chlum-Lipa, even the ever despondent Benedek sensed his advantage and, at làst, weighed a counteroffensive. On his way up from Königgrätz in the morning, he had personally ordered Ramming's VI Corps to the front. Thanks to Prussian prisoners brought in at 10:00 A.M., Benedek knew the exact number of the force he had opposite him, which amounted to less than half his strength.[91] At 11:00, he had two well-fed, blissfully inebriated reserve corps deployed below him on the Königgrätz-Jicin road. Nineteen Austrian battalions were deployed in the Svib Forest, and Fransecki had been pushed back to Benatek, where he was surrounded by thirty-four more battalions ready to pounce. From Chlum-Lipa, Benedek could make out most of this.[92] The Prussian center had been flattened and, at last report, the Saxons were still holding Elbe Army, securing Benedek's single line of retreat for the time being.

BENEDEK WEIGHS AN OFFENSIVE

Paradoxically, *retreat* was as good a reason as any for an immediate Austrian *advance*, for, at 11:45 A.M., Benedek learned finally that several divisions of the Prussian Second Army had crossed to the right bank of the Elbe at 9:00 A.M. and were closing from Königinhof and Josephstadt. Second Army's speed and march direction meant that Crown Prince Friedrich Wilhelm would land in force on Benedek's right flank sometime after 2:00 P.M.[93] Given the proximity of this menacing Prussian *Flügelarmee*, it now became essential for Benedek to do one of two things: either step backward over the Elbe to "refuse" his threatened flank or remove it from danger by escaping *forward*, across the Bystrice. From the stand-

90 Craig, *Königgrätz*, p. 111.
91 KA, AFA 1866, Karton 2291, 13–103, Sopron, December 16, 1866, Capt. Handel-Mazzetti. Nachlässe, B/572: 2 (Nosinic), Timisoara, December 27, 1866, Capt. Woinowitz.
92 KA, AFA 1866, Karton 2275, 13–166, Hohenmauth, July 4, 1866, Capt. Stransky.
93 KA, Nachlässe, B/572: 2 (Nosinic), Timisoara, December 27, 1866, Capt. Woinowitz. B/1109 (Sacken), Vienna, December 20, 1866, Maj. Sacken, "An Generalstab."

point of troop morale and logistics, the latter course was plainly the better one, for it would not crush the spirits of North Army's excited reserves and would not have to be conducted along a single, overcrowded road. When pressed after the war to explain why no one in North Army headquarters prepared a retreat disposition once the advance of Second Army was confirmed, Krismanic replied: "because during the battle we could have committed our reserves to an *offensive*, which would have made a [retreat] unnecessary."[94]

Given the timidity of Benedek and Krismanic, this may have been a lawyer's dodge, but the fact remained that Benedek, who had just circulated orders to his generals to conserve their ammunition for a second battle the next day, could no longer count on one.[95] With a large Prussian flanking column aimed at his right wing and rear, he now had no choice but to escape forward or backward. In his panicky haste to retreat to Olmütz, he had already trucked the reserve ammunition he would need for a reprise of this battle across the Elbe. Moreover, his left wing was about to be turned, and his right wing, even if reinforced by Ramming and I Corps, would probably not have held against four Prussian infantry corps. Fransecki still clung to the northeastern corner of the Svib Forest, which, as an Austrian officer noted, would have permitted Crown Prince Friedrich Wilhelm to "advance huge columns under cover for an assault on Masloved, Cistoves, Lipa and Chlum."[96]

At 10:30 A.M., Benedek had sent a staff officer, Major Adolf Sacken, to find Mollinary and Thun and order them back to their original positions in line at Nedelist and Trotina. Benedek wanted his right wing to "rest on the Elbe." Sacken found Mollinary at Masloved at 11:00 and delivered the order. He found Thun forty-five minutes later near Benatek, just as the advanced guard of Second Army – a few battalions of the 1st Guard Division and a regiment of VI Corps – was peeking over the high ground northeast of the battlefield and just as General Benedek, who, incredibly, never thought to install a field telegraph at his headquarters on Lipa, was receiving late notification of its march.[97] Mollinary considered Benedek's order absurd. After all, Second Army was not going to swim the Elbe. It would need the very ground he had just conquered to infiltrate the Austrian position. Svib Forest and Masloved, as another officer put it, were the critical "outworks" of Lipa-Chlum, like modern contreforts extended to protect an antique citadel from long-range fire.[98] A return to Nedelist and Trotina from the hard-won Masloved plateau would not only be a return to the unfavorable tactical placement of the morning, it would also needlessly expose the Austrian battalions in and around the wood to pursuing fire – the most demoralizing of all – as they countermarched to Nedelist. Benedek's "order spoilt everything," a IV Corps

94 KA, Nachlässe, B/572: 2 (Nosinic), Wr. Neustadt, July 12, 1866, GM Krismanic.
95 KA, AFA 1866, Karton 2270, 8–12a, St. Pölten, August 7, 1866, FML Gondrecourt.
96 Bartels, "Der Nebel von Chlum," p. 22.
97 KA, Nachlässe, B/1109 (Sacken), Vienna, December 20, 1866, Maj. Sacken.
98 Bartels, "Der Nebel von Chlum," p. 23.

officer later testified. "It was incomprehensible." Mollinary considered disobeying it. Why did Benedek not send a cavalry division or two to delay the arrival of Second Army? Once the Austrian right wing pulled back, the Austrian position would be as vulnerable as ever, and "the opportunity for a decisive offensive would be lost."[99]

Benedek, of course, was responding not so much to Mollinary's "insubordination" – if the exercise of initiative by a corps commandant is really to be called that – but to the predictable consequence of his own faulty deployment on the Bystrice, which made it impossible for North Army to attack the Prussians without opening a gap at the salient angle. The "hole" critics later accused Mollinary of opening in the Austrian line, and which Benedek himself later seized upon as a convenient excuse for his defeat, was in fact an unavoidable result of Benedek's own undiscriminating choice of ground. None of the Austrian generals could advance without opening a hole in North Army's front. This, however, was no reason to remain on the defensive, for the Prussian First Army lacked the reserves to exploit a gap in the Austrian line, wherever it might appear. A better general than Benedek would have trusted in the maneuvering power of his army, its ability to defend itself at any stage of Mollinary's proposed offensive against a force as small as Prince Friedrich Karl's.

Though he was no strategist, Benedek's experience of war had taught him something about logistics. His maps of Bohemia suggested that the Prussian Second Army would not arrive suddenly, in a rush, but gradually, in driblets. From Josephstadt and Königinhof down to Königgrätz there were roads enough to move only two corps at a time. The rest of Second Army would have to wait for the routes to clear, in which case they would not arrive at Königgrätz until the fourth, or march cross-country, in which case they would arrive late, exhausted, and incapable of pursuit. In fact, this was precisely Crown Prince Friedrich Wilhelm's predicament on July 3. After assigning the turnpikes between Miletin and Josephstadt to the divisions of the I and VI Corps, he had no choice but to send his Guard Corps, followed eventually by Steinmetz, down the country tracks between these two march columns. His cavalry division – essential for the pursuit of a beaten enemy – would miss the battle of Königgrätz altogether, hopelessly snared in the tangle of supply wagons and gun batteries left behind on the roads from Miletin and Königinhof by the Guards and Bonin's I Corps.[100] Thus, at 11:45 A.M., when a messenger from Königgrätz brought Benedek the frightening news of the crown prince's march, the situation was still far from frightening. The bulk of Second Army was at *least* three hours away, and First Army was badly shaken. With the Austrian left wing already giving ground, with massive Prussian reinforcements on the way, and a single, unprepared line of retreat to the rear, the moment was at hand for Benedek to counterpunch decisively.

99 KA, Nachlässe, B/572: 2 (Nosinic), Vienna, January 6, 1867, Capt. Sembratowicz.
100 Grosser Generalstab, *Feldzug 1866*, pp. 305–8.

On the hill at Lipa, North Army headquarters looked to the legendary Feldzeugmeister for a sign: "*Retreat* dispositions?" Benedek's adjutant, Colonel Kriz, exclaimed after the war. "Until 2:00 P.M., we had excellent prospects for a *victory*. . . . All I heard was talk of an *offensive*."[101] Captain Eduard Hoffmeister, one of Henikstein's aides, overheard a conversation between Benedek and his new operations chief, Alois Baumgarten, at 11:45. A staff officer had just galloped up from the telegraph station in Königgrätz with the news that Second Army was approaching. Baumgarten – who had just ordered Ramming to leave his reserve position behind Gablenz in the center and move into line on the right wing – heaved a sigh of relief: "Then it's a good thing that I ordered [VI Corps] to fill in behind the Second [Corps]," he told Benedek.[102] Perhaps, but this was defensive thinking, and the prospects for an offensive in the center were still excellent. As Ilja Woinowitz, the staff captain who delivered the news of the Prussian crown prince's approach to Benedek, recalled: "At 12 noon, the Feldzeugmeister knew *exactly* how the Prussian army was divided." He had twice Friedrich Karl's numbers and three hours in which to work.[103] Would the "Lion of Solferino" ever show his teeth?

As Benedek and Baumgarten conferred, an officer from the Austrian VI Corps rode up to advise the Feldzeugmeister that though Ramming was turning east in deference to Baumgarten's orders, his brigades were still in position behind Gablenz. This was Benedek's last chance to throw them down the heights at the exhausted Prussian divisions on the Bystrice. The fog had lifted in the meantime, disclosing a clear view of the Prussian base on Dub. Benedek turned to Archduke Wilhelm, the Habsburg prince in ceremonial command of North Army's gun reserve: "Shall I attack with [Ramming's] corps, Your Majesty?"[104] Now this was rum. What on earth did the young archduke know? He was a war ministry functionary and the least experienced man in Benedek's suite. Ramming's galloper, who was standing by awaiting instructions, also thought it remarkable that Benedek did not specify a *direction* for the proposed offensive. He clearly had no idea *where* to commit his reserves, whether up the middle or round one of Moltke's flanks. Archduke Wilhelm, a stripling in jodhpurs, pondered a moment, then replied "no"; Benedek ought *not* hazard an offensive. Baumgarten hastened to agree with the archduke. An offensive would be far too risky. Krismanic and Henikstein said nothing at all. "It was 12 noon," Captain Hoffmeister noted. "Lipa and all the villages below us were in flames."

At that very moment, Colonel August Neuber, Benedek's *sous-chef*, cantered up

101 KA, AFA 1866, Karton 2270, 8–12aa, Budapest, August 12, 1866, GM Kriz.
102 KA, AFA 1866, Karton 2271, 13–1, n.d., Maj. Sacken, "Bericht." KA, AFA 1866, Karton 2270, 12–6, Vienna, December 15, 1866, Capt. Hoffmeister.
103 KA, Nachlässe, B/572: 2 (Nosinic), Timisoara, December 27, 1866, Capt. Woinowitz.
104 "*Soll ich kaiserliche Hoheit dieses Armee-Corps nunmehr vorrücken lassen?*" KA, AFA 1866, Karton 2291, 13–103, Sopron, December 16, 1866, Capt. Handel-Mazzetti. Karton 2273, 13–46, "Operations Journal der Nord-Armee."

to Lipa from Masloved with good news. Mollinary's offensive had cleared Svib Forest. Mollinary himself arrived on horseback a few minutes later and begged Benedek to countermand the retreat order on the right wing and carry an offensive over the Bystrice into the flank of Moltke's First Army instead. Captain Hoffmeister, loitering nearby, pricked up his ears: "It sounded to me as if [Mollinary] were requesting reinforcements." Mollinary in fact was urging Benedek to scramble some of his heavy cavalry regiments up to the heights of Horenoves to slow the advance of Second Army and to deploy Ramming behind them at Masloved. By thus securing the right flank of the Austrian army with forty squadrons of cavalry, thirty-five infantry battalions, and 112 guns, Benedek would have permitted II, III, and IV Corps and his remaining reserve brigades to attack toward Dub and beat Friedrich Karl before Friedrich Wilhelm could arrive on the scene in force. It could all be accomplished quickly, Mollinary insisted. Benedek had only to *act*. "No," Benedek replied crossly. He would not be rushed. Mollinary and Thun must heed their orders and pull back to Nedelist; Ramming was to stand down and remain in reserve behind Langenhof.[105]

---

105 KA, AFA 1866, Karton 2291, 13–103, Sopron, December 16, 1866, Capt. Handel-Mazzetti. Mollinary, vol. 1, pp. 145, 150.

10

Königgrätz: Moltke's envelopment

At midday on July 3, Moltke searched anxiously for a sign of the Prussian Second Army on the eastern skyline. The crown prince's arrival in force would add 110,000 bayonets to Moltke's sagging front, more than enough to shore up the Prussian center *and* turn Benedek's right flank on the Trotinka. For his part, Benedek had wielded an Austro-Saxon army of 240,000 over the 135,000 bowed heads of Moltke's Elbe and First Armies all morning, yet had made *nothing* of this advantage. At noon in Prussian headquarters, Moltke might have said of Benedek what Napoleon had said of Wellington: "This general fights war in a new way: He sits on his ass." Given Benedek's paralysis and his refusal to smite the Elbe and First Armies before the arrival of the Second Army, it was scarcely surprising that, by early afternoon, events and excited subordinates overtook the Feldzeugmeister no less calamitously than they had overtaken Archduke Leopold at Skalice.

In the course of the morning, General Anton Mollinary, commandant of the Austrian IV Corps, had accumulated a quasi–independent command of fifty-three battalions, twenty-eight squadrons and 160 guns. He now wanted desperately to slip the leash and accomplish his bold plan to envelop the Prussian Elbe and First Armies.[1] At least one of Mollinary's brigadiers in the Svib Forest – Duke Wilhelm of Württemberg – was steadfastly refusing to withdraw from his forward position on the northern edge of the wood. The duke had earned a Maria Theresa Cross for disobeying orders under similiar circumstances at Solferino and now saw an even better path to glory here on the Bystrice.[2] In the Austrian center, Gablenz was trying to organize a major offensive off his own bat and was drawing down Benedek's gun reserve.[3] By now, Archduke Ernst was fairly clamoring for an advance to the Bystrice; he too had begun to negotiate secretly with Ramming for the loan of reserve brigades.[4] Leopold Gondrecourt, who had replaced Clam-Gallas as commandant of I Corps that morning, had deployed his regiments in

1 KA, Nachlässe, B/572: 2 (Nosinic), Vienna, January 6, 1867, Capt. Sembratowicz.
2 KA, AFA 1866, Karton 2282, 7–16b, Vienna, December 26, 1866, Col. Döpfner.
3 KA, AFA 1866, Karton 2267, 7–89 1/2, Floridsdorf, July 17, 1866, FML Gablenz.
4 KA, AFA 1866, Karton 2270, 8–12L, Pressburg, August 17, 1866, FML Ramming.

16. General Wilhelm Ramming (1815–76), commandant of the Austrian VI Corps and Benedek's principal rival

march columns facing north toward Dub at 9:00. At 10:30, he had closed up behind X Corps on his own initiative. At midday, the insistent beat of Gondrecourt's drums carried up to Benedek's headquarters on Lipa from the Königgrätz road.[5]

5 KA, AFA 1866, Karton 2291, 13–77, Lemberg, December 15, 1866, Maj. Schmedes. Karton 2278, 7–16a, St. Margareth, July 27, 1866, Martini Regiment Nr. 30.

Ramming too was causing problems. Like Manstein at Dub, he was not even acquainted with North Army's new chief of staff. "Who is General *Baumgarten?*" he demanded impatiently when Major Adolf Sacken brought a second order from headquarters instructing him to redeploy his corps to the right wing. None of the Austrian corps commandants was aware that Krismanic had been deposed. Ramming, whom Gablenz had just invited to join an offensive from Langenhof, ordered Sacken to return to Lipa and inform Benedek that he would begin the front change toward Nedelist all over again but hoped that the Feldzeugmeister would reconsider the order and send his reserves against Sadova and Dub instead.[6] "Ramming's idea," a VI Corps staff officer recorded, "was to beat First Army *before* the arrival of the crown prince. [Ramming] understood that the best defense against an impending envelopment is a breakthrough in the *center*."[7]

The battle of Königgrätz was at its climax. Second Army was approaching but still far in the distance and, owing to the exigencies of its last minute march, scattered forty kilometers from wing to wing. Front to rear, Friedrich Wilhelm's "flanking army" was a bedlam of mixed-up arms, extending all the way back to its cantonments round Königinhof and Josephstadt. Steady rain had reduced most of Second Army's roads to bottomless gullies, forcing infantry battalions to slog single file toward the sounds of fighting on the Bystrice. As morning turned to afternoon, much of the Prussian Guard Corps – Second Army's most advanced unit – was still mired on the Dubenec plateau, hauling its guns and ammunition through ropes of twisted corn and heavy clumps of tillage, fairly mad with frustration.[8]

On the Bystrice, Moltke – whose improvised *Kesselschlacht* appeared to have bogged down – had now ironically to consider committing his only reserve corps to extricate Fransecki, Horn, and Werder from the dangerous "pocket" created by Mollinary's strike at Masloved. To Moltke's left, the crown prince, who was marching in the van of his 1st Guard Division, had his first glimpse of the battle shortly after 11:00. Riding ahead with his staff, he came within view of the Masloved plateau, which, though it blocked his line of sight down to the Bystrice, was lit by flashes from the Austrian batteries deployed on the high ground by Mollinary. Mollinary's guns at Horenoves and Masloved were firing west, down the Bystrice and into Friedrich Karl's flank. Friedrich Wilhelm, who had also assumed that Benedek would stand behind, not before, Königgrätz, now understood that this was no rearguard action. Benedek seemed to be within an ace of enveloping the Elbe and First Armies from Moltke's left. To speed the convergence of his four scattered corps on Benedek's exposed flank, the Prussian crown prince ordered his divisional generals to march not to the "sound of the guns," which might have landed them in *front* of the Austrian position on the Bystrice,

6 KA, AFA 1866, Karton 2271, 13–1, n.d., Maj. Sacken, "Bericht."
7 KA, AFA 1866, Karton 2291, 13–103, Sopron, December 16, 1866, Capt. Handel-Mazzetti.
8 Grosser Generalstab, *Feldzug 1866*, pp. 305–8.

but to a stand of trees clearly visible on the skyline at Horenoves, which would direct the Prussian Second Army into Benedek's right flank.[9]

RAMMING DEMANDS AN AUSTRIAN OFFENSIVE

Meanwhile, in the fields behind Lipa and Langenhof, Benedek's reserves – 50,000 infantrymen and 10,000 cavalry troopers – pressed up behind the front-line formations, high on schnapps and swaying to the "Radetzky March." Virtually everyone on the Bystrice heights awaited Benedek's offensive down to Sadova. The 120 guns of the Feldzeugmeister's reserve were limbered and ready to shoot the infantry through Friedrich Karl's softened line.[10] What on earth was Benedek waiting for?

Between 12 noon and 1:00, Major Sacken – the North Army adjutant shuttling between Benedek and Ramming – raced back to Lipa with Ramming's appeal for an immediate Austrian counteroffensive. "I was excited," Sacken recalled, "and convinced that a powerful thrust would carry the day for us." Sacken rode through the masses of reserve infantry crowding the slopes of Chlum and Lipa to the dairy where Benedek had established his headquarters; he breathlessly recited Ramming's proposal. Now only Baumgarten resisted Ramming's plan. The cautious schoolmaster continued to insist that the Austrians should not hazard an offensive until late in the evening or the following morning. In view of Second Army's impending envelopment, this was a ludicrous suggestion, which Benedek ignored. Sacken noted that Benedek was visibly tempted by Ramming's suggestion. "From the height of Chlum," Sacken recalled, "the enemy appeared to be retiring from Sadova." When Baumgarten ordered Sacken to return to Ramming and *insist* that VI Corps carry out its march to the right wing, Benedek countermanded the order. Ramming should remain in his reserve position on the Königgrätz road. Benedek then sent staff riders down to Gondrecourt's I Corps "to inform the men that the entire Austrian army was concentrated and that the battle was going well." He ordered Gondrecourt to form march columns and advance into the hollow behind X Corps. To all appearances, the Feldzeugmeister was readying a counterattack.[11]

By now, two vital hours had passed since Gablenz and Mollinary had first recommended a counteroffensive. Though Austrian headquarters was still hopeful, the tide of the battle was perceptibly turning. On Dub, more Prussian batteries were arriving from Jicin and Second Army was creeping inexorably closer. At 1:00, five Prussian Guard companies took Horenoves without resistance and the advanced battalions of Mutius's VI Corps pushed down from

9 Craig, *Königgrätz*, pp. 113–18.
10 KA, Nachlässe, B/946 (Coudenhove), July 3, 1866, FML Coudenhove, "Tagebuch."
11 KA, AFA 1866, Karton 2271, 13–1, n.d., Maj. Sacken, "Bericht." Karton 2270, 8–12l, Pressburg, August 17, 1866, FML Ramming. Karton 2278, 7–16a, St. Margareth, July 27, 1866, Martini Regiment Nr. 30.

Sendrasice to Trotina, threatening to slide behind Benedek. Thanks to the exertions of Prussia's Guard artillery in the morning, forty-eight Second Army guns were deployed within range of Chlum by midday. They did not delay in bringing Benedek's masses of reserve troops under heavy fire.[12] In the bowl behind Chlum, General Coudenhove had constantly to rearrange his heavy squadrons, which were being blasted by Prussian shells. By noontime he had his regimental bands going full swing to keep his men's flagging spirits up.[13] These first shots from Second Army paralyzed Benedek with fear. That he first ordered Mollinary to relax his grip on Prince Friedrich Karl's left flank and then advanced Ramming in the center showed that the Feldzeugmeister had not the slightest idea *how* to win the battle before him. Irritated by all the eyes upon him in headquarters, he left Lipa at 12:45 P.M. and rode back to Chlum to get a better prospect of the field and come to a decision.[14] He must have known that the decision would shortly be taken from his grasp, for even as Second Army began to intervene on his right wing, his exhausted *left* was crumpling, opening a path for Herwarth von Bittenfeld's slow-moving Elbe Army to cut finally across his only line of retreat.

ELBE ARMY TURNS BENEDEK'S LEFT

At 1:00 P.M., the Saxons, faced now by two entire Prussian divisions at Hradek and Nechanice, renewed the offensive they had broken off in the morning. Their object again was to thrust between the converging divisions of Elbe Army and, in the process, extend the Austro-Saxon left to the more defensible ground at Hradek. Accordingly the Saxon crown prince descended with two brigades from Problus and began moving southwest to Hradek. In the meantime, however, General Canstein had led his Prussian 30th Brigade to Hradek and turned into the unguarded Saxon flank. While Elbe Army's batteries at Hradek and Lubno flailed the Saxons with bursts of shrapnel, Canstein's brigade began to roll the Saxons up from both flanks.[15] General Weber, commandant of the Austrian VIII Corps at Prim, hurriedly shoved his Schulz Brigade forward to disengage the Saxons only to see it, not the Saxons, bear the brunt of Canstein's attack from Hradek. A single Prussian fusilier battalion infiltrated the Prim Forest and panicked Schulz's entire 74th Regiment, a Czech unit raised in Jicin. Schulz himself was killed as two Prussian battalions drove into the flank of his 8th Regiment, taking 830 prisoners.[16] What remained of the terror-ridden Schulz Brigade – the same unit that had bravely refused to relinquish its position at Skalice five days earlier – stumbled backward into the Saxon 1st Division, ruining Albert's attack on Hradek. Although the Saxons showed good discipline throughout this harrow-

12 Grosser Generalstab, *Feldzug 1866*, pp. 313–17.
13 KA, Nachlässe, B/946 (Coudenhove), July 3, 1866, FML Coudenhove.
14 KA, Nachlässe, B/572: 2 (Nosinic), Timisoara, December 27, 1866, Capt. Woinowitz.
15 Grosser Generalstab, *Feldzug 1866*, pp. 360–2.
16 Fontane, *Der deutsche Krieg*, vol. 1, p. 484. Grosser Generalstab, *Feldzug 1866*, pp. 362–5.

ing episode they came under withering fire from a second Prussian brigade, which drove at them from Lubno. Prussian rifle companies thus curled in on both Saxon flanks and began to mow down Schulz's disoriented stragglers, who scattered into the Prim Forest in panic.

Watching this bungled passage of arms from Prim, General Weber, in mounting desperation, detached his Fragnern Brigade – minus Fragnern, killed at Skalice – to rescue Schulz and the Saxons. As at Skalice, the Fragnern Brigade charged down in half-battalion masses only to be ripped apart a second time and disbanded by Prussian rapid-fire. The brutal defeat of the Austrian VIII Corps in less than thirty minutes opened a yawning gap between the Saxons and Gablenz. With just seven battalions, Canstein had reversed Moltke's strategic predicament of the morning. Now the Elbe and First Armies could join on the left bank of the Bystrice and rupture the connection between Benedek's left wing and center. General Weber described this "unfavorable turn of events," criticized again the lack of a "clear-cut plan" in headquarters, and begged Benedek for reinforcements from North Army's reserve.[17] Gablenz, deployed to the right of VIII Corps, warned Benedek that if headquarters did not send reserve troops to plug the hole, he would have no choice but to leave his place in line and attack southwest to prop up North Army's sagging left wing. The situation at Problus and Prim had become so dangerous for the Austrians that North Army, with the Prussian Second Army closing from the northeast, was now in imminent danger of a *double* envelopment.[18]

At 1:30 P.M., apprised of the "great hole" between Problus and Langenhof, Baumgarten dispatched a staff officer to General Edelsheim with orders to throw his light brigades into the breach "to support [Benedek's] intended offensive in the center."[19] It appeared that Benedek would try a *Flucht nach vorne* after all, but was there still time? The Feldzeugmeister had dithered for hours. The Prussian Guard batteries that had opened fire on Mollinary's wing from the heights of Horenoves at 11:45 A.M. had been preparing for the arrival of Louis Mutius's Prussian VI Corps and the 1st Guard Division from Königinhof and Josephstadt. At noon, with this Second Army vanguard halted two kilometers north of the battlefield awaiting supporting formations, Benedek still had time to attack First Army. He even had time at 1:00, when he received a second telegram from Josephstadt – sent at 12:10 P.M. – describing the "slow progress" of Second Army to the Bystrice.[20] Thereafter, it became a chancier proposition with each passing minute, and quite impossible once Benedek ordered Mollinary and Thun

17 KA, AFA 1866, Karton 2292, 7–25, Bruck, August 1, 1866, FML Leopold. Karton 2293, 13–49, Vienna, August 1866, Lt-Col. Reinländer.

18 KA, AFA 1866, Karton 2295, 7–14, Brübau, July 8, 1866, Col. Mondel. Karton 2296, 13–10, Vienna, December 19, 1866, Capt. Schulz.

19 KA, AFA 1866, Karton 2299, 8–12, Pressburg, August 15, 1866, FML Ramming to GM Edelsheim.

20 Benold, "Österreichische Feldtelegraphie," p. 65.

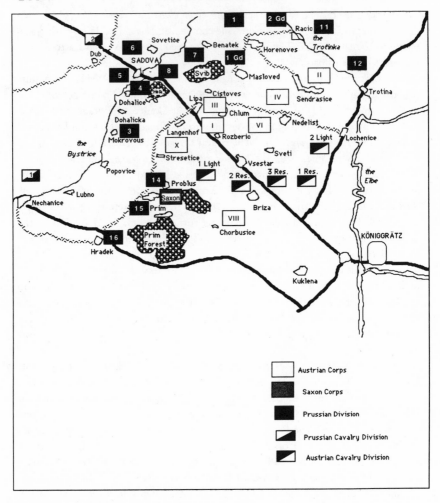

Königgrätz: Moltke envelops Benedek, July 3, 1866

to remove their troops and guns from the Masloved plateau at 1:15 P.M. Fransecki, the prime beneficiary of this unexpected reprieve, plunged back into the Svib Forest. He could now drive toward Chlum unmolested by the artillery fire that had decimated his ranks all day, for Mollinary's units streaming back to their original positions south of the Svib Forest masked the Austrian batteries on Lipa and Nedelist.[21] Prussian gun crews at Horenoves, no less grateful for the respite, rode ahead and shortened their ranges to Nedelist, Lipa, and Chlum. Moltke, now more confident of victory, got First Army's reserve divisions on their

21 Grosser Generalstab, *Feldzug 1866*, p. 351. Craig, *Königgrätz*, pp. 120–1.

feet, broke open his reserve caissons, which he had been husbanding for a last stand, and began pouring shell into the Austrian position.[22]

SECOND ARMY TURNS BENEDEK'S RIGHT

On Benedek's right wing, the four brigades of the Austrian II Corps, which had been preparing all morning for a strike at Fransecki's 7th Division, were surprised by the apparition of the Prussian Second Army on their flank. No one had warned Thun's men of the approach of a *third* Prussian army. Demoralization, the predictable result of this reversal of fortune, was complete. At 12:30, a single Prussian fusilier battalion cleared two of Count Thun's battalions from Horenoves. These Austrians were Poles and Ukrainians of Michael Thom's 40th Regiment, who were bewildered by events around them. One hour earlier they had been the leading edge of Mollinary's drive to Dub. Now they found themselves marooned at the tip of an out-thrust salient. They surrendered easily to a small detachment, proving again the truth of Napoleon's maxim that "morale is to the physical as three is to one."[23] Thom's *Jäger*, mostly Czechs recruited in this very Königgrätz district, offered only token resistance before giving way to five Guard infantry companies. They retreated to Nedelist, leaving 300 prisoners, half their strength, behind.[24] From his vantage point at Dub, Moltke watched his 1st Guard Division sink itself in the Austrian flank at Horenoves, then turned to the king, and said: "The success is complete. Vienna lies at Your Majesty's feet."[25]

While the Prussian Guards took possession of Horenoves, Louis Mutius' Prussian VI Corps swung forward on their left to Racic and Trotina. Here, on the banks of the cold, chest-deep Trotinka River – a natural obstacle that shielded Benedek's right wing – Mutius's Silesians expected to encounter stubborn Austrian resistance. Instead, three battalions of the Prussian 50th Regiment waded the Trotinka and took Racic easily, capturing 250 demoralized Hungarians in the process.[26] Even more alarming was the collapse of General Gustav Henriquez's supposedly élite brigade of Austro-German troops in Trotina, the village that anchored Benedek's right. Henriquez's brigade did not even deploy its batteries and surrendered the trench formed by the Josephstadt road after a brief scuffle.[27] Three companies of Prussian light infantry sufficed to drive Henriquez's entire 27th Regiment out of this important junction and seize the line of the Trotinka. The Prussians later discovered hundreds of Styrian troops skulking in the huts of Trotina. It had been enough, as Tacitus once said, "to defeat their *eyes*" with the

22 Bartels, "Der Nebel von Chlum," pp. 55–8. Fontane, *Der deutsche Krieg*, vol. 1, p. 548.
23 Strachan, *European Armies*, p. 43.
24 KA, AFA 1866, Karton 2282, 13–13, Vienna, December 21, 1866, Lt-Col. Matschenko. Grosser Generalstab, *Feldzug 1866*, pp. 316–26.
25 Craig, *Königgrätz*, pp. 122–3.
26 Fontane, *Der deutsche Krieg*, vol. 1, pp. 550–1.
27 KA, AFA 1866, Karton 2267, 7–177 1/2, Vienna, August 12, 1866, FML Mollinary.

prospect of a flanking attack. With the Prussian Guards and VI Corps solidly established on the Masloved plateau, Benedek at Chlum had to begin unwinding the counteroffensive he had been winding up all morning. As shells from the sixty Prussian guns deployed at Horenoves, Masloved, and Sendrasice burst among the Feldzeugmeister's reserve formations, he was forced to begin moving them backward, fueling the panic and disappointment that now began to course through every Austrian regiment.

With Prussian batteries and rifle companies so near at hand, the squadrons of Prince Emerich Taxis's 2nd Light Cavalry Division – North Army's shoulder on the Elbe – turned and retreated alongside II Corps.[28] Benedek later criticized Taxis for not warning him of Second Army's rapid advance, but Taxis must have wondered why on earth he should have removed his entire division from the battle on the right wing to discover something that Benedek would have learned at 9:00 A.M. if only he had thought to have a field telegraph installed in his headquarters at Lipa.[29] All the bloodshed of the morning had been for naught; Benedek had freely relinquished the gains of 8,000 Austrians killed or wounded in Mollinary's fight for Masloved and the Svib Forest. The Prussian Guards sweeping through Horenoves and Mutius's battalions gathering along the Trotinka could not believe their luck.

Still, these were relatively weak Prussian detachments. They ought to have been held up by Count Thun's four intact brigades. For the moment, Baumgarten and Benedek saw that the more immediate threat was on the Austrian left, where Elbe Army – Philipp von Canstein's marauding 15th Division in the lead – was busy mauling the three Austro-Saxon brigades left intact around Problus. While the Guards took Masloved and Mutius crossed the Trotinka on North Army's right, Canstein's 30th Brigade wrested Ober-Prim from what remained of the Austrian VIII Corps on the left, pressing General Weber's Saxon supports backward and *inward* to Problus, where they were beaten at 2:00 P.M. by the Prussian 14th Division, which came up at last on Canstein's left.[30] If only Herwarth, who still had many of his units on the right bank of the Bystrice, would hurry, Moltke would be able to drive both his wings forward and snap them together *behind* Benedek, trapping all of North Army on the low ground before Königgrätz. As Herwarth's 14th Division bashed in Benedek's left flank – driving the Saxons out of Problus in bitter house-to-house fighting – Moltke, who was now having difficulty keeping himself apprised of his quickening flank attacks, informed the Elbe Army commandant that Second Army was folding back Benedek's right, "cutting his line of retreat to Josephstadt" and threatening North Army with a

28 KA, AFA 1866, Karton 2300, 7–29, Wamberg, July 5, 1866, FML Taxis, "Über Anteil 2. leichte Cavallerie-Division." Karton 2282, 7–16, n.d., FML Philippovic.

29 The message from Josephstadt warning of Second Army's advance was sent at 9:00 A.M., but did not reach Benedek at Chlum until 11:45. Though Benedek had seventy-six kilometers of telegraph wire with him on the third, he deployed none of it. Benold, "Österreichische Feldtelegraphie," p. 13.

30 Craig, *Königgrätz*, pp. 124–9. Grosser Generalstab, *Feldzug 1866*, p. 366–74.

double envelopment.[31] With the defensive potential of Austria's "northern Quadrilateral" thus defeated and the thrilling prospect of a "second Cannae" in sight, Moltke brusquely countermanded Prince Friedrich Karl's second attempt to commit his two reserve divisions to the battle at 1:45 P.M. Prussia's plan, Moltke reminded the prince, was to fix Benedek in the "Bystrice pocket" and crush him, not drive him prematurely backward and out of danger.[32]

From the Austrian perspective, urgent countermeasures were needed. Though Moltke was now confident of victory, Benedek's situation was by no means hopeless. As Bonaparte had always said, and as Ramming and Mollinary were now saying with regard to Moltke's attempted envelopment: "whoever flanks me is *himself* flanked." Archduke Karl, Austria's great theorist of the nineteenth century, had enjoined a whole generation of Austrian officer candidates, Benedek included, that there is "no better defense against flanking columns than a prompt *offensive*, for the faster and farther you advance, the harder it is for the enemy to find your flank. He will hit air instead."[33]

Moltke's center was still vulnerable. Though Fransecki was being reinforced from Second Army, much of the strength of Friedrich Karl's two reserve divisions would be needed to replace losses in the Prussian 3rd, 4th, and 8th Divisions.[34] What had become of Benedek's counteroffensive, which might have split the Prussian princes like a chisel, rolled over Friedrich Karl, and landed heavily atop Herwarth? Though the optimal moment for such a stroke had passed, the opportunity still beckoned. And Benedek really had no choice. He had cancelled Ramming's movement to Nedelist, leaving the "hole" opened by Mollinary hours earlier unplugged. Without organized lines of retreat and sufficient bridges behind him, he *had* to advance. Count Thun's II Corps had simply given up on the right, and the Saxons and VIII Corps had been hacked to pieces on the left. The Prussian Guards alone had already mounted eight batteries on the Masloved plateau and, as Mollinary had foreseen, were landing shells in Chlum-Lipa, sowing terror in the Austrian ranks.

"A bullet that hits you in your back hurts no more than one in your chest," Archduke Karl had assured Austrian generals reluctant to escape *forward* through a gap between enemy columns. Hesitation was the worst possible course. "Men are easily panicked by flank attacks," Karl had warned. "A commandant must act swiftly to prevent this happening."[35] Thun's staff chief, whose brigades were succumbing more to the anticipation of Second Army's flank attack than the force of it, noted after the battle that a "powerful offensive against one or the other of the Prussian armies" would have been Benedek's only hope of salvation. A contin-

31 Groote, "Moltkes Planungen," in *Entscheidung 1866*, pp. 96–7.
32 Grosser Generalstab, *Feldzug 1866*, p. 364–5. Craig, *Königgrätz*, p. 123.
33 [Eh. Karl], "Zur taktischen Offensive und Defensive der Infanterie," *ÖMZ* 1 (1863), p. 286. KA, Nachlässe, B/208: 6 (Fischer), "Charakteristik der Operationen Napoleons I."
34 Bartels, "Der Nebel von Chlum," p. 52.
35 [Eh. Karl] "Zur taktischen Offensive und Defensive der Infanterie," *ÖMZ* 1 (1863), p. 286.

ued "defensive battle" in the horrible position around Chlum "made a catastrophe inevitable."[36]

Still, Benedek vacillated. He had allowed another hour to pass since the exchange with Ramming about an offensive down to the Bystrice. When Gablenz asked for more batteries from the army reserve at 2:00 P.M., Benedek refused. He informed Gablenz that he needed the guns "for the decisive moment" ahead.[37] Yet by now even Ramming had begun to have second thoughts about an offensive. An advance into the Bystrice valley at this late hour might have ended in the annihilation of North Army by the converging Prussian armies. On North Army's disintegrating right wing, Mollinary and Thun had been requesting help from Ramming since 1:00. At 2:00 P.M., Ramming advised North Army headquarters that the Feldzeugmeister would have to do *something* lest "the whole Chlum-Lipa position be rolled up" by Second Army. Even as Ramming corresponded with Benedek, stragglers from the Austrian right wing were stumbling back through his reserve formations from Trotina and Cistoves. Despairing finally of a sign from headquarters, Ramming ordered the Austrian VI Corps to change front and move into line at Nedelist.[38]

At this time, an officer at Benedek's side on Lipa recalled that "the Feldzeugmeister decided once and for all against an offensive." He would revert to his original plan and cling defensively to the Bystrice heights.[39] This, however, was neither as easy nor as sensible as it seemed. As Mollinary had predicted, Benedek's regiments on the Lipa-Nedelist end of the line as well as the reserve formations behind them were already suffering grievously from shells landed in their position by a growing number of Prussian batteries on the Masloved plateau.[40] With Fransecki and the Prussian 1st Guard Division in command of Svib Forest and the commanding height at Masloved, Benedek's regiments would have to retreat or attack. If they remained in their positions around Chlum, they would be blown to pieces like sitting ducks. In view of this fact, General Thun's staff chief could not comprehend why Benedek had scotched Mollinary's promising drive on Dub and surrendered Masloved to the Prussians in the course of the day. "Masloved was an invincible position where the Prussian crown prince was able to assemble his army and throw it at our flank with every advantage of surprise and coordination." Chlum-Nedelist was a "death trap" by comparison.[41] One of Prince Taxis's light brigades, which had hewed to the original disposition and remained on the low

36 KA, AFA 1866, Karton 2282, 7–16b, Vienna, December 26, 1866, Col. Döpfner.
37 KA, AFA 1866, Karton 2296, 13–10, Vienna, December 19, 1866, Capt. Schulz.
38 KA, AFA 1866, Karton 2270, 8–12, Pressburg, August 17, 1866, FML Ramming. Karton 2291, 13–77, Lemberg, December 15, 1866, Maj. Schmedes.
39 KA, AFA 1866, Karton 2270, 12–6, Vienna, December 15, 1866, Capt. Hoffmeister.
40 KA, Nachlässe, B/572: 2 (Nosinic), Vienna, January 6, 1867, Capt. Sembratowicz. Capt. Cristofek, "Meiningen Nr. 46 im Feldzuge 1866," *ÖMZ* 4 (1867), p. 225.
41 KA, AFA 1866, Karton 2282, 7–16b, Vienna, December 26, 1866, Col. Döpfner.

ground behind Nedelist, tried once to disengage Thun's floundering Henriquez Brigade at Trotina but was driven off by Prussian infantry fire. Benedek "deployed us in a *ravine*," an angry hussar snorted.[42] By now Prussian gunners had found the range of Chlum, keypoint of the Austrian position. It caught fire at 2:15 P.M. as the first Guard infantry companies began their advance in skirmish formation from Masloved toward Chlum.

Benedek, lost in thought and bracketed by flames in Chlum and Lipa, was brought to his senses by a storm signal that drifted up from Archduke Ernst's position on the north face of Lipa at 2:30. Ernst's densely packed III Corps was now attracting the fire of thirty rifled guns at Masloved and had two Prussian Guard brigades approaching its front through the Svib Forest. Since Austrian troops were not trained to defend trenches, Ernst thought it best to *attack* the oncoming Prussians with the bayonet. Benedek, who was rapidly losing control of the battle, ordered the counterattack halted. The notion, cultivated by Benedek after the battle, that 12,000 Prussian Guards somehow slipped undetected through the "fog of Chlum" into the heart of his position was as ridiculous as it was improbable. By 2:00 P.M. the sun was shining faintly on the Bystrice valley and the morning fog had lifted. At 1:00 P.M., an officer deployed on Chlum with Ernst's 46th Regiment had turned to his colonel and indicated the Prussian 1st Guard Division descending from Horenoves to the Svib Forest. Colonel Slaveczky, nearsighted and without a telescope, scoffed: "You're as pessimistic as ever." Revealing an unpardonable ignorance of North Army's own deployment, for which he would shortly pay with his own life, Slaveczky insisted that the approaching columns in Prussian blue had to be Saxons. Although more Austrian officers reported the approach of the enemy Guard, Slaveczky still refused to credit the reports. Another III Corps officer, acknowledging that Slaveczky was an imbecile, thought it far more significant that although the colonel had been on the captain's hill since 8:30 A.M., "no one [in army headquarters] had found time to tell him what he was supposed to *do*. Whenever subordinates asked him for instructions, his only answer was a shrug of the shoulders."[43]

To make matters worse, General Karl Appiano, who had extricated Slaveczky's regiment and the rest of his brigade from Cistoves at noontime and returned to Chlum, now found the height untenable. Prussian shells were screaming in from Masloved and bursting among his columns. To slip out from under this Prussian barrage, which was covering the march of the 1st Guard Division to Chlum, Appiano redeployed all but one of his battalions to the reverse slope of Chlum sometime after 1:00 P.M. Since virtually everyone in North Army was still expecting Benedek to attack Prince Friedrich Karl and Herwarth, Appiano made front

42 KA, AFA 1866, Karton 2300, 7–29a, Holice, July 4, 1866, Col. Bellegarde. Karton 2300, 7–29b, Wamberg, July 5, 1866, GM Westphalen.

43 Capt. Cristofek, "Meiningen Nr. 46 im Feldzuge 1866," *ÖMZ* 4 (1867), pp. 225, 230. Lettow-Vorbeck, vol. 2, p. 478.

to the west, with his *back* to Chlum. No one in headquarters had informed him of the approach of the Prussian Second Army.[44]

THE PRUSSIAN CAPTURE OF CHLUM

Ultimately North Army's loss of Chlum may have had less to do with Prussian stealth or firepower than with the shape of Benedek's deployment for battle. The Prussian Second Army hit the northeastern face of Benedek's half-moon front. In such a formation, the face assailed could be easily turned on both flanks, for the assailant could bring his entire force to bear on one-half of Benedek's line without troubling to protect himself against the other. This was just one of the many flaws in Benedek's ungainly Bystrice deployment. If the Prussians took Trotina and Nedelist, they could take Chlum as well, which was precisely what happened.

Second Army's 1st Guard Brigade, echeloned out in companies and platoons, passed easily through Svib Forest and Cistoves. Some of the Guards cleared the Austrian trenches and battery positions on Lipa and Nedelist, meeting little resistance from the III and IV Corps brigades of Colonel Alexander Benedek and Archduke Joseph, while others passed up the sunken roads from Masloved and Cistoves to the village of Chlum.[45] Retreating regiments of the Austrian IV Corps simply ignored the thin lines of Prussian Guards behind them, for by now a battle that had begun with every prospect of success had plainly been lost, and the front change ordered by Benedek at 1:00 P.M. had shattered the tactical cohesion of the Austrian right wing. Thus, the Prussian Guards did not really advance through a "hole" opened by Festetics, Thun, and Mollinary in the morning, an excuse later propounded by Benedek. On the contrary, Prussian troops who reached Chlum had first to move past II Corps on the Masloved plateau, then past retreating elements of IV Corps, then through trenches occupied by III Corps at Lipa. In truth, the Austrian right-center simply collapsed, yielding 8,000 unwounded prisoners and fifty-five guns.[46] In all of his Hamlet-like deliberation, Benedek had never considered the devastating *moral* impact that a late-arriving Prussian army would have on his men, most of whom had been under arms awaiting an Austrian offensive since the morning.[47] Hit suddenly from all sides – front, flank, and rear – Thun, Mollinary, and Taxis could not hold their men, who were

---

44 KA, AFA 1866, Karton 2285, 13–7b, Arad, December 19, 1866, Capt. Hegedus. Grosser Generalstab, *Feldzug 1866*, pp. 328–31. Treuenfest, pp. 448–50. Bartels, "Der Nebel von Chlum," p. 57.

45 KA, AFA 1866, Karton 2267, 7–97a, Holice, July 12, 1866, Infanterie-Regiment Nr. 52, "Gefechts-Rélation." Lettow-Vorbeck, vol. 2, pp. 474–6. Grosser Generalstab, *Feldzug 1866*, pp. 328–38. Craig, *Königgrätz*, pp. 132–3.

46 k.k. Generalstab, *Österreichs Kämpfe*, vol. 3, Beilage 3.

47 Benedek's adjutant, Colonel Ferdinand Kriz, made this point to Albrecht after the war. KA, AFA 1866, Karton 2270, 8–12aa, Budapest, August 12, 1866, Col. Kriz to FM Albrecht.

concerned only to reach their bridges on the Elbe to dodge the heavy, unexpected blow descending from the northeast.[48]

In Chlum, the single battalion of Hungarians detached by Appiano to defend the smoldering village was routed by several companies of the Prussian 1st Guard Regiment shortly before 3:00. Four hundred Hungarians of the Austrian 46th Regiment laid down their rifles and meekly surrendered this central bastion of Benedek's position.[49] Their supporting battalions, deployed on the southwest face of the height, turned round to face Chlum and advanced into enfilading fire. Six hundred of them fell dead or wounded; the rest gave up. Who could blame them? For these men, Baumgarten later wrote, the Prussian Guards "materialized in Chlum as if from thin air."[50] The village was captured so quickly that the bulk of Appiano's brigade, sheltering from Prussian shellfire in the ravines behind Chlum, did not even distinguish the sounds of the firefight above them from the general din of the battle around them. When a passing hussar informed Appiano that Prussian rifle companies had taken Chlum, the Austrian brigadier was dumbfounded. "*Nicht denkbar,*" he snapped before catching sight of Prussian skirmishers loping through the tall grass to his right. They were making for Rozberic at the foot of Chlum, a village athwart the Sadova-Königgrätz road – Benedek's sole line of retreat – and in the midst of the Austrian reserves.

Appiano ordered his *Jäger* to turn round and intercept the Prussians descending toward Rozberic. He then ordered the line infantry he had with him to storm Chlum. These men, Magyars and Rumanians of the 62nd Regiment, had already endured the morning's action at Cistoves, which had reduced them to just four intact companies. As this demoralized rump neared Chlum, Prussian uhlans with couched lances appeared on the summit. For Appiano's Hungarians, this was the wrong side of enough. The brigadier reported that his men "threw off their backpacks and cartridge pouches and ran – deaf to my commands and those of their officers – crashing through the files of the brigade to my left." Stripped of his line troops, Appiano spurred down to Rozberic to see how his light infantry were faring against the Prussian flanking column detected earlier. "Only one company was standing its ground. It was no longer possible to rally [the brigade]." At this moment Appiano himself was overrun by a troop of fleeing

48 A III Corps *Jäger* at Lipa recalled that "IV Corps fled through our position in disorganized heaps." KA, Nachlässe, B/1003: 1 (Hirsch), p. 39. Why? Capt. Moriz Moser of IV Corps explained: "At three o'clock we were hit with a violent barrage from Chlum, Masloved, and Nedelist. Prussian masses appeared on both of our wings; we retreated under a heavy fire to Sveti, thence to Placka, where we crossed the Elbe." Men and officers were worn out and in no mood to change front again and resume the battle. AFA 1866, Karton 2287, 13–60, Vienna, December 20, 1866. Karton 2300, 7–29, Wamberg, July 5, 1866, FML Taxis. FML K. v. Went., "Erinnerungen eines österreichischen Kriegsmannes 1866," *ÖMZ* 3 (1899), pp. 267–8.

49 Grosser Generalstab, *Feldzug 1866*, pp. 329, 375–6.

50 The Prussians took 400 prisoners in the 1st battalion of the 46th, 584 in the 2nd, and 456 in the 3rd. Capt. Cristofek, "Meiningen Nr. 46 im Feldzuge 1866," *ÖMZ* 4 (1867), p. 231. KA, AFA 1866, Karton 2270, 8–12bb, Vienna, August 15, 1866, GM Baumgarten.

Austrian cuirassiers and thrown from his horse. His disbanding units broke completely and fled south to the Elbe.[51]

What remained of III Corps's Kirchsberg Brigade — it had lost several battalions in the suicide attack on Hola Forest five hours earlier — turned its back on the Bystrice and attacked into Chlum from Lipa. The fighting was vicious as Julius Kirchsberg's German *Jäger* locked hand-to-hand with the Prussian Guards, stabbing with their bayonets and discharging their rifles at point-blank range. Their line of retreat to Königgrätz suddenly blocked, many of them were fighting more for a way out of Prussian captivity than for Chlum itself.[52] One of their brigade batteries on Lipa raced back, unlimbered 150 meters from the village church, and poured case shot into the Prussians. Guard musketeers returned fire, killing the battery commandant, fifty-three men, and sixty-eight horses in a matter of minutes. This was Captain August Gröben's legendary "Battery of the Dead," commemorated forever by an eye-catching cenotaph atop Chlum.[53] Four hundred Rumanian *Grenzer*, the residue of III Corps's beaten Prohaska Brigade, took one look at the long waves of Prussians closing from the east and legged it southward.[54]

The Guards had struck from the northeast while General Benedek and most of his headquarters staff had been standing on the southwestern face of Lipa observing the collapse of the Saxons at Problus. By shifting Edelsheim's division from Prim to Langenhof, Benedek had shortened his left wing and opened a path for Herwarth's Elbe Army into the Austrian flank and rear. He was now, belatedly, detaching Ludwig Piret's brigade from I Corps to block that path and relieve pressure on VIII Corps and the Saxons.[55] In the midst of this maneuver, at precisely 2:45 P.M., Benedek's *sous-chef*, August Neuber, rode up and informed the Feldzeugmeister that there was heavy fighting *behind* him, on North Army's right flank and in Chlum itself. A staff captain at Benedek's side recalled that the North Army commandant was thunderstruck.

Colonel Neuber arrived ashen-faced. The Feldzeugmeister was at that moment studying a message from the Saxons. When he had finished reading, the colonel reported: "The enemy is in Chlum; it is burning, and I was fired upon." The Feldzeugmeister stared at him for a few moments in a singular way, then turned to General Baumgarten and said: "You, Baumgarten, ride there and find out what's going on." Almost immediately, however, he changed his mind and galloped off to Chlum himself. Headquarters followed.[56]

51 KA, AFA 1866, Karton 2270, 8–12j, Hodolein, July 11, 1866, GM Appiano.

52 KA, Nachlässe, B/1003: 1 (Hirsch), p. 39.

53 Fontane, *Der deutsche Krieg*, vol. 1, pp. 561–72. Lettow-Vorbeck, vol. 2, p. 476. Grosser Generalstab, *Feldzug 1866*, pp. 375–8.

54 KA, AFA 1866, Karton 2267, 7–97a, Olmütz, July 12, 1866, "Gefechts-Rélation 52. Infanterie-Regiment."

55 KA, AFA 1866, Karton 2270, 8–12dd, Hetzendorf, July 31, 1866, Col. Pelikan. Karton 2270, 8–12q, Vienna, August 14, 1866, FML Edelsheim.

56 "*In Chlum ist der Feind; es brennt im Orte und ich bin angeschossen wurden.*" – "*Sie, Baumgarten, gehen Sie in den Ort und recognosciren Sie was darinnen ist.*" KA, Nachlässe, B/572: 2 (Nosinic), Timisoara, December 27, 1866, Capt. Woinowitz.

By now most of the 2nd Prussian Guard Brigade had joined the 1st on Chlum. Deploying quickly on the summit, they allowed North Army command, which was beating a path through a crowd of Austrian stragglers, to close to 200 meters before they opened *Schnellfeuer*. Colonel Adolf Catty, Archduke Ernst's staff chief, still would not accept the fact that these were Prussians. "Don't return fire," he called to Benedek's dragoon escort. "It *must* be the Appiano Brigade." Though Benedek and Catty had been side by side for most of the day, the Feldzeugmeister had never thought to inform Catty – who was responsible for the defense of Chlum and Lipa – of Second Army's approach.[57] Count Alois Esterházy, one of Benedek's adjutants, was shot from his horse by a Prussian guardsman. Headquarters wheeled wild-eyed into a battalion of Croats – men of the 78th Regiment – who were being literally herded by their officers toward Chlum. "*Our* panic furnished *them* with an excellent pretext to disband," an officer at Henikstein's side drily recalled. After composing themselves, Benedek and his staff drew their sabers and rode in amongst the Croats, driving them toward Chlum. "Most of them," a witness confessed, "would shortly surrender."[58]

Lipa was now strewn with the idle battalions of III Corps, which had been rapidly outflanked and left to ponder their next move. Benedek discovered several hundred of Appiano's routed Hungarians loitering nearby and ordered them to retake Chlum. The men refused. "They were deserting the front," an officer noted, "and taking others with them." The Magyars of the 52nd Regiment behaved more nobly. When they saw Benedek, a fellow Hungarian, approaching, they changed front to face Chlum, fixed bayonets, and began to ascend the height without so much as a word from their officers. Ignoring the fire around him, Benedek rode in amongst them, puffing a cigar and softly calling: "*Ellöre! Ellöre!*" (Forward! Forward!).[59] Having rallied the 52nd, all of whom would be shot down or taken prisoner within minutes, Benedek rode off in search of Gablenz and Ramming.

THE COLLAPSE OF BENEDEK'S FRONT

As Benedek and his staff descended the western face of Chlum, nervous Austrian troops on the Königgrätz road mistook the Feldzeugmeister and his suite for Prussians and opened fire on them at a range of little more than 100 meters. For once Austria's infantry of the line shot straight. Baron Henikstein and six other officers tumbled to the ground astride dead horses. Count Grünne's son was killed, and Archduke Wilhelm was struck in the head by this friendly fire, which, in their embarrassment, Benedek and Austria's official historians would later

57 KA, AFA 1866, Karton 2285, 13–7, Graz, February 5, 1866, Col. Catty. Nachlässe, B/572: 2 (Nosinic), Vienna, January 6, 1867, Capt. Sembratowicz.
58 KA, AFA 1866, Karton 2270, 12–6, Vienna, December 15, 1866, Capt. Hoffmeister.
59 KA, Nachlässe, B/572: 2 (Nosinic), Timisoara, December 27, 1866, Capt. Woinowitz. Lettow-Vorbeck, vol. 2, p. 474.

mendaciously attribute to the Prussian Guards in Chlum. As aides and escorts dismounted to drag Grünne and the wounded archduke to cover, others in head-quarters spurred down the slope to order the Austrian troops below them to cease firing. Benedek took this opportunity to divest himself of most of his staff, galloping up to Langenhof with Baumgarten and Kriz, leaving Henikstein, Krismanic, and Neuber behind in the fading cross fire.[60]

The want of an Austrian retreat disposition was now sorely felt, for Herwarth's Elbe Army had by now taken Prim and Problus and was within striking distance of Benedek's principal bridge and line of retreat at Königgrätz. When I Corps's Piret Brigade — detached by Benedek to reinforce the reeling Saxons — attempted to retake Problus, it was blown back by rifle and shrapnel fire on the edge of the village.[61] The Saxons, Edelsheim's cavalry squadrons and Weber's VIII Corps fell back to Königgrätz while more and more of Herwarth's battalions swarmed through Prim and Problus in pursuit.[62] To their left, Prussian rifle companies boiled out of Hola Forest and Sadova and began climbing toward Langenhof and Lipa. Gablenz looked on in horror. From his central height, he could actually observe the progress of Moltke's *Kesselschlacht*. Prussian columns were knifing through both of North Army's flanks and converging on its only escape route. Gablenz's own forward position was, by 3:00 P.M., almost completely sur-rounded. Herwarth had mounted guns at Problus; the Guards were potting away at him from Chlum, and Prince Friedrich Karl's reserve divisions were ascending from Sadova. The road behind Gablenz to Königgrätz was jammed with reserve troops so numbed by the sudden collapse of Benedek's line that they did not even react when just three companies of Guard fusiliers took Rozberic in their midst.[63]

Gablenz ordered his guns turned round to face Chlum only to find that his fire was masked by the confused masses of Austrian infantry still on the height. As Gablenz weighed his options, Benedek cantered up from the road below and ordered X Corps to take one collective step backward and one to the right to face the Prussian Guard division on Chlum. Yet the more troops Benedek threw at Moltke's Second Army, the less he had to arrest the other two. Count Adolf Wimpffen, posted with his brigade on X Corps's left wing, rode over to Gablenz and informed him that Herwarth's rapid advance was exposing the Wimpffen and Mondel Brigades to fire in their front *and* flank: "We cannot remain here," he warned Gablenz, who, having just turned his guns to face Chlum, now turned them back around to face Problus. All along the line, from Langenhof to

60 KA, AFA 1866, Karton 2275, 13–166, Litomysl, July 5, 1866, Capt. Stransky, "Tagebuch."
61 Grosser Generalstab, *Feldzug 1866*, pp. 397–9.
62 KA, AFA 1866, Karton 2293, 13–49, Vienna, August 1866, Lt-Col. Reinländer. Karton 2298, 7–8, Schloss Saar, July 7, 1866, GM Edelsheim.
63 A VI Corps officer considered this "*Überfall der Schlacht-Reserve inmitten der Schlacht*" to be the most preposterous aspect of Benedek's poorly directed battle. KA, AFA 1866, Karton 2291, 13–78, Prague, December 1866, Capt. Butterweck.

Stresetice, his men were falling in a cross fire, another predictable consequence of Benedek's deployment on the salient angle of Prim-Chlum-Nedelist.[64]

The failure of only one wing on this half-moon front compromised the retreat of the other, for all lines to the rear converged on the same point: Königgrätz. Under these circumstances, it was impossible for Benedek to pull back his threatened wings — the routine defense against an envelopment — without wreaking havoc in his rear. When the Saxons trooped past the Piret Brigade on their retreat from Problus, Piret's regiments fired on them, mistaking their retreating allies for attacking Prussians. "We could not distinguish the retreating Saxons from the pursuing Prussians, so we shot them both," an Austrian private lamely explained.[65] Panicky incidents like this one took place all along the cluttered line to the rear as all of North Army stuck fast in the narrow *Kessel* between the Elbe and the Bystrice. At Sveti, inside the shrinking pocket, General Coudenhove, commandant of Benedek's 3rd Reserve Cavalry Division, skipped in circles on his charger, looking first one way then the next: "Chlum had been taken by the 1st Guard Division and the Saxons had yielded Problus. It was 3:00; the battle had turned."[66]

To say the least: without Chlum, the Prussians would only have enveloped North Army from both wings and threatened its lines of retreat. With Chlum *and* a double envelopment, they were able to pour guns, rifle companies, and reserve cavalry into the center of the Austrian position and roll it up from the inside out. Suddenly the entire Austrian army, not just a rearguard, was at risk. For Benedek, who had entertained reasonable hopes of victory all day long, the battle of Königgrätz had become a catastrophe of epic proportions. At 3:00, he approached a straggling battalion near Chlum and barked: "Stand to! There's no escape."[67]

Indeed, there did not appear to be any. With the Prussians closing from both wings and in his midst, Benedek found himself forced back with six infantry corps, four cavalry divisions, and dozens of gun batteries on a single road. Although in the company of *three* General Staff chiefs — Henikstein, Krismanic, and Baumgarten — throughout the day, the Feldzeugmeister had not found time to take even the most elementary precautions. No gangways had been pegged out to steer retreating units to the rear and keep them from mingling. No staff officers had been posted behind the army with information on roads, sidetracks, bridges, and fords. Gablenz noted that even when Benedek's staff ordered four bridges built in the afternoon, they neglected to mark them with signposts or bring them to the attention of the corps commandants in the front line before the panic of Chlum set in. Since pontoon bridges were not visible over the tall

64 KA, AFA 1866, Karton 2295, 7–13, Floridsdorf, July 17, 1866, FML Gablenz. Karton 2296, 13–10, Vienna, December 19, 1866, Capt. Schulz.
65 KA, Nachlässe, B/1453 (Lebeda), Lauterbach, November 13, 1866, Pvt. Lebeda.
66 KA, Nachlässe, B/946 (Coudenove), July 3, 1866, FML Coudenhove.
67 KA, Nachlässe, B/1003: 1 (Hirsch), pp. 39–40. Bartels, "Der Nebel von Chlum," p. 59.

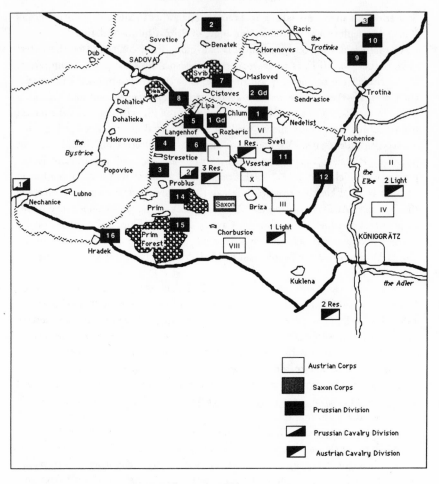

Königgrätz: North Army's collapse, July 3, 1866

banks of the Elbe, many Austrian units would run right past crossings without seeing them.[68]

After the war, General Krismanic suggested that there was far more than just Old Austrian *Schlamperei* at the bottom of this calamity. After spending most of July 3 at Benedek's side, he cited the Feldzeugmeister's listless pessimism as the principal cause of the Austrian rout. Krismanic recalled that even when Benedek learned of the Prussian crown prince's advance at 12 noon, he did not react. "I urged [Benedek] to shore up the front on the left, then ride with reserve troops to the right wing," Krismanic testified. "The army commandant looked at me and

68 KA, AFA 1866, Karton 2270, 8–12p, Floridsdorf, August 16, 1866, FML Gablenz.

nodded, but in an apathetic, fatalistic way that did not bode well. . . . This man had no aptitude whatsoever for the command of large armies."[69] At no time was this more evident than during the ensuing "panic of Königgrätz," the wild descent of tens of thousands of disbanded Austrian troops on the Elbe fortress works, a disorganized flight that shook North Army's morale and structure beyond redemption.

THE AUSTRIAN RETREAT TO KÖNIGGRÄTZ

Fired on from the heart of their position and enfiladed from east and west, North Army's regiments panicked at 3:00 P.M. and began running the ten kilometers south to the Elbe.[70] Chlum was barely 600 meters from the Königgrätz post road, well within the range of even the worst shots in the Prussian army. And who could miss? The road and villages between Chlum and the Elbe were crammed to bursting with Austrian reserve troops. Targets further out were easily ignited and obliterated by shell fire from Chlum and Masloved. Benedek had not thought to buttress the Chlum position with even a single "reply point" round which his army might have rallied.[71] Hard pressed from every direction, Austrian troops shrugged off their equipment and ran south toward the reassuring bulk of Königgrätz. Scavengers would later pick through heaps of abandoned kit around Chlum: tens of thousands of backpacks and haversacks, canteens, cloaks, shakos, spare shoes, ammunition, bayonets, and even rifles. Discarding this last item in the presence of the enemy was a capital offense for which Benedek and Archduke Albrecht would later threaten to shoot every tenth man in North Army.[72]

After conferring hastily with Gablenz, Benedek descended from Langenhof to the Königgrätz road, where he rode in amongst the fugitives and tried in vain to stem the rout. His horse was borne half the way to the fortress in the mob, the Feldzeugmeister shouting encouraging words in a half-dozen languages and crying "*Railliren!*" (rally!) – over and over. Adjutants and staff officers jogged alongside bawling: "*Auf Befehl des Armee-Kommandants soll Alles halten!*" (By order of the Army Commandant, everyone must *halt!*) It was no use. Even Archduke Ernst, the Habsburg prince entrusted with the defense of Chlum, galloped through to the rear surrounded by his suite. Instead of imitating the edifying example of Gröben's "Battery of the Dead," Austrian gun crews with full caissons were packing up and deserting the front, exposing their infantry comrades to the full fury of the Prussian pursuit.[73]

69 KA, Nachlässe, B/572: 2 (Nosinic), Wr. Neustadt, January 2, 1869, GM Krismanic.
70 "Panique und Pflichttreue in der Schlacht bei Königgrätz," ÖMZ 8 (1866). KA, AFA 1866, Karton 2270, 8–121, Pressburg, August 17, 1866, FML Ramming.
71 Bartels, "Der Nebel von Chlum," p. 24.
72 KA, MKSM-SR 1866, 24/4, Vienna, July 17, 1866, FM Albrecht, "Armee-Befehl Nr. 4."
73 KA, Nachlässe, B/572: 2 (Nosinic), Timisoara, December 27, 1866, Capt. Woinowitz. AFA 1866, Karton 2270, 12–8, Innsbruck, December 28, 1866, Capt. Adrowski. Karton 2275,

Benedek and Baumgarten halted at last and decided to compose a long overdue retreat disposition for North Army. In vain: by now Prussian shells were falling from Chlum and Langenhof and exploding around them. An Austrian battery began thudding away over their shoulders. "For God's sake," Baumgarten snapped to an aide, "ride over there and tell them to shut up!" Austrian headquarters shifted to a quieter spot only to be bowled over by more units fleeing the front. By leaving Krismanic and Neuber on Chlum without instructions, Benedek had lamed his own efforts to organize a withdrawal of the army. Now he and his rump headquarters admitted defeat and began to ride aimlessly around the field.[74]

On Lipa, the original center of Benedek's line – now flanked and cut off by the 1st Guard Division in Chlum – staff chief Henikstein had managed to replace his stricken English mare but was proving more of a hindrance than a help. He was engaged trying to persuade an idle III Corps battery to open fire on the survivors of the Appiano Brigade when Ernst's staff chief discovered him in the position and mercifully intervened.[75] Henikstein slipped down to the Königgrätz road and joined the flight to the Elbe. By 3:30, the two brigades of Guards in Chlum had flung the last Austrians out of the village, mounted a battery of guns, and begun firing down on everything that moved beneath them. Bullets, shell splinters and shrapnel pitched into the backs of the fleeing Austrians, spreading panic and terror.

When the Prussians took Chlum at 3:00 P.M., Benedek had sent a staff officer to find General Gondrecourt and order him to "concentrate" I Corps around Chlum. Baumgarten, meanwhile, went in search of Ramming and ordered him to retake Chlum with VI Corps. Unfortunately, Benedek neglected to coordinate the two attacks. His "concentration" of I Corps and Baumgarten's attack with VI Corps were conceived and executed separately, which explained why fifteen exhausted Prussian battalions on Chlum were able to repulse the thirty-five fresh Austrian battalions sent against them by Ramming and Gondrecourt in two distinct stages.[76] Noting Benedek's absence during both storms, Krismanic, who

13–166, Litomysl, July 5, 1866, Capt. Stransky, "Tagebuch." Grosser Generalstab, *Feldzug 1866*, pp. 378–81.

74 KA, Nachlässe, B/572: 2 (Nosinic), Timisoara, December 27, 1866, Capt. Woinowitz: "*Um Gottes Willen, rennen Sie hin. Sie sollen's Maul halten.*" KA, AFA 1866, Karton 2271, 13–1, n.d., Maj. Sacken. Karton 2296, 13–10, Vienna, December 19, 1866, Capt. Schulz.

75 KA, AFA 1866, Karton 2285, 13–7, Graz, February 5, 1867, Col. Catty.

76 The actual order Benedek scribbled for Gondrecourt implicates the Feldzeugmeister in the useless slaughter of I Corps (4,000 dead and wounded, 6,000 missing in less than sixty minutes), for this is all it said: "Concentrate at the latitude of Chlum behind Langenhof." At first, Benedek had written "concentrate beside VI Corps in order to retake Chlum," but he struck this part out. By the time Gondrecourt decided that he was meant to take Chlum, Ramming had already attacked and spent his corps. KA, AFA 1866, Karton 2278, 7–8a, n.d, unsigned. Received for delivery by a staff captain at "circa 3:00 P.M."

was with Ramming throughout, scolded the army commandant for "dropping the reins at this critical juncture."[77]

While the 1st Guard Division consolidated its hold on Chlum, urgently appealing for reloads and reinforcements from Bonin's I Corps vanguard, which, at 3:00 P.M., was collecting itself on the Masloved plateau, Benedek's two reserve corps on the Königgrätz road were still deployed in long march columns facing *away* from Chlum – Ramming toward Nedelist, Gondrecourt toward Sadova.[78] Ramming's VI Corps had therefore to change front for the *third* time that day and form itself into storm columns, a time-consuming process. Gondrecourt, whose I Corps was extended all the way back to Problus on the left wing, dispensed with the latter measure, turned round to the right, and prepared to storm Chlum in *march* columns. His attack would assuredly be a massacre.[79] Gablenz, meanwhile, had no sooner rotated to face Chlum than he was hit in the rear by the Prussian First Army, which – once Gablenz's guns were distracted by the action at Chlum – emerged from cover and began ascending from the Bystrice villages. Colonel Friedrich Mondel, who was struggling to extricate his brigade from the front line, recalled that "we had 40,000 troops packed in the cavity between Langenhof and Chlum, and the Prussians poured fire into us."[80]

Austrian staff officers trying to coordinate the rearguard attacks on Chlum by Benedek's two reserve corps lost touch with the Feldzeugmeister, who, by 3:15, was behaving like La Marmora at Custoza. Instead of taking up a central, fixed post to conduct the retreat, he was galloping breathlessly around the field; hence critical measures were continually postponed, or neglected altogether.[81] Ramming, for example, had lost a number of his guns to the Prussian *coup de main* at Rozberic. When he sent a staff officer to request replacements from the army gun reserve and a brief postponement of the attack on Chlum, the officer rode to Langenhof, where Benedek was *believed* to have moved headquarters after Lipa was overrun, but there drew a blank: "No one knew *where* the army commandant had gone. I rode back and forth across the field looking for him."[82] Benedek had in

---

77 And, by default, delivering them into the hands of Ramming, who, Krismanic said, "was bent on demonstrating *ad oculos* that he was the real army commandant." KA, Nachlässe, B/572: 2 (Nosinic), Wr. Neustadt, January 2, 1869, GM Krismanic.

78 Grosser Generalstab, *Feldzug 1866*, pp. 376–82.

79 Gondrecourt deplored Benedek's negligence in leaving Chlum so lightly occupied: ". . . *diese ungenügende Besetzung, die Vernachlässigung der Deckung und Eklairung der rechten Flanke, die zu späte Verwendung Reserven.*" KA, AFA 1866, Karton 2270, 12–8, Innsbruck, December 28, 1866, Capt. Adrowski. Karton 2270, 8–121, Pressburg, August 17, 1866, FML Ramming.

80 KA, AFA 1866, Karton 2295, 7–14, Brübau, July 8, 1866, Col. Mondel. Grosser Generalstab, *Feldzug 1866*, pp. 401–2.

81 At one point during the retreat, Benedek astonished his suite by steering off the crowded Königgrätz road into the grass to ride away without a word. KA, AFA 1866, Karton 2270, 12–6, Vienna, December 15, 1866, Capt. Hoffmeister.

82 KA, AFA 1866, Karton 2270, 12–8, Innsbruck, December 28, 1866, Capt. Adrowski. Karton 2270, 12–7, Vienna, December 16, 1866, Capt. Pohl.

fact shifted headquarters to a gutted shop on the road beneath Chlum. When a staff officer returned there with a captured guardsman who had precise information on the strength of the Prussian force on Chlum, he discovered that Benedek had abandoned this post too, yet had left no forwarding instructions.[83]

RAMMING'S ATTEMPT TO RETAKE CHLUM

General Ramming, meanwhile, not only had less artillery than he would have liked, he had neither the time nor the space to deploy pincers for a flanking attack on Chlum. And without Benedek's overview of the battle, he had no information on the fluctuating deployment of North Army, so he wasted more precious minutes trying to decide where to place his wings. The wild flight of four Austrian corps around him uncovered his flanks and, as he put it with judicious understatement, "visibly affected [his] troops, who became very unsure of themselves." Ramming later characterized his assaults on Chlum not so much as a serious attempt to take the place, but as suicide attacks "to hold up the Prussian pursuit." Sixth Corps would accomplish this, but with heavy casualties and at the cost of its tactical unity. Instead of making sure that Ramming and Gondrecourt ascended Chlum together, taking the single, exhausted Guard division above them in front and flank, Benedek allowed the seven brigades to go separately, with the remarkable result that while the Feldzeugmeister bobbed south along the Königgrätz road like a cork on a rising tide bawling at his disbanded regiments, his last two intact corps were beaten in detail, I Corps all but annihilated.[84]

Ramming's Rosenzweig Brigade, first to go, was halted by just three Guard fusilier companies barricaded inside Rozberic. Their fire was so thick and fast that Count Gondrecourt's staff chief – who abandoned the concentration of I Corps to join Ramming's assault – was struck by no less than three bullets: one tore away his coat, another dented his saber, and a third grazed his back.[85] After Rosenzweig's skirmishers had been repulsed, his *Deutschmeister* Regiment carried Rozberic, root-

83 KA, Nachlässe, B/572: 2 (Nosinic), Timisoara, December 27, 1866, Capt. Woinowitz:

> I observed VI Corps' assault on Chlum in the expectation that [Prussian] prisoners would be taken. *Richtig!* On the left wing, three *Deutschmeister* brought back a Guard NCO who gave me the following information: "In the village itself there is only a fusilier company and a foot regiment. We marched from Königinhof at 8:00 A.M. We belong to the 1st Guard Division and have uhlans with us. These are all the troops I saw." I thought this information was of critical importance. I raced back to headquarters, but found that it had been moved. No one knew where. Since VI Corps was engaged in what was unquestionably the most significant action on the whole field, I assumed that the Feldzeugmeister would come back sooner or later, so I waited [for an hour] in Rozberic.

> Benedek never returned.

84 KA, AFA 1866, Karton 2289, 7–17, Vienna, August 5, 1866, FML Ramming. Nachlässe, B/572: 2 (Nosinic), Wr. Neustadt, September 8, 1866, GM Krismanic to Untersuchungs-Commission.
85 KA, AFA 1866, Karton 2280, 13–103, Lemberg, December 19, 1866, Col. Litzelhofen.

ing the Prussians out of the village with the bayonet. Reduced by 50 percent casualties and low on ammunition, the Guard fusiliers – young Lieutenant Paul von Hindenburg in their midst – yielded the mud huts of Rozberic and retreated up a sunken path that led to Chlum.[86] This country track, hidden by ramparts of earth and grass and later dubbed the "Way of the Dead," was where Appiano's brigade had sheltered from Second Army's cannonade in the early afternoon. The noise of Rosenzweig's brass bands, which were conducting the Austrian brigade up from Rozberic, attracted the attention of four Prussian infantry companies atop Chlum, who ran over to reinforce the 200 fusiliers stumbling backward up the "Way of the Dead." The Prussians gathered at the mouth of this defile and mounted its banks to pour fire into Rosenzweig's Germans and Ukrainians. Prussian hussars from Prince Friedrich Karl's reserve rode in and slashed at their backs. Two Guard batteries deployed only 100 meters away in the grass between Chlum and Rozberic blasted loads of case shot through their flanks.[87] An Austrian adjutant sent to summon two battalions of Hungarians deployed in support of Rosenzweig's foundering attack found that the men had quietly slipped away: "No one knew where they had gone."

Georg Waldstätten's brigade stepped into the breach and was quickly mauled. His 79th Regiment – the Venetians who had briefly mutinied in June – formed storm columns only to be overrun by friendly cuirassiers, who had ridden up and been panicked by Prussian fire. To disengage Rozenzweig's shattered attack, Ramming, who had located his two battalions of missing Hungarians in the meantime, put himself at their head and charged up the "Way of the Dead." They too were thrown back, Ramming lucky to escape with his life. In less than sixty minutes, VI Corps lost 125 officers and 6,000 men, more than it had lost in five hours of fighting at Vysokov. Ramming's demoralized infantry simply gave up; the *Jäger* of Ramming's Jonak Brigade – unable even to *load* their carbines in the unrelenting Prussian cross fire – were observed surrendering to a lightly armed squadron of hussars.

Rosenzweig's luckless *Jäger* were knocked sideways out of Rozberic and into the path of Gondrecourt's I Corps, which charged up to Chlum a full forty-five minutes after Ramming had gone. These poor men, who had already been ravaged in the streets of Rozberic, were swallowed up by Gondrecourt's columns and subjected to a second storm, this time in Russian-style battalion masses.[88] Whereas Ramming had taken time to deploy batteries and open intervals between his storm columns, Gondrecourt launched his corps in close march order, with most of his batteries trailing uselessly behind the infantry columns. By 4:00 P.M., when Gondrecourt finally struck, fifteen Prussian battalions and

86 Craig, *Königgrätz*, pp. 147–8.
87 Grosser Generalstab, *Feldzug 1866*, pp. 382–5.
88 KA, AFA 1866, Karton 2291, 13–78, Prague, December 1866, Capt. Butterweck. Karton 2289, 7–17, Vienna, August 5, 1866, FML Ramming. Karton 2270, 8–12l, Pressburg, August 17, 1866, FML Ramming.

their batteries were deployed not only on the crest and southwestern face of Chlum but on the valley floor as well, in Rozberic and in Vsestar. The latter place was no more than fifty meters from Gondrecourt's heaving, panic-stricken columns. Even as the Austrians shambled round to face right, they were being cut down by Guard fusiliers and blasts of canister. Their own batteries, attempting to give covering fire, were run down and silenced by Prussian hussars before the infantry even charged.[89] Where the devil was Benedek? Old Radetzky would never have allowed this fumbling attack to jump off. Gondrecourt, a notoriously inept tactician, was presiding over a second Inkerman. In this formation, every Prussian bullet would not only hit, it might drop two men at once. Benedek's beloved troopers were about to be slaughtered, yet their self-styled *"Truppenvater"* was nowhere to be found. Where was he when the men most needed him?

At 4:00 P.M., while Gondrecourt was readying I Corps for its attack on Chlum, an Austrian officer spotted Benedek off to the west on the plain of Stresetice. The Feldzeugmeister was pursuing a regiment of Coudenhove's cuirassiers, who had refused an order to drive back the Prussian First Army units beginning to deploy on the crest of Langenhof and had begun retreating to Königgrätz instead. Benedek, returning from the direction of Problus, galloped into their path, stopped, and pointed north and west: *"Um Gottes Willen, meine Herren! Dort ist der Feind! Dorthin die Front!"* (For God's sake, gentlemen! The enemy is up *there*, so is the front!) The cuirassiers halted. As their colonel turned them around, a shell sailed in from the Bystrice heights and burst beside his horse, blasting splinters into the colonel's chest and face. He fell backward and hit the ground, his boot caught in the stirrup. As Benedek and the men looked on in horror, the horse sauntered off, smearing the bloody corpse through the grass: "Stop that horse! Stop him!" Benedek called to no one in particular. By this time, Prussian batteries had taken the range of these sitting targets and a flurry of shrapnels exploded among the cuirassiers, blowing men and horses to the ground. The men spurred away to the south leaving Benedek alone on the plain.

The Feldzeugmeister, a stickler for discipline, could not tolerate this. Though he would have been far more usefully employed extricating Gondrecourt's brigades from their futile attack on Chlum, he went after Coudenhove's frightened cuirassiers instead. He rode into their column a second time and ordered them to halt and turn around. Ilja Woinowitz, a staff captain at Benedek's side, recalled that "no one would even listen to him. It was a truly heartbreaking sight. [Benedek] stopped, looked to the sky, balled his fists and began to weep. Fat tears streamed down his cheeks. He screamed: 'And now I must bear even this disgrace into my old age, that a cavalry troop would not obey me!' " Woinowitz was deeply moved. "The meaning of these words," be noted, "was to be found not so

89 KA, AFA 1866, Karton 2278, 7–13, Moschtienitz, July 14, 1866, GM Leiningen. Karton 2278, 7–5, n.d., GM Gondrecourt.

much in the words themselves, as in the tone in which they were uttered, and I can find no way to describe that accent."[90]

North Army had dissolved. Thirteen hundred Austrian officers had fallen in the course of the day, and the entire army was migrating south through bursts of pursuing fire and a vacuum of authority. For a moment, Benedek was alone on the plain of Stresetice with Woinowitz, Baumgarten, Kriz, a junior adjutant named Eugen Müller, and a few escorts. There were no other Austrian soldiers in the vicinity. To their right, Gondrecourt, still without instructions from headquarters, was going up Chlum. To their left, the Piret Brigade was being blasted to the four winds at Problus. Benedek, the only man on the field who could have cancelled these senseless attacks, pulled the units back, and made a proper rearguard of them, took no notice. He appeared, Woinowitz noted, "morally and physically crushed," his eyes still wet with tears. At this moment, a stray projectile struck and killed Lieutenant Müller, who had served Benedek for years in Verona and was like a son to the Feldzeugmeister. Benedek peered down at Müller's lifeless body, then glanced dully at his dragoons: "He was my dearest. Lift him up."[91] Turning away from Chlum and Problus, Benedek joined the flight to the rear, giving Königgrätz and the crowd of fugitives before the fortress a wide berth. When he crossed the Elbe downstream that evening, he ordered the four pontoon bridges that had been constructed during the afternoon taken up. It was too early. He stranded thousands of men – including much of his reserve cavalry, fourteen battalions of Saxons, and most of I and VI Corps – on the right bank.[92] While what was left of North Army fought for its life, Benedek put the Elbe behind him and went in search of a telegraph station to wire news of the defeat to Emperor Franz Joseph. "The catastrophe I warned you of two days ago happened today," he cabled the Hofburg. Fog had concealed the Prussian advance. Unworthy subordinates had opened a "hole" in his battle line. Baron Henikstein had fought valiantly. North Army would resume its retreat to Olmütz.[93]

THE "PANIC OF KÖNIGGRÄTZ"

At 5:30 P.M., Captain Karl Stransky, a staff officer who had become separated from Benedek at Chlum two and a half hours earlier, finally arrived before the walls of Königgrätz. Although Ramming had, in the meantime, made a rally line

90 KA, Nachlässe, B/572: 2 (Nosinic), Timisoara, December 27, 1866, Capt. Woinowitz.
91 *"Der ist mir der Liebste gewesen; hebt ihn auf."* KA, Nachlässe, B/572: 2 (Nosinic), Timisoara, December 27, 1866, Capt. Woinowitz.
92 KA, KM 1866, CK, Karton 242, 14–5/33, Wr. Neustadt, September 27, 1866, FZM Nobili, "Untersuchungs-Commission." AFA 1866, Karton 2280, 13–104, Vienna, December 1866, Col. Pelikan. Karton 2270, 8–12q, Vienna, August 16, 1866, FML Edelsheim.
93 KA, MKSM 1866, Karton 343, Holice, July 3, 1866, FZM Benedek to Franz Joseph.

17.   The rout of the Austrians at Königgrätz, July 3, 1866

of North Army's reserve batteries and those extricated from the front line, Stransky found that Benedek's disbanded regiments were by no means reassured. "Men were screaming and firing their rifles in the air," he recalled. "There was no sign of the Feldzeugmeister, who had already quit the field and crossed the river. . . . We could see masses of Prussians advancing behind us [Mutius's VI Corps] and shells were falling everywhere. It was madness. Even army headquarters had no idea where bridges had been constructed!"[94]

The Austrian field hospital on the flat ground between Chlum and Königgrätz was overrun by 8,000 panic-stricken Austrian cuirassiers, who thundered through screaming "run for your lives!" The lazaret literally disappeared along with hundreds of wounded men trapped inside. Survivors who climbed from the wreckage joined the flight to the Elbe, where, as Ramming put it, "the realization that the battle was lost and that there were no fortified bridgeheads to conduct the men to safety crushed morale utterly."[95] Königgrätz itself was inundated and locked up for a siege. Upon reaching the narrow causeway that rose above the flood waters to give access to the fortress, the Austrian line troops, thinking they were home at last, smashed down palisades at the head of the causeway, streamed along it, and pounded on the fortress gates. Since there were Saxons among the Austrians,

94 KA, AFA 1866, Karton 2275, 13–166, Litomysl, July 5, 1866, Capt. Stransky, "Tagebuch."
95 KA, AFA, Karton 2270, 8–121, Pressburg, August 17, 1866, FML Ramming.

garrison troops inside the fortress opened fire, again mistaking their allies for Prussians. Austrians and Saxons on the causeway returned fire. Ramming appeared and demanded that the fortress be opened for the passage of guns and wounded. The fortress commandant refused. He was readying for a siege. "Whole corps are descending on the fortress in wild flight," he wired Vienna. "Defense capability destroyed. Please answer."[96]

Königgrätz was a decommissioned eighteenth-century building with provisions for a brigade and no facilities to receive a beaten army. This explained why at 5:00 P.M. the little garrison sallied briefly against its own field army to restore palisades torn down by Benedek's deranged mob. The fortress commandant himself was spotted clubbing Austrian troops with the flat of his saber to make way. Despite his best efforts, more and more desperadoes threaded through the outworks and onto the causeway of Königgrätz. Men crushed against the walls of the fort suffocated, and the ones along the sides of the causeway tumbled off into the neck-deep water of the moat. All around the fortress works, troops fell to their knees and begged to be let inside. Others swam across to the escarpment and tried to climb the slimy wall.[97] Few of them could swim and most were too frightened to realize that they could stand in this water. The Elbe forked to either side of Königgrätz, forcing the men to cross not one but two rivers: first the Elbe, then the Adler.

What Benedek's court of inquiry called "total panic" ensued. Austrian troops searched along the riverbank for the easiest crossings, an individual quest that destroyed what was left of the army's tactical unity. Gablenz's X Corps and the Saxons crossed the river at three different points in disorganized bands. Eighth Corps became inextricably tangled with I and III Corps. In the end, it was every man for himself: "the water was deep, so I jumped in behind some Venetians," a German of the Austrian 18th Regiment reminisced. "Italians always stick together, so I grabbed one by the coattails and wouldn't let him go. He and his pals *had* to pull me out." Hundreds of less fortunate Austrians drowned. And thousands more would succumb to fever contracted from extreme exhaustion, two cold dunkings, and a night in the open.[98]

GONDRECOURT'S ASSAULT ON CHLUM

As Austrian troops mobbed the works at Königgrätz and kicked and thrashed their way across the Elbe, General Gondrecourt sounded the storm signal at

96 KA, KM 1866, CK, Karton 254, 67–11/1, Königgrätz, July 3, 1866, GM Wigl to FML Franck. AFA 1866, Karton 2270, 12–8, Innsbruck, December 28, 1866, Capt. Adrowski.

97 KA, KM 1866, CK, Karton 254, 67–50, Königgrätz, August 18, 1866, GM Wigl. AFA 1866, Karton 2275, 13–166, Litomysl, July 5, 1866, Capt. Stransky, "Tagebuch."

98 KA, Nachlässe, B/1453 (Lebeda), Lauterbach, November 13, 1866, Pvt. Lebeda. AFA 1866, Karton 2270, 8–12p, Floridsdorf, August 16, 1866, FML Gablenz. Grosser Generalstab, *Feldzug 1866*, pp. 432–3.

Chlum and sent three brigades up the hill. By now, with both Austrian flanks turned, the Prussian 5th and 6th Divisions firing down from Langenhof, and Chlum itself reinforced by the Prussian 1st Division, Count Gondrecourt's attack had no prospect of carrying.[99] Nor did it make tactical sense. Gondrecourt had several Prussian divisions *behind* him at Langenhof and Problus and, at Chlum, was caught in a cross fire. Moreover, since Benedek had detached I Corps's Piret and Abele Brigades to spell the Saxons on the left wing, Gondrecourt no longer had the numbers he would have needed to take Chlum.[100]

This fact merely undermined what was already an aimless mission. There were no Austrian reserve formations available to reinforce Gondrecourt even were he to take the height. Thus, three Austrian brigades went up the southern and western faces of Chlum one beside the other, a lonely smudge of grey in a sea of Prussian blue. Gondrecourt, who led a truly charmed existence, asked nothing of his men that he would not attempt himself and duly conducted a battalion of Slovenian *Jäger* through enfilading fire nearly to the summit of Chlum. In this battalion alone, 500 men fell before Gondrecourt managed to halt the attack and retire.[101] Terrified Austrian troops surged around him, taken from every side by Prussian fire. Though low on ammunition – a scarce commodity all afternoon on Chlum, which was far ahead of Moltke's supply columns – the 1st Guards and Bonin's 1st Division used what they had efficiently. To repulse Gondrecourt's columns, they deployed in firing lines, used cover well, and fired into the flanks of the Austrian columns, negating their "steamroller" effect.[102] Austrian officers foolish enough to appear on horseback fell first. Ringelsheim's 73rd Regiment climbed to within ten meters of the Guards's gun line before being splattered across the slope by loads of case shot delivered into their front and flank at point-blank range. This regiment lost 1,100 men in a few minutes.[103]

Count Leiningen – another stubborn dévoté of shock – stupidly ordered his battalions to close their intervals to two meters before attacking. His first column, Venetians of the 38th Regiment, lost half its strength to wounds and frantic desertions before it had gone 100 steps. When two squadrons of Prussian hussars rode up and began to slash at the men with their sabers, the Italians broke and ran into Rozberic, where they hid among the smoking ruins recently evacuated by the Prussian Guards. Leiningen's second wave, Hungarians and Rumanians of the 33rd Regiment, was literally wiped out. The regimental colonel, 17 officers, all

99 Craig, *Königgrätz*, pp. 151, 159. Grosser Generalstab, *Feldzug 1866*, p. 384.
100 KA, KM 1866, CK, Karton 242, 14–5/33, Wr. Neustadt, September 27, 1866, FZM Nobili.
101 Gondrecourt called it a "murderous, three-way cross fire. Our mission was an impossible one." KA, AFA 1866, Karton 2278, 7–5, n.d., GM Gondrecourt. Karton 2278, 7–14c, Kosteletz, July 8, 1866, 26. Feldjäger-Bataillon.
102 Grosser Generalstab, *Feldzug 1866*, pp. 381–7.
103 KA, AFA 1866, Karton 2278, 7–14b, Geroitsch, July 8, 1866, Infanterie-Regiment Nr. 73. Karton 2278, 7–14, Turnau, July 20, 1866, GM Ringelsheim.

the NCOs, and 612 men fell on the western face of Chlum. Prince Wilhelm Holstein's heavy squadrons, retiring at the run from a failed attack on Langenhof, trampled the survivors.[104]

Ferdinand Poschacher's "Iron Brigade" went up the "Way of the Dead" through heaps of Ramming's dead and wounded. His *Jäger*, who ran along the left-hand lip of the gully to provide a measure of flank protection, were slowed by Guard skirmishers deployed on the slopes of Chlum. While the Prussian fusiliers climbed away backward loading and firing as they went, other Prussian platoons, concealed in the tall grass and broken ground, took Poschacher's light infantry in a well-aimed cross fire. Poschacher and all but five of his officers were killed. The battalion disbanded. Like most Austrian *Jäger* units that day, this one fought and died like line infantry, deploying less than one-fifth of its strength in open-order.[105]

This left Poschacher's Slovakian 34th Regiment alone inside the "Way of the Dead." Or not quite alone. Throughout the action at Chlum, Gondrecourt's columns were buffeted by Austrian stragglers, for once Moltke began sending the Prussian First Army over the Bystrice at 3:30, Austrian front line troops, with the Prussian Guards and Mutius's VI Corps on their flank, abandoned their forward posts and ran back in the direction of Königgrätz.[106] Many of them crossed from Lipa and Nedelist right through the Prussian firing line on Chlum and tumbled down the "Way of the Dead," where those that were not shot in the back by the Prussians slammed headlong into Poschacher's storm columns: "The path was crammed with men fleeing from the right wing [of the Austrian position]," an Austrian officer noted. "Cavalry, infantry, artillery, trains, everything; we couldn't clear them out or restore any kind of order. Our columns were broken up. The enemy directed his fire into this overfilled ravine and every ball hit home. We retreated, leaving thousands of dead."[107]

It was not an alluring prospect for Poschacher's third and final wave, Poles and Ukrainians of the 30th Regiment. They advanced to the edge of Rozberic in three battalion masses, took a few tentative steps up the "Way of the Dead," then broke formation and ran. "Despite the exertions of the officers," a regimental spokesman later wrote, "the men could not even be halted, much less turned around." An Austrian officer tried to deploy a battery to stop the Prussian pursuit. No sooner had he parked his guns, however, than Prince Holstein's *other* panic-stricken heavy brigade, also retiring from the failed attack on Langenhof, overran the battery in its haste to reach the Elbe.[108]

104 KA, AFA 1866, Karton 2278, 7–10, Roketnitz, July 12, 1866, Infanterie-Regiment Nr. 33. Karton 2278, 7–5, n.d., GM Gondrecourt. Karton 2278, 7–13, Moschtienitz, July 14, 1866, GM Leiningen.

105 KA, AFA 1866, Karton 2278, 7–16c, Kokor, July 11, 1866, 18. Feldjäger-Bataillon.

106 Grosser Generalstab, *Feldzug 1866*, pp. 376, 388–90.

107 KA, AFA 1866, Karton 2278, 7–16b, July 1866, Infanterie-Regiment Nr. 34.

108 KA, AFA 1866, Karton 2278, 7–16, Mantern, August 12, 1866, Brigade Poschacher.

It was all over by 5:00 P.M. Gondrecourt spoke reverently of Prussian firepower, which cut down every other man in I Corps: "Those were losses unprecedented in military history. An army corps never lost so many men in so little time." This was partly Gondrecourt's fault, partly Benedek's, who, as the I Corps commandant later charged, "never responded to my two requests for instructions."[109] A few Prussian cavalry squadrons busied themselves hunting Gondrecourt's stragglers along the route to Königgrätz while the most advanced Prussian batteries and foot regiments sent pursuing fire after the Austrians from the reverse slopes of the Bystrice heights. Over at Problus, the Piret Brigade was shot to bits as it attempted to run through a curtain of shrapnel and retake the elevated village from the Prussian 14th Division. Most of Piret's company and battalion commandants were killed in the storm, the brigade routed.[110] Survivors deplored Benedek's absence from the fight. Had he not reprimanded Gablenz for leaving Grivicic to his fate at Rudersdorf? And what had become of Benedek's carefully husbanded reserve cavalry, the 10,000 sabers that the Feldzeugmeister ought to have been unleashing against the Prussian pursuit?

Benedek's critics on the field never found him – nor most of his heavy squadrons – for the Austrian commandant was at this very moment searching for an Elbe crossing in the company of Baumgarten, Kriz, and the entire 2nd Reserve Cavalry Division. At 5:00 P.M., the Feldzeugmeister had made a last stab at dictating a retreat order before being overrun by General Coudenhove's heavy squadrons, which had ridden briefly against the tide of the Prussian advance at 4:00 P.M. but then, like Gondrecourt's infantry, had ebbed away under a hail of well-aimed bullets and shells.[111]

THE CAVALRY BATTLE OF STRESETICE

The uselessness of Austria's heavy cavalry at Königgrätz was a poetic end to a cavalry debate begun in the Austrian war ministry by General Leopold Edelsheim in 1865. Edelsheim, a career hussar, had pointed to the vulnerability of massed formations of horse in an age of rifled muskets and field guns and had recommended that the Austrian cavalry be dispersed into light commandos and rearmed with breech-loading carbines. His suggestions had been easily defeated by more senior cavalry generals like Count Karl Coudenhove and Prince Fritz Liechtenstein, who had emphasized the impact of unflinching shock attacks delivered by massed "walls" of cavalry.[112] Hard-chargers like Coudenhove would have their day

---

109 First Corps would lose 279 officers and 10,227 men in under an hour. KA, AFA 1866, Karton 2278, 7–5, n.d, GM Gondrecourt.
110 KA, AFA 1866, Karton 2278, 7–9, Prerau, July 15, 1866, GM Piret. Grosser Generalstab, *Feldzug 1866*, pp. 397–8.
111 KA, AFA 1866, Karton 2270, 12–6, Vienna, December 15, 1866, Capt. Hoffmeister. Nachlässe, B/1109 (Sacken), Vienna, December 20, 1866, Maj. Sacken, "An Generalstab."
112 KA, KM 1866, CK, Karton 250, 42 1/1, Vienna, December 23, 1865, "Beratung über GM Baron Edelsheim behufs Bewaffnung der Cavallerie mit Gewehren." And Vienna, December 23, 1865, GdC Liechtenstein, "Promemoria über die projektirte Bewaffnung der Cavallerie."

at Königgrätz. Morale was one thing for Coudenhove – a romantic cavalier of the old school – quite another for the more sensible rustics entrusted to his care, who would simply refuse to attack Prussian guns and rifles with their sabers and lances. The famous "Cavalry Battle of Stresetice," unaccountably glorified by Austrian and Prussian propagandists after the war, in fact, attested to the uselessness of massed squadrons of cavalry in the modern age.

Stresetice also attested to a lack of tactical coordination in Moltke's strategic plan to envelop the Austrians in the pocket before Königgrätz. Both Moltke and Prince Friedrich Karl had assumed that Benedek was in the process of retreating over the Elbe on July 3, and had thus launched the *Kesselschlacht* on the Bystrice prematurely, before the three Prussian armies had time to bring their rearmost formations within striking distance of the Austrian positions at Nedelist, Chlum, and Prim. Sadly for the Prussians, their cavalry, much of which ought to have been deployed in advance of the infantry corps, lagged in the rear, and thus arrived late and in small numbers, making the cavalry fight at Stresetice a rather insignificant affair.

To complete the rout of Benedek's army, Prussia's King Wilhelm had ordered the two reserve cavalry brigades he had with him at Sadova to cross the Bystrice at 3:30 P.M. and run what remained of North Army into the ground. This weak Prussian attempt at pursuit stuck immediately in traffic on the Bystrice crossings at Sadova and Sovetice, where Prussian caissons, ambulances, gun batteries, and infantry columns were also trying to cross the river in two directions. After finally extricating itself from the jam at Sadova, a Prussian light brigade – Prince Friedrich Karl in the van, King Wilhelm in the rear – rode up to Lipa. While Friedrich Karl's reserve cavalry joined the fight at Stresetice and the king literally lost himself in the crowd between Lipa and Problus, the First Army commandant met briefly with Crown Prince Friedrich Wilhelm, who had established his headquarters amid the ruins of Chlum.[113] From Chlum, the two Prussian army commandants could actually observe their envelopment of Benedek. By 4:00 P.M., Prussian cavalry, infantry, and guns were closing a ring round North Army from Nedelist, Chlum, and Problus, and some of Prince Friedrich Karl's hussars gleefully joined the fight at Chlum, attacking and breaking up Leiningen's Venetian regiment just as it was setting off up the height.

It was against this threat to the center of the Austrian position, but also to disengage Gondrecourt's Piret Brigade at Problus, that two of the three Austrian heavy divisions trotted forward from their reserve positions behind Sveti shortly after 4:00. Coudenhove's 3rd Reserve Cavalry Division turned west and headed toward Problus, while Prince Holstein's heavy brigades rode to where the Prussian pursuit was thickest, at Langenhof and Chlum. Six of Holstein's heavy

---

113 Grosser Generalstab, *Feldzug 1866*, pp. 399–401. Van Creveld, *Command in War*, p. 139. Craig, *Königgrätz*, pp. 160–1.

squadrons descended on the two Prussian light ones which were attacking Leiningen's regiments and put them to flight.[114]

This, however, was not the proper role for reserve cavalry, which was supposed to attack *retreating* infantry and guns, not the reverse. More useless slaughter ensued. Prussian gunners parked on Chlum and Langenhof found the range of Holstein's cuirassiers and began to lob shrapnel into their midst. Prussian riflemen not occupied in the destruction of the Austrian I Corps trained their rifles on the heavy brigade in Rozberic and began dropping whole troops of men and horses.[115] This brigade broke up and ran back toward Königgrätz, trampling North Army's field hospital in its panic. Holstein's other brigade raced toward Langenhof but was knocked off course and put to flight by rapid firing from a battalion of the Prussian 4th Division hidden inside a barn.[116]

Count Coudenhove had even less luck. The heavy brigade he hurled at Problus was shot down on the skirts of the village by infantry fire. Survivors fled back to Königgrätz, doing far more mischief to their own troops than to the enemy. Coudenhove turned with his other brigade and rode at the line of fifty guns Moltke had deployed on the ground between Langenhof and Stresetice. Shrapnel, canister, and rifle fire from several battalions of Prussian infantry dropped 400 cuirassiers and shattered this brigade as well.[117] Coudenhove's survivors raced back to the Elbe in disorganized bands, one of which paused to drive Benedek to distraction in that memorable incident on the plain of Stresetice. In a matter of minutes, Prussian firepower had routed Benedek's entire cavalry reserve, which retreated pell-mell, overrunning Vincenz Abele's brigade, the only intact Austrian unit left between Herwarth's Elbe Army and the principal Austrian bridge at Königgrätz. In thirty minutes of hard charging, Coudenhove had lost a quarter of his strength: over 700 men and nearly 900 horses. Though Ramming had established a formidable gun line on the ground before Königgrätz, Coudenhove's accidental trampling of the Abele Brigade meant that no more Austrian infantry stood between the Prussians and total victory. The advanced battalions of Moltke's left and right wings had closed to within two kilometers of each other.[118] With no Austrian reserves available to slow Mutius's pursuit from Sveti, or Herwarth's from Problus, the double envelopment and annihilation of North Army on the banks of the Elbe was in sight.[119]

114 KA, AFA 1866, Karton 2278, 7–10c, Roketnitz, July 10, 1866, Capt. John. Fontane, *Der deutsche Krieg*, vol. 1, pp. 611–620.

115 Grosser Generalstab, *Feldzug 1866*, pp. 404–7.

116 KA, AFA 1866, Karton 2278, 7–16, Mantern, August 12, 1866, Brigade Poschacher. Karton 2278, 7–16b, July 1866, Infanterie-Regiment Nr. 34. Craig, *Königgrätz*, pp. 157–8.

117 Grosser Generalstab, *Feldzug 1866*, pp. 409–16.

118 KA, AFA 1866, Karton 2289, 7–17, Vienna, August 5, 1866, FML Ramming. Grosser Generalstab, *Feldzug 1866*, pp. 416–20.

119 KA, Nachlässe, B/946 (Coudenhove), July 3, 1866, "Tagebuch" and "Mémoir 3. Juli 1866," pp. 29–34. AFA 1866, Karton 2278, 7–9, Prerau, July 15, 1866, GM Piret. Karton 2270, 12–6, Vienna, December 15, 1866, Capt. Hoffmeister.

MOLTKE'S FAILURE TO PURSUE

After the war, Moltke and the Prussian military establishment would rue their failure to finalize the victory at Königgrätz. The great cavalry battle at Stresetice never really materialized. Indeed, Moltke's reserve cavalry, which should have led the chase after Benedek, was scarcely tested at Königgrätz. Only 39 of 350 Prussian squadrons actually rode into battle at Stresetice, and none of them made any effort to pursue North Army's panic-stricken infantry after the rout of the Austrian reserve cavalry. No wonder Schlieffen hated this battle, which he considered about as close as one could come to a "*Schlacht ohne Morgen*" (battle without a tomorrow) without actually ringing down the curtain. At 5:00 P.M., the Prussians had more than four hours of midsummer daylight to work with and all of North Army disbanded before them. What remained of Benedek's eight infantry corps, five cavalry divisions, and reserve batteries were stuck, along with their trains, on a single road, the turnpike from Königgrätz southeast to Olmütz. Since even Thun, Mollinary, and Taxis, who had escaped over the Elbe on their own bridges, would have to rejoin this route once they crossed the river, Benedek's passage across the river was agonizingly slow and accomplished only because of the heroic resistance of the Austrian artillery, which sacrificed more than 100 guns and their crews to cover North Army's retreat. Nevertheless, the chief explanation for Benedek's unlikely, almost miraculous escape was not the fury of Ramming's gun line, but rather Moltke's inability to organize a prompt, forceful pursuit.[120]

In the afternoon of July 3, Moltke not only had a rabble trapped by a river barrier before him; he had a bridgehead too. Mutius had by 4:00 succeeded in wresting II Corps's bridge at Lochenice from Thun's bedraggled rearguard, presenting Moltke with the opportunity to pursue North Army on *both* banks of the Elbe. Yet owing to the chaos in his own march columns, Moltke was forced to let the opportunity slip. In 1867, he would regret this failure to "trap the Austrians by the convergent attack of three armies," a failure that not only enabled Benedek to wriggle free to fight another day but also shifted the strategic balance in the war. In the "Bystrice pocket," Moltke had been positioned to encircle and destroy Benedek. Once across the Elbe, Benedek secured himself against a repetition of this maneuver and effectively halted the Prussian pursuit.[121] After Königgrätz, there would be time for North Army to rebuild, and for French Emperor Napoleon III to force an armistice on Berlin.

The fresh reserves of infantry, cavalry, and guns needed to complete Moltke's envelopment of the Austrians at Königgrätz did not arrive in time to affect the outcome. On the Prussian right wing, Herwarth's first cavalry units did not cross to the left bank of the Bystrice until 5:00. His 32nd Brigade, needed to bring the 16th Division up to full strength, did not reach the bridge at Nechanice until

120 KA, Nachlässe, B/1109 (Sacken), Vienna, December 20, 1866, Maj. Sacken, "An Generalstab."
    B/572: 2 (Nosinic), Vienna, January 6, 1867, Capt. Sembratowicz.
121 Grosser Generalstab, *Feldzug 1866*, pp. 423, 430.

nightfall. Elbe Army's only other reserve formation, the 10,000 men of Berlin's Guard *Landwehr* Division, arrived even later.[122] In the Prussian center, the pursuit was no better organized. Moltke's staff had detached one of Prince Friedrich Karl's two cavalry divisions to Elbe Army in the morning without informing the First Army commandant. When the prince tried to deploy this 1st Cavalry Division in the afternoon, he learned that it had been taken from him, and to no good effect, for Herwarth succeeded only in losing it amongst his baggage trains and rear echelons.[123] Prince Friedrich Karl's infantry divisions, which had suffered 5,000 casualties in the course of the day, crossed paths with Second Army in their haste to gain the Bystrice heights. This further delayed the Prussian pursuit, as did the circumstance that much of First Army had to ascend to Langenhof not in a straight line, but roundabout, via Stresetice and Problus, so as not to mask the Prussian batteries mounted in Sadova to silence the last Austrian guns in Langenhof and pour fire into Benedek's retreat.[124]

On the Prussian left wing, Mutius was able to ram through the Austrian trenches on Nedelist and drive his 11th and 12th Divisions all the way to Briza, a suburb of Königgrätz.[125] But the need to advance warily, with two Austrian pontoon bridges on his flank and Ramming's massed batteries before him, robbed this pursuit of momentum as well. His reserve, Steinmetz's V Corps, the last Second Army unit to march from Josephstadt, did not arrive in force at Chlum until 8:00 in the evening. Austrian staff officers interrogating Prussian prisoners after Königgrätz were amazed to discover that Steinmetz's divisions, which had taken some wrong turnings in the course of their march, had walked nearly forty kilometers to reach the Bystrice. Many V Corps units arrived *hors de combat*.[126] Second Army's cavalry division, which ought to have thundered down the left wing to join the *melée* at Stresetice, did not reach the field until after the battle had been decided. Echeloned for the march to Sadova behind the Guards and Second Army's reserve artillery, it hove up to the Bystrice with Second Army's other laggards, Steinmetz, Bonin, and the 2nd Guard Division. Bonin's I Corps, which ought to have committed its entire strength to the battle of Königgrätz, succeeded in deploying only a brigade, half of the 1st Division, which raced ahead to Chlum just as Gondrecourt's final attack jumped off. Since Bonin had enjoyed unimpeded progress on his road to Horenoves from Miletin, Moltke correctly put his late arrival down to incompetence. Bonin had not even broken camp until 9:30 A.M., long after the rest of Second Army was gone.[127]

122　Grosser Generalstab, *Feldzug 1866*, pp. 279, 359, 399–400, 422–3.

123　Craig, *Königgrätz*, p. 99. Grosser Generalstab, *Feldzug 1866*, pp. 302–3.

124　Grosser Generalstab, *Feldzug 1866*, pp. 401–2.

125　Fontane, *Der deutsche Krieg*, vol. 1, p. 607.

126　KA, AFA 1866, Karton 2268, 7–285, Nord-Armee Hauptquartier, July 6, 1866, Col. Tegetthoff.

127　*Moltke on the Art of War*, ed. Hughes, pp. 134–5. Grosser Generalstab, *Feldzug 1866*, pp. 305–10. Craig, *Königgrätz*, p. 119.

It is doubtful whether massive Prussian reserves would have availed much anyway in the "end game" at Königgrätz, for the very success of Prussia's forward units in their push down to the Elbe ultimately halted them. Moltke, who lost all contact with the king and his three army commandants in the rush across the Bystrice, explained after the war that the rapid compression of a Prussian battle line that had extended thirty kilometers from wing to wing in the morning into the four kilometer-wide pocket between Chlum and Königgrätz created severe command and control problems. Prussian troop formations from all three armies clogged this narrow space, and the time and space needed to separate them stopped Moltke's pursuit. At 7:30 P.M., Moltke and the king, who had ridden to the front of the field at Chorbusice, determined that a final attempt to snap the Prussian pincers closed behind the rump of North Army that remained on the Königgrätz glacis would only result in the admixture of Elbe Army's divisions to the already jumbled units of the First and Second Armies. The Prussian columns were therefore halted, permitting Ramming, who, with his rearguard, had kept the pincers from closing, to shift the rest of North Army to the left bank of the Elbe in the night.[128]

The battle of Königgrätz is often cited as a masterpiece of strategic envelopment, and, indeed, it might have been had Moltke launched it a day later. Unfortunately, Prince Friedrich Karl, convinced that Benedek was trying to escape over the Elbe to the safety of Austria's "northern Quadrilateral," set the operation in train prematurely. He moved while Second Army was still far away and unprepared for a march to the Bystrice, reviving Benedek's advantage of internal lines for a day. Until the early afternoon, Benedek had the option of moving his entire strength against half of Moltke's. Indeed, when the battle was later described in detail to Field Marshal Hess in Vienna, his first question was this: "Why didn't Benedek advance his right wing *before* the Crown Prince of Prussia arrived on the field?" The Feldzeugmeister's court of inquiry asked the same question, for a better general than Benedek – Gablenz, for example, or Ramming or Mollinary – would have made Moltke pay a heavy price for the poor timing of his operation.[129] Conventional wisdom, which holds to this day that Benedek was defeated at Königgrätz by insubordinate generals, the "fog of Chlum," and Prussian stealth, is an untruthful reconstruction of the facts. In reality, it was Benedek's failure to grasp the nettle, not Crown Prince Friedrich Wilhelm's flanking column, which condemned North Army to rout, panic, and defeat.

128 Grosser Generalstab, *Feldzug 1866*, pp. 374–5, 425–33. KA, AFA 1866, Karton 2274, 13–61, Berlin, August 1867, "Offener Brief von einem preussischen Offizier." Nachlässe, B/946 (Coudenhove), "Mémoir 3. Juli 1866," p. 34.

129 KA, KM 1866, CK, Karton 242, 14–5/33, Wr. Neustadt, September 27, 1866, FZM Nobili, "Untersuchungs-Kommission." Mollinary, vol. 1, pp. 145, 150. Glünicke, pp. 170–2. Van Creveld, *Command in War*, p. 140.

11

Aftermath: The peace and Europe, 1866–1914

After Königgrätz, Benedek's North Army disintegrated. For two days after the battle, thousands of Austrian stragglers roved the left bank of the Elbe in search of their units.[1] Austro-Saxon casualties in the battle had been severe: 24,000 killed or wounded, 20,000 more taken prisoner. Prussian losses had been slight by comparison, 9,000 in all.[2] With one mighty push, Moltke had driven Benedek from a well-defended position with just one-fifth Benedek's losses. It was a breathtaking accomplishment that utterly destroyed Austrian morale. Emperor Franz Joseph's foreign minister, General Alexander Mensdorff, visited Benedek on July 5 and advised Vienna that North Army – now reduced by 70,000 men, 2,000 officer casualties, and 200 guns – was, for all intents and purposes, a headless, unarmed rabble.[3] One of Benedek's subordinates hastened to concur: "We are turning aimlessly in circles," General Coudenhove wrote his wife on July 9. "My men are exhausted and sick. . . . Our ship is foundering and our pilot is off his head."[4] For Austria, oppressed after Königgrätz by a second Italian invasion of Venetia and the exasperating surrender of all its German federal allies to Moltke's little West Army, the time had come to sue for peace.[5]

While Benedek, whom the emperor formally subordinated to Archduke Al-

1 KA, AFA 1866, Karton 2270, 8–12p, Floridsdorf, August 16, 1866, FML Gablenz. Karton 2275, Mährisch-Trübau, July 7, 1866, Capt. Stransky, "Tagebuch." Nachlässe, B/946 (Coudenhove), Politzka, July 6, 1866. FML von Went., "Erinnerungen eines österreichischen Kriegsmanns 1866," ÖMZ 3 (1899).
2 k.k. Generalstab, Österreichs Kämpfe, vol. 3, Beilage 3. Grosser Generalstab, Der Feldzug von 1866, pp. 434–5.
3 KA, MKSM-SR 1866, 22/10, Vienna, September 1866, "Zu den Sendungen des Majors Baron Fejérváry in das Hauptquartier der Nordarmee." KM 1866, CK, Karton 242, 14–5/33, Wr. Neustadt, September 27, 1866, FZM Nobili, "Untersuchungs-Commission."
4 KA, Nachlässe, B/946 (Coudenhove), Dalecin, July 9, 1866, FML Coudenhove. AFA 1866, Karton 2268, 7–452 1/2, Olmütz, July 12, 1866, FML Ramming to FZM Benedek. Karton 2275, 13–166, Konitz, July 8, 1866, Capt. Stransky, "Tagebuch."
5 KA, MKSM 1866, Karton 342, 69/8, Bornheim, July 10, 1866, Col. Schönfeld. Kitzingen, July 15, 1866, FML Huyn. Waldürn, July 19, 1866, FML Alexander to Lt.-Col. Beck.

Benedek's retreat to Olmütz and Moltke's drive on Vienna, July 1866

brecht on July 10, retired upon Austria's entrenched camp at Olmütz with the beaten, traumatized rump of North Army, Moltke – determined to extort an optimal peace settlement for Prussia's king and Bismarck – organized a vigorous pursuit.[6] He crossed the Elbe with Second Army at Pardubice on July 5 and sent it after Benedek with orders to drive North Army into the fortress works at Olmütz and keep it there. Moltke recognized that Benedek's flight to Olmütz instead of Vienna was a great strategic error, for it enabled Prussia to occupy all of Bohemia and Lower Austria – the Habsburg Monarchy's wealthiest, most industrialized provinces – without resistance.[7] To exploit this gift, Moltke then pushed his Elbe

---

6 KA, MKSM-SR 1866, 22, Vienna, December 1866, Maj. Fejérváry. Lt-Col. Gustav Wolff, "Die Operationen der österreichischen Nord-Armee nach der Schlacht bei Königgrätz," *ÖMZ* 3 (1898), pp. 75–7.

7 Grosser Generalstab, *Der Feldzug von 1866*, pp. 441–2, 469–70. KA, AFA 1866, Karton 2270, 8–12bb, Vienna, August 15, 1866, FML Baumgarten. MKSM 1866, Karton 343, 69/9, Vicenza, July 9, 1866, FM Albrecht to Franz Joseph.

and First Armies past Königgrätz and, after pausing to capture Prague and begin divesting it of its riches, put them on the road south to Vienna.[8]

To make haste, Moltke, who wanted to take Vienna and dictate a peace to the Austrians before the French or Russians – now belatedly concerned about the shifting balance of power in Europe – could find time to intervene in the conflict, ordered his troops to abandon their supply trains and live by requisitioning instead.[9] By mid-July, a British diplomat observed, the three Prussian armies and their insatiable "requisition commandos" had succeeded in reducing Austria north of the Danube to "a vast desert."[10] Faced with this systematized despoliation of his richest crownlands, Austrian Emperor Franz Joseph attempted to purchase an armed French intervention in the war by formally ceding Venetia to Emperor Napoleon III on July 5.[11] When this availed nothing more than France's "good offices," Franz Joseph decided on July 22 to capitulate. The Prussians, who, by late July were losing 200 men a day to cholera – an intestinal infection that spread easily through Prussia's unsanitary camps – eagerly accepted the Austrian surrender.[12]

THE AUSTRO-PRUSSIAN ARMISTICE

The Nikolsburg Armistice ending the Austro-Prussian War was drafted by Bismarck and presented to the Austrians at Foreign Minister Mensdorff's country estate of Nikolsburg, ninety kilometers north of Vienna. Bismarck allayed French, Russian, and British fears of Prussian expansion by making no territorial demands on Austria.[13] According to the terms of the armistice signed on July 26, which would be confirmed in a formal treaty of peace at Prague in August, Prussia agreed to make no annexations in Austria in return for a large cash indemnity and Franz Joseph's pledge to remove Austria from the German Confederation and whatever political structure Prussia might design to succeed it.[14] Thus, though Bismarck had to give back Prussian-occupied Bohemia, Moravia,

8 Grosser Generalstab, *Der Feldzug von 1866*, pp. 445–52.

9 Grosser Generalstab, *Der Feldzug von 1866*, pp. 452–4.

10 PRO, FO 7/709, no. 31, no. 32, Vienna, July 24, 1866, Bloomfield to Stanley. *Augsburger Allgemeine Zeitung*, July 9, 13, 1866.

11 Quai d'Orsay, CP-Autriche, 492, no. 86, no. 89, Vienna, July 7 and 10, 1866, Gramont to Drouyn. PRO, FO 7/708, no. 413, no. 414, Vienna, July 6, 1866, Bloomfield to Stanley.

12 KA, AFA 1866, Karton 2269, 7–740, Nades, July 22, 1866, GM Fleischhacker to FML Joseph. *Protokolle der österrichischen Ministerrates* (PÖM) *1848–67* 6 vols. (Vienna: Österreichischer Bundesverlag, (1970–3), vol. 6/2, pp. 169–71. Ghy., "Der Streifzug der Radetzky-Husaren im Juli 1866," *ÖMZ* 7 (1906), pp. 993–1007. Heinrich Mast, "Die Ereignisse im Rücken der preussischen Armee im Juli 1866," *ÖMZ* 1 (1966), pp. 21–6.

13 Gall, *Bismarck*, vol. 1, pp. 302–5. Pflanze, *Bismarck*, vol. 1, pp. 311–14.

14 Pflanze, *Bismarck*, vol. 1, p. 316. *PÖM*, vol. 6/2, no. 90A, Nikolsburg, July 23, 1866, Károlyi to Mensdorff, pp. 179–82. KA, AFA 1866, Karton 2274, 13–74, Olmütz, December 2, 1872, Maj. Ripp, "Skizze."

and Lower Silesia – later quipping that "my two greatest difficulties were first to get King Wilhelm into Bohemia, and then to get him out again" – Prussia's House of Hohenzollern was amply compensated for its forbearance.[15] In early August, Austria delivered 30 million silver florins ($405 million) to the Prussian state bank in Oppeln, helping Bismarck balance a Prussian budget that had been driven deep into deficit by the war with Austria and Bismarck's own conflict with Prussia's parliament.[16] Bismarck also secured the assent of Austria, France, and the other powers to Prussia's outright annexation of Schleswig-Holstein, Hanover, Hessia-Kassel, Nassau, and Frankfurt – acquisitions that physically linked the eastern and western halves of the Prussian kingdom. As for the sovereignties of north-central Germany *not* taken by Prussia in 1866 – Saxony, Hessia-Darmstadt, the free cities of Hamburg, Lübeck and Bremen, and the scattered duchies of Thuringia and Mecklenburg – Bismarck gained *indirect* control of them through a Prussian-controlled "North German Confederation" fashioned from the wreckage of the old *Bund*.[17]

Though, strictly speaking, these were merely "reforms" of the German Confederate Treaty of 1815, no one in Paris, St. Petersburg, London, or Vienna was in any doubt as to the *real* nature of this new "North German Confederation," for Prussia took exclusive control of its military and foreign affairs. Although Napoleon III still labored under the delusion that, by tolerating Prussia's growth, he was helping to create a new constellation of French client states in Europe, Lucien Murat, one of his more down-to-earth advisors, reminded him that Bismarck would *never* serve as a French "client," and that Bismarck's North German Confederation *really* amounted to *"une Prusse colossale,"* that would one day turn its attentions to France.[18] Though the French emperor did have the good sense to insist at Nikolsburg upon the continued independence of Saxony, Bavaria, Württemberg, Hessia-Darmstadt, and Baden – thereby limiting Bismarck's annexations to 1,300 square miles and seven million industrious souls – Louis-Napoleon could not spare these German survivors the crushing cash reparations demanded by Bismarck. Bavaria's indemnity was nearly as hefty as Austria's: 23 million florins ($303 million) in all.[19] Saxony's was even more onerous, reducing Dresden to a Prussian tributary in the years after 1866.[20]

15 Gordon A. Craig, *The Politics of the Prussian Army, 1640–1945* (Oxford: Clarendon, 1955), pp. 202–3. Gall, *Bismarck*, vol. 1, p. 301. Pflanze, *Bismarck*, vol. 1, p. 314.

16 PRO, FO 7/709, no. 39, Vienna, July 26, 1866, Bloomfield to Stanley. *PÖM*, vol. 6/2, no. 90A, no. 90F, Nikolsburg, July 23, 25, 1866, Károlyi to Mensdorff.

17 Carr, *Origins*, pp. 138–9. Gordon A. Craig, *Germany 1866–1945* (New York: Oxford University Press, 1980), pp. 6–12.

18 KA, AFA 1866, Karton 2272, 13–13, 187, Vienna, July 12, 1866, Belcredi to FZM Benedek. Friedjung, *The Struggle for Supremacy*, p. 302.

19 PRO, FO 9/176, no. 27, Munich, July 24, 1866, Howard to Stanley. *PÖM*, vol. 6/2, no. 90E, Nikolsburg, July 25, 1866, Károlyi to Mensdorff.

20 Bismarck assessed the free city of Frankfurt a staggering 25 million florins, agreeing to reduce the indemnity to 6 million only when the burgher senate of Frankfurt voted for incorporation in

For the old Confederate diet, driven out of Frankfurt by Prussian troops in mid-July, the message of all this was unmistakable. Reduced by secession and annexation to less than one-third its original membership, the diet quietly voted itself out of existence on July 28 in the dining room of the Three Moors Hotel in Augsburg.[21] With the exception of Saxony, this rump of the German Confederation would regroup after the war in a "South German Confederation." Though this southern *Bund* was nominally protected by France, Bismarck insisted at Nikolsburg on the right to forge "national connections" with it. This last, fateful French concession would form the basis of the mutual defense treaties Bismarck forced on all of the south German states in 1867 and 1868, effectively binding them to Prussia in Bismarck's climactic war with France in 1870.[22]

THE ARMISTICE IN ITALY

After the signature of the Austro-Prussian armistice on July 26, Europe's attention shifted to Italy. General Giuseppe Govone, who had negotiated the Prusso-Italian alliance in April and yielded the height of Custoza in June, appeared at Nikolsburg to insist that Bismarck not conclude a separate peace with the Austrians. Govone also requested Prussian support for Italy's annexation of South Tyrol in addition to Venetia. He was disappointed on both counts, for not only did Bismarck refuse to back Italian expansion north to the Alpine watershed – Italy's "natural frontier" – he also took Prussia abruptly out of the war, depriving Italy of the counterweight needed in August to balance Austrian armed force and French political pressure.[23]

The Italians felt betrayed, but Bismarck abandoned them with a clear conscience, for instead of regrouping after Custoza and resuming the war in Venetia, King Vittorio Emanuele II had let two precious weeks pass before trying a second offensive. This delay had permitted Archduke Albrecht to shift 60,000 troops from Venetia to Vienna after Königgrätz to hold the line of the Danube.[24] And once finally on the move, Cialdini's strengthened Po Army of fourteen divisions had crawled through Venetia without meeting an enemy and had taken two weeks just to cross the Adige and reach Vicenza, which ought to have been the work of a

Prussia. PRO, FO 68/144, no. 45, Leipzig, November 20, 1866, Crowe to Stanley. Stern, *Gold and Iron*, pp. 90–2.

21 PRO, FO 30/228, no. 20, Augsburg, July 28, 1866, Malet to Stanley. FO 9/175, no. 23, Munich, July 21, 1866, Howard to Stanley.

22 Pflanze, *Bismarck*, vol. 1, pp. 401–5. Carr, *Origins*, p. 138. *PÖM*, vol. 6/2, no. 90A, Nikolsburg, July 23, 1866, Károlyi to Mensdorff, pp. 179–82.

23 *Documenti diplomatici presentato al parlamento dal Ministro degli Affari Esteri il 21 Dicembre 1866* (Florence: Tipographia Stato, 1866), no. 285, Florence, July 5, 1866, Visconti-Venosta to Barral and no. 286, Paris, July 5, 1866, Nigra to Visconti-Venosta.

24 PRO, FO 45/88, no. 333, Florence, July 31, 1866, Elliot to Stanley. Elliot noted Bismarck's "extreme resentment against Italy for not having prevented this."

few days.[25] Although Cialdini's object was to drive all the way to Vienna to envelop the Austrian capital in conjunction with Moltke, his army was immediately hobbled by supply problems and got no further than Udine.[26] Meanwhile in Habsburg Trentino, Garibaldi's volunteer battalions were easily repulsed by crack Tyrolean *Kaiserjäger*.[27] In all, 30,000 Austrian troops had sufficed to pin down an Italian army of 200,000 for more than a month, wrecking all plans for Prusso-Italian military cooperation on the Danube. To make matters worse, Italy's iron-clad fleet was roundly beaten at the mouth of the Adriatic by an Austrian squadron half its size on July 20. After this sea battle of Lissa, Italy's plans to open a second front on Austria's Dalmatian coast – plans by which Bismarck and Moltke had set much store in June – had to be quietly shelved.[28]

On July 26, the day Bismarck and Mensdorff signed the Nikolsburg Armistice, Cialdini took Udine. That same day, however, Field Marshal Albrecht and General John – their hands freed in the north – began to shift four corps south from the Danube line to the Isonzo, a three-day trip on the *Südbahn* Railway. The long overdue arrival of Benedek's North Army in Vienna during the last week of July put five more corps at Albrecht's disposal. After being driven into the Tatra Mountains east of Olmütz by the Prussian Second Army, Benedek had made a wearisome march south to the Danube, where his corps began crossing to the right bank at Pressburg (Bratislava) on July 22.[29] After briefly resting the Feldzeugmeister's exhausted units, Albrecht bundled them on to troop trains bound for Innsbruck and Trento, a week's trip by rail, wagon, and foot. Meanwhile, Austrian Admiral Wilhelm Tegetthoff – the victor of Lissa – made necessary repairs to his warships and prepared to ferry Austria's Croatian garrisons over

25 Cialdini's Po Army had in the meantime been made the "Army of Operation," La Marmora's Mincio Army stripped and demoted to an "Army of Observation" of just six divisions commanded not by La Marmora, but by Enrico Della Rocca. KA, AFA 1866, Karton 2348, 13–44f., July 1866, Süd-Armee Commando. PRO, FO 45/88, no. 333, Florence, July 31, 1866, Elliot to Stanley.

26 Most of Cialdini's trains foundered in the Polesine. By the time Po Army reached Friuli in August, the men were subsisting on 500 grams of bread and 350 grams of polenta per man per day. Vincennes, AAT, MR 73/1387, Florence, 1866, Col. Schmitz, "Rapport sur la marche des services administratifs faits par l'armée italienne." KA, MKSM-SR 1866, 23/2, "Stellung der k.k. Armee am 27. Juli 1866."

27 Garibaldi had much the worst of his campaign, taking casualties in Tyrol out of all proportion to the Austrians: 6:1 at Rocca d'Anso on July 3, 4:1 at Vezzo on July 4, 14:1 at Bececca on July 21. In one month of fighting, Garibaldi advanced his lines only eight kilometers and managed to lose the most lopsided contest of the war. Vincennes, AAT, MR 27/1537, Paris, September 1866, Col. Rüstow, "La Guerre de 1866." Bartels, *Der Krieg im Jahre 1866*, pp. 65–72.

28 Milan, Museo Risorgimento, Archivio Garibaldino, Plico no. 141, Caprera, June 2, 1866, Garibaldi, "Promemoria al Generale Cialdini." Theodore Ropp, "The Modern Italian Navy," *Military Affairs* (Spring 1941). Lothar Höbelt, "Die Marine," in *Die Habsburger Monarchie*, eds. Wandruszka and Urbanitsch, vol. 5, pp. 694–701. Lawrence Sondhaus, *The Habsburg Empire and the Sea* (W. Lafayette: Purdue, 1989).

29 KA, AFA 1866, Karton 2282, 7–139e, Pressburg, July 21, 1866, Col. Döpfner.

to Venice from Trieste and Pula. With so much force arrayed against him, Cialdini gladly accepted a three-day truce proffered by General Joseph Maroicic, commandant of South Army's rearguard, on July 30.[30]

On August 2, Cialdini agreed to extend the cease-fire until August 10. He hesitated to sign an armistice, for he had finally got round to sending a regular army division up the Brenta River valley to take Trento in concert with Garibaldi's volunteers. He had General Nino Bixio's division standing by to support the operation and still liked his own chances of crossing the Isonzo and seizing Austrian Gorizia for Italy.[31] For their part, the Austrians refused even to consider making peace on the basis of territory in hand (*uti possidetis*) or plebiscites, Cialdini's two proposals. Franz Joseph insisted on having Trento and Udine back and was prepared to fight for them.[32] Vittorio Emanuele, who had surrounded Trento with overwhelming force but had not yet succeeded in taking it, agreed to evacuate Trentino and return to the pre-war borders in this *demi*-German corner of Italy but reminded Franz Joseph that he would never be able to reestablish Austrian rule in Udine, where hatred of Habsburg officialdom was an article of faith. The emperor conceded this point and allowed the Italians to push their border with Austria east to the Isonzo River, but only after King Vittorio Emanuele had agreed to assume Venetia's share of the Austrian state debt, pay cash for the Quadrilateral forts, and surrender eight priceless Tintorettos and Veroneses to the House of Habsburg.[33] On August 12, a four-week armistice was signed on this basis at Cormons, a small town in Friuli between Udine and Gorizia.[34] Austrian and Italian negotiators staked out a demarcation line that, in the Dolomites, was laid over the eighteenth-century boundary stones of the Venetian Republic. The Austrian war ministry won a hard fight for the rights to Cortina d'Ampezzo, a favorite getaway for bureaucrats weary of Vienna, and instructed General Karl Moering, Franz Joseph's negotiator at Cormons, to insist on having

---

30　KA, MKSM 1866, Karton 343, 69–10/4, Gorizia, August 11, 1866, FM Albrecht to Franz Joseph. AFA 1866, Karton 2353, 13–12, Vienna, December 20, 1866, Capt. Schneider, "Bericht." HHSA, IB, Karton 364, BM 1866, 41, Ljubljana, August 3, 1866, FML Habermann to Belcredi.

31　KA, AFA 1866, Karton 2348, 13–44ff., July 1866, Süd-Armee Commando, "Begebenheiten." Bartels, *Kritische Beiträge*, pp. 113–19.

32　PRO, FO 7/709–710, no. 47, no. 52, no. 63, no. 91, Vienna, July 30–31, August 6 and 21, 1866, Bloomfield to Stanley. PRO, FO 45/88, no. 365, no. 388, Florence, July 29, August 6, 1866, Elliot to Stanley. KA, AFA 1866, Karton 2348, 13–44f., July 1866, Süd-Armee Commando.

33　In September, the Austrians added 106 other *objets d'art* to the price of their departure from Venice. HHSA, PA XL, Karton 124, Gorizia, July 28, 1866, Wimpffen to Mensdorff. IB, Karton 364, BM 1866, 41, Ljubljana, August 3, 1866, FML Habermann to Belcredi. PRO, FO 7/714, Venice, October 9, 1866.

34　KA, MKSM 1866, Karton 343, 69–10/5, Gorizia, August 12, 1866, FM Albrecht to Franz Joseph. AFA 1866, Karton 2353, 13–9, Vienna, December 19, 1866, Maj. Wempfling. HHSA, PA XL, Karton 124, Vienna, August 10, 1866, Mensdorff to Wimpffen. PRO, FO 7/710, no. 75, Vienna, August 13, 1866, Bloomfield to Stanley. Wandruszka, *1866*, pp. 288–90.

the summits of all disputed high ground along the new border. In this, Moering was generally successful, conferring an enormous advantage on Austrian arms in the First World War.[35]

The Cormons Armistice was ratified on October 3 with the signature of a formal Austro-Italian peace treaty in Vienna.[36] Austria was forced to accept the French transfer of Venetia to Italy, to recognize the legal existence of the "Kingdom of Italy," and to stop insisting, in the anachronistic style of Metternich, that "Italy" was not a nation but a "geographical expression." General Giuseppe Garibaldi, who could hardly walk after being shot a second time in the foot he had injured at Aspromonte four years earlier, was disgusted with this partial result of Italy's "Fourth War of Union." He blasted the "servile attitude" of King Vittorio Emanuele's House of Savoy and howled in frustration at the continued "degeneracy" of the "Italian nation," which permitted "drunken Germans" to reclaim Trento and the Upper Adige. "Italians," the general implored in a desperate, last minute proclamation, "fight on!" But the great patriot was yesterday's man and no one heeded him. "Garibaldi?" Italy's king shrugged in an interview after the war, *"malheureusement il se fait vieux"* (I'm afraid that he's getting old.)[37]

POLITICAL CONSEQUENCES OF THE WAR

"We have sunk to the level of Turkey" an Austrian general scoffed as he prepared to turn Venice over to the Italians in December 1866. The Pope, Austria's staunchest ally in good times and bad, agreed with this proposition. Königgrätz, Pius IX declared, had reduced the Austrian Empire to the status of "a second rate Oriental Power."[38] This "Oriental" appearance was underscored by the rapid "Balkanization" of the Habsburg Monarchy, which set in as a consequence of the war. Emboldened by the defeat of Franz Joseph's army, Hungary's national party – which represented Austria's second most numerous people – demanded and got home rule for Budapest as well as Magyar domination of the so-called subject peoples of eastern Austria: the Rumanians, the Croats, and the Slovaks. By the constitutional *Ausgleich* or Compromise of 1867, Austria was renamed

---

35 "If we cede the Lombard-Venetian Kingdom, we must obtain an optimal redefinition of the southern limits of Tyrol to protect the *Kaiserstaat*. Wherever possible, we must insist on having the dominant positions . . . especially the highest points around the mountain passes." KA, KM 1866, CK, Karton 248, 35–9/1, Vienna, July 17, 1866, FML Franck, FML Rossbacher to GdC Mensdorff.

36 John W. Bush, *Venetia Redeemed* (Syracuse: Syracuse University Press, 1967), pp. 96–130. Denis Mack Smith, *Victor Emanuel, Cavour and the Risorgimento* (London: Oxford University Press, 1971), pp. 324–35.

37 Milan, Museo Risorgimento, Archivio Garibaldino, Plico 50, Brescia, August 20, 1866, G. Garibaldi, "Corpi Volontari Italiani." HHSA, PA XL, Karton 124, Venice, December 22, 1866, GM Moering.

38 HHSA, PA XL, Karton 124, Venice, December 22, 1866, GM Moering. PRO, FO 43/96B, Rome, July 27, 1866, Odo Russell to Stanley.

"Austria-Hungary" to reflect this demoralizing change, which began the dissolution of multinational Austria into its constituent nations.[39]

Austria, then, was substantially weakened by the war. Internally, the Habsburg Monarchy broke in two pieces. Externally, it lost the province of Venetia to Italy, its control of the German states to Prussia.[40] For its part, Prussia grew to amazing proportions. Once derided as a mean little kingdom of "sand and starveling pines," Prussia in 1866 annexed half the German Confederation and became a great state, far richer than Austria, and France's peer in population, national income, armed force, and the capital and energy reserves vital for industrialization. Though Austria's foreign ministry had assured Emperor Franz Joseph before the Austro-Prussian War that "the Powers would *never* consent to the creation of a great North German State between France and Russia," the non-German Great Powers actually did little to stop Bismarck.[41] At Nikolsburg, Count Richard Belcredi – Austria's minister of state – recorded his "bafflement" at the decision of France and Russia not to contest "the material advantages" Bismarck took from the armistice, material gains that made Prussia "France's equal in many areas and its superior in others." Enlarged Prussia, Belcredi warned, "would henceforth press relentlessly upon [France and Russia]."[42]

In the clinch, Great Power attempts to mediate the Austro-Prussian conflict and limit Bismarck's gains were defeated by the swiftness of Moltke's military campaign. After the war, French statesmen would rue the "*surprise de Sadova*," the disconcerting, preemptive rapidity of Prussia's victory. Moltke's armies beat the Austrians and drove to the Danube before the French could deploy a proper field army on the Rhine.[43] Though the Russians and the British also expressed misgivings about Prussia's "illegal" growth in 1866, which contravened the European treaties signed at the Congress of Vienna in 1815, they too were bowled over by the speed of Bismarck's annexations and thus meekly accepted them. To his credit, Bismarck had planned for this well in advance. He had secured Russia's benevolence by helping the tsar crush a Polish revolt in 1861.[44] As for the British, Bismarck gambled that they would be more interested in building their overseas empire than in committing themselves to a European conflict. British statesmen, Bismarck remarked before the Austro-Prussian War, "know far more

39 Louis Eisenmann, *Le Compromis austro-hongrois de 1867* (1904; Hattiesburg: Academic International, 1971), pp. 403–680. Alan Sked, *The Decline and Fall of the Habsburg Empire, 1815–1918* (London: Longman, 1989), pp. 187–234. Taylor, *The Habsburg Monarchy*, pp. 140–52.

40 F. R. Bridge, *From Sadowa to Sarajevo* (London: Routledge, 1972), pp. 1–29.

41 HHSA, IB, Karton 364, BM 1866, 35, Vienna, May 5, 1866, Belcredi to Mensdorff.

42 HHSA, IB, Karton 364, BM 1866, 35, Vienna, May 5, 1866, Belcredi to Mensdorff. KA, AFA 1866, Karton 2272, 13–13, Vienna, July 14, 1866, Belcredi to FZM Benedek.

43 KA, AFA 1866, Karton 2272, 13–13, no. 180, no. 270, July 10, October 1, 1866, Belcredi to FM Albrecht.

44 HHSA, IB, Karton 365, BM 1866, 75, Cracow, July 3 and 21, 1866, Polizeidirektor. Dietrich Beyrau, "Russische Interessenzone und europäisches Gleichgewicht 1860–1870," in Eberhard Kolb, ed. *Europa vor dem Krieg von 1870* (Munich: Oldenbourg, 1987), pp. 72–5.

about Japan and Mongolia than they do about Prussia!" And indeed the Anglo-Russian struggle for control of Central and South Asia, which, in 1866, took the form of a full-blown war for Turkestan that occupied 200,000 Russian troops and much of Britain's Indian army, ensured that neither power made trouble for Prussia in the crucial months after Königgrätz.[45]

Berlin's conquest of Germany was therefore owed at least as much to the diplomatic isolation and distraction of Prussia's rivals as to Bismarck's boldness. Nevertheless, the complete triumph of Prussian grand strategy in 1866 served to tighten the *political* connection between the Prusso-German state and army.[46] After 1866, the example of Königgrätz suggested that Prussia-Germany could extend its influence and make vast annexations against *any* rival if only it struck fast and hard enough.[47] This thinking, which originated with Clausewitz and Moltke, would be the basis of Prusso-German military strategy in 1870, 1914, and 1939. Between 1866 and 1870, the Prussian army nearly tripled in size, increasing its war strength to 800,000 bayonets by the prompt extension of Prussian conscription into the North German Confederation. In this way, Moltke and Roon created the mighty war machine that crushed France in 1870.[48] By 1914, the German army had grown to a strength of 3 million men under arms. While other powers tended to view war as a question of "defense," the Germans, after 1866, came to relish its *offensive* potentialities.[49]

THE MILITARY LEGACY OF 1866

Moltke's victory in 1866 demonstrated the superiority of Prussian military professionalism and what, by 1914, would routinely be called the "German method of strategy."[50] In terms of professionalism, Prussia-Germany in 1866, 1870, and again in 1914 was peerless. Its well-trained, autonomous, politically influential

45 Peter Alter, "Weltmacht auf Distanz: Britische Aussenpolitik, 1860–1870," in Kolb, ed. *Europa vor dem Krieg von 1870*, pp. 77–90. W. E. Mosse, *The European Powers and the German Question, 1848–71* (Cambridge University Press, 1958), p. 249. Paul Kennedy, "The Tradition of Appeasement in British Foreign Policy, 1865–1939," in idem., *Strategy and Diplomacy, 1870–1945* (London and Boston: Allen and Unwin, 1983), pp. 15–39.

46 Ritter, *The Sword and the Scepter*, vol. 1, *The Prussian Tradition, 1740–1890* (1954; Coral Gables: University of Miami Press, 1969), pp. 193–206. Craig, *Politics of the Prussian Army*, pp. 238–98. Martin Kitchen, *A Military History of Germany* (Bloomington: Indiana University Press, 1975), pp. 138–60. Strachan, *European Armies*, pp. 126–9. Great General Staff, *The War Book of the German General Staff* (New York: McBride, 1915), pp. 1–73.

47 Martin Kitchen, *The German Officer Corps, 1890–1914* (Oxford: Clarendon, 1968), pp. 96–114.

48 Bucholz, *Moltke, Schlieffen*, pp. 47–8.

49 *Moltke on the Art of War*, ed. Daniel J. Hughes, p. 129. "War has the object of executing government policy by force of arms." Friedrich von Bernhardi, *Germany and the Next War*, trans. A. H. Powles (1911; New York: Chas. Eron, 1914), pp. 42–3. "The appropriate and conscious employment of war as a political means has always led to happy results." Jack Snyder, *The Ideology of the Offensive* (Ithaca: Cornell, 1984), pp. 127–50.

50 PRO, FO 120/907, Vienna, December 8, 1913, Maj. Cuninghame to Bunsen.

General Staff – reformed by Moltke in the early 1860s and linked directly to the Prussian crown – attained a level of military efficiency that other European armies – obstructed by courtiers, ministers, and parliaments – could only dream of. The Prusso-German General Staff was unique in Europe because it focussed military planning, mobilization, deployment, and operations in a single agency free of political and administrative interference. Under the Prussian system, the constitutional, politically accountable war minister served as a mere supplier to the secretive "demi-gods" (Bismarck's phrase) of the "Great General Staff" in Berlin. This was in pointed contrast to the predicament of the French General Staff, which was a mere department of the war ministry and – in matters of strategy, tactics, and discipline – was always subject to political pressure from the left-leaning National Assembly.[51]

Whereas the Prussian General Staff could impose iron discipline and devise war scenarios without political interference, and with a minimum of bureaucratic muddle, other powers were less fortunate. From 1870 until 1914, the French command lost its professional focus in a cyclone of politics. From 1870 until 1895, the conservative officers of the French General Staff conspired continually against France's Third Republic. Indeed, until the Dreyfus Affair, it would be fair to say that the French staff interested itself as much in monarcho-clerical intrigues as in war planning. Only in 1895 – when the anti-Republican Dreyfus Affair began to backfire on the very staff officers who had sponsored it – did France's Radical-dominated parliament begin finally to take the General Staff in hand. Yet they managed this only by purging some very good officers and promoting some very bad ones, and by foolishly insisting upon a reversion to shock tactics – the "*attaque à outrance* " – that would ostensibly "democratize" France's army by slaughtering as many officers as enlisted men in headlong rushes at enemy trenches and machinegun posts.[52] These *politically* motivated French storm tactics of 1914 – which were the opposite of Germany's defensive, fire-intensive ones – pointed again to the superiority of the German staff system, which was correctly characterized by its liberal opponents as a coldly professional technocracy, "a state within a state," free of lay meddling.

Like the French, Europe's other Great Powers all admired the efficiency of the Moltkean General Staff, but, for various reasons, all failed to adopt its methods. Although the Austrians were the first victim of Prussia's military professionalism, their efforts to reform themselves along Prussian lines after 1866 made little progress. Austria's new war minister after Königgrätz – Franz Kuhn, the general who had repulsed Garibaldi's attacks on South Tyrol in 1866 – actually abolished the office of General Staff chief in 1869 in order to augment his own power.[53] Although Franz Joseph revived the Austrian staff in 1874 and strengthened it

51 Douglas Porch, *The March to the Marne* (Cambridge University Press, 1981), pp. 105–33.

52 Michael Howard, "Men against Fire: The Doctrine of the Offensive in 1914," in Peter Paret, ed., *Makers of Modern Strategy*, pp. 519–24. Porch, *March to the Marne*, pp. 213-54.

53 Rothenberg, *Army of Francis Joseph*, pp. 78–80.

with the promotion of his confidant – General Friedrich Beck – to the post of Austro-Hungarian staff *chef*, Austrian military professionalism would never rise to the German standard for political reasons. In 1867, the Austrian Empire broke into two separate states – Austria and Hungary – each with its own separate parliament and administration, and each possessed of its own separate armies: the Vienna-based "imperial and royal common army" and Landwehr, and the Budapest-based Hungarian *honvéd* or "home guard." The costly bureaucracy and infighting that flowed from this political makeshift precluded any rational, rigorous Prussian-style war planning.[54] Since Hungarian military authorities refused on principle to brigade their units with Austrian ones or to correspond with Vienna in German – the Habsburg army's administrative language – Austro-Hungarian military cooperation was – in peace and war – loose, disjointed, and accident-prone.

Italian efforts to adopt a Prussian-style staff system after 1866 were even less successful than Austria's. "Without the reform of men, that of institutions is in vain," an Italian military reformer wrote in 1872, and indeed the whole history of the Italian army down to its intervention in World War I in 1915 would be that of royal efforts to wrestle a sullen peasantry into Italy's national army.[55] General Enrico Cialdini, one of the few Italian generals to emerge untarnished from the war of 1866, took the lead in reforming the Italian General Staff after Custoza, but it was a pale imitation of the Prusso-German model. In effect, King Vittorio Emanuele II merely gave the 130 Italian generals on active service in 1873 the collective designation: "General Staff." Though Cialdini was their titular *capo*, he had no authority to implement reforms, which were the province of the king, the war minister, and parliament. Despite the experience of 1866, Italy would not found a proper General Staff until 1882. And even at that late date, the Italian staff would be subordinated to the war ministry and physically attached to the notoriously fickle Italian Chamber of Deputies by a permanent parliamentary commission, which reserved the right to review all military plans and expenditures.[56]

In sum, none of Prussia's rivals successfully adopted Prussia's military organization after 1866. Though awed by the efficiency of Moltke, the French, Austrians, and Italians all failed to recreate it. In Russia, attempts to adopt the Prusso-German staff system after 1866 and 1870 were thwarted by Tsar Alexander II's all-powerful war minister – Dmitri Miliutin – who, like Franz Kuhn in Austria-Hungary, regarded an independent General Staff as a threat to his authority.[57] Ever suspicious of Continental practices, the British did not form a General Staff until 1904, when their parade of mishaps in the Anglo-Boer War admitted of no

54 Norman Stone, "Constitutional Crisis in Hungary, 1903-1906," *Slavonic and East European Review* 40 (1967), pp. 166–81.

55 Gooch, *Army, State and Society in Italy, 1870–1915*, p. 22.

56 Gooch, *Army, State and Society in Italy, 1870–1915*, p. 127.

57 Bruce W. Menning, *Bayonets before Bullets* (Bloomington: Indiana University Press, 1992), pp. 6–18.

other solution.[58] Thus by 1914, all European armies had come to appreciate the need for Prussian-style professionalism, but none of them had effectively copied it. At bottom, the Prusso-German General Staff was a German *political* phenomenon: a genuinely independent, free-spending military authority beyond parliamentary and ministerial control. Given the German General Staff's immense power and its historical ties to the Prusso-German crown, it was hardly surprising that in 1917 Berlin's Great General Staff actually ousted Germany's civilian leadership and replaced it with a military dictatorship. Such had been the tendency of German politics since 1866. Cosseted by secrecy, "iron budgets," and imperial favor, the Prusso-German General Staff would thus intensify the conduct of war every bit as much as the vaunted "German method of strategy," which the Prusso-German staff devised and disseminated to its regiments of the line in the years after Königgrätz.

In general, the "German method of strategy" disclosed in 1866 spurned defensive positions and deep, interlocked formations. Instead, Moltke had cast his army like a net over the densely concentrated Austrian army. The obvious risk of this Prussian approach – that the deeply formed Austrians might have cut through the thin, widespread Prussian net at any point and folded it up from behind – had never materialized. Austrian units, mesmerized by the action on their front, had consistently permitted themselves to be enveloped from their flanks, first at Skalice, then at Jicin, and finally at Königgrätz. The lesson of the Austro-Prussian War seemed to be that well-armed, clever Prussian troops – able, as a French admirer observed, "to act promptly and confidently in all phases of battle" – could be dispersed across very broad fronts with minimal risk in order to facilitate Königgrätz-style envelopments.[59]

The second test of Moltke's new doctrine would be the Franco-Prussian War in 1870, which, again, opposed two radically different styles of war. The French, like the Austrians, were Jominians. They believed in massive concentration and in the orderly, defensive deployment of armies for battle. Enemy formations would be lured past the French outpost line to be set upon in the well-reconnoitered, heavily manned French "concentration area." This watchful, scientific way of war was wholly at odds with the relatively unscientific Prussian approach tested and crowned with success in 1866.[60] In Bohemia, the Prussians had regularly ignored strategic considerations to wrest important tactical victories from the Austrians. Thus, Steinmetz had dived from the strategic safety of the Vysokov plateau into the tactical bedlam of Skalice in the rather unreasonable

58 John Gooch, *The Plans of War* (New York: Wiley, 1974), pp. 1–5.
59 Ardant du Picq, *Battle Studies*, p. 123. In 1914, General Friedrich von Bernhardi would describe the secret of German tactical success thus: "Once [German] troops have come within effective range of the enemy's fire all regular and comprehensive issue of orders ceases . . . self-reliance is everything." Friedrich von Bernhardi, *How Germany Makes War* (New York: Doran, 1914), p. 111.
60 PRO, FO 120/907, Vienna, December 8, 1913, Maj. Cuninghame to Bunsen.

hope that somehow, in the melée, he would land a crippling blow. Old Steinmetz's gamble had succeeded, and his pursuit of North Army down to Königinhof after Skalice had only underlined this Prussian tendency "to kick" – as Schlieffen would later put it – "not tickle." In a similiar vein, Ludwig Tümpling's Prussian 5th Division had plunged ahead to engage the entire Austro-Saxon Iser Army at Jicin without waiting for its supports or even connecting itself with Werder's 3rd Division. Tümpling's bet had been that his tough Prussian infantry would be able to surprise and disconcert the Austrians, endure hard fighting against superior numbers, and, ultimately, shoot their way through to victory. This gamble had succeeded no less marvelously than had Steinmetz's, routing Benedek's Iser Army and securing the strategic crossroads of Jicin for the Prussian First Army. Finally, Chlum: there, in the center of Benedek's line at Königgrätz, a single Prussian Guard *division* had dared penetrate to the very heart of the Austrian position to confront four entire Austrian corps. The 1st Guards had beaten them all, then split Benedek's position open from within at the very moment that Moltke's flanking columns were enveloping it from without. Although Königgrätz had pitted the Prussians against the Austrians, the battle had also matched new Prussian principles of strategy against old French ones. The next war would do the same and enshrine forever Moltke's "*Kesselschlacht* doctrine."

There was, to be sure, nothing magical about Prussia's victory over France in 1870. Incompetent subordinates meddled with, misinterpreted, and sometimes wrecked Moltke's plans as frequently as they had in 1866. Despite Moltke's issuance of new tactical regulations in 1869 that forbade frontal attacks of the sort attempted by Prince Friedrich Karl at Sadova, Prussian army and corps commanders often disregarded them.[61] At Spicheren and St. Privat in August 1870, Steinmetz, now in command of an entire Prussian army, wasted more than 10,000 men in bloody frontal assaults on French positions that might have been easily flanked. At Wörth, elements of Crown Prince Friedrich Wilhelm's Third Army did the same, losing more Prussian dead and wounded in that single frontal attack against French breech-loaders than three entire Prussian armies had lost at Königgrätz.[62] Moltke's plan to envelop and destroy France's two armies in August 1870 thus had to be postponed until September. Nevertheless, it worked. After the battles of Gravelotte and St. Privat – two actions that featured unpardonable blundering by Steinmetz and Prince Friedrich Karl – Moltke succeeded in encircling and disarming Marshal François Bazaine's Army of the Rhine at Metz. Two weeks later, Moltke's widely spaced armies marched round the flanks of Marshal Patrice MacMahon's Army of Châlons – sent by Napoleon III to relieve Bazaine – and took the surrender of 104,000 first-rate French troops at Sedan.[63]

The Franco-Prussian War thus ended with two dramatic *Kesselschlacht* victories

61 *Moltke on the Art of War*, ed. Daniel J. Hughes, pp. 171–224.
62 Howard, *Franco-Prussian War*, pp. 93–7, 107–119, 170–82. Strachan, *European Armies*, pp. 115–16.
63 Howard, *Franco-Prussian War*, pp. 167–223.

that seemed to confirm the wisdom and efficacy of the Moltkean strategy first tested in 1866. The French, like the Austrians at Königgrätz, had tried to repulse the Prussians from concentrated, defensive positions yet had succeeded only in trapping themselves between Prussia's broadcast armies. Even where the Prussians had maneuvered badly in 1870 – at Spicheren and Mars-la-Tour, for example – they had still won through, prompting Moltke to postulate afterward that, in war, "genius is subordinate to the offensive spirit."[64] Prussia's reward for its "offensive spirit" in 1870 was even greater than in 1866. France paid Prussia an indemnity sixty times larger than the one remitted by the Austrians in 1866 and meekly accepted Prussia's absorption of the North *and* South German Confederations to form a unitary "German Empire" ruled from Berlin. Thus began a Prusso-German fascination with *Niederwerfungsstrategie* (overthrow strategy) that would grow stronger despite Moltke's own encroaching pessimism as he approached his death in 1891, warning all who would listen that Germany was no longer bounded by vulnerable, politically isolated Great Powers – the case in 1866 and 1870 – but by two, perhaps three, mutually supportive ones: Russia, France, and England.[65]

To a younger generation of German strategists reared on the legends of Königgrätz and Sedan, such political scruples did not seem to matter. Cautious old Kaiser Wilhelm I died in 1888 and was succeeded by his vainglorious grandson, Kaiser Wilhelm II, who promptly threw Moltke overboard and replaced him with his incautious *sous-chef:* General Alfred von Waldersee.[66] Waldersee believed that German unification – built as it was upon the broken bodies of Austria and France – would never be truly secure until Russia too was broken.[67] He thus spent the 1880s imploring Moltke and Germany's civilian leadership to authorize a vast, preemptive envelopment of the Russian army, much of which was stationed in Russian Poland. In 1891, Wilhelm II replaced Waldersee with an even more aggressive dévoté of the "pocket battle," Field Marshal Alfred von Schlieffen.[68] In the years between 1891 and 1905, Schlieffen devised the German General Staff's notorious "Schlieffen Plan," which was an ambitious scheme first to envelop France's entire army, then to turn the same trick against the slower mobilizing Russians. Schlieffen died in 1913, enjoining the officers gathered round his deathbed to invade France first and "keep the right wing strong." This man – who had tasted battle for the first time at Königgrätz as a young staff

64 Cyril Falls, *The Art of War* pp. 77–80.

65 Kitchen, *A Military History of Germany*, pp. 138–44.

66 In April 1866, Count Waldersee, then a lieutenant-colonel on the Prussian General Staff, was arrested by Austrian police in the Prague railway station after being observed sketching Prague's fortifications. He was released after three days' confinement. HHSA, IB, Karton 370, BM 1866, 979, Vienna, April 13, 1866, Agent-Rapport.

67 Graydon A. Tunstall, Jr., *Planning for War against Russia and Serbia* (Boulder: Social Science Monoraphs, 1993), pp. 33–9. Kitchen, *German Officer Corps*, pp. 64–71.

68 Gunther E. Rothenberg, "Moltke, Schlieffen, and the Doctrine of Strategic Envelopment," in *Makers of Modern Strategy*, pp. 296–325. Craig, *Politics of the Prussian Army*, pp. 238–98.

lieutenant – was so convinced of the infallibilty of the *Kesselschlacht* that he ignored all of its limitations, the most obvious of them being logistics.[69]

In 1866 and again in 1870, German horse-drawn supplies had failed to keep pace with Moltke's field armies once inside enemy territory. This failure of the Prussian supply service had, in turn, caused dangerous, potentially disastrous shortages of food, drink, fodder, and ammunition. It was only the swiftness of the Austrian and French *political* collapses that had saved the Prussian army from thirst and hunger and had made Königgrätz and Sedan decisive battles.[70] With these sobering observations in mind, the Prussian General Staff became obsessed with the problem of supplying mass armies after 1866. In 1890, Waldersee said of Moltke that he never made an important decision "without consulting the German railway guide."[71]

The logistical problems experienced by Moltke in 1866 and 1870 only worsened in 1914, when the tenfold expansion of the German army and its adoption of a magazine rifle, the machinegun and quick-firing artillery resulted in a truly insatiable demand for food and ammunition supplies that slowed the march of German armies to a crawl. No amount of painstaking mobilization planning – another legacy of 1866 – could overcome the essential difficulty of coordinating the delivery of millions of men and the tons and hectoliters of food, forage, drink, and ammunition that they would need to survive in the field.[72] In 1914, it was precisely the slowness of the heavily laden German invasion of France through Belgium that enabled the French army to backpedal out of the slowly closing jaws of the Schlieffen Plan. The same thing happened in the east in 1914. After successfully enveloping the fraction of the Russian army foolish enough to venture up to Germany's East Prussian railheads at Tannenberg, the Russians prudently withdrew beyond the reach of the German army's railway net and successfully held the Germans and their Austro-Hungarian ally in check until 1917, when Russia collapsed not because of a German-wielded *Kesselschlacht* but because of an internal revolution.[73]

The Königgrätz legend and the German dream of decisive flanking maneuvers survived the largely immobile, frontal stalemate that was World War I thanks to General Heinz Guderian and the "German tank school," which was born in the 1920s. Between 1939 and 1945, German armored columns restored mobility to the twentieth-century battlefield and made it possible finally for mechanized troops to race ahead of their horse-drawn supplies and, in the case of the perennially difficult Russian theater, even to track trackless wastes. Thus, in World War II, Moltke's *Niederwerfungsstrategie* rose again. In a sequence of well-executed

69 Bucholz, *Moltke, Schlieffen*, pp. 109–19. Dennis E. Showalter, *Tannenberg* (Hamden: Archon, 1992), pp. 13–35.
70 Howard, *War in European History*, p. 105.
71 Bucholz, *Moltke, Schlieffen*, p. 126.
72 Strachan, *European Armies*, pp. 121–4, 135–8. Snyder, *Ideology of the Offensive*, pp. 150–3.
73 Larry H. Addington, *The Blitzkrieg Era*, pp. 9–27.

German "pocket battles" spearheaded by Guderian's Panzer divisions, France fell in 1940, England nearly did, and Russia was brought to the verge of collapse in 1941. However, as in World War I, German tactical successes in World War II were ultimately undone by strategic errors. At Nikolsburg in 1866 and at Paris in 1871, Bismarck and Moltke had prudently consolidated their tactical gains and settled for limited war aims. Drunk with the legend of German military prowess, their successors – Schlieffen, Ludendorff, Kaiser Wilhelm II, and Hitler – would bid for unlimited world domination, and Germany would collapse in 1918 and again in 1945 under the weight of their vast undertakings.[74]

CHANGES IN BATTLE TACTICS AFTER 1866

Prussian strategy and tactics were always closely related, and after concluding peace with the Austrians in 1866, the Prussians began improving the tactical areas in which they had proven deficient. If Königgrätz had nearly turned in favor of the Austrians, it was in large part because Prussia's old-fashioned artillery was vastly inferior to Austria's in 1866. Therefore, in the years between 1866 and 1870, Moltke rearmed the Prussian artillery with steel, breech-loading Krupp rifles. In Moltke's deft hands, this lighter, more mobile, faster-firing Prussian field artillery became an integral, *new* part of the "pocket battle." At Metz and again at Sedan in 1870, French attempts to break out of Moltke's closing "pockets" were thwarted less by the needle rifle than by the relentless, long-range fire of Prussia's new model artillery, which shattered enemy resistance inside the *Kessel* and permitted the German infantry to encircle and crush it rather easily.[75]

Artillery, then, would claim a much bigger tactical role and much larger budget appropriations after the wars of 1866 and 1870. Prussian infantry corps that had disposed just 72 guns in 1866 would be armed with 144 heavier, more destructive pieces by 1905. At the battle of Mukden in 1905, officers of the Japanese Nambu Brigade were astonished to learn that Russian *artillery* had accounted for 90 percent of their casualties, a devastating firestorm that foreshadowed the events of World War I.[76] While the artillery thus rose to prominence after 1866, cavalry fell. Although saber regiments would have a last fling at Sedan in 1870 – when Napoleon III ordered his heavy squadrons to punch a hole through the closing Prussian envelopment only to see them torn to pieces by Prussian fire – the war of 1866 had already exhibited cavalry's extreme vulnerability to rifled arms. Time and again – at Custoza, at Jicin, and at Königgrätz – "shock cavalry" had proven useless against infantry and guns. Therefore, after

74 B. H. Liddell Hart, *The Revolution in Warfare* (1947; Westport: Greenwood, 1980), pp. 66–9.
    Strachan, *European Armies*, pp. 128–9. Michael Geyer, "German Strategy in the Age of Machine
    Warfare, 1914–1945," in *Makers of Modern Strategy*, pp. 527–97.

75 Howard, *Franco-Prussian War*, pp. 119, 208–17. Addington, *Blitzkrieg Era*, pp. 6–8. Strachan,
    European Armies, pp. 115–19.

76 Bucholz, *Moltke, Schlieffen*, pp. 210–13.

1866 and 1870, most European cavalry regiments would rearm with carbines and confine themselves to "light duties," chiefly picketing and reconnaissance.[77]

Infantry too underwent a profound transformation after 1866. The Prussian victories at Vysokov, Skalice, Jicin, and Königgrätz were so remarkable that by 1870, all the European Great Powers – poor, straitened Italy included – had rearmed with a breech-loading rifle. The new rifles tended to abolish the old distinction between light and line infantry. In Bohemia, the Prussians had sent line troops hot on the heels of skirmishers in order to maximize their firepower and press their attacks home with celerity and force. They refined this hard-hitting, fire-intensive tactic in 1870, this time preparing their infantry attacks with much heavier cannonades. The effect of the Prussian victories in 1866 and 1870 was, a French tactician noted, "to transfer the combat to the skirmishing line, which previously only prepared it." In extending their fronts to envelop first the Austrians, then the French, the Prussians consigned the Napoleonic assault column to oblivion. This Prussian tendency to lengthen and strengthen the skirmish line until it bore the main weight of a battle was imitated by most other European armies. In 1881, even the Russians – who had coined the phrase "the bullet is a fool, the bayonet a smart fellow" – began deploying their line infantry in skirmish formation, a reform copied by the Austro-Hungarians and the Italians.[78] By 1914, all European armies – with the curious, tragic exception of the French – would fight in the Prussian style pioneered in 1866.[79]

However, though all powers appreciated the need for dispersed, fire-intensive troop formations after 1866, they could not all apply these tactical innovations equally. Austro-Hungarian infantry would *never* master the small unit tactics employed by the Prussians in 1866 for reasons deduced by Field Marshal Albrecht in 1869: What was most wanting in the Austrian army, he wrote, was not the right rifle or the right tactic, but simply "*responsibility* at all levels, by far the most important thing in war." After Königgrätz, Albrecht, who would serve as Austrian army inspector until his death in 1895, ordered fewer parades, more practical training, and an end to the rigid *Formalismus* that had set in during Benedek's years in Verona. Austrian officers, Albrecht insisted, would have to learn to plan and execute sensible operations in the Prussian style; Austrian men would have to learn to stand their ground and stop being so exasperatingly *desertionslustig.* [80] All of this, however, was far easier said than done. "Fighting," Clausewitz once said, "is to war, what cash payment is to business," and the Austro-Hungarians – notorious for their indiscipline – would never be particularly good fighters. At Austro-Hungarian fall maneuvers in 1877, France's military attaché was struck by the "unmilitary bearing" of the troops involved, most of whom had to be manhandled

[77] Strachan, *European Armies*, pp. 119–21.
[78] Menning, *Bayonets before Bullets*, pp. 136–43, 259–62.
[79] Falls, *Art of War*, p. 75. Ardant du Picq, *Battle Studies*, pp. 244–5.
[80] KA, Nachlässe, B/208: 6 (Fischer), [FM Albrecht], "Über die Verantwortlichkeit im Kriege."

through their paces by beefy NCOs.[81] At Habsburg maneuvers in 1912, and again in 1913, Britain's military attaché – Major Thomas Cuninghame – made identical observations. He was also struck by the lack of "fire action" and spontaneity in Austrian exercises and by the Austro-Hungarian tendency to mass men in dense, easily managed lines that differed little from the attack columns of 1866. "If the Austrian infantry are going to attempt to do in real war what they often attempted to do in these maneuvers," Cuninghame concluded in 1913, "they are going to suffer very severely indeed."[82] And suffer they did. In 1914, the Habsburg Monarchy's next trial by fire, the Austro-Hungarian army would crumble under Serbian and Russian blows and be revived for the duration of the Great War only by the steady influx of Reich German reinforcements.[83]

A new Italian tactical manual published in 1869 suggested that irresponsibility and *Desertionslust* were problems in Italy no less than in Austria-Hungary. Only long-service *bersaglieri* or light infantry were considered dependable enough to be deployed in open order. After the experience of Custoza, where whole Italian divisions had panicked and dissolved, Italian line infantry would continue to be massed in battalion columns until the turn of the century. As for fire tactics, these involved mathematical calculations beyond the ken of the average *contadino*. "Only a very small number of the men deployed in a line will be permitted to fire at ranges exceeding 600 meters," the Italian manual instructed. "At ranges beyond 300 meters, the men may fire no more than one round per minute. The men may fire at will only when the enemy has closed to within 150 meters."[84] This was the effective range of an eighteenth-century musketeer; in Italy as in Austria poorly trained or refractory troops simply could not be trusted to take full advantage of the latest military technologies.

Fire control was only one question left unsolved by the Austro-Prussian War, in which the Austrians, in their haste to charge the Prussians with the bayonet, had never forced the Prussians to spend their cartridges skirmishing or trading salvos. The Bavarians, in contrast, had demonstrated on several occasions that even fire tactics would shatter against a resolute, well-covered defensive.[85] Indeed, the only remarkable aspect of the Prussian West Army's war in the German states after Langensalza had been the disparity in casualties suffered by the Bavarians of the German VII Corps on the one hand, and the mixed contingents of the German VIII Corps on the other. The brigades of VIII Corps had all practiced Austrian-

---

81 Vincennes, AAT, 7N1123, Vienna, November 1, 1877, Capt. Berghes, "Rapport sur l'instruction dans l'armée austro-hongroise."

82 PRO, FO 120/906, 907, Vienna, January 16 and December 8, 1913, Maj. Cuninghame to Bunsen. Rothenberg, *Army of Francis Joseph*, pp. 108–12, 125–38.

83 Geoffrey Wawro, "Morale in the Austro-Hungarian Army," in P. Liddle, H. Cecil, eds., *Facing Armageddon: The First World War Experienced* (London: Leo Cooper, 1996).

84 Vincennes, AAT, MR 69/1388, Florence, October 4, 1869, Col. Schmitz to Randon.

85 Munich, BKA, HS 817, Munich, July 4, 1900, Sgt. Stegmaier, "Erinnerungen aus dem Feldzuge 1866." KA, AFA 1866, Karton 2269, 7–259, Vienna, July 11, 1866, Maj. Mingazzi.

style shock tactics and, on average, had absorbed eight casualties for every one suffered by their Prussian foe. For their part, the Bavarians had sensibly avoided storm columns and adopted open-order instead, achieving a one-to-one casualty ratio with the Prussians in their last combats despite the fact that the Bavarians, like the Austrians, were armed with a muzzle-loading rifle.[86]

The rough parity in Prusso-Bavarian losses in 1866 begged an important question: What would happen in a future war if *both* sides resolved to make the most of rapid firing from the tactical defensive? How would armies attack?[87] After Kissingen – Bavaria's last clash with the Prussians in July 1866 – Bavaria's staff chief, General Ludwig von der Tann, had argued that it was no longer physically possible to take the offensive against breech-loading rifles and field guns. The era of the trench had arrived, as the American Civil War seemed to attest. Moltke, however, resisted this defensive prejudice, for it would have impeded Prussia's bold operational strokes. In the years after 1866, he insisted that a battle like Königgrätz could be a model for tactical success. The Germans would divert the fire of their enemies with a relatively weak frontal attack, then deliver the main blow from the flank, where the enemy's defensive fire would be thinnest.[88]

As the nineteenth century ground on and a new generation of rifles, machineguns, and artillery cast doubt even upon Moltke's relatively cautious tactics, all manner of schemes were aired to restore mobility to the battlefield and avoid what a French officer called the "hecatomb of the future."[89] Already in 1866, an Austrian officer suggested encasing cavalry – man and horse – in steel jackets, an idea taken up by the French military theorist Ardant du Picq before his own mortal wounding by a Prussian shell splinter in 1870.[90] As for the infantry, an Austrian reformer in 1866 recommended a return to something like the eighteenth-century grenadier system: Swarms of fusiliers would pour rapid-fire into an enemy's trenches to cover the advance of phalanxes of "storm guards" clad in full body armor. An Austrian war ministry official argued for the early introduction of tanks or "*Land-Monitors*," ironclad carriages mounting guns. "The more ghastly and destructive war becomes, the less we will have to fear it," he conjectured. After 1866, European powers considered that each new technological invention was liable to overturn this delicate balance of terror. When the Germans adopted a small-caliber repeating rifle in 1887, the Austrians worried that their ally would go to war with Russia and France to exploit the discovery. When a German inventor forged a bullet-proof steel breastplate in the 1890s, European

---

86 Munich, BKA, HS 2875, Kissingen, July 10, 1866, Capt. Lippl, "Tagebuch." Rolf Förster, "Die Leistungsfähigkeit der bayerischen Armee im Feldzuge 1866" (phil. Diss. Munich, 1987), pp. 155–6.

87 Howard, *War in European History*, pp. 103–6.

88 Strachan, *European Armies*, p. 116. *Moltke on the Art of War*, pp. 201–8.

89 Luvaas, *Military Legacy of the Civil War*, pp. 140–2, 166–7.

90 Ardant du Picq, *Battle Studies*, pp. 199–204.

armies held their breath until it proved too heavy in testing for the average foot soldier.[91]

However, for all of their *fin-de-siècle* agonizing about the "future of war," European armies would, in the end, rather casually brush aside the tactical difficulties posed by modern firearms and the bloody results they had achieved in the Boer, Russo-Japanese, and Balkan Wars.[92] Hence, the "bath of steel" that was World War I: thirteen million would die, mown down by belt-fed, water-cooled machineguns and breech-loading, recoilless artillery lavishly fed with shrapnel, high explosive and gas shells by the industrial states. To most European powers, the Great War did indeed seem to be "the war to end all wars." Moltke's "overthrow strategy" seemed finally to have been ground into the mud by an Entente "strategy of attrition."[93] To the Germans, however, even World War I offered a glimmer of hope. Their final offensives in 1917–18 had featured new "storm tactics" that anticipated the *Blitzkrieg* operations of World War II. German "storm troopers," armed with stick grenades, light machineguns, and flamethrowers, had infiltrated the Entente trenches in dispersed units under cover of intensive gas and shell barrages. Even in small numbers, these well-armed German *Stürmer* had been able to panic and rout much larger French, British, and American formations, bursting through their center and racing round their flanks. These German storm tactics – which had something in common with Prussian tactics at Jicin and Chlum – would supply the Prusso-German army with a ready-made doctrine for Hitler's War, the last terrible gasp of German *Niederwerfungsstrategie*.[94]

* * *

In the end, it is tempting to speculate upon what "might have been" had Austria only won the war of 1866, for Emperor Franz Joseph's war aims are a matter of record. In Italy, he aimed to diminish or dissolve the Kingdom of Italy and to restore as many of the princely states of 1815 as France – Austria's rival in Italy – would tolerate. After a victorious campaign in Italy, Franz Joseph would have sought to restore the Bourbon Kingdom of the Two Sicilies in the south, the

---

91 "Über die Misserfolge der österreichischen Nordarmee," *ÖMZ* 2 (1866), p. 354. Toilow, *Die österreichische Nordarmee*, p. 160. Wondrák, "Trauerspiel 1866," p. 79. The point of Ivan Bloch's six-volume *Future of War* (New York: Doubleday, 1899) was that given the destructiveness of modern technology (magazine rifles, smokeless powder, small-bore cartridges, range-finders, quick-firing guns, peroxilene explosive, etc.) and the industrial organization and discipline of modern European economies, Great Power wars had become *impossible* by the thirtieth anniversary of the Franco-Prussian War.

92 Michael Howard, "Men against Fire: The Doctrine of the Offensive in 1914," in *Makers of Modern Strategy*, pp. 510–26. John Ellis, *The Social History of the Machine Gun* (1976; London: Pimlico 1993), pp. 47–76.

93 Howard, *War in European History*, p. 113.

94 Hans von Luck, *Panzer Commander* (New York: Dell, 1989), pp. 34–91. Addington, *Blitzkrieg Era*, pp. 24–7. Strachan, *European Armies*, p. 145.

Pope in Rome and central Italy, and the Habsburg princes in the northern duchies of Tuscany, Modena, and Parma.[95] Although Austrian statesmen did agree to cede Venetia to France in June 1866, they viewed this as the price of a French neutrality that would permit Vienna – as Austria's military attaché in Papal Rome put it – "to reduce the rotten Kingdom of Italy to rubble."[96]

These destructive Austrian aims in Italy, which seemed graspable after Vittorio Emanuele's rout at Custoza, were ultimately undone by the Habsburg army's own defeat at Königgrätz, where Prussia secured the continued existence of Italy and itself. Before the war, the Austrian emperor had described Prussia as the *"möglichst zu schwächenden Feind"* (the enemy to be maximally weakened) and, for the event of an Austrian victory, he had prescribed crippling annexations at Prussia's expense.[97] Had Austria won the war of 1866, Franz Joseph planned to seize Upper Silesia, the coal-rich, formerly Austrian province around Breslau, which had been lost to the Prussians in 1740. This annexation would have vastly augmented Austria's high-grade coal reserves and, as Austria's war minister noted in May 1866, "grievously wounded Prussia's vital interests."[98] To reward Austria's German federal allies, Franz Joseph planned to restore Lusatia to Saxony and to divide Berlin's Rhine provinces among the states of Hanover, Hessia-Darmstadt, Bavaria, and Württemberg. For Vienna, such a radical redrawing of the German map would have served two purposes: it would have substantially weakened Prussia and reinforced the tendency toward regional particularism in Germany, thus slowing the spread of nationalism – the bane of the Habsburg Monarchy – in Europe.[99]

Had the Austrians won the war, the Prussians could have expected no mercy. Barring French or Russian intervention, they might have been reduced to something like the Tilsit frontiers of 1807. If Austria's rough handling of Turin after the Austro-Piedmontese War of 1849 gave any clues as to Habsburg policy in 1866, Franz Joseph would surely have looted the Prussian treasury after an Austrian victory to pay his war costs.[100] Before the mobilizations of 1866, the

95 Geoffrey Wawro, "Austria versus the Risorgimento: A New Look at Austria's Italian Strategy in the 1860s," *European History Quarterly* 26 (January 1996).

96 KA, MKSM 1866, Karton 338, 33–1/14, Rome, June 8, 1866, Maj. Frantzl to FML Crenneville. Heinrich Srbik, ed., *Quellen zur deutschen Politik Österreichs*, vol. 5, nr. 2760, Munich, May 20, 1866, Blome to Mensdorff.

97 KA, MKSM 1866, Karton 342, 69–8, Vienna, June 7, 1866, Franz Joseph to Saxon Crown Prince.

98 KA, KM 1866, CK, Karton 252, 51–6/49, Vienna, May 29, 1866, FML Franck to FZM Benedek.

99 KA, MKSM 1866, Karton 342, 69–8, Vienna, June 7, 1866, Franz Joseph to Saxon Crown Prince.

100 After Radetzky's victory at Novara in 1849, Emperor Franz Joseph had wrested a 25 million florin ($337 million) indemnity from the Piedmontese. Adolf Beer, *Die Finanzen Österreichs im neunzehnten Jahrhundert* (1891; Vienna: Verlag des wissenschaftlichen Antiquariats, 1973), pp. 204, 221.

emperor's finance minister had warned him that only big post-war indemnities from Berlin and Florence would "stave off an Austrian bankruptcy."[101] Vienna would have stunted Prussia's economic growth by a debilitating schedule of reparation payments, the amputation of industrial provinces like Silesia, Lusatia, and the Ruhr, and by the forcible attachment of the underdeveloped Austrian Empire to the Prusso-German *Zollverein*.[102] With its north German rival thus constrained and diminished, great, wobbly Austria might have continued to exercise its rather harmless leadership of the multistate German Confederation.

It was this vision of a Germany led by muddling Austria, not rigorous Prussia, that led an English historian to argue in 1902 that had Benedek only prevailed at Königgrätz, "the history of Prussia, of Germany, of Europe, and now we may say even of Asia Minor – even of Asia – would have been different. There would have been no Spicheren, Wörth, Gravelotte, no German unity, no Baghdad railway, no Germanized Africa, Near East or Orient."[103] Preoccupied as he plainly was with the turn-of-the-century German threat to British colonial interests, this historian perhaps overstated his case. Nevertheless, a great Austrian victory at Königgrätz would, at the very least, have *lengthened* the Austro-Prussian War and thus given France or Russia time to intervene in the conflict to enforce Europe's delicate balance of power.[104] Surprised by the rapid Prussian conquest of Germany in 1866, neither France nor Russia seriously contested it. Noting this curious, fateful fact, Austria's minister of state in 1866 correctly predicted that Bismarck "would not neglect the opportunity to show the world – and France in particular – the immense power of his new position."[105]

101 Heinrich Benedikt, *Die wirtschaftliche Entwicklung in der Franz-Joseph-Zeit* (Vienna and Munich: Verlag Herold, 1958), pp. 72–3. Friedjung, *Struggle for Supremacy*, pp. 133–4.

102 KA, MKSM-SR 1866, 22/5, Vienna, August 1865, Evidenz-Bureau, "Machtverhältnisse." Srbik, *Quellen*, vol. 5, pp. 27, 306. PRO, FO 7/714, Venice, January 8, 1866, Perry to Clarendon.

103 A. D. Gillespie-Addison, *The Strategy of the Seven Weeks War* (London: Scheinemann, 1902), p. 37.

104 KA, AFA 1866, Karton 2272, 13–13, Paris/Vienna, June 14 and 24, 1866, Belcredi to FZM Benedek: "Austria need win but a single victory over the Prussians and all France will stand with us."

105 KA, AFA 1866, Karton 2272, 13–13, Vienna, July 14, 1866, Belcredi to FZM Benedek.

Bibliography

UNPUBLISHED DOCUMENTS

Austria Haus-Hof-und Staatsarchiv (HHSA), Vienna. Consulted: Politisches Archiv (PA): *Acta Secreta* and *Interna* and correspondence with the German and Italian states, Prussia, France, Russia, Great Britain and Turkey. Informationsbüro (IB), police archives under the rubrics of "BM-Akten" and "Actes de Haute Police."

Kriegsarchiv (KA), Vienna. Consulted: Alte Feld-Akten (AFA) for 1864–6. Militärkanzlei Seiner Majestät (MKSM), 1865–6. Kriegsministerium (KM), Centralkanzlei (CK), 1860–6. Papers (Nachlässe) of Krismanic, Franck, Nagy, Nosinic, Beck, Gablenz, Coudenhove, Fischer, Hirsch, Bartels, Lebeda, Arno, Paic, Sacken.

France Archive du Ministère des Affaires Etrangères (Quai d'Orsay), Paris. Consulted: Correspondance Politique (CP) for Austria, Prussia, the German states, Italy and Papal Rome, 1860–6.

Archive de l'Armée de Terre (AAT), Vincennes. Consulted: Mémoirs Reconnaissances (MR). Army attaché and war ministry reports on Austria, Prussia and Italy, 1840s to 1870s.

Germany Bayerisches Kriegsarchiv (BKA), Munich. Consulted: Generalstab (GS), 1859–66, Handschriften-Sammlung (HS), B-Akten (field reports) and various unpublished manuscripts.

Great Britain Public Record Office (PRO), London. Consulted: Correspondence of the ambassadors, ministers and consuls in Vienna, Berlin, Paris, Frankfurt, Munich, Leipzig, Stuttgart, Florence, Rome, Venice, Trieste, Dubrovnik, Budapest and Belgrade, 1864–6.

Hungary Magyar Honvédség, Hadtörtenélmi Levéltár (Hungarian Army Archive), Budapest. Consulted: Papers of General Gideon Krismanic.

Italy Archivio Centrale dello Stato, Rome. Consulted: Ministero Interno Gabinetto, Atti Diversi, 1849–95. Police and administrative acts and reports on Austrian espionage.

Archivio di Stato, Rome. Consulted: Ministero delle Armi, Affari Riservati, 1865–7. Papal army records.

Archivio di Stato, Naples. Consulted: House of Bourbon Archive, 1860–6.

Archivio di Stato, Venice. Consulted: I.R. Presidenza Luogotenenza, 1865–6. Venetian civil and military affairs.

Museo del Risorgimento, Milan. Consulted: Archivio Garibaldino. Garibaldi's correspondence, orders-of-the-day, proclamations and polemics, 1861–6. Archivio Guastalla. Details of the administration and battles of the Italian Volunteers in 1866.

PUBLISHED DOCUMENTS

Die auswärtige Politik Preussens, 1858–71. Edited by Rudolf Ibbeken and Erich Brandenburg. Berlin, Munich: Oldenbourg, 1931–45.

Documenti diplomatici presentato al parlamento dal Ministro degli Affari Esteri il 21 Dicembre 1866. Florence: Tipographia Stato, 1866.

k.k. Abgeordnetenhaus. *Stenographische Protokolle über die Verhandlungen des Abgeordnetenhauses.* Vienna: k.k. Haus-Hof-und Staatsdruckerei, 1862–5.

k.k. Central-Commission für Statistik. *Statistisches Handbuchlein des Kaiserthumes Österreich für das Jahr 1865.* Vienna: k.k. Hof-und Staatsdruckerei, 1867.

k.k. Herrenhaus. *Stenographische Protokolle über die Verhandlungen des Herrenhauses.* Vienna: k.k. Haus-Hof-und Staatsdruckerei, 1862–5.

k.k. Kriegsministerium. *Militär-Schematismus des österreichischen Kaiserthumes für 1866.* Vienna: k.k. Hof-und-Staatsdruckerei, 1866.

Militär-Statistisches Jahrbuch für 1872. Vienna: k.k. Hof-und Staatsdruckerei, 1875.

Statistischer Jahresbericht über die Sanitären-Verhältnisse des k.k. Heeres im Jahre 1869. Vienna: k.k. Hof-und Staatsdruckerei, 1871.

Statistisches Handbuchlein des Kaiserthumes Österreich für das Jahr 1866. Vienna: k.k. Hof-und-Staatsdruckerei, 1868.

Militär-Administrations Karte des österreichischen Kaiserstaates. Vienna: Verlag Wm. Braumüller, 1865.

Die Protokolle des österreichischen Ministerrates (PÖM), 1848–1867. 6 vols. Vienna: Österreichischer Bundesverlag, 1970–3.

Quellen zur deutschen Politik Österreichs, 1859–1866. 5 vols. Edited by Heinrich Srbik. Berlin: Verlag Gerhard Stalling, 1934–8.

SECONDARY SOURCES

Abasi-Aigner, Ludwig. *Die ungarische Legion in Preussen 1866.* Budapest: Pester Lloyd Gesellschaft, 1897.

Addington, Larry H. *The Blitzkrieg Era and the German General Staff, 1865–1941.* New Brunswick: Rutgers, 1971.

Patterns of War Since the Eighteenth Century. Bloomington: Indiana University Press, 1984.

Allgemeine deutsche Biographie. 56 vols. Leipzig: Duncker, 1875–1910.

Alten, Georg. *Handbuch für Heer und Flotte*. 6 vols. Berlin, Leipzig, Vienna: Bong, 1909–14.

Alter, Wilhelm. *Feldzeugmeister Benedek und der Feldzug der k.k. Nordarmee 1866*. Berlin: Paetel, 1912.

Amon, Gustav. *Geschichte des k.k. Infanterieregiments Hoch-und Deutschmeister Nr. 4*. Vienna: Mayer, 1879.

Apfelknab, Egbert. *Waffenrock und Schnürschuh*. Vienna: Österreichischen Bundesverlag, 1984.

Ardant du Picq, Charles. *Battle Studies*. Translated by J. Greely. 1880. New York: Macmillan, 1921.

Aresin [pseud.]. *Das Festungsviereck von Ober-Italien*. Vienna: k.k. Hof-und-Staatsdruckerei, 1860.

Arneth, Alfred. *Aus Meinem Leben*. 2 vols. Vienna: Holzhausen, 1892.

Arno, Wolf Schneider von. "Der österreichisch-ungarische Generalstab." Vienna Kriegsarchiv Manuscript, in B/197, Arno Nachlass.

Arrivabene, Count. *The Finances of Italy*. London: Wm. Ridgway, 1865.

Bartels, Eduard. *Der Krieg im Jahre 1866*. Leipzig: Otto Wigand, 1867.

Der Krieg im Jahre 1859. Bamberg: Buchner Verlag, 1894.

Kritische Beiträge zur Geschichte des Krieges im Jahre 1866. Zurich: Caspar Schmidt, 1901.

"Der Nebel von Chlum" (In KA, Nachlässe, B/157).

Österreich und sein Heer. Leipzig: Otto Wigand, 1866.

Baxa, Jakob. *Geschichte des k.u.k. Feldjägerbatallions Nr. 8, 1808–1918*. Klagenfurt: Kameradschaftbund, 1974.

Beer, Adolf. *Die Finanzen Österreichs im neunzehnten Jahrhundert*. 1891. Vienna: Verlag des wissenschaftlichen Antiquariats, 1973.

Benedek, Ludwig. *Benedeks nachgelassene Papiere*. Edited by Heinrich Friedjung. Leipzig: Grübel und Sommerlatte, 1901.

Benedikt, Heinrich. *Die wirtschaftliche Entwicklung in der Franz-Joseph-Zeit*. Vienna, Munich: Verlag Herold, 1958.

Kaiseradler über dem Appenin. Vienna and Munich: Verlag Herold, 1964.

[Benkert, Carl-Marie.] *Moderne Imperatoren: Diskretes und Indiskretes aus dem Tagebuche eines politischen Agenten Franz Joseph I*. Cologne: Ahns Verlag, 1867.

Benold, Josef. "Österreichische Feldtelegraphie 1866." Vienna Kriegsarchiv Manuscript, 1990.

Bernhardi, Theodor von. *Germany and the Next War*. Translated by A. H. Powles. Orig. 1911; New York: Chas. Eron, 1914.

How Germany Makes War. New York: Doran, 1914.

Blaas, Richard. "Die italienische Frage und das österreichische Parlament 1859–66." *Mitteilungen des österreichischen Staatsarchivs (MÖSA)* 22 (1969).

"Vom friauler Putsch im Herbst 1864 bis zur Abtretung Venetiens 1866." *MÖSA* 19 (1966).

Bloch, Ivan S. *The Future of War.* Translated by R. C. Long. New York: Doubleday, 1899.

Blumenthal, Albrecht. *Journals of Field-Marshal Count von Blumenthal for 1866 and 1870–71.* Translated by A. D. Gillespie-Addison. London: Edward Arnold, 1903.

Böhme, Helmut. *Deutschlands Weg zur Grossmacht.* Cologne: Kiepenheuer und Witsch, 1966.

Boyer, John W. *Political Radicalism in Late Imperial Vienna.* Chicago and London: University of Chicago Press, 1981.

Brandt, Harm-Hinrich. *Der österreichische Neoabsolutismus: Staatsfinanzen und Politik, 1848–60.* Göttingen: Vandenhoeck und Ruprecht, 1978.

Bridge, F. R. *From Sadowa to Sarajevo.* London: Routledge, 1972.

The Habsburg Monarchy among the Great Powers, 1815–1918. New York: Berg, 1990.

Brüning, Günter. "Militär-Strategie Österreichs in der Zeit Kaiser Franz I." phil. Diss., Münster, 1982.

Bucholz, Arden. *Moltke, Schlieffen and Prussian War Planning.* New York and Oxford: Berg Publishers, 1991.

Bush, John W. *Venetia Redeemed.* Syracuse, N.Y.: Syracuse University Press, 1967.

Calza, Pio. *Nuova luce sugli eventi militari del 1866.* Bologna: Zanichelli, 1924.

Carr, William. *The Origins of the Wars of German Unification.* London and New York: Longman, 1991.

Chiala, Luigi. *Ancora un po più di luce sugli eventi politici e militari dell'anno 1866.* Florence: G. Barbèra, 1902.

Cenni storici sui preliminari della guerra del 1866. 2 vols. Florence: Carlo Voghera, 1870–2.

Clardy, J. C. "Austrian Foreign Policy during the Schleswig-Holstein Crisis of 1864." *Diplomacy and Statecraft* 2 (July 1991).

Clark, Chester Wells. *Franz Joseph und Bismarck.* Cambridge, Mass.: Harvard University Press, 1934.

Clausewitz, Carl. *On War.* Translated by J. J. Graham. Edited by Anatol Rapaport. Orig. 1832; New York: Penguin, 1985.

Coppa, Frank J. *The Origins of the Italian Wars of Independence.* London, New York: Longman, 1992.

Corpo di Stato Maggiore. *La Campagna del 1866 in Italia.* Rome: Carlo Voghera, 1875.

Craig, Gordon A. *The Battle of Königgrätz.* Philadelphia: Lippincott, 1964.

The Politics of the Prussian Army, 1640–1945. Oxford: Clarendon Press, 1955.

War, Politics and Diplomacy. London: Weidenfeld and Nicolson, 1966.

Czoernig, Karl. *Das österreichische Budget für 1862.* Vienna: Prandel, 1862.

Deák, István. *Beyond Nationalism.* New York: Oxford University Press, 1990.

Delbrück, Hans, and Emil Daniels. *Geschichte der Kriegskunst im Rahmen der politischen Geschichte.* 7 vols. Berlin: Georg Stilke, 1907–36.

Derndarsky, Michael. "Das Klischée von 'Ces Messieurs de Vienne,' " *Historische Zeitschrift* 235 (1982).

Deutsch, Wilhelm. *Habsburgs Rückzug aus Italien.* Vienna: Adolf Luser, 1940.

Dicey, Edward. *The Battlefields of 1866.* London: Tinsley Brothers, 1866.

Diószegi, István. *Österreich-Ungarn und der französisch-preussische Krieg 1870–71.* Budapest: Akadémiai Kiadó, 1974.

Ditfurth, Moritz. *Benedek und die Taten und Schicksale der k.k. Nordarmee 1866.* 3 vols. Vienna: Seidel und Sohn, 1911.

Douglas, Norman. *Old Calabria.* London: Martin Secker, 1915.

Duffy, Christopher. *The Fortress in the Age of Vauban and Frederick the Great, 1660–1789.* London: Routledge and Kegan Paul, 1985.

The Military Life of Frederick the Great. New York: Atheneum, 1985.

Eisenmann, Louis. *Le Compromis Austro-Hongrois de 1867.* 1904. Hattiesburg: Academic International, 1971.

Elrod, Richard Blake. "The Venetian Question in Austrian Foreign Relations, 1860–1866." Ph.D. diss., University of Illinois, 1967.

"Realpolitik or Concert Diplomacy: The Debate over Austrian Foreign Policy in the 1860s." *Austrian History Yearbook* 17 (1981).

Enciclopedia Italiana. Rome: Giovanni Tecanni, 1929–.

Engel-Janosi, Friedrich, and Helmut Rumpler, eds. *Probleme der franzisko-josephinische Zeit, 1848–1916.* 2 vols. Vienna: Verlag für Geschichte und Politik, 1967.

Esmarch, Friedrich von. *Über den Kampf der Humanität gegen die Schrecken des Krieges.* Stüttgart and Leipzig: Deutsche Verlags Anstalt, 1899.

Eyck, Erich. *Bismarck and the German Empire.* 1950. New York: Norton, 1964.

Falls, Cyril. *The Art of War.* London: Oxford University Press, 1961.

Fischer, Fritz. *Germany's Aims in the First World War.* London: Chatto and Windus, 1967.

War of Illusions. London: Chatto and Windus, 1975.

Förster, Rolf. "Die Leistungsfähigkeit der bayrischen Armee im Feldzuge 1866." phil. Diss., University of Munich, 1987.

Fontane, Theodor. *Der deutsche Krieg von 1866.* 2 vols. Berlin: Verlag der königlichen geheimen Ober-Hofbuchdruckerei, 1870–1.

[Fontane, Theodor]. *Von der Elbe bis zur Tauber: Der Feldzug der preussischen Main-Armee im Sommer 1866.* Bielefeld, Leipzig: Verlag von Belhagen und Klasing, 1867.

Franzel, Emil. *1866 Il Mondo Casca.* 2 vols. Vienna: Verlag Herold, 1968.

Frauenholz, Eugen. "FML Alfred Freiherr von Henikstein im Jahre 1866." *Münchener historische Abhandlungen* 2/3 (1933).

Friedjung, Heinrich. *Der Kampf um die Vorherrschaft in Deutschland.* 2 vols. 1897. Stuttgart and Berlin: J. G. Cotta, 1911.

Historische Aufsätze. Stuttgart and Berlin: J. G. Cotta, 1919.

The Struggle for Supremacy in Germany, 1859–1866. Translated by A. J. P. Taylor. 1897. London: Macmillan, 1935.

Gallenga, Antonio. *The Invasion of Denmark in 1864*. 2 vols. London: Bentley, 1864.

Gall, Lothar. *Bismarck: The White Revolutionary*. Translated by J. A. Underwood. 2 vols. Frankfurt 1980; London: Allen and Unwin, 1986.

Gallouédec, L., and Maurette, F. *Nouveau cours de géographie: Les Grandes Puissances du monde*. Paris: Hachette, 1918.

Geschichte des k.u.k. Infanterie-Regimentes Mollinary (Haugwitz) Nr. 38, 1725–1891. Budapest: Verlag des Regiments, 1892.

Gillespie-Addison, A. D. *The Strategy of the Seven Weeks War*. London: Scheinemann, 1902.

Glaise-Horstenau, Edmund von. *Franz Josephs Weggefährte: Das Leben des Generalstabschefs Grafen Beck*. Zurich and Vienna: Amalthea, 1930.

Glünicke, George J. R. *The Campaign in Bohemia 1866*. London: Swan Sonnenschein, 1907.

Goldinger, Walter. "Von Solferino bis zum Oktoberdiplom." *Mitteilungen des österreichischen Staatsarchivs* 3 (1950).

Gooch, John. *Army, State and Society in Italy, 1870–1915*. London: Macmillan, 1991.

Good, David F. *The Economic Rise of the Habsburg Empire, 1750–1914*. Berkeley and Los Angeles: University of California Press, 1984.

Great General Staff. *The War Book of the German General Staff*. Translated by J. H. Morgan. New York: McBride, 1915.

Gregorovius, Ferdinand. *The Roman Journals, 1852–74*. Edited by Friedrich Althaus. Translated by Mrs. G. W. Hamilton. London: Geo. Bell, 1907.

Groote, Wolfgang, and Ursula Gersdorff, eds. *Entscheidung 1866*. Stuttgart: Deutsche Verlags Anstalt, 1966.

Grosser Generalstab. *Der Feldzug von 1866 in Deutschland*. Berlin: Ernst Mittler, 1867.

Gründorf von Zebegény, Wilhelm Ritter von. *Mémoiren eines österreichischen Generalstäblers, 1832–1866*. 2 vols. Stuttgart: Verlag Robert Lutz, 1913.

Gruner, Wolf D. *Das bayerische Heer 1825 bis 1864*. Boppard: Harald Boldt, 1972.

Guastalla, Enrico. *Carte di Enrico Guastalla*. Edited by B. L. Guastalla. Rome and Milan: Alfieri and Lacroix, 1921.

Hamley, Edward Bruce. *The Operations of War*. Edinburgh and London: Wm. Blackwood, 1866.

Hamann, Brigitte. "Erzherzog Albrecht: Die graue Eminenz des Habsburgerhofes: Hinweise auf einen unterschätzten Politiker." In *Politik und Gesellschaft im alten und neuen Österreich*. Edited by Isabella Ackerl. Vienna: Verlag für Geschichte und Politik, 1981.

Hasek, Jaroslav. *The Good Soldier Svejk and his Fortunes in the World War*. Translated by Cecil Parrott. 1923. New York: Penguin Books, 1981.

Heller, Eduard. "Benedek und Benedek-Legenden." *Militärwissenschaftliches Mitteilungen*. Vienna, 1937.

Helmert, Heinz. *Kriegspolitik und Strategie*. [East] Berlin: Deutscher Militärverlag, 1970.

Militärsystem und Streitkräfte im deutschen Bund. [East] Berlin: Deutscher Militärverlag, 1964.

Preußischdeutsche Kriege von 1864 bis 1871. [East] Berlin: Militärverlag, 1975.

Henderson, W. O. *The Zollverein*. London: Frank Cass, 1984.

Hess, Heinrich. *Schriften aus dem militärwissenschaftlichen Nachlass*. Edited by Manfried Rauchensteiner. Osnäbruck: Biblio Verlag, 1975.

Hönig, Fritz. *Österreichs Finanzpolitik im Kriege von 1866*. Vienna: Steinmann, 1937.

Hof-und Staatshandbuch 1866. Vienna: k.k. Hof-und Staatsdruckerei, 1866.

Hoffman, Georg. *Die venezianische Frage zwischen den Feldzügen von 1859 und 1866*. Zürich: Verlag Leemann, 1941.

Hohenlohe-Schillingsfürst, Chlodwig. *Denkwürdigkeiten des Fürsten Chlodwig zu Hohenlohe-Schillingsfürst*. 2 vols. Stuttgart and Leipzig: Deutsche Verlags Anstalt, 1906.

Hommon, William Scott. "The Diplomatic Recognition of the Kingdom of Italy, 1861–1866." Ph.D. diss., University of Pennsylvania, 1973.

Howard, Mary Katherine. "The French Parliament and the Italian and Roman Questions, 1859–1865." Ph.D. diss., University of Pennsylvania, 1963.

Howard, Michael. *The Franco-Prussian War*. 1961. London: Granada, 1979.

War in European History. Oxford: Oxford University Press, 1976.

Hozier, Henry Montague. *The Seven Weeks' War*. Philadelphia, London: Lippincott, Macmillan, 1867.

Hundert Jahre metrisches Maßsystem in Österreich, 1872-1972. Vienna: Bundesamt für Eich-und Vermessungswesen, 1972.

Jahnel, A. *Chronik der preussischen Invasion des nördlichen Böhmens im Jahre 1866*. Reichenberg: Selbstverlag, 1867.

Jenks, William A. *Francis Joseph and the Italians, 1849–1859*. Charlottesville: University Press of Virginia, 1978.

Kählig, Eduard. *Vor und nach Custozza: Alte Tagebücher aus dem Feldzüge 1866*. Graz: Verlag Leykam, 1892.

Karl, Erzherzog. *Militärische Werke*. 3 vols. Vienna: k.k. Hof-und-Staatsdruckerei, 1862.

Kennedy, Paul. *Strategy and Diplomacy, 1870–1945: Eight Studies*. London, Boston: Allen and Unwin, 1983.

Kennedy, Paul, ed. *The War Plans of the Great Powers, 1880–1914*. London, Boston: Allen and Unwin, 1979.

[Kerchnawe, Hugo]. *Die Vorgeschichte von 1866 und 19??*. Vienna, Leipzig: C. W. Stern, 1909.

Kitchen, Martin. *The German Officer Corps, 1890–1914*. Oxford: Clarendon, 1968.

A Military History of Germany. Bloomington: Indiana University Press, 1975.

k.k. Generalstab. *Der Krieg in Italien 1859*. 3 vols. Vienna: Verlag des k.k. Generalstabs, 1872–6.

Österreichs Kämpfe im Jahre 1866. 5 vols. Vienna: Verlag des Generalstabs, 1867–9.

Koch, Klaus. *Franz Graf Crenneville: Generaladjutant Kaiser Franz Josephs*. Vienna: Österreichischer Bundesverlag, 1984.

Kohn, Ignaz. *Österreichs Eisenbahn Jahrbuch*. Vienna: Tendler, 1868.

Kolb, Eberhard, ed. *Europa vor dem Krieg von 1870*. Munich: Oldenbourg, 1987.

Komlos, John. *The Habsburg Monarchy as a Customs Union: Economic Development in Austria-Hungary in the 19th Century*. Princeton: Princeton University Press, 1983.

Kramer, Hans. *Österreich und das Risorgimento*. Vienna: Bergland Verlag, 1963.

Krauss, Alfred. *Moltke, Benedek und Napoleon*. Vienna: Seidel, 1901.

La Marmora, Alfonso. *Un po più di luce sugli eventi politici e militari dell'anno 1866*. Florence: G. Barbèra, 1873.

Lemoyne, J. V. *Campagne de 1866 en Italie: La Bataille de Custoza*. Paris: Berger-Levrault, 1875.

Lettow-Vorbeck, Oscar. *Geschichte des Krieges von 1866 in Deutschland*. 3 vols. Berlin: Mittler, 1896–1902.

Liddell Hart, B. H. *The Revolution in Warfare*. 1946. Westport: Greenwood, 1980.

Lónyay, Carl. *Ich Will Rechenschaft Ablegen*. Leipzig and Vienna: Joh. Günther, 1937.

Lorenz, Reinhold. "Ludwig Freiherr von Gablenz." In *Neue österreichische Biographie, 1815–1918*. Vol. 8. Vienna: Amalthea, 1935.

Luvaas, Jay. *The Military Legacy of the Civil War*. Chicago: University of Chicago Press, 1959.

Lutz, Heinrich. *Österreich-Ungarn und die Gründung des deutschen Reiches*. Frankfurt am Main, Berlin and Vienna: Propyläen, 1979.

McDonald, Michael Joseph. "Napoleon III and His Ideas of Italian Confederation, 1856–1860." Ph.D. diss., University of Pennsylvania, 1968.

Mack Smith, Denis. *Italy and its Monarchy*. New Haven: Yale University Press, 1989.

Modern Sicily after 1713. New York: Viking, 1968.

Victor Emanuel, Cavour, and the Risorgimento. London: Oxford University Press, 1971.

Mahon, John K. "Civil War Infantry Assault Tactics." *Military Affairs* (Summer 1961).

Malet, Alexander. *The Overthrow of the Germanic Confederation by Prussia in 1866.* London: Longman's, Green. 1870.

Marraro, Howard R. *American Opinion on the Unification of Italy, 1846–1861.* New York: Columbia University Press, 1932.

Mechtler, Paul. "Die österreichische Eisenbahnpolitik in Italien 1835–66." *Mitteilungen des österreichischen Staatsarchivs* (1961).

Menzel, Wolfgang. *Der deutsche Krieg im Jahre 1866.* 2 vols. Stuttgart: Verlag Adolph Krabbe, 1867.

Mertal, Walter. "Graf Richard Belcredi, 1823–1902: Ein Staatsmann aus dem Österreich Kaiser Franz Josephs." phil. Diss., University of Vienna, 1962.

Meyer, Bernhard. *Erlebnisse.* 2 vols. Vienna and Budapest: Verlag Carl Satori, 1875.

Mollinary, Antoine. *Quarante-six ans dans l'armée austro-hongroise, 1833–79.* 2 vols. Paris: Fournier, 1913.

Moltke, Helmuth. *Moltkes kriegsgeschichtlichen Arbeiten.* Edited by Grossen Generalstabe. 3 vols. Berlin: Mittler, 1904.

Strategy: Its Theory and Application. 1907. Westport, Conn.: Greenwood Press, 1971.

Mosse, W. E. *The European Powers and the German Question, 1848–1871.* Cambridge University Press, 1958.

Müller, Rudolf. *Entstehungsgeschichte des roten Kreuzes und der genfer Konvention im Anschluß an un Souvenir de Solferino.* Stuttgart: Greiner und Pfeiffer, 1897.

Müller, Wilibald. *Geschichte der königlichen Hauptstadt Olmütz.* Vienna and Olmütz: Eduard Hölzel, 1882.

Neue österreichische Biographie, 1815–1918. 22 vols. Vienna: Amalthea, 1923–87.

Nipperdey, Thomas. *Deutsche Geschichte 1800–1866.* Munich: Verlag C. H. Beck, 1983.

Paret, Peter, ed. *Makers of Modern Strategy.* 1943. Princeton: Princeton University Press, 1986.

Pflanze, Otto. *Bismarck and the Development of Germany, 1815–71.* 1963. Princeton: Princeton University Press, 1990.

Pieri, Piero. *Storia Militare del Risorgimento.* Turin: Giulio Einandi Editore, 1962.

Pollio, Alberto. *Custoza 1866.* Città di Castello: Unione Arti Grafiche, 1914.

Porch, Douglas. *The March to the Marne: The French Army, 1871–1914.* Cambridge University Press, 1981.

Posselt, Oskar. *Geschichte des k.u.k. Infanterie-Regiment Ritter von Pino Nr. 40.* Vienna: Gerold, 1913.

Presland, John. *Vae Victis: The Life of Ludwig von Benedek, 1804–81.* London: Hodder and Stoughton, 1934.

Rauchensteiner, Manfried, ed. *Clausewitz, Jomini, Erzherzog Carl.* Vienna: Österreichischer Bundesverlag, 1988.

"Zum 'operativen Denken' in Österreich: Von Solferino bis Königgrätz." *Österreichische Militärische Zeitschrift (ÖMZ)* 5 (1974).

Redlich, Joseph. *Das österreichische Staats-und Reichsproblem.* 2 vols. Leipzig: Neue Geist, 1920.

Regele, Oskar. *Feldmarschall Radetzky.* Vienna, Munich: Verlag Herold, 1957.

Feldzeugmeister Benedek und der Weg nach Königgrätz. Vienna, Munich: Verlag Herold, 1960.

"Staatspolitische Geschichtsschreibung erläutert an Königgrätz 1866." *MÖSA* 3 (1950).

Riall, Lucy. *The Italian Risorgimento: State, Society and National Unification.* London and New York: Routledge, 1994.

Ritter, Gerhard. *The Sword and the Scepter.* 4 vols. 1954–68. Coral Gables: University of Miami Press, 1969–73.

Rogge, Walter. *Österreich von Világos bis zur Gegenwart.* 3 vols. Leipzig, Vienna: Brockhaus, 1872–3.

Rothenberg, Gunther E. *The Army of Francis Joseph.* W. Lafayette: Purdue University Press, 1976.

"The Habsburg Army and the Nationality Problem in the Nineteenth Century, 1815–1914." *Austrian History Yearbook* 3/1 (1967).

"Toward a National Hungarian Army: The Military Compromise of 1868 and its Consequences." *Slavonic Review* 31 (1972).

Sawallich, Astrid. "Die Geschichte der päpstlichen Armee unter dem Pontifikat Pius IX, 1849–1870." phil. Diss., University of Vienna, 1970.

Scherr-Tosz, Arthur. "Erinnerungen aus meinem Leben." *Deutsche Rundschau* 10 (1881).

Schlichting, Sigismund. *Moltke und Benedek.* Berlin: Ernst Mittler, 1900.

Schlieffen, Graf General-Feldmarschall. "Benedeks Armee-Führung nach den neuesten Forschungen." *Vierteljahrshefte für Truppenführung und Heereskunde* 8 (1911).

Schmidt-Brentano, Antonio. *Die Armee in Österreich: Militär, Staat und Gesellschaft 1848–67.* Boppard: Harald Boldt, 1975.

Scirocco, Alfonso. *Il Mezzogiorno nella crisi dell'unificazione, 1860–1861.* Naples: Società Editrice Napoletana, 1963.

Il Mezzogiorno nell'Italia Unita, 1861–1865. Naples: Società Editrice Napoletana, 1979.

Sheehan, James J. *German History, 1770–1866.* Oxford: Clarendon, 1989.

Showalter, Dennis E. "Mass Multiplied by Impulsion: The Influence of Railroads on Prussian Planning for the Seven Weeks' War." *Military Affairs* 38/2 (1974).

Railroads and Rifles: Soldiers, Technology and the Unification of Germany. Hamden, Conn.: Archon, 1975.

"The Retaming of Bellona: Prussia and the Institutionalization of the Napoleonic Legacy, 1815–76." *Military Affairs* 44/2 (1980).

"Soldiers into Postmasters: The Electric Telegraph as an Instrument of Command in the Prussian Army." *Military Affairs* (1973).

Tannenberg: Clash of Empires. Hamden, Conn.: Archon, 1992.

Sked, Alan. *The Decline and Fall of the Habsburg Empire, 1815–1918.* London: Longman, 1989.

The Survival of the Habsburg Empire. London: Longman, 1979.

Snyder, Jack. *The Ideology of the Offensive: Military Decision Making and the Disasters of 1914.* Ithaca, N.Y.: Cornell University Press, 1984.

Sondhaus, Lawrence. *The Habsburg Empire and the Sea: Austrian Naval Policy 1797–1866.* W. Lafayette, Ind.: Purdue University Press, 1989.

Srbik, Heinrich. *Aus Österreichs Vergangenheit.* Salzburg: Otto Müller Verlag, 1949.

Deutsche Einheit. 4 vols. Munich: F. Bruckman, 1935–42.

Stato Maggiore dell'Esercito. *L'Esercito italiano dall'unità alla Grande Guerra, 1861–1918.* Rome: Ufficio Storico SME, 1980.

Steefel, Lawrence. *The Schleswig-Holstein Question.* Cambridge, Mass.: Harvard University Press, 1932.

Steinitz, Eduard. "Aus den Tagen vor Königgrätz." *Militärwissenschaftliche und technische Mitteilungen* 8 (1926).

Stern, Fritz. *Gold and Iron: Bismarck, Bleichröder and the Building of the German Empire.* 1977. New York: Vintage, 1979.

Stone, Norman. "Army and Society in the Habsburg Monarchy, 1900–1914." *Past and Present* 33 (1966).

Europe Transformed, 1878–1919. Cambridge, Mass.: Harvard University Press, 1984.

Strachan, Hew. *European Armies and the Conduct of War.* London: George Allen and Unwin, 1983.

Streith, Rudolf. *Geschichte des k.u.k. Feldjäger Batallion Nr. 26.* Innsbruck: Wagnersche Universität, 1892.

Sybel, Heinrich. *Die Begründung des deutschen Reiches durch Wilhelm I.* 7 vols. Munich and Bern: Oldenbourg, 1889.

Taylor, A. J. P. *The Course of German History.* London: Hamish Hamilton, 1945.

The Habsburg Monarchy, 1809–1918. 1948. London: Pelican, 1988.

The Struggle for Mastery in Europe, 1848–1918. Oxford: Clarendon, 1954.

Teuber, Oskar. *Feldmarschall Erzherzog Albrecht.* Vienna: Seidel, 1895.

Teuber, Oskar, and Rudolf Ottenfeld. *Die österreichischen Armee, 1770–1867.* 2 vols. Vienna: Verlag Berté und Czeigler, 1895–1900.

Toilow [F. Karl Folliot-Crenneville]. *Die österreichische Nordarmee und ihr Führer im Jahre 1866.* Vienna and Leipzig: Wm. Braumüller, 1906.

Treuenfest, Gustav Amin. *Geschichte des k.u.k. Infanterie Regimentes Nr. 46 FZM Féjerváry.* Vienna: Verlag des Regiments, 1890.

Turnbull, Patrick. *Solferino.* London: Robert Hale, 1985.

Ulloa, Girolamo. *L'Esercito italiano e la Battaglia di Custoza.* Florence: Tipografia Gaston, 1866.

Van Creveld, Martin. *Command in War*. Cambridge, Mass.,: Harvard University Press, 1985.

Supplying War. Cambridge University Press, 1977.

Technology and War. New York: Free Press, 1989.

Wachenhusen, Hans. *Tagebuch vom österreichischen Kriegsschauplatz*. Berlin: Lemke, 1866.

Wagner, Arthur L. *The Campaign of Königgrätz*. 1889. Westport, Conn.: Greenwood Press, 1972.

Wagner, Walter. *Von Austerlitz bis Königgrätz: österreichische Kampf und Taktik im Spiegel der Reglements, 1805-1864*. Osnäbrück: Biblio Verlag, 1978.

Wandruszka, Adam. *Schicksalsjahr 1866*. Vienna: Verlag Styria, 1966.

Die Habsburger Monarchie, 1848–1918. 6 vols. Vienna: Verlag der österreichischen Akademie der Wissenschaften, 1973–89.

Wawro, Geoffrey. "An 'Army of Pigs': The Technical, Social and Political Bases of Austrian Shock Tactics, 1859–1866." *The Journal of Military History* 59 (July 1995): 407–34.

"Austria versus the Risorgimento: A New Look at Austria's Italian Strategy in the 1860s." *European History Quarterly* 26 (January 1996): 7–29.

"The Habsburg *Flucht nach vorne* in 1866: Domestic-Political Origins of the Austro-Prussian War." *The International History Review* 17 (May 1995): 221–48.

"Inside the Whale: The Tangled Finances of the Austrian Army, 1848–1866." *War in History* 3 (February 1996): 42–65.

"Morale in the Austro-Hungarian Army." In P. Liddle and H. Cecil, eds. *Facing Armageddon: The First World War Experienced*. (London: Leo Cooper, 1996).

Wehler, Hans-Ulrich. *The German Empire, 1871–1918*. Translated by Kim Traynor. 1973. Leamington Spa and Dover: Berg Publishers, 1985.

Werkmann, August. "Erzherzog Albrecht und Benedek." phil. Diss., University of Vienna, 1946.

Whittam, John. *The Politics of the Italian Army, 1861–1918*. London and Hamden, Conn.: Croom Helm, Archon, 1977.

Woinovich, Emil. "Benedek und sein Hauptquartier im Feldzuge 1866." Vienna Kriegsarchiv Manuscript, 1911.

Wondrák, Eduard. "Die Wahrheit vom Trauerspiel 1866: Das Leid und Elend im sogenannten deutschen Krieg." Private Manuscript, Olomouc, 1990.

Wrede, Alphons. *Geschichte der k.u.k. Wehrmacht*. 5 vols. Vienna: Verlag Seidel, 1898–1903.

Wyatt, W. J. *A Political and Military Review of the Austro-Italian War of 1866*. London: Edw. Stanford, 1867.

Zorzi, Alvise. *Venezia Austriaca, 1798–1866*. Rome and Bari: Laterza, 1985.

Index

Abele, General Vincenz, 186, 266, 270
Albert, Crown Prince of Saxony, 125, 128; at
    Jicin, 182, 184, 189–90; at Königgrätz, 210,
    213, 230, 242; Iser operations, 132–5, 157
Albrecht, Archduke of Austria (Austrian South
    Army commandant in 1866), 45, 57, 61,
    257, 274–5, 278–9, 291; appointed South
    Army commandant, 65–7; at Custoza, 102–
    9, 115–22; plan for Custoza, 95–9; plan for
    war with Italy, 67–71, 82
Alexander, Prince of Hessia, 74, 77
Alexander II, Tsar of Russia, 42, 282–3, 285
Amadeo, Prince of Italy, 111, 113
Appiano, General Karl, 220, 249–51, 253
armistices of 1866, 276–81
artillery, 7, 118, 220, 290–1
August, Prince of Württemberg (Prussian
    Guard Corps commandant in 1866), 136,
    160, 162–3, 193
Ausgleich of 1867, 281–2, 285

"battery of the dead," 252, 257
Bauer, Col. Ferdinand, 108
Baumgarten, General Alois (Austrian "opera-
    tions chief" at Königgrätz), 210, 219, 236,
    240–1, 243, 246, 251–2, 254–5, 258, 263
Bazaine, Marshal François, 287
Beck, Lt.-Col. Friedrich, 204, 212, 284
Belcredi, Count Richard (Austrian minister of
    state, 1865–7), 135, 282, 296
Benedek, General Ludwig (Austrian North
    Army commandant in 1866), after
    Königgrätz, 273–5, 279; at Königgrätz,
    202–7, 212–15, 219, 220–2, 227–31,
    233–8, 240–3, 246–50, 252–60, 262–5,

268, 271; conduct of war until Königgrätz,
    124–8, 135–7, 144–5, 151–5, 165–9,
    175–81, 183, 189, 192–9; friendship with
    Henikstein, 27, 213; rapid promotion, 25–
    6, 45, 49; reputation, 25, 53, 56–7; tactical
    ideas, 35
Bernhardi, Theodor, 87–8, 92
Beyer, General Gustav, 76
Bismarck, Count Otto von (Prussian minister-
    president in 1866), 14–15, 148, 199–200,
    217–18, 275–9, 282–4, 296; army crisis of
    1862, 13, 16–17, 80; strategic aims in
    1866, 39–44
Bittenfeld, General Karl Herwarth von (Prus-
    sian Elbe Army commandant in 1866), 53–
    5; at Königgrätz, 199–202, 208, 212, 214–
    16, 228, 230–1, 242, 246, 252, 254, 270–
    2; Iser operations, 129–31, 134, 158, 183
Bixio, General Nino, 104–6, 280
Blumenthal, General Albrecht (Prussian Second
    Army staff chief in 1866), 126, 200–1, 216
Bonin, General Adolf (Prussian I Corps com-
    mandant in 1866), 136–7, 145–51, 160,
    163, 167, 193, 259, 272
Britain, role in 1866, 282–3
Bruck, Ludwig, 38–9
Burkersdorf, battle of, 154, 160–4, 170, 175–
    6, 204

Canstein, General Philipp von, 230, 242–3,
    246
Carlo Alberto, King of Italy, 116
Catty, Col. Adolf, 227, 253, 258
cavalry, 268, 290–1
Cavour, Count Camillo Benso di, 48

Cerale, General Enrico, 99, 102, 107–8
Chlum, Prussian capture of, 187, 250–7, 287
Cialdini, General Enrico (Italian Po Army commandant in 1866), 70, 72; dispute with La Marmora, 87–95; role in war of 1866, 98–9, 113, 118–19, 278–80, 285
Clam-Gallas, General Eduard (Austrian I Corps commandant in 1866), 62; at Jicin, 181–4, 186–7,189–91, 197; Iser operations, 125–6, 128,132–5, 151, 154–5, 165, 180, 204
Clausewitz, Carl von, 10, 283, 291; legacy, 13, 16; *On War*, 7, 9, 30
Congress of Vienna (1815), 36–7, 45, 48, 277, 282
Cormons armistice, 278–81
Coudenhove, General Karl, 63, 179, 181, 205, 215, 242, 255, 268–70, 274
Crenneville, General Franz Folliot, 29, 61, 212–13
Custoza, battle of: Albrecht's plan, 95–9; Austrian attack, 95–104; Austrian failure to pursue, 116–23; Italian plan, 87–95; Pulz's charge, 104–7; struggle for Mincio heights, 107–16

Danish War, *see* War of 1864
Daun, Field Marshal Leopold, 196, 197
Degenfeld, General August von, 29
Delbrück, Rudolf, 39, 51
Della Rocca, General Enrico (Italian III Corps commandant in 1866), 102, 104, 109–10, 115, 121, 279n
Dubenec position, 181–2, 193–9
Durando, General Giacomo (Italian I Corps commandant in 1866), 97, 102, 104, 108, 114

Edelsheim, General Leopold: at Jicin, 187, 191; at Königgrätz, 203, 206–7, 210, 214, 230, 243, 252, 254, 268; Iser operations, 125, 128, 131
Ernst, Archduke of Austria (Austrian III Corps commandant in 1866), 181, 186, 190–1; at Königgrätz, 217, 220, 227, 232, 238, 249, 257

Fabrice, General Georg (Saxon staff chief in 1866), 184, 190
Falckenstein, General Eduard Vogel von (Prussian West Army commandant in 1866), 19, 54–5, 78–9, 131

Festetics, General Tassilo (Austrian IV Corps commandant in 1866), 166, 169, 193, 203, 221–2, 224, 227, 250
Flies, General Eduard, 79–80
Fragnern, General Gustav, 170–1, 204
France, role in 1866, *see* Napoleon III
Francesco II, King of Naples, 120, 123, 294
Franck, General Karl, 28, 61
Fransecki, General Eduard von, 131, 134; at Königgrätz, 218, 221–7, 229, 234, 240, 244, 247
Franco-Austrian War, *see* War of 1859
Franco-Prussian War, 286–91
Franz Joseph I, Emperor of Austria: choice of Benedek for high command, 25–7; post-war activity, 284; resistance to army reforms, 29, 32; role in 1866, 63–5, 118, 125, 196, 202, 212–13, 219, 263, 274, 276, 280, 282; tactical notions, 31–2; war aims in 1866, 294–6
Frederick the Great, King of Prussia, 13, 15–16, 39, 57, 209; tactics, 6–7, 22; wars with Austria, 20, 60, 166, 193, 196
Friedjung debate, 3–4
Friedrich Karl, Prince of Prussia (Prussian First Army commandant in 1866): command of First Army until Königgrätz, 55, 125, 129–31, 151, 153, 156, 158, 165, 175, 182–3, 186, 190–1, 199–202, 210; conduct at Königgrätz, 211–12, 215–17, 223, 226, 228, 231–3, 247, 254, 269, 272–3; in 1870, 287
Friedrich Wilhelm, Crown Prince of Prussia (Prussian Second Army commandant in 1866): command of Second Army until Königgrätz, 55, 126, 128, 135–6, 138, 145, 151, 160, 165, 199–202; conduct at Königgrätz, 212, 215–16, 233–5, 240, 250, 269, 273; in 1870, 287

Gablenz, General Ludwig (Austrian X Corps commandant in 1866), 45; at Königgrätz, 199, 204–5, 229, 232, 238, 240–1, 243, 248, 254, 257, 259, 273; at Trautenau, 137, 145–51, 153–5; Burkersdorf fiasco, 160–5, 175–6, 179–80
Garibaldi, General Giuseppe (Italian Volunteer Corps commander in 1866), 48, 68, 70, 84–6, 89, 92–3,119, 123, 279–81
Gastein Convention (1865), 42–4

German Confederation, 15, 30, 36–40, 44, 72–9, 277–8, 295–6
German Empire, founding of, 288
Goeben, General August, 75, 78
Gondrecourt, General Leopold, 129, 184–5, 187, 189–92, 205, 238, 241, 258–63, 265–9, 272
Govone, General Giuseppe, 111, 115, 278
Grivicic, General Georg, 137, 147, 150, 160–1, 163–5
Gröben, Capt. August, 252, 257
Guderian, General Heinz, 289–90

Hanover, Kingdom of, 75–81, 175, 277
Hartung, General Ernst (Austrian IX Corps commandant in 1866), 71, 96–9
Henikstein, General Alfred (Austrian General Staff chief in 1866), 45, 61; appointed staff chief in 1864, 27–8, 57; role in Königgrätz campaign, 136, 151, 189, 195, 212–13, 219, 236, 253–5, 258, 263
Henriquez, General Gustav, 245
Herwarth, General Karl, *see* Bittenfeld
Hess, Field Marshal Heinrich, 25, 31, 64, 116, 273
Hindenburg, Lt. Paul von, 261
Hitler, Adolf, 290, 294
Hoffmeister, Capt. Eduard, 236
Holstein, Prince Wilhelm, 199, 267, 269–70
Horn, General Heinrich, 131, 216–19, 226, 240
Hühnerwasser, skirmish at, 129–30, 134, 154, 158

infantry, *see* tactics
Iser Army: at Jicin, 165, 179–80, 181–4, 189–91, 196, 287; at Münchengrätz, 151, 154, 156, 158–9; at Podol, 128–35; formation, 62–3, 74–5.
Italian War, *see* War of 1859

Jicin, battle of, 153, 157–8, 181–92, 196, 204, 287
John, General Franz (Austrian South Army staff chief in 1866), 45, 67, 279; at Custoza, 102–9; plan for Custoza, 95–9, 121
Jomini, Antoine Henri, 18–21
Jonak, Col. Johann, 141–2
Joseph, Archduke of Austria, 250

Karl, Archduke of Austria, 25, 29–30, 65, 99, 116–17, 120, 247

Karl, Prince of Bavaria, 77
Kirchsberg, General Julius, 252
Kissingen, battle of, 293
Knebel, Col. Albert, 147, 150, 162–3, 204
Königgrätz, battle of: Austrian "council of war," 204–7; Austrian retreat; 257–60, 263–5; Benedek's torpor, 212–13, 233–7, 247–8; Bystrice position, 202–4, 208–10; cavalry battle at Stresetice, 268–70; Elbe Army flanks Benedek, 242–5, 254; fighting on the Bystrice, 215–21, 229–33; Krismanic's battle plan, 212–15; Mollinary attacks Svib Forest, 221–9, 233–7; Moltke's battle plan, 210–12; Moltke's failure to pursue, 271–3; near collapse of the Prussian First Army, 238–41; Prussian capture of Chlum, 250–7, 260–3, 265–8; Ramming's restlessness, 241–2; Second Army flanks Benedek, 245–57, 260–3, 265–8
Königgrätz legend, 283, 286–90
Königinhof position, 193–9
Kreyssern, General Leopold, 171–3
Krismanic, General Gideon (Austrian North Army "operations chief" until Königgrätz): appointed operations chief, 57–62; at Königgrätz, 211–15, 219, 234, 236, 240, 254–6, 258–9; role before Königgrätz, 136, 144, 151–5, 161, 165–9, 179 195–6, 198, 204, 205n, 207
Kriz, Col. Ferdinand, 61, 236, 250n, 254, 263
Kuhn, General Franz, 119, 284

La Marmora, General Alfonso (Italian Mincio Army commandant in 1866), 70–1, 84–5, 121, 259, 279n; at Custoza, 102–7, 110–11, 118–19, 122; plan in 1866, 87–94, 95–9
Landwehr (Prussian), 7, 16, 80–1, 272
Langensalza, battle of, 79–81
Leopold, Archduke of Austria (Austrian VIII Corps commandant until Königgrätz), 126; at Skalice, 144, 153, 155, 165, 169–76, 178, 181, 199, 230, 238
Liechtenstein, Prince Friedrich, 67, 268
Lissa, battle of, 279
Litzelhofen, Col. Eduard, 154, 186, 191
Ludendorff, General Erich, 290

MacMahon, Marshal Patrice, 287
Manstein, General Albrecht von, 231–2
Manteuffel, General Edwin von, 75, 81

Maroicic, General Joseph (Austrian VII Corps commandant in 1866), 71–2, 96–9, 111, 115, 117, 123, 280

Mars-la-Tour, battle of, 288

medical matters, 123, 150, 224, 276

Mensdorff, General Alexander (Austrian foreign minister in 1866), 42–4, 52, 274, 276, 279

Miliutin, General Dmitri, 285

Moering, General Karl, 98, 100, 114, 118, 121–2, 280–1

Mollinary, General Anton (Austrian IV Corps commandant at Königgrätz), 45; at Königgrätz, 221–2, 224–9, 234–8, 240, 243, 246–8, 250, 271, 273, 275

Moltke, General Helmuth von (Prussian General Staff chief in 1866): appointed staff chief, 12–13, 15; army crisis of 1862, 16, 80; at Königgrätz, 211–12, 217–18, 226–7, 229, 231–3, 238, 240, 244–7, 269, 271–6; conduct of war until Königgratz, 124–8, 131, 135, 148, 151, 156–7, 160, 174–5, 182, 199–202; drive to Vienna, 279; military legacy, 282–93; mobilization in 1866, 50–7, 59–60, 62; operations in Germany, 78–80; preference for Cialdini, 88–92, 102; reforms, 13, 16, 32; strategic ideas, 16–21, 30–1, 178; tactical ideas, 21–5

Mondel, Col. Friedrich, 137, 145–7, 162–3, 254, 259

Müller, Lt. Eugen, 263

Münchengrätz, battle of, 151, 154, 156–9, 165, 182

Murat, Lucien, 83, 277

Mutius, General Louis (Prussian VI Corps commandant in 1866), 136, 166–8, 241, 243, 245–6, 264, 267, 270–2

Nachod, battle of, *see* Vysokov

Napoleon I, Emperor of France, 7–8, 30, 36, 46, 120–1, 238, 245, 247

Napoleon III, Emperor of France: French policy in 1866, 42, 52, 82–3, 135, 192–3, 200, 211, 271, 276–8, 281–2; war of 1859, 11–12; war of 1870, 287, 290

Neuber, Col. August, 57–9, 195, 236–7, 252, 254, 258

Ney, General Edgar, 119

Nikolsburg armistice, 276–9

North German Confederation, 277, 282–3, 288

Olmütz: Austrian camp in 1866, 58–63; Benedek's retreat after Königgrätz, 274–6; punctation of, 14–15, 38

Pelikan, Col. Joseph, 190

Petitti, General Agostino, 92–4, 108, 114

Pettinengo, General Ignazio, 87

Pianell, General Giuseppe, 108

Piret, General Eugen, 100, 107–8, 114

Piret, General Ludwig, 187–8, 191, 204, 252, 255, 268

Pius IX, Pope, 119, 123, 281, 295

Podol, battle of, 131–5, 154

Pöckh, General Karl, 225–6

Poschacher, General Ferdinand, 133, 158, 186, 191, 204, 267

Prusso-Italian alliance (1866), 43–4, 49, 52, 87–8

Pulz, Col. Ludwig, 100, 104–5, 110, 114–15, 117

Quadrilateral forts, 1, 12, 30, 46, 69–70, 72, 89–90, 280

Radetzky, Field Marshal Joseph, 47, 90, 116, 118, 120–2, 262

Ramming, General Wilhelm (Austrian VI Corps commandant in 1866), 45; at Königgrätz, 195, 199, 205, 207, 232–3, 238–41, 247–8, 258–65, 270–3; at Skalice, 165, 169; at Vysokov, 137–8, 139–45, 153–4

rifles, 10, 123; Prussian "needle rifle," 21–2, 129–30, 133–4, 144–5, 150, 164, 171, 174, 187, 191, 195, 204, 221, 293

Ringelsheim, General Joseph, 158, 186, 190, 203, 266

Rodakowski, Col. Joseph, 105–7

Rodic, General Gabriel (Austrian V Corps commandant in 1866), 71, 96, 100, 105, 108, 114, 117

Roon, General Albrecht von (Prussian war minister in 1866), 12–13, 16, 80, 182, 199, 283

Rouher, Eugène, 83

Rudersdorf, battle of, 164–5, 268

Rupprecht, General Friedrich, 102, 105, 107, 112

Russia, role in 1866, 42, 282–3

Sacken, Major Adolf, 234, 240–1
Sadova, battle of, *see* Königgrätz
St. Privat, battle of, 287
Saxony, Kingdom of, 19–20, 73–4
Schleswig-Holstein question, 17, 40–4, 52
Schlieffen, Field Marshal Alfred von, 121, 144,
   271, 287, 290; Schlieffen Plan, 288–9
Schulz, General Karl, 167, 171, 173
Schweinschädel, battle of, 193
Scudier, General Anton, 111–12, 114
Sedan, battle of, 287–9
Sirtori, General Giuseppe, 99, 102, 108, 112
Skalice, battle of, 153, 154, 160, 165–74,
   176–7, 204, 231, 238
Soor, battle of, *see* Burkersdorf
South German Confederation, 278, 288
Spicheren, battle of, 287–8
Steinmetz, General Karl, 56, 136, 138–9,
   143–5, 160, 166–74, 193, 272, 286–7
Stransky, Capt. Karl, 195, 263–4
strategy: conflicting schools, 17–19, 29–31,
   286–90
Stresetice, cavalry battle of, 262, 268–72

tactics: fire tactics, 21–5, 32, 34, 224–5, 230,
   268, 290–4; shock tactics, 7–8, 11–12, 23,
   31–5, 224–5, 249, 267, 291–3
Tann, General Ludwig von der, 293
Taxis, Prince Emerich Thurn und, 127, 181,
   199, 227–8, 246, 250
Tegetthoff, Admiral Wilhelm, 279–80
Thom, Col. Michael, 177, 245
Thun, General Karl (Austrian II Corps comman-
   dant in 1866), 125, 176–8, 197, 205, 222,
   225–9, 234, 237, 243, 245–6, 250, 271
Töply, Col. Johann, 115, 117
Trautenau, battle of, 137, 145–51, 154–5,
   160, 167–8, 204
treaties of peace, 276–81
Tümpling, General Ludwig, 183, 185–6, 188,
   191, 287
Turnau, skirmish at, 134

Umberto, Crown Prince of Italy, 104–5
Usedom, Count Guido, 88, 92

Vittorio Emanuele II, King of Italy, 48, 278–
   81, 285, 295; at Custoza, 108, 110, 113;
   supreme command in 1866, 83–4, 87–99
Voigts-Rhetz, General Konstantin (Prussian
   First Army staff chief in 1866), 158, 201,
   211
Vysokov, battle of, 137, 139–45, 154, 204,
   261

Waldersee, General Alfred von, 288–9
Waldstätten, Col. Georg, 143, 261
War of 1859, 48; lessons of, 11–13, 18, 31–2,
   188, 190; Prussian attitude, 12, 15
War of 1864, 17, 40–2; lessons of, 23–4, 31,
   34–5
Weber, General Joseph (Austrian VIII Corps
   commandant at Königgrätz), 230–1, 242–3,
   246, 254
Weckbecker, General Hugo, 97, 100, 109
Wellington, Duke of, 228, 238
Welsersheimb, Col. Otto, 115, 117, 123
Werder, General August, 182–3, 186, 189–
   91, 219, 240, 287
Wilhelm, Archduke of Austria, 236, 253–4
Wilhelm I, King of Prussia, 44, 51–2, 59,
   128, 288; army reforms, 12–16; role in
   1866, 182, 212, 217–18, 226, 229, 233,
   245, 269, 273, 275, 277
Wilhelm II, Emperor of Germany, 288, 290
Wimpffen, General Adolf, 147, 163, 254
Wimpffen, Col. Alfons, 142
Wörth, battle of, 287
Woinowitz, Capt. Ilja, 236, 262–3
Wrangel, Field Marshal Friedrich von, 19, 23–
   4, 55, 78

Zollverein (Prussian Customs Union), 38–9,
   296
Zychlinski, Colonel Franz von, 224